THANKS FOR
WATCHING

THANKS FOR WATCHING

AN ANTHROPOLOGICAL STUDY OF VIDEO SHARING ON YouTube

Patricia G. Lange

UNIVERSITY PRESS OF COLORADO
Louisville

Published by University Press of Colorado
245 Century Circle, Suite 202
Louisville, Colorado 80027

 The University Press of Colorado is a proud member of
the Association of University Presses.

The University Press of Colorado is a cooperative publishing enterprise supported, in part, by Adams
State University, Colorado State University, Fort Lewis College, Metropolitan State University of
Denver, Regis University, University of Colorado, University of Northern Colorado, University of
Wyoming, Utah State University, and Western Colorado University.

ISBN: 978-1-60732-947-3 (hardcover)
ISBN: 978-1-60732-948-0 (paperback)
ISBN: 978-1-60732-955-8 (open-access PDF)
ISBN: 978-1-64642-009-4 (open-access ePUB)
https://doi.org/10.5876/9781607329558

Library of Congress Cataloging-in-Publication Data

Names: Lange, Patricia G., author.
Title: Thanks for watching : an anthropological study of video sharing on YouTube / Patricia G.
   Lange.
Description: Louisville : University Press of Colorado, [2019] | Includes bibliographical references
   and index.
Identifiers: LCCN 2019025981 (print) | LCCN 2019025982 (ebook) | ISBN 9781607329473 (cloth) |
   ISBN 9781607329480 (paperback) | ISBN 9781607329558 (ebook)
Subjects: LCSH: YouTube (Electronic resource) | Online social networks—Social aspects. | Internet
   videos—Social aspects. | Mass media and anthropology. | Mass media and culture.
Classification: LCC HC79.T4 L364 2019 (print) | LCC HC79.T4 (ebook) | DDC 302.30285—dc23
LC record available at https://lccn.loc.gov/2019025981
LC ebook record available at https://lccn.loc.gov/2019025982

An electronic version of this book is freely available, thanks to the support of libraries
working with Knowledge Unlatched. KU is a collaborative initiative designed to make high-quality
books open access for the public good. More information about the initiative and links to the open-
access versions can be found at www.knowledgeunlatched.org.

Cover illustrations: Smartphone image © studioZEVS/Shutterstock; vlogger image © Jacob Lund /
Shutterstock.

CONTENTS

Acknowledgments   vii

CHAPTER 1: Introduction   3

CHAPTER 2: YouTube Initiation: Participating through a Camera   32

CHAPTER 3: Growing Closer: Sharing Time and Space   69

CHAPTER 4: Syncing Up through Reciprocity   107

CHAPTER 5: What Defines a Community?   145

CHAPTER 6: Portals to the Posthuman   187

CHAPTER 7: Living with Arrhythmia: Prospects for Renewal   225

CHAPTER 8: Conclusion   253

Notes   283
References   309
Index   339

ACKNOWLEDGMENTS

I am deeply grateful to my husband, Andrew Lange, and to my children, Catherine and Alexander, for their steadfast support of my projects. I also wish to thank my parents, Jay and Lilia Gonzalez, as well as my sister, Leah Jarlsberg, and my brother, Michael Gonzalez, for their lifelong encouragement. Special thanks also to Chris Jarlsberg for his support. Thanks to the Lange clan, especially Janet and Jay Lange, as well as Colin Lange, Tessa Tinney, and Jonathan Lange.

I wish to extend thanks to Virginia Kuhn, Holly Willis, Gabriel Peters-Lazaro, and all the staff of the Institute for Multimedia Literacy at the University of Southern California (USC), for their encouragement. I am grateful also to USC's Department of Anthropology. I would like to acknowledge the encouragement I received from Nancy Lutkehaus and Jenny Cool. Special thanks also to Lanita Jacobs for her friendship and support.

I am grateful to the John D. and Catherine T. MacArthur Foundation for its support of my research on YouTube. For their intellectual inspiration and leadership, I wish to thank Mimi Ito and the late Peter Lyman. Thanks also to Wesley Shrum, Executive Director of Ethnografilm 2014. For encouraging my filmmaking endeavors, I would like to thank Heather Horst. Special thanks to Bonnie Nardi for her generous mentorship.

I am grateful to my colleagues at California College of the Arts (CCA) for their support of my work. I would like to thank Stephen Beal, Tammy Rae Carland, Tina Takemoto, Emily McVarish, Tirza Latimer, Juvenal Acosta, Kim Anno, J

Carter, Mitchell Schwarzer, Jackie Francis, Max Leung, Rebekah Edwards, Stuart Kendall, Ignacio Valero, Barry Katz, Jeanette Roan, Beth Mangini, and Brook Hinton. Special thanks also to Teri Dowling and Bobby White. At the Columbus College of Art & Design, I'd like to extend my thanks to Melanie Corn for her support. At the San Francisco Art Institute, I would like to acknowledge the support of Rachel Schreiber.

From fields ranging from media studies to filmmaking to video blogging, I would like to thank Henry Jenkins, Michael Wesch, Howard Rheingold, Mindy Faber, Jean Burgess, Joshua Green, Ryanne Hodson, Jay Dedman, Micki Krimmel, Michael Verdi, Steve Woolf, Zadi Diaz, Markus Sandy, Alicia Shay, Mike Ambs, Roxanne Darling, Lan Bui, Vu Bui, Jen Proctor, Rick Rey, Eric Rey, Kent Nichols, and Jonathan McIntosh.

I wish to thank all the people of YouTube who participated in my ethnographic research project and who contributed videos that provided insight on sharing the self through media. I would like to express my special thanks to OhCurt for making me feel welcome to YouTube and encouraging me to keep the camera rolling. Special thanks also to robtran, whose commentary about community and its limits provided crucial insight about our increasingly posthuman condition. Thanks to Joe "Mystery Guitar Man" Penna for his kind support of the project. I would also like to acknowledge the support and enthusiasm of thetalesend and ZenArcher, bright spirits who truly made a difference to the YouTube community and whose presence is greatly missed.

At the University of Michigan, I would like to thank Conrad Kottak, Bruce Mannheim, and Ruth Behar for their intellectual inspiration and generous support. I am also extremely grateful for interactions I have had over the years with Jan English-Lueck and Chuck Darrah at San José State University.

I am also grateful to Julie LaFramboise and our mutual friend for providing emotional support and friendship while juggling research and motherhood. I cherish our friendship deeply!

As a long-term San Francisco Bay Area resident, I wish to thank the friends who made Los Angeles seem like a magical place while I lived and worked there. I would like to thank Ann-Marie and Keith Fine, Jenny and David Madariaga, and Rose and Behram Parekh.

For attending my preview screening at CCA and encouraging my filmmaking, I would like to thank Sally Rayn, Brian Cheu, Padric McCaig, Eric Share, and the intrepid attendees from Platypus: the CASTAC Blog, notably Jordan Kraemer and Michael Scroggins. CASTAC stands for the Committee for the Anthropology of Science and Technology, a division of the American Anthropological Association.

Special thanks also to Gwen Dewar and Adrienne Young for sharing many anthropological insights. For their contribution to the field of media studies and their kind support, I wish to thank Annette Markham and Theresa Senft.

I also wish to acknowledge the ongoing support of my friends Chris and Jan Cooke, Kevin Carter and Che Johnson, and Matthew Carhart and Matthew DeCoster.

Thanks to all the members of the Bay Area Anthropology and Philosophy Group and the Dumbarton Circle, especially Melissa Cefkin, Mazyar Lotfalian, and Shreeharsh Kelkar, for helping participants to deepen our knowledge about the philosophical roots of anthropology.

I wish to thank the anonymous reviewers for their insightful comments and suggestions. Thanks also to the entire team at the University Press of Colorado for their care and attention to my book. Finally, I wish to thank my editor, Charlotte Steinhardt. I am grateful for her guidance in helping to bring this book into its final form.

THANKS FOR WATCHING

1

INTRODUCTION

For many people, YouTube is a website for watching wacky videos. For the people profiled in this book, YouTube is a state of mind. It is not just a video-sharing website but rather a perspective that welcomes video makers of all abilities into a mediated, social space. Even with its challenges in hostile audiences and policies privileging commercialization, interviewees characterized the YouTube experience as much more than posting videos. People forging social ties considered themselves part of a YouTube community by interpersonally sharing videos on topics that were important to them.

People in this self-identified community came from many walks of life, including office administrators, technical writers, nurses, homemakers, social workers, comedians, documentarians, and actors. They connected in order to have fun and improve the craft of making videos. YouTube participants—defined here as those who posted comments or videos—became friends through the media they made and the experiences they shared. Themes that helped people connect included everything from mourning a loss to sharing excitement about the personal and social benefits of making and globally distributing one's own media. The idea of "YouTube" is analyzed the way many YouTubers saw it—as an attitude about what it means to engage democratically through video.

After opening to the public in December 2005, YouTube enabled creators to share their vernacular, pre-professional, or professional voice through video. The site quickly moved toward commercialization in 2007 with the addition of ads and

DOI: 10.5876/9781607329558.c001

monetized partnerships. Popular media makers were exclusively invited into the partnership program.[1] The monetization effort expanded in late 2007[2] to allow applications to the program and again in 2012, enabling anyone to monetize single videos.[3] It was restricted in 2017[4] and again in 2018 in favor of larger, ad-friendly creators.[5] Interviewees did not necessarily perceive monetization as incompatible with sociality, but the way monetization rolled out negatively impacted some YouTubers who became disenchanted and left the site. Nevertheless, interviewees in the study often remained connected to their YouTube friends—even after migrating to other social media.

This book deals with a concept of "YouTube" as an orienting framework for people socially interacting through videos and other social media. When YouTube participants gathered in person, they recorded their activities with an eye toward posting and enjoying the videos online. Back on YouTube, viewing meet-up footage encouraged people to interact again in person so that YouTube's connotations threaded online and off in a "mediascape,"[6] often in cyclical ways.

Thanks for Watching uses an anthropological approach to explain how interpersonal dynamics are mediated through video. Anthropologists often make the familiar strange and the strange familiar. To those who see it as a familiar video-watching site, the concept of YouTube in this book may seem strange; it functioned socially for people. Given that so many people from around the world of different ages and types were vlogging, they sometimes playfully referred to YouTube in a way that was analogous to a fictional country with its own customs and values called "YouTubia."[7] To those who feel that sharing so much of the self through video is strange, the book empathetically examines why personal media-sharing practices were so compelling. As a media-shy person, I initially considered such intimate sharing odd and discomforting, and thus my perspective resonates with the more traditional anthropological approach of studying lifeways that are distinct from one's own.[8] During a multiyear project, I became a YouTuber and participated in a video-sharing culture to understand its rhythms and sociality. Although I never disclosed highly personal information, I did share videos about one personal passion—the anthropological study of video-sharing practices. Over the course of the project, I came to appreciate why people bonded through video.

This book's title—*Thanks for Watching: An Anthropological Study of Video Sharing on YouTube*—reflects how I, as an anthropologist, analyzed YouTube's participatory dynamics. It also examines found visual materials from YouTubers who produced video blogs (vlogs) in ways that articulated their goals and dreams for YouTube's participatory and social potential. On YouTube the term "participation" exhibits various meanings.[9] For YouTubers, participation often dynamically moved from watching to commenting and eventually to making and sharing videos. Although interviewees believed that even non-video-making activities such as commenting were community-building, a strong social pull existed for YouTube participants to make their own videos and share their individual perspectives.

YOUTUBE'S CULTURAL INFLUENCE

YouTube is a massive and ever-changing entity. Since videos come and go every minute, no two instantiations of YouTube are ever the same. Policies about monetization and privacy also continually change—sometimes reportedly without warning or explanation. What remains consistent is its popularity and sustained cultural influence. YouTube's participatory statistics are staggering. Founded by former employees of the online payment system PayPal in 2005, YouTube was purchased by Google for an estimated $1.65 billion in 2006.[10] As of 2007, six hours of video were uploaded to the site every minute.[11] Receiving 1 billion monthly visitors by 2013,[12] YouTube continues to see dramatic increases in video postings and viewership. In 2017, YouTube viewers were watching 1 billion hours of video per day, a figure that threatens to surpass television viewing time.[13] By 2017, 400 hours of video were uploaded *every minute* to the site,[14] which represents four times the amount of video uploaded in 2013.[15] According to the Pew Research Center, YouTube is the second most used social networking site, behind only Facebook. In a 2014 study of US internet usage, Pew reported that 77 percent of adult internet users participated on Facebook, compared with 63 percent who used YouTube. YouTube was also far more popular than LinkedIn (25 percent) or Twitter (21 percent).[16]

Pew's statistics suggest that YouTube maintains a strong position in the public imagination. However, such generalized statistics tell only part of the story. When we ethnographically examine YouTubers' individual stories, we see that ultimately the idea of YouTube is many things to different people. Many viewers use it to relax and watch funny videos. Other YouTube participants use it to professionalize creative work, learn how to make videos, and to socialize. Even to a single individual, YouTube's multiple connotations change at different times in life, a fact that is revealed by the temporal approach taken in this book. Sometimes YouTube participation means watching videos alone; during hard times it involves telling painful stories to connect with others dealing with similar circumstances.

Mass media have largely presented only a partial view of YouTube that emphasizes its viral, profit-centric, video-of-the-week fare. Past scholarly assessments of YouTube have similarly focused on topics such as popular videos, prospects for monetization, and YouTube "stars." It is difficult to think about YouTube without picturing funny viral videos. In scholarly presentations in which I include YouTube video clips, viewers often have trouble recognizing quiet vlogs as true YouTube videos. During my talks I have been bewildered by the question of why my presentation contains no clips of YouTube videos with piano-playing cats or boys with lasers in their garages!

Although exploring the impact of virality and celebrity culture is important, the standard focus on the site's outrageous forms impacts how public discourse is shaped to deal with vernacular video voices. YouTube greatly facilitates promoting crass and outré videos, making it difficult for scholars to locate and discuss everyday vernacular work. Mass media and news sources focus on the most outrageous examples and use denigrating and dismissive language in a way that comparatively showcases their own assumed professionalism and levels of quality vis-à-vis the vernacular. For example, as media scholar Henry Jenkins has stated, if news outlets only ever quote silly or disturbing videos instead of thoughtful ones, such a choice helps identify the news program or other professional media as exhibiting superior quality in comparison to vernacular messages.[17] Professional media discourse often obscures views of YouTube that are thoughtful, insightful, and compelling for the story of human mediation.

Popular discourses have so thoroughly focused on crassness, comedy, and video virality that viewers have difficulty accepting contemplative videos as authentic "YouTube videos." Yet many YouTubers are often productively self-reflective and eloquent about their life experiences. Popular works tend to drown out subtle videos of sociality that have always been a cornerstone of the site. *Thanks for Watching* shines a light on everyday video statements and, more importantly, the processes by which people create and share them.

THE GOALS OF THIS BOOK

YouTube may have started life as a "visual repository,"[18] but its uses for sociality and learning have considerably expanded. The first major goal of this book is to analyze everyday media practices by offering a behind-the-scenes look at videos produced by people who formed a community of video enthusiasts. Unlike prior studies, it provides an analytical account that moves beyond the site itself and critically examines not just videos but practices that people engage with over time, including meeting up in person. By moving beyond the 'Tube and taking a temporal approach that examines interactive dynamics, the book illustrates just how deeply media are intertwined with contemporary sociality.

In anthropology it has long been acknowledged that it is not possible to study a whole culture. A research project can reveal only what anthropologist James Clifford called a "partial truth" of a vast cultural world.[19] This book can present only a partial view of YouTube—but one that crucially offers an "alternative narrative" to the dominant YouTube celebrity and monetization stories.[20] Although a few YouTube stars make cameos when analytically appropriate, this book focuses on people who shared an interest in improving their craft and found it meaningful to socialize with other YouTubers. The stories told here are just as true as those that emphasize video virality and celebrity, but they provide a lasting alternative narrative because they challenge common assumptions about how mediated sociality works. Making media is now inseparable from experiencing and even creating many of the events that we are trying to mediate.

Anthropological concepts such as participant-observation, reciprocity, and community were originally developed through the study of small-scale societies. A second goal of this book is to investigate whether such theoretical concepts resonate in the highly technologized and mediated idiom of YouTube. The book argues that many of these concepts still apply, but in new form. In some cases the concepts have been re-theorized within anthropology itself and take on different connotations and meanings. In other cases video-sharing dynamics invite reformulations of anthropological concepts. For example, anthropologists who studied cyborg anthropology in the 1990s explored the intimate way in which technologies are integrated into the body and influence life. This book elaborates on this project and investigates whether we are entering a "posthuman" era in terms of humans' deep involvement with technology. Although anthropologists continue to study humans, immersion in technological forms often subjectively yields discomforting as well as connective posthuman experiences that this book examines.

By studying YouTube sociality anthropologically, the third goal of this book is to take seriously how temporalities frame and influence mediated interaction. Many media studies focus on identity work and self-presentation by examining videos at a single point in time—a framework that has productively analyzed mediation. However, this book takes a different approach by focusing on temporal patterns and how they provide clues about culturally influenced interaction. Rather than only interpreting video content, this book's rubric takes into account *processes* of video sharing. It concentrates on patterns of participation over time and analyzes how people deepen their sociality, deal with tensions on the site, and use publicly temporal orientations to create a shared sense of history within a concept of "YouTube."

YOUTUBE'S PARTICIPATORY RHYTHMS

How might one meet the challenge of studying a *concept* of YouTube ethnographically and anthropologically? This book draws on several modes of visual production and digital participation to identify key interactive rhythms that subtly operate amid a heterogeneous mass of visual images and comments. It analyzes these rhythms and patterns and how they play out to examine how we use media not just to express the self but to show our affection for others.

Analyzing behavioral rhythms is important for understanding cultural organization and conflict. Philosopher and sociologist of everyday life, Henri Lefebvre used an approach that he termed "rhythmanalysis" to encourage attention to cultural rhythms and their origins and effects.[21] His rubric inspires this book's approach, which involves developing sensitivity toward appreciating life's rhythms, processes, conflicts, and temporalities and their meanings in everyday life.[22] Lefebvre's rubric has proven especially useful for exploring nontraditional forms of ethnography and their loci of study.[23] The current project is not concerned with addressing all of Lefebvre's terms but rather draws inspiration from his rubric to see how rhythms and various trajectories of media-making influence participation in digital milieus.

For Lefebvre, rhythm was present whenever there was "interaction between a place, a time and an expenditure of energy."[24] He was particularly concerned with examining repetitions of actions, determining whether behavioral trajectories were linear or cyclical, and analyzing how actions exhibited temporal stages, including "birth, growth, peak, then decline and end."[25] Similarly, this book will follow one Lefebvrian cycle for a social group that came together on the site. It traces how they moved from initiation to intensification of participation. It analyzes how YouTubers reached a peak of sociality through perceived community formation but saw participatory decline and ruptures through monetization, haters, death, and digital migration. The book also supplements the Lefebvrian rubric by examining prospects for rebirth or renewal as creators returned from video-making hiatuses or envisioned new sites that more closely mapped to their idea of a useful, socially oriented, video-sharing platform.

Video-sharing practices exhibit multiple experiential temporalities. The term temporality "designates how beings experience such processual qualities in different sociocultural contexts."[26] Rhythms of interaction occur at several layers of analysis, including the micro level of response to a single video. For example, YouTubers believed that in social-sharing circles, a video's most intensive viewership—or what this book calls its *pace of receptive vitality*—is usually a few days; most commentary and views tended to appear within that window. An activity's timing is important and exhibits specific meanings. A comment posted in the first blush of a video's posting may be read quite differently than the same comment posted years later.

Rhythms occur at broader levels of observation as well. Online sites often have a participatory rhythm that begins with contributors' initial excitement, moves to intensive participation, and invites feelings of connection. Yet participants may ultimately experience disillusionment after problems ensue and more popular services emerge.[27] Sometimes sites become associated with older populations, and young people migrate to media with more youthful connotations. Sites emerge, enjoy intensive use, and ultimately fade from supporting a critical mass. They may even be shut down, thus effectively dying.

Humans and media exhibit both similar and distinctly different rhythmic patterns, which are punctuated by diverse forms of beginnings and endings. Humans, for instance, have a linear life trajectory. We are born, meet new people, have experiences, and die. Digital media, however, enable parts of us to continue as representations possibly in perpetuity, thus existing long past the human life-cycle rhythm. The perpetuation of media enables us to become "posthuman," such that alternative versions of ourselves, or our "alters," live on. These asymmetrical temporalities and desires for our alters' futures create tensions that are analyzed in this book. While some video makers hope their media will linger forever, others prefer it to be terminated in a contemporaneous way with the end of their life cycle. Attending to varied rhythms and their tension points enables insight into human mediation.

Rhythm analysis reveals nuances of "participation," a word that characterizes how people engage in creative production on social media sites. The book explains how mediated rhythms influence specific characterizations of participation on YouTube. It analyzes how interactive tensions may emerge when participatory rhythms are, in Lefebvre's terms, "polyrhythmic"[28] or operate according to multiple cultural beats. For example, some people encourage other YouTubers to subscribe to their videos right away. Since YouTube's opening in 2005 and continuing to 2018, to subscribe to another YouTuber has simply meant pressing a Subscribe button for a particular video maker and then being alerted at no cost when new videos from that creator are posted. Other creators resented such immediate demands for reciprocity and preferred to "discover" videos in their own time. Polyrhythmic differences in video viewing could result in "arrthymias" or asymmetrical rhythms that translated into participatory pathologies and conflicts. Understanding cultural and social rhythms and patterns offers an insightful way to anthropologically examine how interactive opportunities and tensions might be addressed to broaden participation, sociality, and knowledge exchange through media.

To develop his ideas, Lefebvre philosophically gazed out of his window to observe lively rhythms of behavior on local Parisian streets. Similarly, scholars may productively identify how people perceive rhythms of mediated life and analyze the meanings of alternatively harmonious and conflicting rhythms in everyday interaction online. But we need to do more than "look out the window" or, in this case, glance at our screens and "watch" or "read" YouTube videos. To gain a deeper understanding, it is beneficial to participate directly within circles of sociality. Participating in networked groups involves meeting people, as well as recording and sharing digital media, in order to experience the effects of mediation in YouTube-centric, social milieus.

PRIOR SCHOLARLY APPROACHES

By analyzing and mediating a concept of YouTube, the book joins an ongoing scholarly conversation that initially sought to analyze YouTube by "reading" and "watching" videos on the site. In their book (first published in 2009 and updated in 2018), media scholars Jean Burgess and Joshua Green engaged in close readings of a survey of thousands of popular videos on the site.[29] They identified key patterns that emerged within the first few years of YouTube's launch. They focused on how YouTube was structured as a media system and how it related to commercial media. Their foundational text insightfully lays out key debates and challenges that YouTube participants and YouTube as an entity faced, including disruptions to old media and cultural politics.

Using a method that also concentrates on video content, communication scholar Anandam Kavoori approached this terrain by "reading" and conceptualizing YouTube videos and their related discourse (including comments) in order to produce a thought-provoking taxonomy.[30] Kavoori focused on the viral aspect of YouTube, including how videos promote and organize celebrity culture and how such culture shapes future experiences. For example, watching viral videos about childhood begins to shape our experiential understanding of childhood itself.

While Kavoori was concerned with "reading" videos, communication and media scholar Michael Strangelove "watched" YouTube to investigate its social uses.[31] He analyzed issues of great interest to this book, including investigating prospects for community and challenging the online and offline dichotomy. This book shares Strangelove's philosophy of approaching vernacular video not in terms of judgments about supposedly failed quality, but rather taking these works and interactions "seriously" and studying them "sympathetically" as part of life. His goal is to understand videos' cultural role, a move that follows a larger trajectory in communication and media studies. I agree with Strangelove that ultimately "an amateur video on YouTube should be analyzed not merely as a text but as a process," in part because video meanings relate to community interactions and responses.[32] *Thanks for Watching* studies processes of video making and sharing in a central way.

In addition to media scholarship, this book continues a decades-long tradition of digital ethnography in which researchers become part of an online community and observe interaction to analyze patterns of sociality.[33] Recent examples of this approach from anthropologists include Tom Boellstorff's *Coming of Age in Second Life* (2008), which studied key aspects of online culture, including racism, sexism, commercialization, relationships, and antisocial behavior within the digital environment of Second Life. In contrast, the present study engaged with people both online and at in-person gatherings to see how video making was processual and interwoven across different media modalities. Another anthropologically motivated digital ethnography is Bonnie Nardi's *My Life as a Night Elf Priest* (2010), which explores cultural and gaming dynamics such as sexism and addiction to the game of *World of Warcraft*. My book *Kids on YouTube* (2014) focuses on how young people used the site to learn participatory skills and to develop a technologized identity. In contrast to works that analyze identity formation using digital media, *Thanks for Watching* examines adults' participatory dynamics through the interactive choices they make to accomplish video sociality.

Thanks for Watching departs from prior approaches in terms of its detailed attention to the video-making process, including discussing dynamics such as interpersonal reciprocities and migratory patterns into and out of the site. This book investigates how the acts of *making* and *sharing* videos are situated within a larger interactive field that includes varying levels of mediation and participation. In contrast to many prior works in digital environments, *Thanks for Watching* is less centrally concerned with identity formation through media creation than it is with analyzing how video creation and sharing support or challenge mediated sociality. The focus is not solely on reading or watching videos but on participating directly over time and attending carefully to how interaction and interwoven modalities influence the dynamics of a particular cultural group.

ETHNOGRAPHIC APPROACH

Thanks for Watching lies at the intersection of digital media studies and visual anthropology, an interdisciplinary terrain that some scholars refer to as "digital visual anthropology."[34] In addition to examining digital milieus and participating across modalities, the book also draws on traditional visual anthropology approaches as outlined by anthropologists Jay Ruby and Richard Chalfen. Under this rubric visual anthropology includes one or more of the following: (1) recording or collecting visual materials of people, things, and events to analyze human behavior (in this case recording observations and interviews); (2) studying found visual artifacts (in this case YouTube videos); and (3) using visual media to present data and research findings (in this case vlogs and a feature-length video).[35] Anthropologists Howard Morphy and Marcus Banks argue that visual anthropology is not just a method for interpreting visual materials but also enables analyzing visual systems and visual cultural forms.[36] A key line of evidence includes studying YouTubers' own videos, which reveal how they are "expert witnesses" of their mediated experiences.[37]

According to anthropologists Nancy Lutkehaus and Jennifer Cool, scholars are increasingly studying their own culture in an attempt to encourage "intelligent dialogue across ethnic, class, and cultural lines, among individuals different from one another, but who nonetheless can benefit from attempting to convey their differences."[38] In one sense I was studying my own culture of fellow media enthusiasts in the United States. However, in several key ways I was quite different from the people whom I studied. Some interviewees were advanced media makers or technologists who knew much more about making media than I did. Unlike some interviewees who struggled financially in low-paying jobs, I am an academic with access to considerable resources. My goal was to promote meaningful dialogue across various cultural lines, especially with regard to transmitting one's message through video blogging.

The book draws on multiple lines of evidence to understand how people share the self through media and how their interactive choices confirm or challenge anthropological concepts such as participant-observation, chronotopes, reciprocity, emplacement, community, digital migration, and even being "human." The analysis draws on evidence collected from 2006 to 2018. It combines the following data collection activities:

- Interviewing 152 people who engaged at various levels with video making and/ or YouTube
- Participating in ten gatherings in diverse locations, including New York City; Marietta, Georgia; Los Angeles (Hollywood); San Francisco; San Diego; Minneapolis; Philadelphia; Toronto, Canada; Santa Monica; and Anaheim, California (VidCon)
- Attending twenty video-themed events, such as the video festival Pixelodeon in Los Angeles and the *Ask a Ninja* DVD release party in Hollywood
- Analyzing more than 300 YouTube videos
- Maintaining two research video blogs (both called AnthroVlog, which stands for Anthropology Video Blog), one on YouTube and the other on a separate video blogging site called WordPress
- Recording, directing, and producing an ethnographic film entitled *Hey Watch This! Sharing the Self through Media* (2013),[39] which includes interviews and observations of people at meet-ups
- Analyzing my video-recorded footage from gatherings that did not appear in the film or in the video blogs but provide insight about YouTube interaction.

A cornerstone of anthropology includes participant-observation, in which a researcher becomes part of a community to gain insights that are difficult to glean from analyzing artifacts alone. As part of the ethnographic project, I established my own channel on YouTube. A YouTube channel is similar to a social media profile page. It is required to post comments or upload videos. Each channel includes information supplied by the YouTube service, such as a list of videos that the account holder has posted, the date that creators opened the channel on YouTube, and the number of views that the videos accumulated. The channel also contains information supplied by the account holder, such as a textual description of the account and playlists (thematically curated groups of videos). Each channel also has a Discussion section enabling public comments.

I created a video blog called AnthroVlog to engage in participant-observation on YouTube. On each video's text description, I stated that the channel was a research site and that posted comments might be used in research. According to most research standards, public commentary of this type is open to analysis, but a note about the vlog's status as a research site was included. Although the name AnthroVlog was not particularly novel, it reiterated to anyone whom I met that I was an anthropologist attending meet-ups and interviewing people about their YouTube experiences. It provided a recognizable, stable identity on the site and reminded people that I was collecting data through my encounters.

Studying YouTube anthropologically meant accepting vulnerability by showing my work in progress to the world and by broadcasting a series that I called "open video fieldnotes," which included recorded video interviews and observations as I encountered them to stimulate discussion and further data collection. As of July 2018, AnthroVlog on YouTube had 670 subscribers, which reflects a social rather than mass following. Most of the videos received a few hundred views. However, videos in which I interviewed well-known YouTubers, academics, or media experts received several thousand views.

In total I interviewed 152 people who were mostly from the United States.[40] I interviewed 57 females and 95 males who ranged in age from being in middle-school to having grandchildren. This book focuses on analyzing case studies of adults who formed an interwoven social network. It also includes material from YouTube videos on themes addressed in the book. Most of the people discussed in the study were early adopters; they joined within the first year of the site's launch. As of 2015, reports indicate that most YouTube viewers are thirteen to thirty-four years old (although viewers under thirteen are not tracked).[41] Most of the people profiled in this book are in their twenties to thirties, although I also interviewed YouTubers in their forties and fifties. The research protocol was structured so that adult interviewees over eighteen could choose whether they wished to be referred to in the research by their official name, their channel name, or a researcher-selected pseudonym. Official name here refers to a consistent name appearing on public documents and reported sources about a person, such as a Wikipedia page, press report, personal web page, or social media site. Since interviewees profiled in this book were not compensated, this gesture enabled adult vloggers to advertise their work in the research. Most interviewees chose their channel name. If interviewees preferred that I refer to them using their official name or a researcher-assigned pseudonym, this is so indicated throughout the book.

The semistructured interview protocol included questions aimed at understanding people's participatory trajectory, processes of video sharing, and experiences on the site over time. Typical interview questions included:

- How did you get started on YouTube?
- How did you find YouTube as an environment for posting your videos?
- Is YouTube a community? How so? If not, why not?
- Do you feel you must comment back to people who have posted comments to your videos? Why or why not?
- Does posting comments count as participation on YouTube?
- What do you think of the practice of "sub for sub" whereby people agree to subscribe to your YouTube account and watch your videos if you promise to do the same for them?
- What do you owe your subscribers, if anything?
- Why did you attend this meet-up?
- Have you been to meet-ups before? Which ones? How did they compare to this one?
- (If interviewing a meet-up organizer) What prompted you to organize this meet-up? What were some of the benefits and challenges of organizing a meet-up? Did you receive support from YouTube?
- What have been your biggest challenges in posting videos on the site?
- What would be the best outcome of participating on YouTube?

Thanks for Watching takes a diachronic view that examines creators' experiences at multiple stages of their YouTube journey. This approach revealed that associations with fellow YouTubers often continued on other media and showed how YouTube became a socially orienting framework rather than only the name of a website. By recording, curating, participating in, and mediating a social slice of YouTube, this book draws attention to subtle interactive rhythms and engages with intelligently mediated life in the vlogosphere.

LIFE IN "YOUTUBIA"

The purpose of the study, which was initially funded by the MacArthur Foundation, emerged from an interest in understanding digital media use in the United States. When I selected YouTube as my research site and launched my study in 2006–2008, the United States dominated the YouTube scene. In 2008 anthropologist Michael Wesch created a Digital Ethnography research program at Kansas State University and observed that video makers in the United States uploaded five times more videos to the site than did video makers from the country with the next largest number of uploads, the United Kingdom.[42] Wesch and his team also noted patterns of sociality and communication that were occurring between participants and constituted an important video genre on the site. In terms of popular content, in 2010, five years after YouTube's launch, the top five most-subscribed channels on YouTube were all males from the United States, each with roughly 2 million subscribers.[43] In 2016, when measured as the number of monthly active users of YouTube, the United States reportedly accounted for more than double the view traffic from the next largest country, which was Brazil.[44]

Social activities profiled in this book include video makers commenting on and viewing each other's work, hanging out at public meet-ups, and making videos together. One could visually see how interconnections were being formed and solidified through media. For example, in one video two women living on opposite coasts in the United States document their trip to the Vatican. Comments might initiate chains of interactions, such as one in which a commenter offered to get together, saying: "BTW, I'm going to be in LA on Monday if you wanna hang out :)." In videos, YouTubers described how they became close to their YouTube friends. Friendship might begin by posting comments to each others' videos. Interaction then moved off of YouTube to other platforms such as social media and email. Friends began meeting in person at larger meet-ups as well as making private visits to each other's homes. These gatherings and hang-out sessions were continually occurring across the network of interviewees profiled in this book.

Demographic information and video data (such as view counts and subscriber numbers) are included throughout the book to broadly index each video maker's type of work and audience size. To standardize comparisons, video statistics were collected at roughly the same time in June–July 2018. Services that track YouTube statistics claim that about half of all YouTube videos peak at 500 views, even after being posted for months, and that 60 percent of YouTube videos never go beyond 1,000 views.[45] A video maker in the study who regularly receives a few thousand views on each video likely has a robust social following. Creators of a video receiving tens of thousands of views or more may be eligible for monetizing their YouTube-related work.

Subscriber numbers are provided but serve only as a guide. Creators generally have more subscribers than views on videos. Watching videos regularly involves a more intensive level of commitment than just clicking a Subscribe button. One interviewee who vlogged about her religious faith and health issues noted that about 24 percent of her subscribers actually "tuned in" and kept watching and commenting on her work as regular viewers. If accurate, her estimate reflects a strong viewer/subscriber ratio, especially for a socially oriented vlog. Media specialists estimate that a healthy viewer-to-subscriber ratio is usually from 10 percent to 14 percent for those who wish to commercialize their YouTube account. Professionals typically need to intensify social interactions, such as responding to comments, to keep viewers engaged.[46]

This book analyzes a wide variety of video makers. Some creators had a knack for making videos and developed a sufficient following to contemplate a new career in making media. Others did not expect to professionalize; they simply had fun through a camera. For example, I interviewed a white woman and social worker in her early thirties who had been on the site for about two years. She had become popular on YouTube under the channel name NutCheese. She vlogged, often humorously, about topics such as awkward moments in church, interacting with other YouTubers, collaborative videos (collabs) such as montages of YouTubers burping, hanging out with her nephews, her YouTube addiction—and her trip to the Vatican with a fellow YouTuber. She regularly receives thousands of views on each of her videos and had amassed 6,547 subscribers as of June 2018. Although she had a respectable following for a nonprofessional media maker, during her interview NutCheese said that she did not have professional aspirations. She intended to participate on YouTube only as long as "it was fun."

Interactive dynamics invite reflection on whether this social group constituted a video-sharing "culture." Anthropologists often define culture as sets of "traditions and customs, transmitted through learning, that form and guide the beliefs and behavior of the people exposed to them."[47] Yet the concept remains contested in terms of its varied definitions and whether people operating in a culture really agree on its norms and values. One objection is that culture, when used as a noun, has the connotation of being "some kind of object, thing, or substance" in a way that suggests homogeneity among people who presumably belong to a specific culture.[48] The anthropological record demonstrates that social phenomena are much more complicated. People contest cultural rules and values, and they often do not follow the precepts of their supposed culture. In addition, people do not belong to just a single culture but to multiple cultures that may intersect, run in parallel, or unpredictably conflict. Anthropological studies now tend to privilege the adjectival form of the word. The idea is to emphasize differences that groups wish to express so that people may mobilize distinctive, collective identifications.[49] Similarly, this book does not analyze a single culture but rather cultural practices and ideals associated with a particular video-motivated social group.

I joined YouTube early in its life cycle in 2006 and analyzed materials until 2018, a time span long enough to observe the site's changing dynamics and impacts. I watched how YouTubers negotiated new cultural expressions and tensions due to monetization within a technical and economic infrastructure. When YouTubers from the United States first arrived, they brought ideas from their cultures to media making. At the same time, they had to contend with specific technical features, people, and commercialized motivations on the site. Examining these interactions and confrontations provided a window into how YouTubers envisioned a video-sharing site that would more directly support their desires.

FACILITATING THE THIRD WAVE OF NETWORKED ACCESS

The site's corporate decisions have complicated the vernacular focus that fueled its initial popularity. YouTube moved toward professionalized fare, such as paid subscription services that offer television programs and films online.[50] YouTubers interested in sociality reacted negatively to many of the changes that facilitated commercialization. However, this book does not argue that the mediated configuration of sociality that it analyzes is idealized; in fact it addresses opportunities and tensions that were present from its inception.

As we move into increasingly mediated futures, the stories in this book provide a harbinger for how video may be used for sociality as well as commercialization. It provides a "history of the future," as the post-phenomenologists say.[51] The idea is to "search for the roots of [future] possibilities in the very recent past" so that "the focus [is] on the potentialities that are waiting to be realized, referring to the present as a condition for the future."[52] This book's "history of the future" outlines practices and features that supported and complicated sociality. From a techno-science studies perspective, it analyzes events to discuss "potentialities and trajectories"[53] of what future sites interested in social video sharing and learning might accomplish. Developing usable platforms is particularly salient given that vernacular voices are fighting to retain productive, expressive, and interconnected mediated milieus.

Thanks for Watching adds to the discourse of addressing the "third wave" of internet access, which involves ensuring user-friendly, digital arenas of media exchange.[54] Whereas the first wave of networked access aimed to achieve widespread physical access to the internet, the second wave addressed concerns about expanding access to include making content. While these concerns have not remotely been successfully addressed, we are nevertheless seeing a third wave of discourse, which concerns creating and implementing meaningful platforms that facilitate vernacular exchange. Platforms have politics in that they are the "curators of public discourse."[55] Therefore it is important to understand how platforms impact vernacular expression among intersecting participatory populations. Of course, features by themselves do not guarantee sociality. Much depends on interactive choices, and this book deals with the problematics of having asymmetrical expectations about what constitutes appropriate video exchange.

Cultural expression is "dialogic," meaning that video makers continually co-create their cultural forms through conversations, interactions, practices, and communicative choices.[56] Cultural expression has an "emergent quality"[57] that cannot be predicted simply by being familiar with video makers and the variables they contend with in new encounters. Just because a site offers a technical feature does not mean people will use it or believe that it promotes meaningful community. Tensions often emerged because YouTube simultaneously enabled a platform for sociality and for self-promotion. *Thanks for Watching* is concerned with the stories of those who negotiated such tensions by engaging in multiple, interactive modalities. For socially oriented video makers, a connection to "YouTubia" was never far away.

CHALLENGING TENACIOUS DISCOURSES

A set of common assumptions about everyday digital interaction has run in parallel to scholarly observations about how such experiences work. These suppositions perniciously hang on despite contrary evidence emerging from multiple disciplines over the last few decades. Presumptions about the separateness of so-called online versus offline experiences, a tendency to fault anonymity rather than underlying prejudices for precluding productive discourse, and the belief that video is inherently narcissistic are not possible to sustain amid contrary evidence. Although these assumptions have taken root in the popular imagination, the book will challenge these discourses by examining YouTubers' video sociality. It is vital to address the problematics of their generalizability in order to craft more user-friendly designs of creative, networked platforms.

Maximizing Modalities

So-called online and offline worlds and experiences are real, interwoven, and linked.[58] Yet scholarly works and popular discourses struggle with determining what constitutes an online versus an offline field of interaction. When YouTubers recorded a video at a gathering, the concept of YouTube deeply influenced that activity, thus entangling modalities. But when YouTubers constantly record themselves in a public park or live-stream the action, does this constitute "online" or "offline" interaction? This book argues that we need to wean ourselves away from these terms, even though they are entrenched and difficult to avoid, especially when citing prior studies, popular discourses, and remarks from interviewees.

Scholars have long recognized that multiple, mediated modalities exist. Modalities broadly refer to forms of sensory media that yield particular types of interaction. Within YouTube there are multiple modalities of interaction. Some people were happy to post text comment to videos; others preferred to interact through recording video responses. During in-person gatherings, various intensities of mediation also appeared. Sometimes people carried a camera and recorded everything they could; at other times the camera was mostly packed away. Modalities were chosen for specific purposes. For instance, at times YouTubers sought live, simultaneously connected links to each other rather than waiting for asynchronous YouTube videos. They hung out using a live chat service separate from YouTube.

Despite contemporary media inter-threadedness, it is striking to observe that news stories and research projects that acknowledge the link between the online and the offline continue to label online interaction as "not real." This discourse pervades the public consciousness, which is ethically problematic as digital phenomena such as online bullying and stalking are not taken seriously. Consider a recent headline proclaiming, "Real v. Online World: Teens Do Not Distinguish."[59] This headline portrays youth as on the digital leading edge, in part because they cannot differentiate (as adults supposedly can) the implied difference between what is assumed to be "real" (in-person interaction) and what is assumed to be not real (online interaction). The assumption is that teens *should* be able to differentiate and that, indeed, *online interaction is not real.* A moral undertone implicitly judges young people for their inability to tell the difference. Although there are clearly experiential differences across modalities, all of these experiences are equally real.[60] An email from one's boss is an actual communication, for instance. It cannot be conveniently ignored because it appears in digital, networked form.

It is far more productive to speak of "degree of intensity" and "type" of mediation rather than perpetuating an online (implied unreal) versus offline (implied real) binary. Moral undertones pervade characterizations of digital milieus. For example, one rubric equates "real life" with "lived reality," whereas online experiences are termed "digital life."[61] Even though the point of this rubric is to illustrate "blurriness" between these categorical experiences, the terminology risks reinforcing the idea that "digital life" is somehow not a part of "lived reality." Yet experiences such as cyberbullying (often conducted by people whom the sufferers know from school) demonstrate that what happens online cannot simply be dismissed as "unreal" or somehow separate from young people's "lived reality."

Different modalities of mediation are real; yet they exhibit different properties that this book acknowledges and critically examines. Socially oriented YouTubers demonstrated that emotions underlying different modalities of experience were often fungible or interchangeable. In other words, communication through videos online as well as videos made together at a meet-up felt interchangeably meaningful and emotionally important to interactants. Yet YouTubers sometimes experienced frictions in engaging with particular modalities. For example, YouTube participants might lose internet access or might have difficulty justifying the expense and sacrifice of taking time off from work to travel to gatherings. It is important to acknowledge instances of emotional fungibility between different modalities of expression while confronting frictions across physical modalities that result in asymmetrical access to resources and sociality.

Strict dichotomies between so-called online versus offline behaviors and interactions have been problematized by scholars in numerous fields.[62] However, they do not always agree on terminology.[63] Some researchers oppose the term "virtual" to a host of other terms, including the "real," the "actual," or the "physical."[64] One proposal involves referring to computer-mediated interaction as "online" interaction but using the term "onground" to underscore place-based aspects of interaction.[65] Gaming scholars have used the term "synthetic worlds" to refer to environments crafted by people to facilitate large-group interaction.[66] In computer science and design, one approach conceptualizes interaction not as a binary between mediated and unmediated interaction, but rather in terms of how people experience augmented forms of networked interaction in everyday life.[67] As anthropologist Bonnie Nardi has eloquently stated, "Perhaps language is still catching up to technologies that have altered human possibilities in ways we are only beginning to grasp."[68]

Drawing from her work on experimental digital media studies (such as Second Life and simulated virtual environments), Beth Coleman concluded that, for many people, being connected creates a pervasive, networked atmosphere that is "no longer distinctly virtual or real but, instead, representative of a diversity of network combinations."[69] Universal access has clearly not been achieved.[70] Yet, for many of us having the constant presence of devices that connect us to ideas and other people now augments our experiences and interactions such that we may properly accept "an end of the binary logic of virtual and real."[71]

Approaching the subject from the field of digital anthropology, Daniel Miller and his colleagues argue in a study of social media that "by now it is very evident that there is no such distinction—the online is just as real as the offline. Interactive media has already become such an integral part of everyday life that it makes no sense to see it as separate. No one today would regard a telephone conversation as taking place in a separate world from 'real life'"[72]—nor, I would add, would they refer to phone calls as "virtual" conversations. The difference is that telephone calls are familiar and do not carry moral undertones of being less than or parasitic to in-person experiences in the way that computer-mediated experiences often are.

Binary terminology does not exhibit globally consistent connotations. For instance, Miller and his team found that interviewees used the term "offline" to refer to sharing photographs via WhatsApp, a messenger application for phones that use the internet to share text, audio, images, and video.[73] This appears to be "online" behavior because images are digitized and distributed over a network. Yet interviewees drew on private connotations of using WhatsApp to send photographs to close friends such that they conceptualized this behavior as being conducted "offline."

In their videos many YouTubers describe how their participation is actually situated within larger media ecologies of interaction. Their practices, which exhibit varied intensities and types of mediation, ultimately contribute to YouTube as a larger mediascape that inter-threads multiple forms and degrees of mediation. Within this mediascape it is time to pay greater attention to videos that offer everyday commentary across modalities, thus challenging recurring fantasies and fears about digital interaction.

The Importance of Anonymity

A corollary to digital and moral dualisms about online interaction being "fake" is the idea that most mediated interactions are anonymous and that anonymity is the cause of degraded online discourse.[74] The anonymity debate has been researched in a variety of contexts, including legal issues and privacy.[75] My experiment in public anthropology (see chapter 5) showed that a proportion of anonymous discourse posted to my video *What Defines a Community?* was quite productive in exploring prospects for community on YouTube. Notably, the most *productive* commentary came from individuals *whom I did not know*. Eliminating anonymous commentary would likely have complicated an ability to methodologically reach beyond previously invested YouTube participants to examine diverse views on the subject.

The fantasy/fear of online anonymity is more difficult to maintain than one might assume. As media sociologist Lori Kendall observed, online interaction that is called anonymous is often actually *pseudonymous* because people exhibit similar behavior patterns over time using a consistent pseudonym.[76] Commenters to my videos and other YouTubers' work often left clues about their identities. "Haters" exhibited pseudonymously consistent behavior that reflected underlying societal prejudices that are ultimately more important to tackle than anonymity in and of itself.[77] Is the problem truly anonymity, or is it the fact that people are racist, sexist, or homophobic? If the latter, how might forms of connected learning such as those discussed in this book address widespread prejudices?

People often forget how much interaction is mediated between *known interlocutors* in digital contexts. Given enough motivation and resources, people's identities can be discovered by dedicated individuals or governments, even in the most secret realms, such as those of hackers.[78] Writing from the perspective of sociology and communication, Barry Wellman and Milena Gulia observed twenty years ago that "hackers are reluctant to change their pseudonyms regularly because the status associated with a particular nickname would be lost."[79]

In fact, conceptually we may ask, how well do we really know anyone? Husbands, wives, partners, children, parents, and friends all have their secrets. The more important question is, how much do we need to know someone to interact, accomplish collective goals, or persuade people to act or vote in certain ways? In fact, when the temporal approach of this book is applied, people clearly must deal with initially anonymous others in order to advance key goals, such as persuading others of civic positions or exploring potential future relationships. This book offers a rubric that suggests that knowing someone involves (1) assessing the *relevance* of knowing particular identity information; (2) having a *desire* to gain this information; and (3) having access to the *resources* to reveal the specific identity information we require.

Much of the angst about online interaction follows from the assumption that anonymity is equivalent to accountability. But it is possible to be anonymous to many people and still be accountable for one's actions. Examples include receiving reactions and commentary from individuals who protest inappropriate media. For instance, fellow YouTubers once alerted me to a horrific video of a headless person of color. Many of us reported this video, and it was immediately removed. A person may be anonymous to viewers but not to site administrators, who have access to more details about individuals and their accounts than does the average YouTube participant. Severely problematic accounts may be traced back to households or individuals who are reported to authorities, even when people continue to reopen new accounts.[80] It is important to distinguish between "anonymity" and "accountability," which are related but not equivalent terms.

Conversely, when we meet someone in person, identities are not necessarily as obvious as we might believe. In professional and everyday contexts, misinterpretations about identities are continually exposed—and these are only the ones we know about because they were revealed after our initial assumptions were incorrectly solidified in our minds. For example, tensions surfaced in a high-profile case in 2015 in which a person accepted as being black in her daily life reportedly grew up as a white person.[81] Her identity presentation—which was widely accepted—was not conducted online but *in person*. Many people (perhaps most of us) engage in a kind of *interpretive arrogance* that assumes that our analysis of someone must be correct when we see them in person. In fact many misconceptions remain hidden. Sociologist Erving Goffman powerfully proved this fact in his work on hidden "stigmas" such as mental illnesses, which are not necessarily visible to casual observers.[82] Writing in the 1950s—long before the emergence of the internet as we know it—Goffman cleverly called these mistaken assumptions "virtual" identities because they included characteristics that were assumed to be true about people whom we met *in person*, whether or not they were correct.[83] We need to move beyond interpretive arrogance when analyzing digital interaction. We need to acknowledge that access to a person's identity depends on whether it is *relevant* and immediately *desir-able* to have it and whether we have the *resources* to gain access to information about a person for specific purposes.

Anonymity exists on a temporally oriented, interactive continuum. YouTubers sought to move far beyond anonymity and form friendships. But meaningful connections are typically developed within publics only after we are willing to experience an *initial state* of *relative anonymity* vis-à-vis another person who exhibits potential interpersonal value. Further, creating "publics"[84] that exchange information or form coalitions to deal with social issues includes appealing to and persuading people whom we will *never really know*. If we wish to change the world or even accomplish basic tasks such as sharing information, then dealing with anonymity is inevitable and arguably desirable. We cannot really know and intimately support all the people whom we wish to persuade to vote in certain ways. For interviewees, video sharing crucially decreased anonymity and brought visibility to thoughtful but less seen videos—even as extreme and celebrity-driven videos were gaining most of the attention.

Sociality versus Self-Promotion

Despite continued fears of anonymity leading to disruption of online discourse, a paradoxically opposite anxiety involves concern about people sharing too much information about themselves to narcissistically gain attention. Yet if we are all sharing too much information online, how could anonymity realistically be a widespread concern in digital milieus? These contradictory and very polarized discourses obscure more common, everyday patterns of mediated interaction, social connections, and friendships.

When reflecting on media scholarship using a temporal framework, it is clear that narcissism concerns tend to recur when new forms of media appear. Narcissism was said to be an inherent property of video when the technology emerged in the 1970s.[85] The claims resurfaced when video blogging appeared on the scene in the early 2000s.[86] Yet another wave of narcissism claims emerged in the 2010s with the arrival of the selfie genre.[87] Because such claims tend to accomplish different sociological work across technologies and populations, it is important that scholars analyze them individually as well as collectively. For example, such claims leveled at YouTubers in part emerged from anxieties about how vernacular voices may successfully compete with corporatized broadcast media. Calling home videos narcissistic became a way to discourage nonprofessional forms of expression. When narcissism accusations resurface, scholars need to investigate whether the claims have merit; they should also examine their effects in particular technologized and cultural contexts.

Among the social group I studied, tensions existed with regard to what degree people should self-promote or engage in interpersonal sociality. That self-centered forms of attention occurred was evidenced by the fact that organizers of meet-ups frequently took steps to actively set a tone for gatherings that de-emphasized self-promotion. At the same time, the YouTube case reveals that viewers are often far more tolerant of vernacular and do-it-yourself media than media industries and artistic elites claim.[88] Aligning with broad accusations of narcissism on YouTube risks curtailing everyday, mediated voices by overgeneralizing what constitutes narcissistic (read: poor quality) and therefore "inappropriate" forms of self-expression.

We must be careful to avoid overgeneralizing the term "narcissist." Psychological terms are often overlaid onto disparate forms of experience. People will say they are "so OCD" (meaning they have obsessive-compulsive disorder) simply because they double-check that their front door is locked. Although it is a common phrase, it risks minimizing the problems that actual OCD sufferers face. Such expressions shape discourse in ways that prompt nonsufferers to dismiss real problems when they occur. Subtle psychological generalizations also infiltrate research studies. For instance, according to the Merriam-Webster dictionary, a voyeur is defined as "one obtaining sexual gratification from observing unsuspecting individuals who are partly undressed, naked, or engaged in sexual acts." As media scholar Theresa Senft has argued, the term has been overgeneralized.[89] If people invite you into their living room for a public vlog, they are exhibiting certain aspects of themselves willingly. This is a different level of video engagement than that of someone who is being spied upon in vulnerable situations against their will. Overgeneralizations of psychological terms risk misrepresenting mediated experiences and obscuring pathways to addressing specific problems.

Simply needing human attention is quite different from being narcissistic, which implies desiring so much attention that one cannot adequately admit their mistakes or function in healthy interpersonal relationships. Concerns about narcissism, although sometimes legitimate, run the gamut from general unease about basic vanity to seeing new media as enablers of an underlying epidemic.[90] A study released in 2014 suggests a more complex picture in which social media are seen to promote both selfishness and empathy.[91] In addition, gendered assessments appear in which male narcissists are perceived positively, as potential leaders, in contrast to females.[92]

Many everyday experiences discussed in YouTube videos deserve public attention. For example, vlogs may involve exploring societal problems or personal tragedies. Most people would not accuse people of "narcissism" simply because they made videos about significant life issues, such as a struggle to afford college. Narcissistic behavior exists on a spectrum and is ultimately interpretive. Vlogs are not inherently narcissistic as a genre; much depends on how they are used.

Narcissism is often determined through a "moral" lens, even though such assessments are not recognized as morally motivated. In other words, if a person "deserves" attention, the video maker will not be termed narcissistic. If they are judged not to merit attention, they risk being labeled as selfish narcissists. Arguably, it is easier to brand someone a self-centered "narcissist" and dismiss the kind of pain discussed in video blogs rather than deal with a person's loneliness or struggles with health or finances that reflect broader and sometimes seemingly intractable societal problems. This book argues that we need to pay more attention to what is said in a wider variety of everyday videos in order to find solutions and move toward equitable participatory trajectories.

OVERVIEW OF CHAPTERS

This book takes as its point of departure the idea of "meeting up"—in person, through video exchanges, and through inter-threaded modalities—to interrogate anthropological conceptualizations of mediated sociality. À la Lefebvre, the book is organized in a way that mirrors the temporal and rhythmic stages of how mediation occurs over time on YouTube. The book moves from analyzing video makers' "birth" or arrival to the site to examining digital death and possible rebirth, all in ways that highlight this YouTube group's cultural distinctiveness and interpersonal connections.

Chapter 2 analyzes YouTubers' mediated initiation as they joined the site and began making videos and posting comments. It critically interrogates what participation means in a video-sharing milieu and the multiple pathways that YouTubers embarked on to make videos. Despite YouTubers' rhetoric that watching and commenting were legitimate forms of participation, interviewees nevertheless continually pulled people into a circle of video mediation. These interpersonal centripetal forces offered a sense of social closeness rather than distance, which is often feared amid discourses of video narcissism. YouTube "lurkers" were encouraged to move from the shadows and join in the fun by contributing their own video-mediated statement.

The chapter analyzes how observation through a camera was legitimized as a form of participation on YouTube. A common perception and understandable fear is that when experience and mediation become conflated, we are unable to truly appreciate life's moments. In some cases it is wise to put down the camera and sensually experience wonders such as natural vistas. This position assumes that lived experiences always exist apart from mediation—an assumption that does not bear out in video-sharing cultures in which mediation fundamentally constitutes experiences. The data also invite philosophical reflection on the participant-observation method, which is criticized based on the assumption that people cannot deeply experience a moment that they are simultaneously trying to analytically record. Yet for many YouTubers—and the visual ethnographer—it was not only possible but a social expectation to observe and simultaneously participate through a camera. Observation via technologized mediation was an acceptable and desired participatory form, in part because observation and participation became inseparable in genres such as vlogging.

In Lefebvrian terms, chapter 3 analyzes how YouTubers grew closer together by attending meet-ups, engaging in broader communicative mediascapes, and creating shared histories by documenting their experiences. The chapter illustrates how a concept of YouTube became emplaced, thus shining analytical light on the intimate relationship between place and mediation. In this book emplacement refers to how mediated experiences become conceptually, emotionally, or practically linked to physical places. For instance, YouTubers may take over a section of a public park so that a place becomes temporally infused with the idea of "YouTube." Conversely, place-based, video-recorded interactions were digitally shared to whip up excitement for future gatherings. Meet-ups functioned as chronotopes, a term that integrates ideas about time and place in a single concept.[93] To create a sense of shared history, YouTubers chronotopically met up in ways that cyclically emplaced the internet in specific locations.

The chapter introduces the concept of *chronotopic chains* of rhythmic sociality that conceptually anchored YouTube to specific points across time and space, thus connecting and inviting new cycles of interaction. For instance, a historic early gathering was dubbed by its organizers as "777" because it took place on July 7, 2007, in New York City. The meet-up "888" was deliberately created in reference to the "777" meet-up so that people could gather for a reunion one year later, on August 8, 2008, in Toronto. YouTubers collectively invented their history and future traditions to produce a distinctive cultural form. Studying these temporal framings of sociality provides a way for designers and policy makers to create new infrastructures that encourage and accommodate vernacular dynamics.

Patterns of intensifying sociality through reciprocity are addressed in chapter 4. It analyzes how people engaged in or withheld video reciprocities to enhance their relationships and maintain a creative aura for the site. Contrary to fears about the "loss of reciprocity" in digital realms, instances abound in which quiet videos exhibited reciprocal video sharing, emotional support, and mutual aid. The chapter examines several levels of reciprocity, ranging from comments to mutual viewing and subscription pledges to donating footage for "collab" videos that promote a worthy cause. The investigation digs deep into the anthropological record to critically interrogate how traditional nuances and dimensions of reciprocity take shape in a video-sharing environment. Enacting reciprocity was important in YouTubers' conceptualizations of mediated sociality, but their patterns played out differently in comparison to traditional ethnographic descriptions. Although interviewees did not always characterize reciprocities as "obligations," interviewees rather systematically did address the emotional debt that appeared to enter the interactional record when commenters took the time to engage with a video.

Chapter 4 also draws on revised anthropological models of reciprocity by showing how strategic withholding of reciprocity could be as crucial for maintaining creativity and sociality as was bestowing it. In certain circumstances YouTubers resisted mutual viewing pledges unless other participants' videos exhibited emotional or creative merit. The chapter draws on anthropologist Annette Weiner's observation that certain items are difficult to exchange because of their inalienable quality, which refers to how artifacts may be imbued with the characteristics of the person exchanging them.[94] In the digital environment of YouTube, features that technologize emotion and sociality, such as likes and comments, originate from particular individuals. Thus their interactional value is not necessarily interchangeable. A "like" from one person is not necessarily perceived as equivalent to a "like" from another. Video makers who requested reciprocity but were perceived as undeserving were denied to ensure the site's robustness as a space for collectively making and sharing creative works.

Chapter 5 addresses the Lefebvrian idea of reaching an experiential "peak," which in this case revolves around how sociality fosters intense feelings of community—one of the most traditional concepts in anthropological research. Indeed, YouTubers' activities could not be contained in a single concept of community. Their interactions exhibited several types, such as imagined communities deriving from shared interests, which are addressed in chapter 5. They displayed creation of communities of practice in a core-periphery configuration of video sharing, as discussed in chapter 2. YouTubers also experienced emotional forms of ritualized bonding that anthropologist Victor Turner called "communitas,"[95] as analyzed in chapter 3.

Chapter 5 examines an experiment in public anthropology by analyzing comments I received on my video *What Defines a Community?* The video consists of observational meet-up footage and interviews with YouTubers who offered their perspective on whether the site was a community in traditional and new conceptualizations of the term. Most interviewees characterized the site as a community or as exhibiting the possibility of facilitating it.

YouTube editors selected my video to be featured on the YouTube welcome page for one week,[96] where it garnered more than 1 million views and 1,906 comments. A random sample of the comments revealed a small but intriguing discourse in which commenters struggled with conceptualizing and reconciling notions of community with their video-sharing experiences. Interestingly, a nominally larger number of commenters engaged interactively with the video in contrast to producing spam or hate. Further, the most active commenters were people completely anonymous to me (as far as I knew—indeed, anonymity works both ways). This experiment suggests that community is a recurring discourse that must be approached anew as waves of networked participants dealing with new media sites and modalities make sense of their social experiences. Although some scholars advocate dismissing the term, community still exhibits vitality as an orienting sociological framework, as seen through YouTubers' struggle to define it and to apply it to their video-mediated idiom. The chapter argues that the term should be retained in research but not in a categorical, definitional sense. Rather, it should be viewed as an exploratory, interactive proxy that invites collective discourse on its meaning for specific social groups. Sharing these ethnographic materials provided cautious optimism that, under the right circumstances, it is possible to promote online discourse on organically meaningful anthropological topics.

The end of the Lefebvrian participatory cycle through disenchantment, digital migration, and death is addressed in chapter 6. The discussion provides a window into video-sharing conflicts and people's experiences of the "posthuman." The posthuman is a controversial but theoretically productive term that refers to a state in which our identities resemble informational patterns that reside in the body by an accident of birth.[97] As we mediate ourselves, aspects of our identities become detached from our bodies and traverse digital realms in ways that provide opportunities and discomforts. Although some scholars see the rubric of "posthumanism" as dismissive of human agency or as confined to futuristic science fiction, this chapter argues that YouTube is already a site of the posthuman if this concept refers to a feeling-tone of participation rather than a bodily label. The version of posthumanity discussed in this chapter concentrates on how informational versions of ourselves, or "alters," roam about in mediated ways. The argument is not that humanity has disappeared; in fact, humans have been evolving in technologized ways for millennia. But the concept of the "posthuman" is a good one to "think with" in temporal terms because it reveals the social and personal implications of having our alters continue in perpetuity.[98]

Staying connected through alters creates reassurances and anxieties. We can feel reassured that we are in a collective that is concerned for our well-being. Conversely, unintended alters may cause distress in terms of how our persona may be wrongly interpreted. For example, one interviewee describes how his videos were manipulated by "haters" who remixed his videos to contain anti-Semitic sentiments that he obviously did not share. The YouTube viewing algorithm lists them alongside his authentic videos, such that viewers encounter these mash-up videos simultaneously or even prior to seeing his original work. These deleterious mash-ups function as posthuman, violative "alters" that risk broadcasting harmfully false representations about his character. The anthropological approach to the posthuman clarifies why the narcissism argument falls flat in many vernacular contexts. Individual voices may need more attention rather than less in an increasingly dehumanized, mediated field in which original works are ignored or become difficult to locate. Posthuman encounters challenge ideas about agentive "participatory" cultures in contexts in which we (sometimes erroneously) assume we have creative control over our work.

Chapter 6 also analyzes what happens to our digital "traces" when we are no longer human because we have passed away.[99] In interviews YouTubers articulated diverse responses about their envisioned, temporally situated, "posthuman," digital alters. While some interviewees expected loved ones to close their account, others hoped their account would be left up intact so that people could visit their page to mourn their loss. YouTubers talked about visiting their departed friends' YouTube pages and videos in this way. These poignant stories show a range of preferences for people's digital legacies, and they signal potential conflict as friends and family disagree on how to deal with honoring or reconciling their own and their loved one's digital desires. Since one cannot discuss these matters after passing away, these interviews provide *pre-posthuman* visualizations of individual and collective futures. Developing the technical and emotional tools to deal with the lingering aspects of our "posthuman," digital selves will be an ongoing process as individual desires and cultural expectations change.

Media's participatory rhythms are punctuated by beginnings and endings. Chapter 6 concludes with a theoretical discussion about how YouTube is not a singular site but has its own "alters." People often migrate to other forms of media. The concept of a YouTubian-inflected imagined community may live on through other sites such as Facebook, Twitter, and Instagram. A concept of a post-YouTube, which has already exceeded the parameters of a website, filters through other media and situates socially connected interactants.

Chapter 7 supplements the Lefebvrian rubric by examining the prospects for renewal or revitalization of a platform that more closely maps to YouTubers' ideals for the site and for videos that linger on. A YouTube video may never really die but rather asymptotically exhibits the potential for interaction that may dissipate in interactive energy over time. But videos may never entirely disappear. Someone somewhere may interact with a video, or a video maker may one day return anew.

The chapter critically examines YouTubers' reaction to the site's monetization trajectory in a way that analytically highlights their concept of an ideal YouTube. The argument is not that profiting from one's creative labor and engaging in sociality are incompatible. Nevertheless, video makers did face complications as YouTube's particular monetization pathways intensified. The chapter analyzes crucial events, including the site's migration from video sharing to commercial video streaming, changes to partnership terms and support, monetization of meet-ups, the rise of multichannel/multiplatform networks, temporal padding of content to increase revenue, and the problem of YouTube burnout. The chapter outlines the environment that continuing veterans, returning video makers, and newcomers all face when trying to post social videos on a commercialized platform.

Augmenting the Lefebvrian cycle that moves from birth to death, the chapter considers possibilities for rebirth and explores which features should be retained or avoided in designs of sites that wish to emphasize sociality. It poses the question of whether it is possible to speak of creating an idealized video-sharing platform. The chapter argues that the march toward monetization is but one possible narrative in a continuing saga of video sharing. The teleological belief that the YouTube experience as it unfolded was the natural or only way that the story might have played out should be resisted. Tensions raised in the chapter will likely reoccur and should be addressed in future instantiations of video-sharing sites that seek to support sociality and offer material benefit for one's creative work.

Finally, chapter 8 sums up the lessons learned by engaging in a visual anthropology project on a new media site. Core anthropological concepts retain vitality but require modifications. Sometimes YouTubers' experiences illustrate how changing theories in anthropology occur in a mediated milieu. In other cases YouTubers' unique experiences invite reconsiderations of anthropological theorizations. Concepts such as community and the posthuman are vital but function as illustrative metaphors rather than as categorical social science. YouTube sociality exhibits opportunities and challenges for reworking accepted notions of networked participation.

Thanks for Watching argues that we must understand videos as they are situated within a YouTube participant's "lived experience,"[100] which involves a complex array of criteria that include technical and commercial factors, cultural perspectives, dialogic interaction with interlocutors, media dispositions, and in-person interactions. Particularly useful are diachronic views that exhibit temporal sensitivity to participatory rhythms and patterns. The book concludes by proposing a framework for studying video sharing, one that focuses on empathy, temporalities, emplacement, and nuances, such as attending to technical details of particular sites. Features matter, and video makers work within and around the parameters of technical options and commercial constraints to accomplish interactivity.[101] The book's final chapter proposes that different "media generations"—which often exhibit much faster cycles than human generations—must grapple with constant mediated change.

The stories of the YouTubers profiled in this book offer crucial case studies for creating more usable platforms that support future vernacular voices. We need to engage in a form of "anti-memory"[102] and "forget" certain types of success related to monetization if we wish to create equitable participatory spaces. Dominant YouTube discourses of virality and celebrity do not represent the only—or the most interesting—version of events that transpired in video-making milieus. *Thanks for Watching* constructs a history of the future for more socially supportive platforms. By shining a light on quiet, social videos and the rhythmic dynamics of video sharing, we may achieve deeper appreciation of human mediation and sociality.

2

YOUTUBE INITIATION

PARTICIPATING THROUGH A CAMERA

Colleagues and friends of mine are often surprised to learn about the depth of sociality that emerged from participating on YouTube. Being stunned by this sociality is itself astonishing given that cycles of interaction emerging from digital milieus have appeared over the last three decades. Participation on YouTube exhibited multiple trajectories. Some YouTubers began by jumping in feet first and uploading videos. However, YouTube participants often needed encouragement; even the most enthusiastic creators began modestly by posting comments and gradually increased their participation over time. An advantage of YouTube's openness was that it enabled newbies to mingle with and learn from advanced amateurs and pre-professionals or people working in media industries.[1]

In terms of the Lefebvrian rhythmic cycle, this chapter analyzes the dynamics of "birth," or more precisely, "initiation" into video cultures. It explains how people are drawn closer to core activities of YouTube participation, typically moving from being watchers to adding comments and then becoming video makers. The chapter examines underlying rhythms and patterns that encourage video creation and sharing. It critically interrogates what constitutes participation in video-sharing milieus, and it proposes conceptual rubrics aimed to inform the design of user-friendly, media-exchange sites.

The chapter begins by detailing my arrival on YouTube and my video-making approach. I quickly learned to accommodate YouTube sociality by accepting camera-driven forms of participatory sociality. The chapter then maps out how researchers

DOI: 10.5876/9781607329558.c002

have discussed participation in media scholarship. It argues that the term's multiple connotations encourage a broad array of meaningful experiences in mediated groups. The chapter ethnographically analyzes participants' prototypical initiations into the video-sharing space. YouTube participants were often drawn in by a wish to go beyond watching and move toward interacting with other YouTubers. While no two initiation stories were identical, common elements included being drawn in through sociality and moving toward creating one's own video statements.

The chapter draws on ethnographic evidence to argue that narcissism claims—which are often assumed to be rooted in the medium of video itself—are overstated in social milieus. Certainly, narcissism exists in digital spaces and should be addressed where it is harmful. However, making videos does not inevitably prove that one is narcissistic, especially in light of the dynamics of the social group under study. Analyzing emotional content of videos using a temporal approach suggests that narcissism is difficult to sustain over time if one is interested in sociality. Narcissistic traits such as aggressive and competitive forms of attention-seeking were not central to this social crowd, who directed energy toward inspiring others to contribute their own video message. In a revealing case study, the chapter analyzes how veteran creators exhibited a centripetal force–based dynamic to encourage newcomers to make videos. Drawing participants closer to core video-making activities is one characteristic of robust participatory cultures that invite people of different abilities to be seen and heard.

Newcomers and veterans alike embraced the practice of conducting interactions through a camera. This chapter shows how observing through a camera and bestowing attention to other YouTubers constituted crucial participatory forms. The chapter challenges the idea that observation and participation are always distinct experiences. In this environment participating by observing through a camera integrated both activities into a single act—both socially and in visual ethnography research. The chapter draws on ethnographic evidence to critically interrogate critiques of the participant-observation concept in anthropology. Critics argue that the term is an outdated and obfuscating oxymoron. The YouTube case shows that in certain mediated milieus observation and participation cannot be separated but are rather productively intertwined, not only among participants but in visual ethnography projects.

Finally, the chapter concludes by drawing on an exemplary participatory activity known as the drum circle, in which people collaborate to spontaneously create music. The drum circle—an activity I observed at a YouTube meet-up—provides an inspirational metaphor for conceptualizing future video-mediated and more welcoming participatory spaces. A key advantage of the drum circle is that it requires simultaneous observation of others while participating by making one's own music.

Observation and participation ideally become inseparable if collectively produced creative environments are to thrive.

Notably, the drum circle offers constant mutual visibility of all other participants—whatever their level of creational skills. This is a crucial attribute that made YouTube so compelling for inviting participation and sociality. Observing creators of introductory skill gave newbies courage to try their hand at making media. Seeing video makers of advanced skill inspired YouTubers to improve their craft. The intermingling of multiple ability levels was fundamental for encouraging video creation and sharing. Designing future socially motivated, networked spaces means revising popularity-based schemes that may fuel narcissism and instead offering opportunities to provide visibility of everyone's media message in equitable and participatory ways—much the way drum circles invite contributors to produce and enjoy the fruits of everyone's collective labor. The drum circle metaphor suggests that video sociality benefits from inviting disparate creative voices into an integrated, participatory whole.

ARRIVING ON YOUTUBE

My participatory arc resembled initiation stories I heard from interviewees. When I arrived on YouTube in May 2006, I opened an experimental account and created a channel page—the social media equivalent of a profile page. This book defines early adopters as those who joined within the first year. I also joined early—six months after YouTube's public launch in December 2005. Initially, my experimental channel page was very quiet. I did not start posting videos until April 2007. I then posted regularly—usually once a week—because that was the video-blogging standard at the time and I wanted to improve my skills. I looked around and saw YouTubers' channels filled with videos and comments; they were lively and participatory. I elected not to publicize my experimental channel so that I could learn how to make videos in a semipublic way. I used an account name based on a former character of mine in an online gaming research project. I oriented my channel around practicing voiceover vlogging (without my image). My most viewed video was a car-show vlog about the fictional superhero car in television and films called the Batmobile (107,500 views). The video depicts images of the car while I narrate my reactions.

In May 2007, I felt ready to debut a more public-facing vlog that listed my name, contact information, and data about my research project. Beginning with my experimental vlog and continuing with my new vlog, I posted weekly videos for about one year. I created two vlogs, one on YouTube and another on WordPress, a blog-hosting site. I called both vlogs AnthroVlog. On YouTube I digitally migrated to AnthroVlog and no longer posted to my earlier experimental YouTube channel, choosing instead to focus on my research vlog. I left the older account open, but I did not provide a link to it. Over time, it is common for YouTubers to start over with a new account that is updated to their current video-making efforts and persona. Interviewees may not wish to disclose the name of a prior channel, which may be deleted. Nevertheless, clues appear in videos when other YouTubers refer to a fellow video maker's former channel. By creating and posting videos and comments and interacting with video makers, over time AnthroVlog became more socially integrated into the site. My most viewed video was called *What Defines a Community?*, which received over one million views and is discussed in detail in chapter 5. Interviewees and other YouTubers whom I interacted with for this study began posting encouraging commentary, which spurred me on.

In recording interviews and observational footage, I initially used a recording setup that aimed to maximize video image and sound quality. I used a lav mic for myself and a shotgun mic mounted on top of a Sony hand-held camera for recording interviews. Initially I used a tripod whenever possible when conducting interviews. I quickly discovered that pieces of equipment become "actors" in mobile encounters in which the presence of a camera influences interaction.[2] Using a tripod at meet-ups complicated my ability not only to be nimble when following action but also to connect interpersonally with video bloggers. Their standard was generally to avoid tripods, and many of them could not afford high-end cameras or sound equipment. However, they might use tripods in specific circumstances, such as taking group photographs or observational footage.

Some documentary filmmakers advocate the creation of an "invisible wall" such that the filmmaker records events in a way that distinctly separates them from the action being recorded.[3] The idea is to avoid people mugging for the filmmaker or changing the very behavior that the documentarian wishes to record. However, writer-director Barry Hampe argues that context may influence whether such a separation makes sense. Visual ethnographers note that creating such an invisible wall not only is unnecessary in many situations but also presents a loss of participatory opportunities.[4]

Writing from the perspective of sociology and video ethnography, Wesley Shrum and his colleagues characterize interviewees and researchers as operating in a "videoactive context." Similar to an "interactive context," the videoactive context is a "social situation with potential and known recording capacity, created by the presence of a loaded camera."[5] Under this rubric the "wall" becomes more fluid or disappears, and roles may become interchangeable between the mediator and the mediated. The filmmaker relinquishes the desire for explanation and, in its place, "[seeks] out revelatory moments, those flashes of connection between what would otherwise be lost to flux."[6] In observational mediation one becomes more attuned to the "improvisatory character of lived experience."[7]

According to Shrum and his colleagues, using an "invisible wall" approach privileges observational detachment over participatory empathy.[8] Striving to avoid changing the action creates the type of remoteness that produces unempathetic ethnographies. They argue that while the role of "observer" arises due to differences between researchers and interviewees, the role of "participant" arises because of their sameness. A trend in visual anthropology is to promote observational forms of ethnography that encourage nimble and interactive forms of filming. Filmmakers move around with subjects and become more intimate with them through a camera, perhaps walking and talking together while recording.[9]

The video blogging stylistic included creating intimate visual connections using devices operated by a steady hand. I noticed that having a tripod situated me as an outsider and observing researcher in this milieu. Over time I found myself using a tripod less and less and instead opted for more nimble arrangements that placed me closer to the ethnographic action. I used a more personal recording style—even for interviews.

The experience demonstrated that observing action through a camera could be intimately interwoven and inseparable from what is considered active participation in a heavily video-mediated, social milieu. A dominant paradigm in research is that wielding a camera is a cool, detached, observational act. Yet, in this milieu, recording people in socially motivated circumstances could be interactive and participatory. Still, YouTubers typically needed to ramp up their participation in ways that required social encouragement to expand their engagement.

PARTICIPATORY CULTURES

The term "participation" is frequently central to analyses of social media and creative production. Yet the term has many connotations across contexts. To anthropologists everyone "participates" in some way within their culture. Writing from the fields of media and fan studies, Henry Jenkins coined the term "participatory cultures" to describe groups of people who make their own socially connected media and operate outside of professional media outlets.[10] This chapter illustrates how a centripetal dynamic invited people to intensify their participation over time.

Media scholarship prior to research in participatory cultures focused on viewers' spectatorial engagement with mass media such as films and television, which broadcast circumscribed amounts and types of content.[11] In contrast, in participatory cultures people mediate their own ideas and share their messages globally. Barriers to entry are low, and people receive strong social support and mentorship for their work.[12]

Participation often connotes making rather than only viewing media. Yet research by media scholars and anthropologists have problematized analytical divisions between supposedly passive (spectatorial) and active (production-driven) forms of engaging with mass media. Revisions to the scholarly record show that people engaging with mass media did not simply absorb media messages without active interpretations. For example, a study of female readers of romance novels revealed interpretive strategies that readers brought to their processing of books' narratives.[13] The act of reading novels became a form of active protest in that female readers refused to succumb to the gendered demands of housework while reading. Being "participatory" with media takes many forms, ranging from internal, conceptual engagement with mass media to creating one's own works, as well as points in between. All of these practices are active experiences that do not passively accept standardized or surface meanings of mass media or vernacular works.

Although YouTube is too diverse to label it a "participatory culture" in Jenkins's sense, subgroups have used the platform to produce and circulate socially relevant or thematically inspiring video content. The participatory culture concept has found broad acceptance in studies that analyze how people distribute self-produced media to serve personal and collective interests.[14] The term "participatory culture" implies control over one's vision for producing media. Yet agentive challenges are apparent on YouTube. For example, in videos and at gatherings, YouTubers discussed "camera envy" when they saw another video maker with a better-performing (and usually more expensive) device. Not everyone could afford cameras that yielded high production values. In addition, participation in core activities requires a comfort level to share the self as well as skills to produce and circulate acceptable media. Scholars investigating participatory cultures are aware of these challenges and advocate the development of digital literacies to increase the distribution of voices through media. Robust participatory cultures encourage multiple levels of ability in media creation to facilitate skill development and sociality.

TRAJECTORIES OF VIDEO PARTICIPATION

Video participation has grown substantially in the United States. Pew reports that the percentage of adult internet users who posted videos online doubled from 14 percent in 2009 to 31 percent in 2013.[15] Still, nationwide statistics offer only one view of what people are doing and feeling when they post videos. In the present study a typical participatory trajectory began when a person watched YouTube videos through links that friends had sent. Note that the initial discovery of the site itself as well as individual videos were socially oriented for many people. Moved by a particular video, they might obtain an account in order to comment and begin creating and posting their own work. The length of time it might take from watching other videos to making one's own videos varied by individual; a few of the respondents had not yet made videos. This section investigates the varied participatory pathways that people traveled.

Commentary was an important initial step for many people. Interviewees insisted that contributing comments was just as legitimate and important to sociality on the site as was video creation.[16] The first time one posts a comment to the site can feel, if not momentous, at least personally significant in that a participatory divide of sorts is being crossed. Should comments continue, a new understanding of one's role in a social group may develop.

For instance, an interviewee named Lorraine (a researcher-assigned pseudonym) affirmed that YouTube facilitated social connection, in part through posting comments. Lorraine was a white woman whom I spoke to in 2007 at the SouthTube meet-up in Georgia.[17] She stated: "I think people definitely feel connected. Even if you're not making [videos] and you're just commenting, you feel a part of that person that you're always commenting with."

One common motivation that inspired people to move from the shadows was an attempt to achieve personal self-healing. An example is found with an interviewee who requested that I refer to her in the study as Veronica. She was a young, white woman who had been on YouTube just over two years when she shared her story during a video interview with me at a meet-up in Philadelphia in 2008. Veronica told me she was a newcomer to meet-ups. Her video views vary, receiving a few dozen to a few hundred views each. She often vlogged about a variety of subjects, such as attending college, providing inspirational words, dying her hair, and attending meet-ups. One of her meet-up videos received a few thousand views. She had forty-four subscribers as of July 2018. Similar to other YouTubers, Veronica began by watching videos. Inspired by comedic and charming videos on the site, she gradually escalated her participation to seek support after a serious injury. Veronica stated:

> I actually started as just a watcher. I was in a car accident four years ago. And I lost my ability to walk. And there wasn't much that I could do but play video games and play on the internet. That was my thing, and seeing other people go through, like, difficult times really [allowed me] to see that, okay, I'm not alone. You know, and then watching, like, nalts and Mugglesam and people like that, like, it was, like, "oh wow, they're so adorable," or "they're so funny," or something like that. But I got to see a real human side of people. And then I remember one of my first videos was a response to *nalts gets fit* and I had just gotten cleared to start working out. And it was in the beginning of this year, and I figured, you know what, this is going to be my time to start getting the support that I need.

Veronica recounts how seeing others experiencing hard times helped her heal. She drew inspiration for working out by watching funny videos on the site. A comedic video about fitness prompted her to become more physically active and to increase her YouTube participation. Notably, her connection to making videos and improving her health stemmed from comedic viral videos. It is not only contemplative vlogs that pull people in socially; it is quite common to bond over mass-media fare.

Interviewees' trajectories sometimes emerged from prior patterns of sharing the self using other media. The act of making videos was situated within a larger media ecology. An advantage of the media ecology metaphor is that it highlights how technical, cultural, and social factors are mutually influencing and interrelated.[18] For example, anakin1814 (his YouTube channel name) noted that participating on YouTube was an extension of a longer life trajectory of blogging and journaling that began as a child and continued as new technological platforms appeared. Anakin1814 was a white man in his mid-thirties who had been on YouTube for just over two years when I interviewed him in Minneapolis in 2008. He worked as a freelance photographer and graphic designer, but he did not appear to be using his channel to drum up business through topics (such as how to design a website) that would invite mass audiences.

In his videos he often directly addressed the camera in very personal ways to discuss topics such as art, guilty pleasures, YouTube community issues, birthday greetings, the environment, and music. His audience tended to be more intimate, with each of his videos garnering a few hundred views, although a few reached a thousand views. As of June 2018, he had 2,490 subscribers. His media-making did not suddenly emerge when YouTube launched but was informed by other types of media that he created. In his interview he detailed his participatory motivations and prior media histories. In response to my question about how he got started on YouTube, anakin1814 stated:

> The idea [was] to share my life with people and get a response. Actually, I've been writing journals my whole life, in notebooks for years since like sixth or seventh grade. Eventually I took that online, kind of doing a blog thing. And then the whole podcasting thing came out and video podcasting, and there was this site called YouTube where I could [put] my videos so I could make them easy to look at and view, this site called YouTube, and I could embed them on MySpace, and my journal and all that stuff. And eventually this community formed, and now I've been on YouTube for a couple of years, and it's just amazing how it's changed. And I see it as like a big grand scheme art project. Me sharing my life and getting feedback for it.

Anakin1814 describes how his entry into YouTube was motivated by receiving responses to his work. He alludes to how YouTube's environment saw increased social activity as well as individual improvement. In many of his videos, anakin1814 is thoughtful and reflective about the participatory patterns he has observed over the course of his two years of participation. He posted a contemplative video on March 15, 2008, called *YouTube Community: Season 2*. Anakin1814 describes how people improved their technical and participatory skills. He stated:

> When you see the lives of how people have changed, *their* story lines, you know if you want to look at this in terms of a movie or TV show. But look at each other's story lines that are actually real life. Or look at the talent that people are developing, the editing skills, or the musical skills, or the craft. Or the way people are getting more relaxed and being themselves in front of a camera and really finding their thing. But everybody has something special going on, on their channel, big or small, and we all have to remember that.

Anakin1814 references people's personal stories and how they developed editing and musical skills as well as the craft of making videos. Rather than focusing on himself, his insightful video urges viewers to take note of *other video makers* on the site and honor their experiences and stories, whether "big or small." He also provides insight about the development of digital literacies. He observes that through practice, people became more "relaxed" and found their public voice. As a video blogger, anakin1814 values sharing life experiences and details through video. It is through interpersonal forms of sharing that people may significantly improve their technical and participatory skills.

The YouTube experiment in sociality demonstrated that audience members are more tolerant of vernacular video content than is often assumed, even if video production values are not perfectly polished.[19] YouTube's search engine facilitates finding videos that exhibit virality, crassness, and lack of quality. However, clear discourses of learning, quality, and improvement are also visible on the site.[20] Notably, it was YouTube's unevenness that invited wide access. The varying abilities of YouTubers that anakin1814 described in his video often inspired people to find the confidence to make their own videos. It is arguably more intimidating to begin as a novice when one's peers make videos with superior production values.

Potential contributors who see a wide range of video quality tend to feel *encouraged* to experiment with making their own media and developing media literacies.[21] Put simply, "bad" videos inspire *increased* video making. A successful YouTuber named Olga Kay (her YouTube channel and stage name) reflected on her early entry into YouTube despite lack of formal film training. Olga Kay was a white woman in her mid-twenties. Born in Crimea, she identifies as Russian-American. Her work includes comedic videos and vlogs meant to drive traffic through stimulating visual content, such as trying Japanese candy, promoting her colorful, self-designed sock line called Moosh Walks, engaging in a dancing fail, creating a challenge ingesting odd foods on pizza such as tuna fish juice, and juggling audience-requested items such as GoPro cameras or wet soap. Indeed, each of her videos routinely garners tens of thousands views, with some reaching hundreds of thousands or a million views. She had been on the site for about a year and a half when I interviewed her in Hollywood in 2008. As of June 2018, she had 824,413 subscribers, which indexes a professionally driven, mass following.

Kay used the site to parlay her activities into a successful career, including earning money through merchandising. In a media interview she recalled being inspired to get started by the poor quality of YouTube when she joined in June 2006. She stated: "I remember thinking, I can do it better—if only I knew how."[22] She spent considerable time going to gatherings, talking to people, handing out business cards, and parlaying her talent for juggling and being filmed while doing it. She spoke about learning by doing, given that she had been a circus performer who had no formal training in cinematography or editing.[23]

Seeing modest videos arguably removes the pressure of having to conform to professional standards and gives some video makers the social confidence to develop their own media literacies. As media scholar David Gauntlett astutely explained, beginners—including himself—actually enjoy modest videos and become emboldened to participate on YouTube if they see videos of modest quality; they feel inspired to try their own video experiments.[24] Gauntlett relates the impactful experience of seeing modest videos posted by renowned expert Chris Anderson, who was formerly the editor of *Wired* magazine and author of *The Long Tail* (2006), a highly influential book. Gauntlett reports seeing a video in which Anderson depicts a radio-controlled blimp aimed at the blimp community. Although the video was shaky with poor audio and focus, Gauntlett observed how as a viewer he *"did not mind"* (emphasis original).[25] Viewers interested in connecting socially through shared content see such videos as interesting and potentially "liberating," as Gauntlett noted, for giving one's own media a go.

MusoSF (his YouTube channel name) was an interviewee who characterized his participatory trajectory as fairly similar. Videos on the site made him feel as though he could make videos himself. MusoSF was a white man from San Francisco whose videos garnered a few hundred views each, with a few reaching thousands of views. As of June 2018, he had 1,722 subscribers. In his videos he vlogs, sings, and talks about subjects such as gay marriage, his love of music, sending birthday greetings to YouTube friends, and reflections on YouTube meet-ups. His video about growing up in the 1970s suggests he was in his thirties to early forties. He had been participating on YouTube for about two years when I interviewed him in Minneapolis in 2008. During the interview he explained how he moved from watching to commenting to making videos:

It started with the typical, [somebody] would send me a link to some funny video and I would come look at it. I didn't have an account. But then I read a news article about geriatric1927, being the 87- or something-year-old guy who is on YouTube, and so I thought, "oh that sounds interesting, I'll go check that out." And I watched a video of his and then I wanted to comment, and I realized you have to have an account to comment, so I created an account, and then I started watching his videos when I had subscribed to him. And then I started finding other people that he talked about, and eventually I started thinking, "maybe I can do this." So a few months later I started making my own videos.

Notably, musoSF expressed a desire to socially engage through commenting after seeing a video by a famous YouTube participant from the United Kingdom called geriatric1927, otherwise known as seventy-nine-year-old Peter Oakley, who passed away at eighty-six in 2014.[26] It is not only videos but also people and sites that go viral as word about them spreads. Many people were charmed by the enthusiastic yet modest efforts of an older man who shared personal thoughts on YouTube. His humble and relatable videos that referenced a YouTube "community" resonated with younger and older audiences alike.[27] Commenters provided Oakley with technical tips that Oakley took seriously. Film and media studies scholar Bjørn Sørenssen argues that "the changes in production qualities and techniques in subsequent videos provide evidence of the results of his learning."[28] Although he began humbly, Oakley improved through receiving social support. In turn he inspired other YouTubers such as musoSF to begin their video journey.

Interviewees observed that even a few supportive comments could make the difference between giving up and being encouraged to continue. For example, after discussing his frustration over receiving stereotypical hater comments such as "You suck" and "Go die," one white, male teenager profiled in my book *Kids on YouTube* (2014) described in a voice-only Skype interview how even receiving a few positive comments significantly influenced his willingness to participate on YouTube. He explained: "But then even when you get one good comment, that makes up for 50 mean comments, 'cause it's just the fact of knowing that someone else out there liked your videos and stuff, and it doesn't really matter about everyone else that's criticized you."

Paying attention to other people is a kind of interpersonal gift.[29] As anakin1814 noted, it is important to pay attention to people's individual stories. His enthusiasm for watching others displays a warmth and interpersonal friendliness that reiterates the importance of giving human attention to other people. These YouTube stories demonstrate that the visibility of introductory videos of uneven quality served as an inspiration to share one's message and connect with others. Mutual visibility and active attention to others was a crucial part of socially motivated YouTube participation.

RETHINKING NARCISSISM

Scholars studying narcissism have labeled YouTube as "ground zero" for gaining attention.[30] Exposure to media has been faulted for fueling what popular and scholarly discourses refer to as "narcissism."[31] At times these arguments assert that the medium of video itself is inherently narcissistic—or at least is a key culprit in its dissemination online. The term narcissism as it has been applied to digital realms, and specifically to video sharing, has been defined in ways that range from the clinically pathological to the broadly colloquial, often functioning as a synonym for vanity.

Sigmund Freud, the founder of psychoanalysis, argued that narcissism was characterized by "megalomania," or inflated self-esteem and dominance over others, as well as *withdrawal* from people and things external to the narcissist's world.[32] Communication scholar Jessica Maddox argues that the phenomenon that media discourse labels "narcissism" is better classified as "exhibitionism."[33] According to Maddox, reflection on the original myth shows that Narcissus—who pined away to his death while staring at his beautiful image—actually chose not to interact with others whom he saw as incapable of truly appreciating him. Maddox contends that a literal interpretation of the myth would imply that people would be disinclined to share their image with others. When articulating fears of degraded social interaction, narcissism discourse has tenaciously focused on the myth's moralism against obsessive "self-love." Maddox believes that exhibitionism is a more appropriate concept for the digital era. Exhibitionism is about drawing attention to the self from others through sustained media sharing as facilitated by digital infrastructures.

Social media usage has prompted fears that we are living in a narcissistic "epidemic" and that videos and sites such as YouTube are prime facilitators of this condition.[34] Bolstering this view is the fact that numerous disturbing and mean-spirited videos are routinely posted to YouTube.[35] In addition, politicians exhibit arguably narcissistic tendencies on social media—behavior that can be tricky to diagnose but clearly has disturbing impacts.[36] To the extent that narcissism complicates one's ability to connect or prompts abusive behavior in powerful people, such claims should be addressed.[37] However, simply posting videos does not prove that a person is a narcissist or an exhibitionist or that they became so through social media.[38] Adjudicating narcissism outside of clinical contexts quickly becomes laden with interpretive and moral portrayals about what is right or wrong when expressing the self through media.[39]

According to historian and social critic Christopher Lasch, a problem with defining narcissism is that the term often becomes morally laden and overgeneralized. He states: "Theoretical precision about narcissism is important not only because the idea is so readily susceptible to moralistic inflation but because the practice of equating narcissism with everything selfish and disagreeable militates against historical specificity."[40] When creators post technically substandard videos or videos that general audiences have difficulty connecting with, it is but a short step away to calling those videos—and by implication the video maker behind them—"narcissistic." Yet a series of shaky, poor-quality blimp videos does not make a creator narcissistic. As the vloggers say, if viewers do not enjoy a video and become angry at the video maker for wasting their time, it is possible that the video was not meant for them. Assuming that all videos should satisfy an individual viewer's needs may be defined as *viewership narcissism*. Overgeneralizations are unproductive for diagnosing true problems and inappropriately suppress vernacular videos and their social messages.

Effects of Temporality on Narcissism Claims

Interviewees described diverse reasons for intensifying their participation—from extending prior media ecologies to socializing and flirting. For example, Susan (a researcher-assigned pseudonym) was a white woman in her thirties who had been participating on the site for two years when I interviewed her in Philadelphia in 2008. Notably, her work focused on very personal vlogs about her deep religious faith. She also sang songs, performed songs in sign language, and vlogged about serious health issues that she experienced. Her videos each garnered a few hundred to a thousand views. Her account does not list subscriber numbers. However, in a video posted in 2009, she relates that of her 3,300 subscribers, about 800 are estimated regular viewers.

Susan told me she joined YouTube because she was attracted to a man whom she saw on the site and wished to flirt with him. After a time they became good friends, and she also became friends with his girlfriend. She eventually broadened her participation to make religious videos. What began for Susan as a flirtation ended up being an intensely meaningful activity in which she shared her faith. Certainly flirtation and romance through media are a natural part of life and are thus not surprising to see. But first forays into making media do not represent the totality of a person or their mediated engagement. As of 2018, these videos were no longer on her channel, which focused on her religious views.

Scholars often read flirtatious or even self-focused female media such as selfies as evidence of today's rampant narcissism. Narcissism claims are cyclical in that they often emerge with new waves of media. Discussing the selfie phenomenon, media scholars Theresa Senft and Nancy Baym argue that although selfies are associated with narcissistic young girls, in fact many types of selfie genres exist, including political selfies, jokes, sports themes, fan selfies, illness selfies, and military selfies.[41] Narcissism accusations can become a way of adjudicating female sexuality and romance as well as complicating women's ability to create and control their own images.[42] Because narcissism accusations may be doing different work as they target various populations, it is incumbent upon researchers to investigate such claims anew as they reappear to see if they are valid and to understand their effects. Narcissism accusations sometimes target regulation of female sexuality and are temporally bound, as a participant's video content may change over time.

In Susan's case, to read an initial flirtation video in isolation as self-centered narcissism may have the effect of not only attempting to regulate female romantic impulses; it also ignores how these initial videos functioned as important milestones within Susan's media-making temporal trajectory. In starting something new, one may not be ready to begin with a deeply personal *magnum opus*; one may prefer a modest initial foray. A few flirty videos may represent a less threatening way to begin participating and building the trust of potential audiences. Once she makes friends, a video maker may feel empowered to take risks and share more central aspects of the self, as happened with Susan. When getting to know people or social situations for the first time, one is taught in US culture not to plunge immediately into religion or politics but to start with "small talk" before gaining interactive traction to share deeper aspects of the self, which in Susan's case revolved around her faith. Temporality should be considered in assessments about media making.

Interestingly, when temporality is considered, assumptions about narcissistic behavior change. For instance, communication scholars Maggie Griffith and Zizi Papacharissi conducted a study of ten vloggers in which narcissistic tendencies were reportedly a common theme.[43] In this analysis narcissism was equated to "unwarranted" self-promotion. However, they noted that narcissism was harder to sustain over time. Vlogs tended to include more complex and generalized topics to retain audience interest. Assessments about narcissism are interpretive and involve a matter of degree. Scholarly reflection will be required in an ongoing way to determine what constitutes "unwarranted" bids for attention in videos, especially if psychological terms are used to judge mediated self-expression and, by implication, the media makers behind them.

Personal Content as Important Forms of Self-Expression and Healing

Like selfies, video blogging as a genre has been interpreted as having inherent narcissistic tendencies.[44] The study of ten vloggers noted above equated narcissism with a self-centered tendency of vloggers to talk about their "interests and concerns" and to self-promote in an "unwarranted" way. The researchers argued that although self-promotion in "business" contexts is "understandable," in personal contexts it becomes "narcissistic indulgence." Judgments about narcissism were equated with what is unacceptable in interpersonal interactions. Yet people implicitly self-promote in personal contexts all the time. People wish to be seen as successful among family and friends. At what point does talking about the self to facilitate human connection or to solve personal problems morph into, as Freud called it, "megalomania" or, as Maddox labeled it, "exhibitionism"?

Using psychological terms such as "narcissism" in interpretive contexts may yield unsupported conflations between media and the psychology of creators. Historically, attempts to diagnose psychological conditions from media alone without in-person consultation have seen controversy.[45] Such conclusions are notoriously difficult to make accurately through selected media alone. Interestingly, one of the interviewees profiled in the study of ten vloggers whose work was identified as having narcissistic tendencies was Ryanne Hodson, a white woman in her late twenties whom I interviewed in 2006, about two years after she had started vlogging. Ryanne was a coauthor of a book on vlogging called *Secrets of Videoblogging* (2006).[46] She was a former television producer and editor who worked for WGBH, a PBS (Public Broadcasting System) station in Boston. She turned to video blogging in part because she wished to promote the democratization of vernacular media. Although she joined YouTube in 2007, her mediated center of gravity was not on that site. She had been vlogging on her own website since 2004, before the launch of YouTube. Although her vlog Ryan Edit went quiet in 2010, she was a pioneer among the first generation of vloggers who had worked out video compression methods to share videos on their own websites. Much of her work involved vlogging on issues in her life as well as people, places, and events of personal interest.

Ryanne spent considerable energy traveling the world and helping other people share their messages by teaching them to vlog. Her book focuses on providing tips for improving the craft of making videos. Rather than remaining inwardly self-focused, her vlogs discussed issues of individual and civic importance, such as personal experiences of sexism. It is concerning that readers of scholarly accounts might assume that the creators of media with purportedly narcissistic tendencies are narcissistic—ultimately an interpretive assessment that draws on terminology from a serious psychological disorder. My interaction with Ryanne showed how hard she worked to give others the gift of developing their own mediated self-expression.

According to Griffith and Papacharissi, vloggers' self-presentations become narcissistic (whether intentional or not) when they become "unwarranted" forms of self-absorption. The turn of phrase here invites scholarly reflection on what constitutes "unwarranted" attention. Analyses of narcissism tend to focus on the mediated subject (thus giving them more attention), and not on watchers or those who make decisions about who merits attention. Vlogs that discuss problems may in fact facilitate connections to others who share similar concerns, such that the personal becomes social and sometimes political.[47]

Assessments of narcissism need to consider the variety of digital, vernacular content and the ways in which vloggers express personal problems to engage in collective forms of healing. As noted above, Veronica connected to other YouTubers through particular affinities, in her case exercise and health.[48] YouTube participants who suffered health problems or serious tragedy reported initiating interaction on YouTube to seek emotional support. Indeed, two interviewees for my project, Jane (a researcher-assigned pseudonym) and bnessel1973 (his YouTube channel name), bonded with other YouTubers partly by sharing their experiences in losing a child. Bnessel1973 (whose story is discussed in terms of comment reciprocity in chapter 4) lost his son through SIDS (sudden infant death syndrome); Jane lost her infant son soon after birth.

Jane was a white woman and mother of young children. Her videos focused on family moments such as a baby learning to walk, child haircuts, birthday greetings, and well wishes for sick friends. In one video she lights a candle and wishes a sick friend well. She also created a few comedic videos such as providing tips on how to attract women. She talked about going to nursing school rather than aiming for a media career. Each of her videos garnered a couple of hundred views, although a few saw a thousand views. As of June 2018, she had 134 subscribers.

In a poignant video, Jane created a memorial to her prematurely born son. She posted the video on June 26, 2008, the day he would have turned three years old. She had been participating on the site for fifteen months when she posted the video, which received 2,639 views as of July 2018. Jane states in the text description that she is well aware that her video is not exciting to most people because it does not have funny animals or clever jokes, but it does contain all the photos she had of her son. For Jane, her son's life was deeply integrated with mediation.

In a picture vlog set to music, the first image is that of the commemorative hospital card on which her son's first footprints were inked, next to a picture of a cartoon stork. As a song plays, images appear of Jane's hospitalized son connected to a nest of wires and tubes. As the singer arrives at the lyric "holding you," a touching image appears of Jane holding her son, who is not in an incubator but swathed in a hospital blanket in her arms. The image cuts to close-ups of the baby's face and of Jane's face gazing down to her son's. Photos show her husband sitting next to her and looking sadly on. The video ends with images of memorial sculptures such as an angel and a woman holding a baby.

Visually, the format is similar to those of many memorials on YouTube, which often consist of photographs accompanied by music and captions.[49] Songs are chosen to provide an emotional context and to link loved ones to the person who has passed away. According to cinema studies researcher Malin Wahlberg, slideshow memorial videos often seek to visually portray idealized versions of the deceased.[50] Jane's images include traditional depictions of mother and son together, including Jane holding the baby and ending the video with an image of a mortuary mother-son sculpture, thereby eternally extending the idea of her mother and son bond. The moment and its mediation are poignantly collapsed as one experience at the time of his passing. Moral assessments about the appropriateness of self-focused mediation become questionable and interpretive in these cases. Jane's son's life and his mediation were all too brief, and images helped Jane and her family work through their grief and preserve her son's memory.

Commenters thanked her for the video, calling it "touching," and they extended condolences, such as "My heart breaks for you and your family. I am so sorry for your loss. Peace." Another commenter said, "Words just aren't enough at times like these, but I'm so sorry for your loss. God Bless you." She also received compliments on how beautiful the video and her son were and what a fine tribute the video was to him. Of the thirty comments that other people posted on her video, Jane responded to fourteen, which represents nearly a 50 percent reciprocation rate on commentary. Drawing support from them, she thanked commenters and stated that "if other people see his face and know a little bit of who he was, it makes his death a little bit less pointless." The video's integration of life experience and mediation facilitated connection to other YouTubers. At what point does it become narcissistic to share self-interests such as one's pain to socially connect and begin a journey of healing? How will scholars adjudicate what is appropriate to publicly share? Scholars are not always privy to the back channels in which vloggers help each other to cope with loss, to heal, and to achieve self-actualization through media.

The atmosphere that engaged socially driven YouTubers included touching video content. Elements such as uneven quality of videos, prior media trajectories, and a wish to connect in order to heal were all key initiators into the YouTube experience. They often helped viewers transition into making broader video content. The generalized assumption that videos are narcissistic becomes difficult to sustain as content is often made and received socially rather than through self-centered exhibitionism. The poignancy and connection of such videos throws into analytical relief how interpretive narcissism claims can be and how overattention to such claims threatens to overshadow recognition of how YouTubers encouraged an array of participatory voices.

Centripetal Forces

Although video exchange is gaining traction in digital milieus, many people are uncomfortable *being on camera*, which further challenges widespread narcissism claims. Not everyone who posts a casual video wants to make videos on a regular basis, nor do they wish to participate in video-sharing cultures. In the video realm, statistics similarly show how fears of self-focus may be overinflated at the moment. A survey by the Pew Research Center found that in late 2012, even though 95 percent of US teens between the ages of twelve and seventeen were online and 91 percent posted photos of their own image, only 24 percent of them posted *videos* of themselves.[51] It is possible that rates of posting videos will dramatically increase; growing numbers of people are posting videos online and to YouTube. As stated above, adult internet users posting videos increased from 14 percent in 2009 to 31 percent in 2013.[52] Young people are still more likely to post than older folks; 41 percent of people between eighteen and twenty-nine posted or shared videos online compared with 18 percent of people aged fifty and older.[53]

However, posting about the self appears to exhibit a slow trajectory; only 18 percent of adult internet users post videos that they have created *themselves*.[54] Even when people post their own videos, Pew states, they tend to repost other people's content, or they post videos of family and friends rather than of themselves. Posting media of *other people* shows engaged sociality and defies assumptions of narcissistic withdrawal from socially driven life experiences merely due to the availability of video sharing.

Among the YouTubers whom I studied and observed, various trajectories of participation occurred, with some being more interested in self-promotion than others. Perhaps the most dramatic outlier in terms of aggressive self-promotion was a white man whom I have assigned the pseudonym of "Todd." I encountered Todd at a San Francisco gathering about three months after he had opened his YouTube account. Most of his work includes comedic videos, skits, pranks, and parodies aimed for general audiences. According to his channel description, he formerly worked in a professional media context. As of July 2018, he appeared to have roughly 30,000 subscribers. At the gathering he had set up a table to promote his work—an unusual move in such settings. He used a megaphone to announce prize winners of a contest that he ran. Even future stars such as LisaNova and OlgaKay (their YouTube channel names) who worked the sociality angle professionally did not tend to use such aggressive tactics at meet-ups to generate attention to themselves. As the gathering was concluding, I wandered by Todd's table. He basically demanded that I interview him—which I found off-putting. In service to the project, I agreed to talk to him on camera. I found myself rather mechanically asking questions as he talked about his work without engaging me in dialogue. Notably, such aggressive self-promotion was not the norm.

The tendency among socially driven YouTubers was to include others through interactive engagement with participants' work—often through mutual recordings of conversations or reciprocal interviews. A more recognizable pattern was exemplified in an encounter that occurred with a "lurker," an adult white man (whom I estimated to be in his thirties) who attended the Midwest gathering in Minneapolis in 2008. Due to his camera shyness and his claim to not have a YouTube account, he sparked encouragement from fellow YouTubers. Their encounters illustrate how YouTubers used a centripetal social force to pull people from the periphery to core video-making participation.

Lurkers watch videos but do not post their own work or even text comments. Jenkins argues that because lurkers are doing important work, lurking is a useful dynamic in participatory cultures. Lurkers serve as an audience and feedback mechanism for others to showcase their creative works, and they also learn what it takes to participate by observing how to create media and interact. In a video interview for my project, Jenkins explained:

> A lurker is first of all seen as a potential participant in most cases. Unless the lurker becomes a troll or a stalker, right? [Lurking] is a way of learning. It's peripheral exposure to the activities of the group, and over time the lurker learns what it takes to become fully a participant. Now for many cases, a large chunk of the population are lurking, in the sense that they are not actively contributing yet. But they provide an audience for the performance and the creative expression of other members.
>
> And so, if [you post] your stuff on YouTube, the percentage of people who post stuff is much lower than the percentage of people who comment on stuff, is much lower than the percentage of people who watch stuff, or send out links to videos to their friends and so forth. But each of those people [is] doing important work that sustains the creative community. Now, generally, a participatory culture takes as its value, bringing more people into the center of that, increasing participation. And so [there] is a kind of pull or tug on a lurker over time, at least in a fairly robust social community of participatory culture, to join and become more public with their participation.

According to Jenkins, the percentage of people who post videos is relatively low, suggesting that narcissism through video is not a widespread societal problem but rather attracts attention in specific high-profile cases. Pundits similarly state that the average comment-to-view ratio is 5 percent, such that for every 100 views, one might expect to receive about 5 comments.[55] Jenkins argues that the more "robust" types of participatory cultures invite media makers of varied abilities and comfort levels to move closer to the core of mediated social action. YouTube is generally more interesting the more it contains a variety of content and voices from both video makers and commenters. YouTubers therefore continually seek new and interesting content with which to engage.

The camera-shy man was teased and was dubbed "the Midwest Lurker." He repeatedly evaded the plethora of video cameras that buzz through YouTube meet-ups. I requested an interview with him for my ethnographic film, *Hey Watch This!* (2013), which details YouTubers' trajectory of participation on the site. He declined, so I did not record him. I warned him that someone would probably record his activities and the videos would be all over YouTube, probably in a matter of hours. He understood but declined my request to be interviewed on video—eschewing attention even when offered.

"The Midwest Lurker" was interested enough in YouTube to attend a meet-up, but he was reluctant to be recorded. Contrary to broad discourses of narcissism claiming that people make videos to satisfy inwardly focused self-aggrandizement,[56] this study suggests that at least some individuals exhibited alternative "mediated dispositions"[57] with regard to their acceptance of being recorded and seeing their image distributed globally.

In this context mediated dispositions "refer to the types of media, communicative channels, and devices that people generally prefer to use to communicate."[58] My book *Kids on YouTube* (2014) found that despite the rhetoric that all youth were equally well versed and enthusiastic about all forms of digital media in the early 2000s, in fact they had very different preferences as to which type of media to use. Even for a video project on young people's media, some interviewees preferred watching over making videos. Indeed, a few had almost no interest in putting their image or activities in a video, despite participating heavily online. Nuances in mediated disposition and temporal trajectories in video-oriented participation should be acknowledged and analyzed. One's mediated disposition is just as important as age for shaping individual mediation and interaction through video.

YouTubers downplayed the lurker's protests and recorded him in a way that illustrates common dynamics of active participatory cultures in a socially motivated, video-sharing idiom. One might argue that people should respect a person's wish not to be recorded, even if it means forgoing mentorship, friendship, and encouragement to mediate self-expression. Another interpretation of events is that by attending a meet-up that he must have known would be populated by camera-wielding enthusiasts, the Midwest Lurker was publicly exhibiting curiosity about being pulled into the social group. His attendance potentially signaled a willingness to at least explore increased mediated interaction. He was opening up to being coaxed into overcoming his camera shyness.

As I predicted, several YouTubers relentlessly pursued him and video-recorded him on camera, whether or not that was part of his original plan. At one point a few of us were gathered on a Minneapolis city street and the lurker began walking toward us. One of the gathering's attendees shouted, "Here comes the gray-shirted lurker!" This comment was amusing, as it reminded me of nature films in which an unusual or interesting specimen is observed in the wild. As YouTubers amusedly looked on, the YouTuber also shouted, "We're making your first video now, lurker!" which was greeted by a burst of laughter from the group.

Despite idealistic YouTube rhetoric that watchers and commenters were equally accepted as true YouTubers, it was nevertheless clear that YouTubers spent considerable energy strategizing ways to increase the lurker's participation, including urging him to open a YouTube channel, which at least enables commenting and eventually posting videos. Typically, narcissism is said to be marked by "rampant materialism," "aggression toward others," and a "rabid desire for attention and fame."[59] Veteran video makers already have lurkers' attention. If seeking attention is the principle goal, why encourage a lurker to make videos?

The term "communities of practice" characterizes multiple levels of participation centered around an activity. Communities of practice are groups or networks of participants with various "core" and "peripheral" roles that seek to achieve shared goals within a setting, such as a workgroup or a digital site.[60] In a video milieu a core participant may make many videos, give newcomers advice, and arrange meetups. A peripheral participant may be someone who mainly watches or perhaps comments on a few videos. Strangelove argues that YouTube exhibits a "core-periphery" social structure in which "a small minority of users produce videos that provide thematic content" through which viewers connect.[61] If only a small minority is posting videos, how can video narcissism be rampant throughout the population?

A key ethnographic question involves how participatory roles change over time. How does a person move from the periphery to the core? The Midwest Lurker was pursued in a way that seemed good-natured rather than predatory. Not surprisingly, he was recorded by other video makers. A video of him appeared in which YouTubers said that they could set up an account for him. After smiling, he unconvincingly said he would "look into it." In a good-natured way, YouTube participants encouraged him to join in the video fun. In the video, YouTubers urged him to "come to the dark side" and walked toward him with outstretched zombie arms, droning "join us" and laughing.

Even when he was not present, a group of YouTubers continued to brainstorm about how he might increase his participation on the site. Supportive encouragement did not ensure that he would open a channel and thus maintain a social link to them. Even if he did establish an account, they might have difficulty locating him later amid YouTube's heterogeneous sea of videos. One meet-up attendee suggested making an account for him and sending him the password. In that way they would know which channel was his, and they could connect with their new friend back on YouTube. Once he had the password, he ultimately had control of the account.

Attendees debated potential YouTube channel names that would identify the lurker to them, such as "the Midwest Gathering's Lurker." Another suggestion was "Lurker 6-7-8," which would temporally associate him with the gathering we were attending in Minneapolis, which took place on June 7, 2008. The binary that is assumed to divide experiences and their mediation is challenged by the fact that having fun in person did not feel complete until the Midwest Lurker could be identified for further mediated interaction in digital milieus after people at the meet-up had returned home.[62] Rather than insist on self-centered attention, the vignette illustrates YouTubers' outward focus and desire for mutual visibility.

YouTube's participatory cultural style and mediated centripetal force applied to people on the margins, such as the Midwest Lurker, as well as to those who were already making videos, as happened with another YouTuber at the Minneapolis gathering whose YouTube channel name was BroJo Ghost (pronounced Bro-Joe Ghost). Engagement on the site could intensify through camera-driven interactions that collapsed an experience with its mediation. BroJo Ghost, a man in his early twenties, found himself being filmed by a group of video makers who were having fun through a camera on a city street. BroJo Ghost had been participating on YouTube for about two years and had made a few videos that captured moments with friends. As of 2018, his channel content focused on the theme of druidism. His video views were modest; each of his videos typically saw 100 to 200 views. One video on bookbinding amassed over 8,000 views. As of June 2018, he had a subscriber base of 1,870.

Certainly this moment of video interpellation did not represent the first moment that BroJo Ghost had put himself on camera. Within his YouTube oeuvre, vlogs that he had posted prior to the interaction depicted events in his life, including hanging out with friends. However, most of his early videos were not about himself but rather depicted things and places he had experienced, as well as people with whom he interacted—illustrating a pattern that Pew noted was common among US video posters.

YouTubers enjoyed conducting simultaneous interviews with people about their experiences and feelings. They often used a casual video-blogging style in which a person operates a camera while asking questions or chatting with the person being interviewed. At one point, several people trained their cameras on BroJo Ghost, the man in black in figure 2.1. BroJo Ghost took out his camera, thus creating four intersecting cameras and points of view (the fourth viewpoint is mine as I filmed the interaction). As BroJo Ghost pulled out his camera, an onlooker cheerfully commented, "Now we know it's YouTube!" referring to the number of cameras one sees at meet-ups as well as the proliferation of videos posted to YouTube.

FIGURE 2.1. BroJo Ghost experiences being recorded by others at the Midwest Gathering, Minneapolis, June 7, 2008. Screenshot by Patricia G. Lange from *Hey Watch This! Sharing the Self through Media* (2013).

A YouTuber at the gathering asked BroJo Ghost what it felt like to have so many people record him at once. BroJo Ghost said that he is usually the one behind the camera; he was not used to recording himself or being recorded. In this interaction, he himself was not the impetus for the recording. Rather, other people socially engaged him through their video cameras. However, they did not simply turn the focus back to themselves—a common practice among narcissists. Their attention demonstrated their affection and potentially budding friendship for him through media. One YouTuber humorously tried to soothe BroJo Ghost's discomfort by saying that the encounter only involved a few people. After all, a quiet, social video on YouTube would probably only attract a few viewers. Of course, this was partly a joke, because although only a few people appeared in the encounter, having the video version posted on YouTube makes it available to the entire connected world. One YouTuber suggested that all of the cameras must be creating a "parallel universe," as BroJo Ghost admitted to feeling a bit uncomfortable at being recorded at once by so many people.

Despite the encouragement by fellow YouTubers, BroJo Ghost displays awkward body language as he notices he has forgotten to remove his camera's lens cap. He removes it and trains the camera on himself in video-blogging style. After introducing himself, a common practice in the video-blogging genre, he is caught up in the interaction rather than mugging for the camera. BroJo Ghost's movement along a participatory trajectory did not appear to be motivated by a wish to exhibit himself on camera as much as a desire to join in the mediated sociality that was spontaneously created by fellow YouTube participants.

BroJo Ghost received additional encouragement through comments posted to his compilation video, called *Midwest Gathering Shindig*. Anakin1814, who is also profiled in this book, stated: "COOL video with some great shots! I'm really glad we got to chat for a bit during the day as well as hang out at the video game place for a while! What a great, great day! :)." Other comments praised BroJo Ghost's editing, choice of music, and shot selection. Learning about what makes a good video may be gleaned through compliments and social reinforcement of competent technique as much as corrective critique. BroJo Ghost had been making videos prior to attending the meet-up. Yet invitations to participate more intensely illustrate how participatory cultures exhibit a social pull to deepen participants' contributions.

YouTubers invited potential participants at multiple stages and comfort levels into more core video-making activities. For many YouTube participants, the payoff was high, as they not only enjoyed meeting other YouTubers but developed important self-expression skills, such as being more comfortable with appearing on camera, sharing their message, and developing new technical skills. Discourses of narcissism tend to focus analytical energy on creators rather than on recognizing that viewers have choices in terms of whom they will watch, support, and encourage. Creating videos in robust, participatory groups is often social and spontaneous. Moments of mediation are inexorably integrated with experience, such that people are invited to increase their participatory intensity over time.

MEDIATED OBSERVATION AS PARTICIPATION

Scholarly and popular debates about mediation often revolve around when to record something and when to put down the camera and fully appreciate the moment. Media skeptics believe that an unmediated experience is purer and more authentic than a mediated one. In video-sharing cultures where mutually recorded interviews routinely occur, this assertion leads to several theoretical questions. Is it possible to wield a camera and still feel connected to life experiences at the moment that they occur? If one is observing life through a lens, is one truly living one's own life?

Like discourses of narcissism, criticisms of failing to live life fully when mediated are cyclical and appear alongside waves of new media. Long before the selfie or YouTube, renowned writer and philosopher Susan Sontag expressed concern about life mediation when she observed that tourists often mindlessly take snaps of famous places without stopping to fully appreciate these embodied experiences at a moment in time.[63] Having a life experience, she powerfully argued, often becomes distractingly intertwined with mediating that moment, thus deteriorating the sensuous and connected quality of experience. Such dynamics exhibited particular temporalities; people tend to experience life moments more fully later, through recorded media, rather than at the moment of occurrence.[64] Concerns about mediation are still abundant. Their recurrence is perhaps rooted in generalized fears of media. In response to people recording a funeral, Pope Francis reportedly warned people to avoid letting the "Internet" distract from the quality of life.[65]

A key underlying assumption of this suspicion of mediation is that an experience can be separated from its mediation. Yet these dichotomies do not take into account experiences that physically originate from or are culturally intertwined with mediation. To begin with an obvious example, it is not possible to talk about forgoing mediation when video blogging, as that experience by definition involves making media. For other things it is possible to technically avoid media, but culturally it would present complications. For example, for many people in the United States who wed, recording images of the marriage ceremony and reception is de rigueur.[66] Of course, one can forgo taking photographs or recording video, but to many it would seem as though something important were missing. Finally, even when it is possible and desirable to forgo recording something, people often conceptually retain the idea of mediation during an experience. When we conceive of life in our mind's eye cinematically or "like a movie," or when we gaze at a beautiful vista without a camera yet still imagine ourselves "taking a picture in our mind," the conceptual divide between living an experience and its mediation becomes even more slippery.

Sontag's persuasive arguments about the inauthenticity of mediated experience continue to resonate as pundits fear that social media and video are creating sensory deprivation and promoting disconnectedness from one's own life.[67] The dichotomy of "pure" versus "inauthentic" experience is revealed as what anthropologist Ilana Gershon calls a "media ideology," or belief about how media structure communication and our interpretations of it.[68] Sontag's media ideology was highly critical of mediation as inauthentic experience. Indeed, media and visual culture theorist W.J.T. Mitchell argued that Sontag's book *On Photography* would more appropriately have been entitled *Against Photography*.[69] According to this view, why should one spend time fumbling for a camera at midnight on New Year's Eve rather than joining in the countdown, kissing a special someone, and truly savoring the moment? Is life not better "lived" than "viewed"?[70]

Even YouTubers and vloggers who heavily mediate their lives sometimes struggle with whether or not to record their experiences. Should they pull out a camera or simply absorb and enjoy the experience of a gathering and the people they are meeting? For example, I attended one event in which a video-blogging show was being recorded live and broadcast over the internet. In this instance the video bloggers invited people to their home for the live broadcast. During the taping the vloggers conducted interviews on camera. After the live show concluded, some of us stayed afterward to socialize with the hosts. As the evening progressed, the conversation took on a serious tone, and I noticed that everyone had put down their camera. I sensed that if I picked up my camera and started recording, it would seem odd. Even the most enthusiastic video bloggers had boundaries for what should be recorded and when. Conversely, I met a few video bloggers who fantasized about walking around with a head-mounted camera to instantaneously record interesting things that they encountered in daily life. Their thoughts echo that of one pundit who proclaimed, "Life is footage."[71] Nevertheless, certain interactive encounters were coded as inappropriate for recording interactions.

Relatively private moments among media makers discussing serious issues created an aura that did not invite mediated recordings. However, intimacy alone was not necessarily a deterrent to putting down the camera. I observed instances in which video-blogging enthusiasts were happy to record and post what they felt were intimate moments. For example, one prominent early video blogger and author named Jay Dedman recorded his partner, Ryanne Hodson, while she was sleeping. The video had crossed a line, Ryanne later said in an interview with me, simply because she did not know he had recorded and posted it. Jay was a white, male, ex-television producer in his early thirties who co-wrote the book *Videoblogging* (2006)[72] and was also a first-generation vlogger, having launched his own site prior to YouTube.

In his interview, Jay called the video "beautiful" and "cool" and felt that it captured "something you rarely see." Notably, Ryanne, who was a dedicated vlogger, said that if she had known in advance, it would have been fine to circulate. The offense lay not necessarily in capturing a private moment but rather in not consulting with her before posting it. Clearly, video bloggers had their mediated limits, and sometimes interpersonal media skirmishes ensued as people argued about what was appropriate to record and post or leave off camera.[73]

For the most part, however, observing through a camera was a core activity for YouTubers. In these moments one cannot rationally speak of separating the moment of experience from mediation because they are ontologically intertwined. For example, during a meet-up at SouthTube in Marietta, Georgia, a mock "paparazzi" moment occurred when a popular video blogger whose YouTube channel name was lemonette began joking around. Lemonette was a white woman from the South in her early fifties who had joined the site about a year before I interviewed her. She was something of a celebrity in the YouTube circles that I traveled in. Her videos were often comedic, down-to-earth vlogs recorded from a camera mounted to the dashboard of her car. She shared her opinions on topics such as cursing, going to YouTube gatherings, health issues, finding her "mojo," and aging. Her videos regularly garnered several thousand views each. As of June 2018, she had 5,828 subscribers, a sign of popularity among the social-vlogging set.

When she began joking around, several cameras were instantly trained on her impromptu comedic performance, resembling the dynamics of paparazzi. To engage in a parody of being "paparazzi" ostensibly requires the clicking and whirring of cameras that are trained on their target, much the way one might see paparazzi photograph celebrities in public. Putting down the camera would have meant changing the action being observed because without cameras, one is no longer creating, by definition, a parodic paparazzi experience. Mediation often changes what is mediated, perhaps even defiling the moment. Here it might be argued that *lack of mediation* equally would have altered the experience because the abundance of cameras trained on an individual is what created the experience itself.

Paparazzi moments have distinctive characteristics and rhythms. I witnessed my first live and rather disconcerting paparazzi event when I was living in southern California. My family and I were leaving a children's hair salon in one of the numerous mini-malls that blister the California landscape. As in many parking-restricted areas of L.A., valet parking was the only rational option. While waiting for our car, another car pulled up to the valet station. I sensed before I actually saw several people circling the car. The circlers had cameras, some of them quite small and not particularly professional-looking. It was an odd sensation to feel such movement around people simply getting out of their car. I soon realized that I was watching a woman who appeared to be the actress Jennifer Garner. She was holding a child, whom I surmised was her daughter Violet. The photographers followed them, and they were soon joined by a man who appeared to be Garner's then husband, actor and director Ben Affleck. To my eye, Garner and Affleck hardly seemed to register or react to the paparazzi, who kept their distance but steadfastly followed them with their cameras. They stopped following once the actors entered a children's party facility at the mini-mall. If there was ever an argument for never becoming famous, to me this was it! I could not imagine this kind of invasive lifestyle, especially with regards to children. I did not envy the celebrities their fame.

The word "paparazzi" reportedly originated from *La Dolce Vita* (1960), a famous film directed by auteur director Frederico Fellini. In the film a character named Paparazzo follows celebrities around to take their pictures and sell them.[74] Indeed, paparazzi continue to take lucrative photographs and video.[75] Publications and media firms may pay photographers several hundred to thousands of dollars for images of celebrities.[76] In 2012 one agency reportedly received $250,000 for a photograph of Kate Middleton, the Duchess of Cambridge, looking fit while engaged

FIGURE 2.2. YouTubers surround lemonette as she holds a mock press conference, SouthTube, Marietta, Georgia, September 23, 2007. Screenshot by Patricia G. Lange from *Hey Watch This! Sharing the Self through Media* (2013).

in athletic activity.[77] Photographs may also fetch quite high sums if the celebrities are caught in acts that contrast with their public personae or status.[78]

What motivates a paparazzo is typically the economic value of a particular image as assessed by its perceived cultural interest.[79] However, the paparazzi parody that I witnessed at SouthTube had a very different tone; it was friendly and aimed to focus attention on lemonette rather than to stalk or embarrass her. In this instance, video makers creating the parodic paparazzi moment exhibited admiration in a social and respectful way. Indeed, veneration is said to be a motivation for taking public images.[80]

The mock paparazzi moment began when lemonette started to play around with a gourd that another family had brought for fun. Lemonette pretended that the gourd was a microphone. As seen in figure 2.2, onlookers excitedly began recording her antics and encircling her. Suddenly facing a bank of cameras, lemonette improvisationally began to hold a mock "press conference" in which she offered the eager, pretend-reporters the bold "news flash" that she was "wearing women's underwear." Lemonette engaged in a rather amusing parody and tacit social commentary of the vacuousness of news conferences that ostensibly aim to answer questions from journalists but that often parrot stale sound bytes or offer trite news.[81] Lemonette's "announcements" became part of the parodic experience.

After lemonette's "news flash," a few video makers mockingly reacted with "shock" to her news, shouting exclamations such as "Oh!" and "My God!" and, of course, the ominous, revelatory musical lilt "Dun Dun Duuuun!" that resembles cinematic parodies of dramatic moments. A SouthTube attendee noticed the many cameras on the scene and requested that YouTubers begin circling around until lemonette was fully surrounded by "paparazzi" photographing and enjoying her comedic antics.

A paparazzi moment is often distinguished by the value that an image is expected to fetch. In this instance the mock paparazzi moment metaphorically indexes lemonette's entertaining and interpersonal value to YouTubers who enjoyed the sociality of making videos together. Outside of this context, lemonette's picture would not likely fetch much money. YouTubers visually enacted diversity through their choice of imagery. Of course, one might argue that spicing up one's channel with mediated moments from a popular YouTuber such as a lemonette might bring eyeballs to videos within an "attention economy."[82] Nevertheless, this experience radiated interpersonal sociality. The YouTubers' mediation displayed affection for lemonette, who was a social force to be reckoned with, especially when doling out her infamous "neck hugs." She projected a fun, kind, and welcoming persona, even to me as an anthropologist at the gathering. Because this type of image-making was executed in a way that celebrated her humor and interpersonal sociality, it became a playful and socially acceptable way to express affection and admiration for her. YouTube paparazzi demonstrated that lemonette was worthy of attention and of being recorded.

Scholarly treatments concerned with narcissism or, perhaps more accurately, exhibitionism might emphasize the fact that lemonette garnered a lot of attention for herself. But to focus only on one person in this vignette ignores all of the other people in the room who *chose to record her*. Focusing only on lemonette would perversely attribute too much attention to the mediated subject rather than recognizing the agency and actions of those who elected to bestow attention to her. In this context images were created and coded as special moments between mediators and the mediated, and their communicative value arguably occurred because of the use of cameras. During the incident there were many more people recording lemonette than jumping in front of the cameras to ensure that they were seen.

One might argue that it is possible to have enjoyed this "moment" without mediation. But what constitutes this "moment"? Those who maintain a dichotomy between the pure, unmediated moment and the inauthentic or derivative mediated experience would argue that YouTube participants could have eschewed cameras and simply watched lemonette joking around, or used pantomime to pretend being paparazzi using a camera. Lemonette initiated the moment by pretending that the gourd was a microphone, which in itself is an act of mock mediation. She used her fake microphone to "amplify" her message for the cameras in front of her, thus co-constructing an experience in which she could be recorded in a parodic way.

Yet refraining from mediating the moment would have created a different experience altogether. One cannot set down the camera in this context and create the same event because the experience and the mediation occurred together. To judge a moment as purer because it is unmediated is a media ideology that exhibits certain beliefs about the ethics of media. Conversely, the idea that mediation is a legitimate

FIGURE 2.3. A video blogger records herself and fellow YouTuber while they interact on camera in Hollywood on January 19, 2008. Screenshot by Patricia G. Lange from *Hey Watch This! Sharing the Self through Media* (2013).

form of sociality is also a media ideology that is neither true nor false but a type of belief that structures communication and our ideas about what is appropriate to record.

Even when YouTube participants are not engaged in obvious mediated genres such as parodies of paparazzi and news conferences, one might argue that on YouTube, and among many avid video bloggers, mediation is central to sociality. Much of their participation is rooted in observing through a camera. It is part of the video-blogging idiom to record interaction and conduct video interviews with people. In figure 2.3 one sees a typical video-blogging setup in which the camera becomes an extension of the body, thus creating not only a physical integration but also recordings that add to the world of networked images. To urge people to put down the camera to have a more authentic experience is to miss the point that video blogging requires having a camera or you are not having a "video-blogging experience" at all. Bringing these observations into the open reveals how media ideologies structure our moral interpretations of mediated interactions.

Vlogging activities and ideologies highlight the fact that certain moments of experience are now thoroughly mediated across certain facets of US culture. When expected interpersonal mediation fails, people may view the sociality of the moment as having failed as well. For example, parents who are expected to record their children's championship game or musical recital may be judged harshly if they refuse to capture the event for posterity. Sontag once lamented that "cameras go with family life," such that the mediation becomes just as important as the words in a ritual.[83] A child who gazes out over the bank of "parentrazzi"[84] during their big event only to find them missing in action experiences a social disruption. While other parents click away and lovingly record their child, the forlorn, unmediated youth stands alone and feels neglected. Parents who focus on fully experiencing the moment for themselves and who therefore do not record their child's event may be judged as lazy, incompetent (at working media), or downright neglectful to a child who expects mediation of this proud moment.

Conversely, social media research suggests that young people are increasingly asking their parents to refrain from recording them to obnoxious degrees,[85] suggesting that some parents may prize "parentrazzi" moments more than their children. These findings contradict discourses that identify unrelenting mediated exhibitionism as a generational phenomenon that is taken for granted in younger sets. Whether disappointment over lack of media is read as a culturally driven, childhood need for attention or parental technical failing is a matter of interpretation that differs according to individual media ideologies and mediated dispositions.

The point is neither to praise nor to condemn mediation but to assert that whether one seeks it or rejects it, specific media ideologies and mediated dispositions are motivating these decisions. The YouTubers' experiences in these examples underscore how mediation is intertwined in the lives of video bloggers, but it can also be seen more commonly in everyday life, such that the "internet" is inseparable from daily "life." In many instances it is the audience that seeks to encourage media making rather than participants crassly attempting self-aggrandizement. What seems like odd video-blogging behavior appears to be less so when we consider the role of media in a broader swathe of our interactive lives. Surely it is possible and socially desirable to separate mediation from experience, as when one puts down a camera to appreciate a private moment or a sensual experience. In the YouTubers' case, however, participation and mediated observation were deeply entwined in ways that created, through the act of mediation, a particular moment of experience.

INTERROGATING PARTICIPANT-OBSERVATION

Anthropologists have long debated the viability of experiencing moments while mediating them. This section draws on the YouTube case to apply important lessons to ethnographic work. "Participant-observation" is recognized as a central methodological approach for many forms of ethnography. The term connotes a researcher's ability to simultaneously participate in and observe interactions and events in order to analyze underlying cultural phenomena. Just as YouTubers negotiated observing through a camera and participating, so too have visual ethnographers dealt with what constitutes appropriate simultaneous participation and observation. YouTubers' experiences invite a moment of analytical reflection about whether the term "participant-observation" still resonates as a meaningful methodological approach in anthropology.

Scholars have posited that participant-observation is an oxymoron because it is not possible to sensorially participate in and analytically observe interaction and behavior at the same time.[86] This view echoes criticisms found in Sontag and others who see participation as purer when it is not observed or recorded. Even if one does not use any recording devices (until later, when memory may be less trustworthy), doubt remains over whether one can participate to the fullest extent if one is mentally and analytically processing events and experiences as they occur.

For some anthropologists, participant-observation remains a wayward ideal that can never be adequately executed. As anthropologist Benjamin Paul observed, "Participation implies emotional involvement; observation requires detachment. It is a strain to try to sympathize with others and at the same time strive for scientific objectivity."[87] Anthropologist Ruth Behar keenly observed that it may even paradoxically require that anthropologists deeply appreciate insiders' worldviews but avoid going "native" and embracing other lifeways.[88]

Perhaps accepting participant-observation as a productive oxymoron becomes one way to raise sensitivity about how one observes and studies people in other cultures and life circumstances. Anthropologist Barbara Tedlock argues that the participant-observation rubric has yielded detached ethnographies that futilely aimed for objectivity.[89] Ethnographies based on participant-observation typically wrote the experiences and emotions of the ethnographer out of the equation. Instead, she advocates a conceptual shift from engaging in participant-observation to the observation of participation, which involves far deeper reflexive engagement and narrative description of ethnographic experiences. Focusing on the observation of a researcher's own participation, she argues, prompts meaningful self-reflection and increases cultural sensitivity as we engage in interactions. In this way greater cultural insight may be achieved.

At the same time, characterizations of participant-observation as an oxymoron raise the specter of the philosophical Descartian mind-body split,[90] in which it is assumed that one cannot participate in something in an embodied way while observing it analytically in the mind. Labeling participant-observation as an oxymoron risks reifying conceptual mind-body dualisms that may impede understanding of interaction. Mindful observation is arguably just as embodied an act as so-called participation, which in turn requires active, ongoing observation to understand how to respond as events unfold in real time. In this sense observation is a necessary form of participation.

Despite criticisms, participant-observation remains a stalwart ethnographic method. Perhaps this is because the rubric encourages researchers to observe with fidelity while participating empathetically. Integrating participation and observation becomes especially visible when the observation involves recording action. With my ringside view (see figure 2.2), I became part of lemonette's paparazzi pack and recorded attentional, YouTube-driven dynamics. I wielded another camera that gave the impression of many cameras trained on a person. As a group, we co-created the mediated moment and underscored lemonette's value to the group through the affectionate parody of circling her with cameras. Criticisms about participant-observation as an oxymoron seem less tenable when participation requires observing action through a camera, thus overtly challenging mind-body dualisms.

My camera was not detached in the sense of simply observing research subjects. We were all recording lemonette as she joked around with her gourd. By keeping focused on the action, I viscerally felt the excitement of the moment as I helped co-create the effect of many people recording her. To engage in a Sontagian avoidance of mediation would not have created a purer or more authentic engagement of the experience. As Tedlock might say, I observed myself participating and noted my excitement in engaging in a cultural activity that I had never imagined could produce mutual feelings of pleasure. The participatory excitement of helping to create a mediated moment in which lemonette was visually honored constituted a different feeling than would a detached camera silently recording on a tripod a few feet away.

Scholars who are understandably concerned about unreflective recordings and their effect on human experience call for deeper consideration about when to record and when to put down the camera. Mediation is not a neutral act; some parties obviously may benefit far more than others. Yet we may conversely ask, is forgoing mediation always an ethically or morally superior position? Is it truly desirable for parents to put down cameras during their child's college graduation so that they can fully experience the moment for themselves? For some it might be, but such a conclusion would likely conflict with those who hold the media ideology that graduation merits historical and familial recording. It is therefore productive to carefully consider how people are invited to mediate and be mediated in particular contexts.

Criticisms about participant-observation as an oxymoron do not always bear out when we examine video-sharing experiences, which sheds doubt more generally on these criticisms beyond mediated milieus. Claims about oxymoronic participation-observation risk bolstering a false Descartian dichotomy that separates body from mind. The YouTube examples indicate that it is not only possible but culturally desirable to recognize that observation through a camera and participation at times intertwine in life and in ethnography. The aura that is created within particular mediated interactions suggests that YouTube participants used cameras to co-create meaningful interaction with their fellow video enthusiasts, often in ways that unselfishly bestowed attention on their fellow YouTubers.

VIDEO DRUM CIRCLES

A powerful metaphor for applying the lessons of this chapter to create socially friendly video-sharing environments is the "drum circle." At a meet-up at the Ontario Science Centre in Toronto, a group of YouTubers participated in a drum circle exercise, an activity that is popular in museums and science centers (figure 2.4). The basic philosophy behind a drum circle is that people need not be professional musicians to make and collaboratively enjoy music.[91] Each contributor is given an instrument such as a drum or other percussion device, and a facilitator initiates the action by beating out an orienting rhythm. The facilitator does not "teach" others how to drum, as this make students conscious of "being a student" and inordinately focuses on initial lack of skills.[92] Instead, the facilitator helps people manipulate the instruments to create their own sounds in a collective and interactive way. The interaction is not simply bidirectional with the facilitator but rather draws in all members of the group. As discussed in prior sections, observation of others is required to effectively participate and provide one's own creative contribution. Observation and participation are intertwined and inseparable.

During the drum circle, YouTubers expressed delight at hearing and appreciating the effect of their collective, rhythmic interventions. Applying Lefebvre's analysis, we see polyrhythmic or multiple rhythms, each indexing different participatory, experiential contributions. In this case the circle functions as a "bouquet" of rhythms structured around a single pulse that nevertheless enables each participant to express their unique voice. The result emphasizes harmony and participatory aesthetics. Seen through Lefebvre's lens, holistic activities that unite diverse forms of polyrhythmia may yield feelings of "eurhythmia," which reflect "rhythms [that] unite with one another in the state of health."[93] Lefebvre used the analogy of the human body in which different organs exhibit a multiplicity of rhythms but operate simultaneously in a nourishing way.

The drum circle philosophy serves as a useful metaphor for creating future video-based, participatory cultures. It invites the possibility of bestowing attention equally to diverse participants. Just as drum circle contributors join together in an improvised, spontaneous expression of co-created sound (whether or not they have musical training), so too did people feel invited to participate within certain social parameters on YouTube (whether or not they had prior experience making videos).

FIGURE 2.4. YouTubers participate in a drum circle, Ontario Science Centre, Toronto on August 9, 2008. Screenshot by Patricia G. Lange from *Hey Watch This! Sharing the Self through Media* (2013).

Notably, the shape of the circle is significant. The fact that everyone "can see and hear everyone else equally" means that each creator has a relatively equal position in the activities.[94] Insofar as YouTube initially provided a platform for anyone to post videos, creators had an opportunity to see others' work and interact through videos and comments. On YouTube the size and shape of the metaphorical participatory circle could expand and contract according to creators' needs. YouTubers could expand their interactivity by creating videos that appealed to a wide number of viewers or could target their message to a few friends. Of course, not all YouTubers were treated equally by video creators, viewers, or the corporate entity of YouTube. Popular video makers were given greater visibility and resources to promote their work as well as entry into the partnership program, by which video makers might share a portion of revenue generated from advertisements placed on their videos.

Examining social forms of YouTube participation provides inspiration for a "history of the future."[95] Future platforms might draw on these examples to create more participatory environments that support vernacular diversity. The metaphor of the open drum circle, in which everyone exhibits an equal position both in terms of media creation and *mutual visibility*, represents an ideal that is decreasingly available amid commercially oriented forms of video sharing. Designers of socially driven media exchange sites might create video-sharing mechanisms that facilitate the serendipitous discovery of videos that have merit or are worthy of attention even if they do not captivate mass audiences. A key lesson from the drum circle activity is that mediated delight results from collaborative co-creation of something interesting that exceeds the skills of any single participant, wherever their abilities lie on an evolving digital literacy trajectory.

In a drum circle, as on YouTube, creators are both entertainers and audience members. It is common for a popular video maker to promote the work of a newcomer whose work shows promise or has technical or artistic merit. "Shout-outs," in which a popular YouTuber calls attention to new video makers and their work, are useful mechanisms for increasing visibility. Yet they rely on popular video makers. Design features might enact serendipitous shout-outs in ways that promote new creators widely and consistently. The drum circle infrastructure offers the opportunity for members of a vibrantly participating group to produce a spirit of camaraderie and a "feeling of wellness among the participating population."[96] A crucial dynamic of the drum circle is that video makers feel validated when others notice them and share their work, whether they are advanced video makers or rank novices.

In drum circles people feel empowered to participate, given that "the quality of the music is based more upon the group's relationship with itself rather than the group's rhythmical or musical abilities."[97] In thriving participatory cultures, as in drum circles, what drives a community spirit is not only the final product of a video but the latent *possibility* for participation—and improvement. Not everyone brings the same skill set to the activity, but all are encouraged to feel as though they could contribute and that each contribution is welcome. As Henry Jenkins outlined in his video interview for my project:

> What we see are spaces where lots of people are making contributions; they have a sense that their contributions matter to other participants. There are sometimes formal or informal critiques that are taking place, which allow people to acquire skills and improve at them. Often it's a case where newbies are learning from more experienced players, but not with a fixed hierarchy or predetermined trajectory. It's not like schools where there's teachers and students; it's more like mutual mentorship, [which] emerges in those kinds of environments. There is a sense that not every member needs to contribute, but every member should feel like they could contribute, and that they feel that their contributions are going to be recognized and valued within the groups.

However, learning to make videos and move along a participatory trajectory carries reputational risk. Film and television scholar Eggo Müller has used the term "participation dilemma" to describe how new participants are encouraged to make videos but then are criticized by media elites for their lack of skills.[98] This dilemma also produces a "prideful conundrum": how does one learn in public without overemphasizing one's mistakes to the world?[99] Newcomers may even invite accusations of narcissism for posting work that elites feel does not merit attention. In response, educators and policy makers strive to train creators while sensitively realizing that developing literacies takes time and that there is actually value in accepting diverse voices. Central to this dynamic is creating a social space that enables networked participants to draw people from the periphery into core forms of video making.

Contrary to discourses of narcissism, not everyone is poised to take their place in the spotlight, but what YouTubers seem to understand is that in order for a video "drum circle" aura to emerge, opportunities for participation and improvement should be made available.

Mediation is now an intimate part of daily life, such that patterns of sociality are often motivated by media and their orienting experiential metaphors. In video cultures, participation cannot be separated from observation and recording; they are often parts of a single experience within which visual ethnographers can participate and help co-create. Studying YouTube's dynamics highlights how imbricated media are becoming in daily life. A space is opened for visual ethnographers to reflect on their own mediated interactions and media ideologies. Vloggers' experiences suggest that ethnographies that dismiss participant-observation as untenable may be denying how such activities are deeply intertwined in practice and how criticisms may rely too heavily on outmoded mind-body and possibly elitist dualities.

Robust participatory cultures centripetally drive newcomers closer to core activities, such as making videos, attending gatherings, exchanging communicative commentary, and ensuring that diverse voices receive attention. This case study serves as motivation for a "history of the future," such that sites seeking to broaden creativity would benefit from incorporating design features and mechanisms that encouraged inclusion of diverse vernacular voices, tools for learning about video craft, and techno-cultural mechanisms to make worthy but little-known videos more visible to the entire group, or at least relevant subgroups. YouTubers in these social circles worked together to create mediated, interactional experiences in which a concept of "YouTube" was never static but which dynamically materialized in sometimes unexpected places.

3

GROWING CLOSER

SHARING TIME AND SPACE

At a YouTube meet-up called SouthTube I experienced southern hospitality at its finest. Attendees socialized on white rocking chairs on the porch of a resort in Marietta, Georgia. Activities included dance parties and a hot dog roast in a beautiful, wooded park. In Minneapolis a group of us unleashed our deep-seated media nostalgia as we belted out the lyrics to *The Mary Tyler Moore Show* theme song on city streets. In Philadelphia I caught the gaming action at Dave & Buster's video arcade and saw the Liberty Bell, which I had not seen since I was a child. At the Ontario Science Centre in Toronto I learned about science during the day and sang songs at night around a hotel piano. In Santa Monica I sat by the ocean and shot the breeze amid a breathtaking coastal setting. These are a few of the many experiences I had when traipsing around the country following YouTubers as they gathered together. This chapter analyzes how YouTubers intensified their participation through meeting up with other video makers. In terms of the Lefebvrian cycle, it builds on the prior chapter's analysis of initiation to address the growth phase by examining how YouTubers gathered in person to create a sense of belonging.

Meet-ups were extremely important to YouTubers. Opportunities for attending large-scale gatherings were limited, which prompted them to cherish them all the more. Part of what made the gatherings rewarding was that YouTubers could share in a collective sense of togetherness with other people who felt marginalized. YouTubers complained that family and even most friends were not interested in videos or YouTube. Meeting up stimulated feelings of connection with others who

DOI: 10.5876/9781607329558.c003

held similar interests and with whom YouTubers had been interacting through other media and back channels.

This chapter argues that YouTube is productively conceptualized as a mediascape rather than a single website. Analyzing how YouTubers emplaced the site by meeting in specific locations at gatherings reveals how they drew on multiple, mediated modalities to intensify sociality. According to anthropologist Sarah Pink, an "emplaced ethnography" is one that "attends to the question of experience by accounting for the relationships between bodies, minds, and the materiality and sensoriality of the environment."[1] Although ethnographers may never experience exactly what others feel and sense, we can co-experience place to develop a deeper understanding of mediated human experience.

In line with a growing chorus of digital scholarship, this chapter's position is that online and offline binaries present problems for understanding contemporary mediated experience. So-called online and offline experiences are integrated in our lives and temporally inter-threaded. Internet studies scholar Annette Markham referred to internet life as a "way of being."[2] YouTubers did not gather in person because they saw being online as a flawed experience but because they wished to continue interaction across different forms of mediation that interwove various sensorial and experiential dimensions. At the same time, YouTubers' experiences were not always seamless as they attempted to interact across multiple modalities.

This chapter argues that YouTubers conceived of the site in democratized ways. Studying their forms of emplacement reveals that their models of participation embraced access for all. They rejected hierarchical forms of celebrity and conceptualized meet-ups in ways that invited diversity. They often saw in-person gatherings as reunions, a key way in which YouTubers sought to renew their sociality among people from diverse demographic groups—who happened to share an interest in YouTube.

The chapter will begin by describing the ethnographic context of the research. It will then show how gatherings enact scholarly ideas of emplacement through YouTubers' transformation of spaces into places of socialization. It will analyze how meet-ups illustrated YouTubers' goals for democratized participation. Dynamics of emplacement reveal how YouTube exceeds the parameters of a website and becomes more of a social ideal. The chapter will demonstrate how emplaced interaction stimulated feelings of communitas, or joy of being together in a place away from society and from those who marginalized the YouTube experience.

The chapter will introduce several theoretical concepts that assist in analyzing the relationship between time, place, and mediation. It draws on the idea of the chronotope, which literally means "time/space." Chronotopes integrate notions of time and space in ways that express cultural values.[3] A classic example is the idea of a "threshold," which holds meaning as a person crosses a temporal and spatial divide in personally significant ways. YouTubers oriented around meet-ups as chronotopes because each gathering occurred at a particular time and place and exhibited strong cultural and social connotations. The chapter introduces the theoretical concept of *chronotopic chains of sociality*, which link ideas of time and place to explain how YouTubers regenerated interpersonal connections.

YouTube sociality illustrates how people coming together from disparate backgrounds create collective spatiotemporal frames of reference. The chapter will demonstrate how chronotopes and subsequent chronotopic chains of interaction enabled YouTubers to build shared histories and collective memories. Given that space and time are inevitably linked, the chapter will also show how YouTubers' own videos about gathering in places display strong temporal dimensions that reveal how YouTubers conceptualized the video-sharing platform as an organizing framework for participatory sociality.

The chapter analyzes multiple forms of modal fungibility to illustrate the multi-threaded character of mediated interaction. The chapter introduces the notion of *participatory fungibility*, which refers to whether properties of interaction are interchangeable. The data reveal three types of fungibility: emotional, experiential, and physical. The chapter argues that YouTubers articulated emotional fungibility in which strong feelings became interchangeable across various modalities of communication. At the same time, many people experienced frictions such as an inability to afford long-distance travel, which revealed a lack of physical fungibility between interactive modalities. Such challenges meant that when video makers could attend a meet-up, a tangible sacrifice was made and appreciated. The chapter will conclude by analyzing participatory frictions and how YouTubers dealt with them to intensify their collective sense of belonging in a video-sharing group.

ORIGINS AND DYNAMICS OF MEET-UPS

This chapter draws on observations and interviews conducted at nine grassroots YouTube events. The nine gatherings were held in the following cities: New York City (2007); Marietta, Georgia (2007); Los Angeles (Hollywood; 2008); San Francisco (2008); San Diego (2008); Minneapolis (2008); Philadelphia (2008); Toronto, Canada (2008); and Santa Monica (2009). I also attended one commercial event, VidCon (2016), in Anaheim, California. Informal YouTube meet-ups were occurring at least once every other month during the primary research period in the United States and Europe. For practical purposes many YouTubers only attended one or two major gatherings per year. A search for YouTube meet-ups on the site in 2018 revealed informal gatherings continuing to occur in New York City (2017), Phoenix, Arizona (2017), Raleigh, North Carolina (2016), and Kobe, Japan (2013).

At meet-ups I hung out with YouTubers and engaged in activities such as attending dinners and sight-seeing. In Toronto I even briefly braved the chaos of a jumpy house while the event's organizer (also an interviewee) kindly watched my purse. I conducted video-blogging-style interviews that examined how meet-ups were conceived and why individual organizers chose to helm one. Organizers typically selected a venue that set the tone for the gathering. For instance, the gathering at the Ontario Science Centre was launched to promote the facility's goals, which included supporting science education.

Making and sharing videos at gatherings was a crucial activity at all events. Throughout this chapter—and in a section specifically addressing video temporality—the analysis draws on an examination of a corpus of meet-up videos made by YouTubers. To select appropriate videos for the research, I used a "purposeful sampling approach" by searching for keywords and phrases such as "Philadelphia meet-up" or "Midwest gathering." Using YouTube's "relevance filter," I examined roughly the first five videos returned for each keyword, for a total of 50 videos. I limited my analysis to videos for which I had context of the event. "Purposeful samples" differ from random samples in that the former require selecting relevant examples according to the needs, parameters, and research questions of a particular study.[4] Rather than relying on a random sample that returned videos from people and meet-ups outside the study, the idea was to examine videos from events organized and attended by interviewees and the researcher. YouTubers' videos document interviewees' experiences. They depict how YouTubers engaged in inter-threaded interactions that included past reflections as well as anticipation of future meet-ups in ways that highlighted their social dynamics.

Most of the meet-ups that I attended were organized by YouTubers to meet people, make videos, and expand people's video-based networks. Even meet-ups with hundreds of attendees were organized in a grassroots way. According to the people whom I interviewed, YouTube did not arrange or provide financial support for such gatherings, other than at times donating modest gifts to be distributed at the meet-ups, such as free T-shirts with YouTube logos. One organizer said he received funds for a small dinner that a few of us attended after a gathering. Organizers chose a venue and publicized the meet-up through promotional videos that provided information and raised enthusiasm for forthcoming events. Videos included practical information such as hotels, directions, nearby activities, and lists of attendees. While some meet-ups involved hanging out in public places such as parks, others were more ambitious and organized social mixers, dinners, and activities.

Obtaining precise attendance figures was difficult given that tickets were not sold and people traversed them fluidly, coming and going in parks and public squares.

Organizers estimated about a thousand people attending the meet-up in New York City. The Toronto, Marietta, and San Francisco meet-ups were also quite crowded with what appeared to be hundreds of attendees. Of the meet-ups I attended, the Santa Monica gathering saw the fewest YouTube participants. About fifteen people showed up to chat by the beach.

Notably, people sometimes came from far away to attend the larger gatherings. Videochick770 (her YouTube channel name) was a white woman in her forties who organized the meet-up at the Ontario Science Centre in Toronto after she had been participating on the site for about two years. She operated a channel on behalf of the center, posting videos about science that each received thousands of views. As of June 2018, the site had 819 subscribers, although she has since moved on to other projects. She told me that hundreds of attendees for that gathering came from places as far away as the Netherlands, Trinidad, Argentina, England, Ireland, and Australia to meet up with friends whom they initially encountered on the site.

Interviewing people at meet-ups presented challenges. Time was at a premium during meet-ups, which often took place over an afternoon. The larger meet-ups occurred over the course of a couple of days. Although many YouTubers generously agreed to participate in my study by being interviewed on camera, I tried to remain sensitive to their time constraints and kept video interviews at gatherings relatively brief (under twenty minutes on average). I preferred interviewing people in person, as this felt warmer, facilitated my visual ethnography project, secured an immediate interview, and provided a way for the interviewee to share impressions about activities at gatherings as they were occurring in real time.

The first gathering I attended was the historic meet-up in New York City in 2007. At the time, I was on my way to Europe from California for an academic conference. After seeing some promotional videos about it on YouTube, I decided to make a stop in New York for the gathering. I had no idea what to expect. A feeling tone of palpable excitement permeated promotional videos as well as experiences during the event. Posting videos easily without corporate or institutional assistance had only just become possible for experienced video makers prior to YouTube's launch in 2005, but the site greatly helped nonspecialists share videos widely. It became apparent that YouTubers saw the gathering as a historical moment in the trajectory of vernacular video and that meet-ups of this kind were an important locus of study for understanding the YouTube experience. Seeing the excitement and depth of feeling that attendees exuded at the New York gathering inspired me to travel to other meet-ups to compare their activities, rhythms, and forms of mediation. Of particular importance was analyzing how YouTube became more than a video-sharing platform; it became temporally ensconced in physical places in ways that highlighted YouTubers' social investment in the site.

EMPLACEMENT

Over the past few decades, the role of place in anthropological research has undergone revision. Doing "fieldwork" by conducting research in a circum-scribed location has changed as anthropologists now study diverse social arrange-ments such as diasporic cultures, migrant workers, and people who interact across media, to name just a few.[5] Provocations about place and emplacement have also appeared within the emerging field of sensory ethnography. Drawing on scholar-ship in anthropology, human geography, and philosophy, anthropologist Sarah Pink describes how place is not a physical location but rather is highly conceptual. Under this rubric the concept of place "occurs" as a kind of "event" that gathers and weaves together entanglements of animate and inanimate people and things. Whether this type of gathering together is planned or *ad hoc*, it creates intense feelings and memories.[6]

Pink proposes that ethnographers become more attuned to how interviewees and ethnographers are emplaced and how these entanglements with place influ-ence interviews, ethnographic encounters, and ethnographic representations of people in places. She argues that ethnographers cannot escape conducting research in embodied and emplaced ways. By becoming more sensitive to their own and their interviewees' sensations and rhythms, ethnographers can "begin to become involved in making places that are similar to theirs and thus feel that [they] are simi-larly emplaced."[7] Attending to ever-changing and co-constructed aspects of place is important for achieving interpersonal understanding. Pink argues, "By sitting with another person in their living room, in *their* chair, drinking *their* coffee from one of *their* mugs, or when drinking together in a café, one begins in some small way to occupy the world in a way that is similar to them" (emphasis original).[8]

According to the *Oxford English Dictionary*, the word "emplacement" entered the lexicon from the French in the nineteenth century to combine the notion of *em* (in) with place. Emplacement traditionally refers to relocating and positioning a physical thing such as a sculpture into a fixed place where it will remain over the course of time. Such everyday connotations of the fixity of emplacement does not adequately convey the more dynamic vision of how place is conceptualized and experienced by YouTube participants.[9] In the YouTube case, places, interactions, and their representations through videos were constantly in flux.

In this chapter the term emplacement engages with a more dynamic connotation as implied by Pink and others. Emplacement in the video-making context refers to how sets of mediated interactions or experiences become meaningfully associ-ated with or influenced by physical places. Mediated interaction is infused into places, and experiences that occur within places subsequently influence mediated participation such that mediation is inter-threaded to various degrees. Given that emplacement works in multiple directions, the chapter analyzes the *process* of how such experiences become intertwined.

Meet-ups emerging from internet interaction have been observed and analyzed in numerous early internet studies since at least the mid-1980s. Studies include those by social studies of science scholar Sherry Turkle, communication studies scholar Howard Rheingold, new media and communication studies scholar Nancy Baym, sociologist Lori Kendall, internet studies scholar Annette Markham, and linguist Lynn Cherny, among many others.[10] These studies largely disturbed notions of an online-offline binary, given participants' in-person sociality and multi-threaded interaction. Interviewees in the present study often described how previous behavior in their mediated ecologies influenced their YouTube participation. For example, an interviewee whom I spoke with in Philadelphia organized a YouTube gathering because he had enjoyed similar meet-ups with ham radio enthusiasts years earlier. Such patterns of meeting through media and then gathering while still retaining the connotations of a mediated milieu is a phenomenon that repeats over time and across different media and mediated groups.

The internet and underlying communication networks do not operate above or separately from the physical structures that exist in particular places to make them work. The notion of "cyberspace," once conceived as amaterial and aspatial,[11] is influenced by internet networks' material configurations, spatial situatedness, and local cultural factors. Research on internet cafés around the world shows that people and technologies in specific places greatly influence what constitutes "the internet" for individuals.[12] Even people sitting at a computer interact in embodied and emplaced ways, given that access differs according to people's locations. YouTube and associated mediated interactions are similarly spatially influenced.

Places are constituted from "meshworks"[13] that include the physical and communicative infrastructures that facilitate interaction. Drawing on their research on internet ethnography, anthropologist Daniel Miller and sociologist Don Slater observed that "the Internet as a meaningful phenomenon only exists in particular places."[14] Anyone who has suddenly lost mobile phone or internet coverage when traveling from one place to another has viscerally experienced emplacement's fluidity. Emplacement also occurs as networks efficiently hand off signals across distances, thereby providing smooth coverage. Emplacement may not be overtly visible when communications networks function well, but it is occurring nonetheless. The YouTube case throws into relief how emplacement works and why studying emplacement makes an important contribution to understanding contemporary sociality.

Emplacement dynamics have been studied in diverse ways (sometimes without necessarily referencing this term) in anthropological and ethnographic research.

Researchers found that internet activity may influence perceptions of locational culture and interaction. For instance, groups of Inuit peoples have expressed cultural identity by creating web pages that perpetuate representations of their physical "remoteness." Web pages and posted images create connotations of isolated places, while, ironically, the internet facilitates more intense connections with people in remote areas.[15] In addition, techno-cultural representations of places such as digital, interactive maps assert the tangibility of groups such as place-oriented but physically displaced diaspora. Dispersed groups may retain images and other material artifacts of cherished home countries to keep their memories of places alive.[16]

A large-scale ethnographic project that addresses influences of place is the *Why We Post* study led by anthropologist Daniel Miller at University College London. This collaborative project significantly contributes to the anthropological record, drawing from the research of nine anthropologists who studied social media for fifteen months in locations around the world, including England, China, India, Turkey, Chile, Trinidad, Italy, and Brazil. Although the studies do not address YouTube, they offer the relevant argument that cultural groups located in different places use social media quite differently, such that digital media usage cannot be universalized. Their work constitutes a "plea for greater sensitivity to regional and social differences and their consequences."[17] In addition to studying usage in particular locations, the research also engages with dynamic effects of place on populations as they move. For example, researchers observed how Chinese migrant workers mentally envisioned a world beyond a grim existence involving low-paying industrial labor. Using social media, they created a sense of self that enabled them to connect with others and express their dreams for the future.

Each YouTube meet-up exhibited a particular character, in part based on the physical location in which it took place. YouTubers wished to intensify their interaction by meeting up. Yet they did not believe that networked interaction was not real. They deployed multiple interactive modes to express their sociality. Studying rhythms of mediated emplacement in particular places sheds analytical light on how multi-modal, inter-threaded interaction plays out in particular mediated contexts, as each meet-up exhibited unique as well as similar interactive characteristics.

CONSTRUCTING MEDIASCAPES

Video makers' interactions produced a cross-modal concept of YouTube. During meet-ups, video played a central role as people recorded each other interacting and having fun. Just as the idea of "YouTube" permeated so-called offline interaction, so too did place-based offline interactions find their way back to the site through the meet-up videos that people recorded. Jill, an organizer of the New

York City meet-up, astutely made a similar observation. Officially known as Jill Hanner, she also had a YouTube channel of the same name—her channel had previously been labeled xgobobeanx. Jill was a white woman in her early twenties who vlogged about various topics, including health, pets, dating, interviews with other YouTubers, and debriefs about YouTube meet-ups. Jill participated quite socially across several YouTube gatherings. However, as of 2018 her channel had changed direction and had focused more exclusively on health, fitness, and weight lifting. Jill's videos typically saw 5,000 to 10,000 views each. As of June 2018, she boasted 27,688 subscribers.

Jill had been participating on YouTube for just over a year when she helped organize the groundbreaking gathering in New York City. It was a major achievement and attracted YouTubers from around the world. In her interview she insightfully observed that such gatherings offered the feeling of "taking [YouTubers] away from their computer but still having the computer," which made the meet-up experience "really fun." A concept of "YouTube" became temporally emplaced by being instantiated in physical places, thus eroding the boundaries of its status as an exclusively digital platform.

Rather than a binary online-offline characterization, this type of threaded interaction is more productively characterized as occurring within a "mediascape" of interactional forms. For anthropologist Arjun Appadurai, "*mediascapes* refer both to the distribution of the electronic capabilities to produce and disseminate information (newspapers, magazines, television stations, and film-production studios), which are now available to a growing number of private and public interests throughout the world, and to the images of the world created by these media"[18] (emphasis original). In addition, mediascapes, "whether produced by private or state interests, tend to be image-centered, narrative-based accounts of strips of reality."[19] Under this rubric mediascapes are real and are a part of everyday life.

In a video entitled *Talkin' about OhCurt*, which was posted on April 2, 2009, a YouTuber named anakin1814 (his YouTube channel name) illustrates how interaction traverses mediascapes. Anakin1814 details how he began interacting with fellow video maker OhCurt (his YouTube channel name), whom he says is the first real "internet friend" whom he met in person at a gathering in Minneapolis. Even as he depicts challenges to a strict online-offline binary through his own inter-threaded sociality, his use of terms such as "internet" friends who were "real" and whom he met in person demonstrates how difficult it still is for even leading-edge, heavy media users to move beyond online-offline binary conceptualizations. Anakin1814, a white man in his mid-thirties, vlogged on topics such as art, guilty pleasures, YouTube community, birthday greetings, the environment, and music. He had been on the site for about three years when he posted his video. Each of his videos garnered a few hundred views, with a few reaching a few thousand views. He had 2,490 subscribers as of June 2018.

Their interaction began when OhCurt responded to one of anakin1814's videos. Anakin1814 in turn commented on one of OhCurt's videos, which often revolved around humorous observations. OhCurt was a white man who opened his account in August 2007 and had 2,648 subscribers as of January 2009. His videos often discussed his opinions on life and views about YouTube culture. Due in part to a YouTube commenting glitch, they began chatting on other social media sites and sending long emails to each other. Anakin1814 mentions several times that OhCurt is an inspiration to him. All of these modalities together create a participatory mediascape that circulates images but also includes interactions that are conducted through media while influencing its creation.

Updating Appadurai's concept for the digital realm requires analyzing how experiences traverse modalities and places. Anthropologist George Marcus offers several proposals for contemporary anthropological study, including following movements of people, things, and concepts that exhibit cultural salience.[20] For example, YouTube sociality included interacting in person and through back channels such as direct messaging, emails, and video chat services such as Stickam.[21]

To study a mediated group, one must therefore trace interaction as it moves around a mediascape. For example, inter-threaded content from YouTube videos appeared in a Mentos and Coke demonstration at the New York City gathering. The activity echoed the viral videos that depicted people putting a Mentos mint candy in a Diet Coke bottle to create an explosion. The mint candy caused the Coke to gush upward in a fountain effect, making for dramatic visuals. Mentos and Coke videos were all over YouTube at the time of the gathering in 2007 and thus were associated with the site. At the gathering, the Mentos and Coke demonstration included lines of soda bottles poised to release explosions that people could watch and record. A concept of a "YouTube" activity became emplaced in the park where the meet-up occurred. The "star" in this case was not a person but a shared viewing *activity* that could be reenacted socially on a large scale in a specific location. The activity was distinctly YouTube-flavored, and the demonstration conceptually integrated YouTube and a New York City park in a single event.

Attending these events provided insight into the dynamics of emplacement and how interaction and participatory identity became inter-threaded and multi-modal. For example, videochick770 (her YouTube channel name), the organizer of the Ontario Science Centre meet-up, used a name that was itself an act of emplacement. It evoked the address of the science center where she worked, which was 770 Don Mills Road in Toronto. She and a few colleagues added this number to their YouTube channel names to create a connected subgroup on the site. Here the emplacement trajectory emerges from a geographical place to create mediated identities of a social group of creators within YouTube's mediascape.

General media discourses often highlight conflict and fear of meeting in person. Casual searches in the news reveal that cyberbullying, stalking, and other meet-ups gone wrong provide temptingly provocative headlines. However, for all of the talk of online "stranger danger," the reality is that contemporary sociality for many people with internet connection is commonly dispersed. People meeting at gatherings had already gotten to know each other through many different forms of interaction. Gatherings thus facilitated catching up with close friends, hanging out with acquaintances, and meeting new people. For YouTubers, meeting up often involved reuniting with people whom they had already encountered and interacted with amid a YouTube-inflected mediascape.

EMPLACING YOUTUBE

Emplacement dynamics reveal that when YouTube participants gathered together, their activities were influenced by the experiences they had on the site, their social and participatory goals, and the locations in which a meet-up occurred. Video makers' embodied experiences constituted an emplaced concept of "YouTube." Whether at their computers in their homes or at a meet-up making videos, people gathered together with other people and things in an "enmeshed" way.[22]

Each place of a meet-up became a "YouTube" place, at least as long as YouTubers hung out in that location or remembered their shared experiences there. A meet-up video that was posted by GeneticBlend (his YouTube channel name) on July 12, 2007, well illustrates this point. He was a white man in his mid-thirties who worked on a comedy pilot script with another YouTuber, bnessel1973. In his work GeneticBlend refers to bnessel1973 as "literally like a brother" to him. His videos suggest that he had worked in real estate but eventually became a holistic health counselor who wrote several books—such as *The Definitive Way to Go Gluten Free* (2012)—using his official name of Joe Rignola. GeneticBlend's videos saw several thousand views, and as of June 2018 his subscriptions totaled 2,776. His videos included thoughtful vlogs on topics such as YouTube's changes, YouTubers to check out, a description of a new camera, comedic compilations, health issues, and the challenges of vlogging.

Entitled *NYC Gathering 777*, GeneticBlend's video was posted about ten months after he initially joined the site. The video is a compilation of events that took place at the meet-up in Washington Square Park in New York City. GeneticBlend explains how a place became infused with a concept of YouTubers gathered in the park. Gesturing across the meet-up in the video, he states, "This whole crowd is YouTube. Pretty much like half the park. We own half the park right now." At a

FIGURE 3.1. YouTubers hang out at a resort in Marietta, Georgia, during SouthTube on September 22, 2007. Screenshot by Patricia G. Lange from *Hey Watch This! Sharing the Self through Media* (2013).

specific time and place, YouTubers "took over" the park and "owned" it for a while. The park became a "YouTube" place. GeneticBlend's video invoked an idea of place-inflected sociality within YouTube's interactive mediascape.

As predicted by scholars studying emplacement, meet-ups in different geographical areas exhibited varied activities and feeling tones—ones that were often commensurate with connotations about the physical place in which they occurred. For example, the event dubbed "SouthTube," which occurred in Marietta, Georgia, invoked cultural tropes of the American South. The organizers of SouthTube emphasized southern hospitality in their choice of venue and in their democratizing motto, which was "SouthTube: Where Everybody Is Somebody."

The name "SouthTube" also connoted a concept of the YouTube website—more specifically the social milieu of "YouTube." The SouthTube event evoked cultural associations with interacting in southern milieus, such as hanging out in rocking chairs at the resort in ways that resemble leisurely hanging out on one's own or a neighbor's front porch (figure 3.1).

According to an organizer, the sites for the gathering were chosen because they were beautiful, casual, and would help people "to experience Southern hospitality at its finest." While the night before the gathering was certainly a form of "party-ville," as one YouTube participant described it, the next day's gathering at a park saw many families who brought their children to enjoy the barbecue (figure 3.2), thus

FIGURE 3.2. YouTubers attend a barbecue at Red Top Mountain State Park during SouthTube on September 23, 2007. Screenshot by Patricia G. Lange from *Hey Watch This! Sharing the Self through Media* (2013).

showing the gatherings' mixed-age aura. The organizers appeared to achieve their goal of offering warm social experiences in a laid-back atmosphere.

In addition to experiencing grassroots gatherings, I attended a commercial gathering called VidCon in 2016. YouTubers' reactions to VidCon and similar events within the changing landscape of YouTube's monetization trajectory are addressed in detail in chapter 7. This discussion references VidCon in terms of emplacement. Originally launched in 2010 by two vlogging brothers, Hank and John Green of the vlogbrothers YouTube channel, the event became an expanded commercial enterprise. In stark contrast to grassroots gatherings, VidCon's ticket price structure hierarchically emplaced participation at the Anaheim Convention Center where it took place. The least expensive tier was the Community pass ($100),[23] which provided access to a lottery to meet famous YouTube stars at meet-and-greet events. The second badge (which I purchased at the rate of $175) was the Creator pass, which permitted attendance to informational conference panels on subjects such as understanding viewing metrics, promoting social causes, dealing with critical comments, securing advertising deals, and working with industry partners. The expensive Industry pass ($500) provided access to additional events, panels, and social mixers that facilitated business arrangements, such as connecting video makers to appropriate commercial sponsors.

FIGURE 3.3. Large crowds gathering at food trucks outside the convention center, VidCon, Anaheim, California, June 23, 2016. Photograph by Patricia G. Lange.

At VidCon, emplaced conference participation was hierarchically enforced. Security guards stood by the escalators, only permitting those with Creator and Industry badges onto the higher floors of the convention center for panels and private parties. At lunch a Community pass holder observed to me that those with Creator badges were lucky because they could go to the second floor, even just to explore. She understood participation spatially, in terms of where people with different levels of access could go. One place in which all attendees could mingle was the area between two lines of food trucks outside of the convention center (figure 3.3). Attendees could eat at picnic tables positioned between the trucks and dine with friends or meet new people with any type of pass.

In contrast, the grassroots gatherings were more fluid. Tickets were not sold; people interacted in more directly accessible ways. Indeed, places became video stars in their own right. YouTubers recorded themselves in front of historical monuments, works of art, parks, and even street corners. Meet-up footage often captured key highlights, events, and things that made an event geographically distinctive. For example, on our way to a meet-up in a park in Minneapolis, we noticed a statue of Mary Tyler Moore that commemorated her eponymous 1970s television show. Moore's statue portrays the show's main character, Mary Richards, a television newswoman in Minneapolis. Media nostalgia, including familiarity with old television shows, was a popular topic of conversation at YouTube dinners and social gatherings. Despite age, geographic origins, or socioeconomic class, many of us could readily bond by talking about media.

As we gazed at the statue commemorating the hopeful spirit of a television character, several of us recalled the show's theme song, "Love Is All Around" (written and performed by Sonny Curtis). As the song played in the opening title sequence of the show, a montage depicted the character of Mary Richards arriving in her new neighborhood, excited about her new job in news media.[24] At the end of the opening sequence, Mary Richards threw her hat into the air as a symbol of her positivity and exuberance. The hat toss in the original opening of the show has remained an iconic symbol of the optimism of its title character beginning a new job—notably in media. In 2002 a statue was placed in the area where the hat toss was filmed in Minneapolis. The statue honors the show and the character, who is reassured in the theme song that she will succeed.[25]

As a group of us passed by the statue on the way to the gathering, we paused to interact with it. A few people climbed onto the statue and hugged it, while others delightedly video-recorded these antics. One man threw his hat in the air, mimicking the optimistic act of the newswoman aiming to be a successful media professional. Soon we began belting out the lyrics to the Sonny Curtis tune. The song is about love and reassurance when starting something new, in this case within a mediated idiom. I found myself excited and swept up in the moment of singing a rather infectious and optimistic song that I have always liked with fellow YouTubers—who liked it too.

Many of us felt a participatory optimism about making media and sharing our voices on a broader scale, and the democratized aspects of meeting up underscored these feelings. Our pop culture nostalgia was initiated by interaction with objects in a particular place—which intertwined with our own hopes for the future. We had fun in a way that only a few of our friends and family would likely appreciate. Only a few people I know could recall the theme song to the old *Mary Tyler Moore Show*. (For the record, many of us forgot the words too.) The show's message of mediated success and self-actualization resonated with YouTubers.

A place, such as a section of a street, an area of a public park, or a hotel lobby became emplaced as "YouTube places" for a time to those video makers who came together to socialize. YouTubers created YouTube places by interacting with combinations of people, things, and ideas that were simultaneously evocative of the place and of the interests of the people who gathered there. At times, intense feelings of bonding resulted from gathering in one place to celebrate the experience of making videos together.

COMMUNITAS ON YOUTUBE

YouTube's emplaced activities offered inclusive and democratizing dynamics by inspiring a sense of collective togetherness. Although interviewees often spoke about the sense of community they experienced (see chapter 5), anthropologist Victor Turner's concept of "communitas" arguably provides an insightful way to characterize the sociality that radiated through the emplaced gatherings within YouTube's mediascape. Communitas refers to the deep camaraderie and social bonding that occurs during rituals or moments that feel out of time to people who may feel disparaged by society.[26] Although Turner applied the term to feelings emerging during sacred and secular rituals, he also observed that marginalized social groups often displayed the characteristics of communitas. Examples included "beat" generations and "hippies" who exhibited communitas because they had difficulty accepting hierarchical social orders. Turner characterized communitas as "spontaneous" and "immediate," emerging in ways that protest restrictive social orders.

Interviewees described feeling marginalized because of their video making and YouTube activities. Meet-ups provided a way for people to experience participatory validation. Close friends and family did not readily understand people's need to make or watch YouTube videos, much less meet the people who made them. Such a position was publicly articulated at a gathering by Cory Williams, a white man in his mid-twenties. He was a public figure whose YouTube channel name was SMPFilms. He also went by the nickname "Mr. Safety."

Cory was a very successful YouTuber and organizer of several meet-ups that he labeled "As One" gatherings, including two in Hollywood in 2007 and 2008 and two in San Francisco in the same years. At a small dinner for those of us who stuck around after the Hollywood event in 2008, Cory said that he considered As One as a brand that he worked hard to establish. At the gathering the security guards did not want us to film inside the mall at Hollywood and Highland streets, so people milled around on the public street in front of the mall to meet up.

At the time of his interview with me in Hollywood in 2008, Cory had been participating on the site for about three years. He was a very early YouTube adopter. Cory joined during the beta phase of the site in October 2005,[27] just six months after YouTube's first trial video, *Me at the Zoo*, was posted by YouTube co-founder Jawed Karim.[28] Cory's videos each received tens of thousands to hundreds of thousands of views. As of June 2018, he had accrued 628,541 subscribers, which indicates a mass audience. His videos contained meet-up footage as well as comedic videos on topics aiming for widespread appeal, such as a rubber band stunt, a rap-based response to haters, pranks, and bathing in ramen noodles. Perhaps his most popular video is *The Mean Kitty Song*, which depicts him rapping and staging scenes that make his cute cat seem to act out in mean ways. This video received over 88 million views between its original posting in September of 2007 and June 2018.

Cory organized events that facilitated both sociality and self-promotion. He himself leveraged sociality quite astutely to gain visibility. He achieved early financial success on YouTube, reporting in 2008 that he was earning $17,000 to $20,000 per month on income from YouTube-related work. Half of his income from YouTube was reportedly generated from video advertisements, with the other half coming from sponsorships and product placements within video content.[29] By 2016 he claimed to be earning roughly $100,000 per year.[30]

Several interviewees expressed skepticism about Cory's true commitment to the YouTube community, given the intensive commercialization of his YouTube work and the way he leveraged sociality for material success. Still, it was clear that Cory brought people together socially by organizing well-attended gatherings. Many of us who were interested in YouTube sociality benefited from his efforts.

At a meet-up that he helped organize in Hollywood, Cory made a clever speech and shared a personal vignette that was widely relatable to many of us, certainly stimulating feelings of communitas. He said he had told a friend about YouTube and tried to share the experiences of viewing and making videos. Sadly, he relates, his friend did not join in his enthusiasm. When Cory urged his friend to watch a cool YouTube video, his friend's disappointing response was: "dude, whatever." These outsider friends "walk away," Cory stated, leaving a YouTuber to realize that most of their non-YouTube friends "just don't get it." During the gathering Cory emphasized that "today we get it," meaning that YouTubers could bond in part through feelings of marginality and ostracization that they experienced when non-YouTube friends did not understand the site's participatory appeal.

Feelings of bonding and communitas with other YouTubers became particularly visible during the Toronto meet-up. A group of us informally gathered around a piano in a hotel lobby and sang popular songs in a way that communally emplaced YouTube experiences with other people who shared similar cultural knowledge and emotions (figure 3.4). In some ways hanging out in the lobby made it easier to socialize than it was to interact at the larger gathering the next day at the Science Centre. The actual gathering was filled with stimuli, including many attendees and exhibits to see and experience. The hotel lobby gathering was more casual. People filtered in slowly after attending a pre-party at the center. The energy and positive spirit mounted as YouTubers played the piano, drank, and sang songs.

According to Turner, communitas was often a temporary dynamic. After events ended, marginalized people returned to normal life and became reabsorbed into the structures they had challenged. What makes such spontaneous events (bitter)sweet is perhaps the knowledge that they ultimately must end as people return home to

FIGURE 3.4. YouTubers sing and video-record themselves and each other around a hotel piano in Toronto, August 8, 2008. Photograph by Patricia G. Lange.

the status quo where it might be difficult to be "heard" amid the critical voices that crowd them out. Still, YouTubers maintained their relationships over time. Even if acceptance back home was slow to arrive or never materialized, memories were preserved through videos that recorded a concept of YouTubers' communitas, which video makers repeatedly experienced over time and across media.

GOING TO THE REUNION

Characterizing YouTube gatherings as "reunions" exhibited another important way that video makers reiterated their commitment to democratized media making. YouTube gatherings and reunions exhibited similar cyclical, rhythmic practices and diverse connotations. A reunion is an interesting characterization for YouTubers to make because it connotes the idea of reuniting with people known from prior interactions who have specific things in common. In US society, reunions are often motivated by experiences such as having attended the same club, college, or high school.

YouTube gatherings—like US high school reunions—were marked by diversity. Even as they united people with a shared interest in making videos, they also brought together a kaleidoscope of people with other interests and diverse demographics. Several interviewees talked about the wide variety of people whom they met and learned from by participating on YouTube. One video maker observed that at gatherings one sees a "cross-section of society, that goes from race, creed, religion, sexual orientation, you name it." Scholars of high school reunions state that such events connect groups of people with different backgrounds, interests, and careers, thus resembling a "society in miniature."[31] Part of the reason for reunion diversity is that public high schools in the United States are among the few places, scholars argue, where people of different socioeconomic backgrounds are placed in the same setting. High school reunions are thus characterized by people gathering around a specific variable, much the way YouTubers from very different backgrounds united around video-making interests.

YouTubers referenced diversity and inclusiveness in shaping the parameters of an emplaced gathering. Marty, a white woman in her forties from the South, organized the SouthTube meet-up that I attended. She explained the origins of the event's motto, which was, as mentioned earlier, "SouthTube: Where Everybody Is Somebody." Although Marty has since deleted her YouTube account, at the time of her interview she had made social connections on YouTube and told me that the gathering started with a few local YouTubers talking about having a "weenie roast" and that attendance mushroomed to include hundreds of people. As excitement grew for the gathering, people realized that it would include diverse YouTube participants, from newcomers to celebrities. In response to this diverse mix, Marty developed the gathering's slogan. She stated:

> When we started realizing that everybody was coming, there were people that did not have videos, there were people that were new to YouTube that were coming, there were celebrities via YouTube that were arriving, and there was a little bit of concern that people who may not have any videos or nobody knew them, that they may not want to participate because they thought it might be focused on a celebrity event, and I started thinking, "You know, this is going to be an event where everybody is somebody!" You know, it doesn't matter if you don't have videos or if you have hundreds of videos or if you have no subscribers or you have 10,000 subscribers. So it was just kind of an epiphany one day. I just did "SouthTube: Where Everybody Is Somebody."

Marty firmly believed, as did many interviewees, that all YouTubers—whatever their video-making status—were equally welcome at a gathering. Events at SouthTube sometimes included activities that resembled those at school or workplace reunions. For example, when many of us arrived at the resort, we participated in an organized "break the ice" game in which we had to find other attendees from YouTube who were on our list. Of course, high schools have cliques, and it was evident that smaller groups were gathering privately behind the scenes as well.

A YouTuber named ItalianStallionette (her YouTube name) organized a San Diego meet-up that she playfully dubbed "Best Tube." In her interview she stated that she wanted the gathering to feel "more like a reunion" rather than "advertising people." She aimed to set a warmer, more interpersonal tone than that which encouraged heavy self-promotion—and by extension, hierarchies of popularity. ItalianStallionette was a white woman who lived on the East Coast and had been on the site for about a year and a half when I interviewed her in San Diego. Her videos were often humorous or thoughtful vlogs that each received thousands of views (her subscriber count is unlisted). In one video she describes the famous "Christmas Truce," which was an unofficial ceasefire in World War I in which soldiers sang Christmas carols.[32]

ItalianStallionette appeared to achieve her vision of creating a casual, social event. The San Diego meet-up was attended by perhaps a few dozen people. Attendees made vlogs and took photographs of each other, much the way one does when attending a reunion and seeing old friends. As I traveled through the crowd with my camera, I both *co-created* the emplaced event and experienced it. People waved, mugged for the camera, and interacted with me much as one would in home movies of the past. The photograph in figure 3.5 is representative of the reunion-type photos that were taken at the San Diego meet-up as well as other gatherings.

For most readers, such a photo merely adds documentary proof that I, as an anthropologist, attended the events I describe. For attendees, the photograph takes on quite a different emotional and temporal patina, as it brings to mind a larger field of social interactions and experiences across time. Film theorist Vivian Sobchack provides an insightful conceptualization of three nuanced readings of visual materials. She draws on the phenomenological philosophies of Jean-Pierre Meunier to frame her analysis.[33] Phenomenology is the "study of human experience and of the ways things present themselves to us in and through such experience."[34] According to Sobchack, as spectators we experience the people and things in narrative fiction films as "irreal" because they are characters in a story; we know about them only through specific media. The next level is that of the documentary genre, for which people accept the reality of events as things that have occurred or could conceivably occur at other times and places. These people and events are accepted as not present but as real, even though viewers did not personally experience them. For readers of this book, the photo constitutes visual documentary, as most readers will accept that this image depicts events that occurred during my study of YouTube. However, most readers will likely feel emotionally distant from the people in the image.

According to Sobchack, on the opposite end of the spectrum from the fiction film is the "film-souvenir" or home movie, in which viewers know the filmic subjects and interpretively bring to the image much more information than that contained

FIGURE 3.5. YouTubers gather to video-record and photograph each other in San Diego, April 19, 2008. Photograph by Patricia G. Lange.

within a single photograph or video. Readers who experience this image as a "*photo-souvenir*" (to adapt Sobchack's phrase) see "through" the image across time. Rather than seeing only the things depicted in the photo itself, participants recall many other visual and associated sensorial memories. Looking at the photo, I remember how we interacted together at other gatherings and on YouTube.

Ethnographers who feel similarly warm feelings toward their interviewees gaze on such images and experience them not just as a documentary of a single moment in time but rather as visual souvenirs of connected events. We see "through" these images to many other times, places, and emotions. In looking at this photograph, I remember not just the sociality of that afternoon but also the times I interviewed particular YouTubers and hung out with them at other gatherings over time. For example, after the San Diego meet-up, many of us went out for a delicious Mexican dinner. The photo helps me recall meeting some YouTubers for the first time at that dinner as well as connecting with others whom I had met before. Meeting up felt like a socially welcoming, democratized reunion for those who had interacted within the YouTube mediascape.

CHRONOTOPIC INTERACTION

The concept of the "chronotope" well illustrates how YouTube's mediascape framed interaction. According to philosopher and semiotician Mikhail Bakhtin, chronotopes combine ideas of time and place to reveal cultural and interactional meanings.[35] Originally used to study literary conventions in novels, the chronotope concept has been widely extended to other studies to analyze subtle cultural and interactive variation, particularly of dynamics that are not easily visible.[36] Bakhtin used the example of a "threshold" to illustrate this concept. A threshold is a chronotope because it connotes the *place* between the inside and outside of a house. Simultaneously, it also refers to the moment in *time* that lies between the past (when one was outside of the house) and the future (when one will arrive inside the house). In common parlance, being on the "threshold" of doing something new may produce feelings of personal and cultural significance. An example is found in the ritual of a groom crossing a threshold with a bride. This is a momentous occasion because they are metaphorically starting a new life together and experiencing a major change in their status.

Chronotopes contain "inseparable" spatial and temporal dimensions that are "always colored by emotions and values."[37] On YouTube, chronotopic emplacement moved beyond individuals' experiences and helped reify a collective temporal history through co-participation in events that people experienced together at the same time. Simultaneously "shared happenings" are crucial building blocks of sociality.[38] Whether or not viewers attended gatherings, they could still experience them through videos and interactive comments.

Gatherings functioned as collective chronotopes because they collapsed time-space concepts that were interpersonally, culturally, and historically meaningful to video makers who co-created YouTube history. Chronotopic aspects of place were evident in the naming of many gatherings. Meet-up names often echoed attributes and cultural connotations of a gathering's physical place. For example, the Midwest Gathering, which I attended in Minneapolis, directly refers to the larger geographic area in which the gathering occurred. It broadly invites a larger crowd from the "Midwest" to attend.

Human sociality is rhythmic, given that it marks annual, spatiotemporal experiences such as reunions, anniversaries, and birthdays. It was thus not surprising to see several meet-up videos that depicted activities at multiple SouthTube gatherings. A search for the term "SouthTube" identified videos that depicted yearly SouthTube gatherings between 2007 and 2012. Meet-ups exhibited a chronotopic cyclicality that culturally anchored interactions across time.

When meet-ups are chronotopically instantiated, time "thickens, takes on flesh, [and] becomes artistically visible," Bakhtin wrote, while simultaneously "space becomes charged and responsive to the movements of time, plot and history."[39] Names sometimes echoed cultural resonances with the city in which the gathering took place. For example, the name of the Philadelphia gathering that I attended was called "Yo' Tube," a phrase that recalls the famous *Rocky* films that were set in that city. The films' title character is a boxer named Rocky who calls out to his girlfriend and eventual wife with the famous line, "Yo, Adrian!" The name "Yo' Tube" thus humorously connects a cultural homage to an emplaced YouTube gathering.

One memorable promotional video, which was posted on March 1, 2008, was entitled *The 2008 Philadelphia YouTube Gathering*. It aimed to raise enthusiasm for the Philadelphia meet-up. The video depicts images associated with the city, including scenes, people, and locations from American history, entertainment, food, and sports. A soundtrack pipes out the pulsing theme song of the *Rocky* films. Connotations of "Philadelphia" in the video spur YouTubers' anticipatory excitement to participate. For instance, one commenter stated, "Whoo-hoo Philadelphia! Attending is on my to-do list. This is a very well-done promo—congratulations." In the video a title card boasts that hundreds of YouTubers with video cameras will gather, "for the greatest collaborative historical documentation the World has ever seen." This amusingly hyperbolic claim implies that the gathering's events will yield both "collaborative" and temporally significant documents in YouTubers' social trajectories. These ideals echo the characteristics of Philadelphia as a richly historical—and ostensibly democratized—US city.

For certain gatherings, YouTube place-based meet-up names overtly included a temporal component. Playful numerology characterized (and helped attendees remember!) forthcoming dates. Examples include 777 (the early, large-scale meet-up that took place in Washington Square Park in New York City on July 7, 2007) and 888 (a meet-up held on August 8–9, 2008, in Toronto). The Midwest Gathering in Minneapolis occurred on June 7, 2008, which is represented as 6-7-8 when written numerically. The Santa Monica gathering that I attended occurred on August 8, 2009, exactly one year after the large-scale 888 meeting in Toronto.

Philosopher and sociologist Henri Lefebvre referred to collective rhythms as "public" rhythms.[40] Calendars, ceremonies, and celebrations marked by time serve as social rhythms that coordinate interaction. Clever chronotopic nomenclature was especially important as YouTube was a new site, without specific dates to anchor its history to sociality. The meet-up names helped craft important, shared historical moments that intertwined individual YouTubers' histories with those of YouTube.

Chronotopes emotionally framed interaction through references to cities, events, and shared histories as seen in the Yo' Tube gathering, or they could evince a personal tone, as happened for ItalianStallionette. She organized a meet-up to celebrate her survival after having a kidney transplant in San Diego three years earlier. The meet-up served as a commemorative and very personal chronotope because it spatiotemporally associated her operation with the time and place of a YouTube meet-up. During an interview I asked her why she organized the gathering.

ITALIANSTALLIONETTE: Three years ago I received my second kidney transplant, and it's the anniversary of it, and [I had] my kidney transplant
in San Diego, so I live out on the East Coast, so I wanted to come back
and celebrate, the past three years and that I'm still here!

PATRICIA: Wow! I wasn't anticipating that.

ITALIANSTALLIONETTE: (laughs) Yeah.

PATRICIA: Um, it seems like you've gotten some pretty positive reaction to
putting it on.

ITALIANSTALLIONETTE: I hope so, I mean when I did it, I've been to other
gatherings, but I wanted this one to be [more like] a reunion, not advertising people, just to play and get along. 'Cause that's really what it's all
about. So I thought that'd be kind of fun. Yeah, I'm happy. Everybody
seems happy and relaxed. I like that.

For ItalianStallionette, the San Diego gathering became a chronotopic emplacement of significant life events. The gathering marked the time and place of
her personal healing. It was also positively associated with YouTube sociality.
ItalianStallionette chose an area far away from where she lived, but one that had
personal, spatiotemporal meaning. ItallianStallionette's choice of venue demonstrates how powerful chronotopic time-place associations can be and suggests why
she might be sensitive to ensuring that the gathering had a social rather than overly
self-promotional vibe.

Organizers created YouTube events that yielded strong associations of equality,
accessibility, sociality, and sometimes even healing as they sought to socialize with
like-minded YouTubers. Each gathering exhibited similar social interactions, yet
they varied in feeling tone with regard to their location, time, and style. YouTubers'
values, such as exhibiting a welcoming and collaborative spirit, were reproduced
through specific chronotopes of gatherings, which associated ideas about place
with accessible sociality.[41] Each act of emplacement accomplished important work
by establishing sets of connected points along a historical chain that intertwined
video makers' personal trajectories with YouTube's interactive timeline.

CHRONOTOPIC CHAINS OF SOCIALITY

Shared histories are important for building relationship continuity and outlining
the parameters of social groups. But how are such dynamics accomplished in new
mediascapes? Building on Bakhtin's theories, this chapter proposes the concept of
chronotopic chains of sociality, in which chronotopes are linked together in ways

that provide important cultural resonances over time. For YouTubers, chronotopic chains resulted from experiencing a cyclical pattern of gatherings. Chronotopic chains are significant because each new gathering received participatory energy in part through its connection to prior socially inspired chronotopes along the chain. In the absence of historical trajectories that are typically constructed from public events such as political conflicts in nation-states, chronotopic meet-ups oriented interactants into the mediascape of YouTube.

Chronotopic chains perpetuate the notion of a coherent, regenerating social group. One such chronotopic link appeared in a video entitled *Experience: As One Gathering*, which was posted on March 14, 2008, by NorCalCorsello (his YouTube channel name). NorCalCorsello was a white man in his mid-thirties whose work focused on comedic videos and vlogs on serious issues of the day, such as transparency in government, high-speed train proposals, globalization, bridge suicide barriers, bike lanes, and border patrol. He also posted videos that experimented with form, such as one on "reality TV" in which his image appears on a large-screen television in a friend's living room as they provide running commentary on it. His videos each receive a few hundred to a thousand views. As of June 2018, he had 619 subscribers.

NorCalCorsello organizes his meet-up video around his reflections of a San Francisco gathering. He and another YouTuber, kenrg (his YouTube channel name), reenacted a shot that they had executed together at the San Francisco gathering a year earlier. NorCalCorsello had been participating for a year and four months when he posted this video. Kenrg had been on YouTube for about a year and a half when they recorded their reenactment. Kenrg was a white man in his late forties whose videos included vlogs on topics such as the meaning of Thanksgiving, information about himself, opinions about fair use, equal rights, songs, movie parodies, and footage of gatherings he had attended. His videos each received several hundred to a thousand or even a few thousand views. As of June 2018, he had 4,122 subscribers.

NorCalCorsello begins his video by saying that when he attended the YouTube gathering in San Francisco in 2007, he did not know many people, even famous YouTubers. He relates how he spent much of his time gathering names of channels and subscribing to them upon his return home. Enacting the inter-threaded aspect of meet-ups, he kept up with these channels and their videos so that when he attended the San Francisco meet-up one year later in 2008, he was more familiar with YouTubers and their work. His video is structured such that he cuts back and forth from images of his footage from the event to his current post-meet-up reflections as he narrates them while facing the camera.

About halfway through the video, NorCalCorsello says he was excited to see kenrg, whom he had met one year earlier. The image cuts to footage taken at the event. In this sequence NorCalCorsello trains his camera on kenrg, who recalls, "This is what we did last year." NorCalCorsello moves closer to him so that they appear on camera together to more closely emulate the shot they had taken one year prior. Kenrg states that they will "recreate the same shot from last year." They recreate the shot with one exception: they both noted that instead of having the same model of camera, they have each upgraded to a new one. They reenact a common type of selfie video in which they are both in the frames of each other's footage.

NorCalCorsello and kenrg bond through their shared recollection of their interaction as it was being mediated. This moment of interaction was fundamentally constituted through a mediated act. Temporally speaking, they were repeating a "shared happening"[42] that occurred at the current event as well as a past one. The recreation was chronotopic in that it collapsed the time and place of a meet-up at a pier in San Francisco. The reenactment is a chronotopic link because it connects two different meet-ups over the period of a year. Their reenactment was thus a creative way in which a chronotopic chain of sociality not only tied together an act of recording together but also solidified emotional ties through a collaborative, mediated act of remembering.

TEMPORALITY AS AN ORIENTING FRAME OF SOCIALITY

YouTubers' videos provide a crucial line of evidence that demonstrates the interthreaded character of meeting up in video makers' social constellations. They also show how chronotopic frameworks created YouTubers' shared histories. The first meet-up video that I encountered was entitled *Renetto + Boh3m3 = YouTube History 101*, which was reposted on July 16, 2015. The text description notes that it was originally uploaded around September 22, 2006. Notably, the video is depicted as "History 101," which symbolically characterizes it as an early, culturally significant moment in YouTube's interactive timeline. The video depicts two video-blogging stars known by their YouTube channel names of renetto and boh3m3 (pronounced bo-heem), who were early members of the YouTube partner program. Boh3m3 says in the video that his name is a reference to his interest in art and to the "Bohemian art revolution in Paris"—and, I would add, also references an unconventional lifestyle. Note the 3s serving as backward *E*s, an identity marker initially associated with elite computer geek speech and later with geek emulators.[43]

Renetto and boh3m3 informally met and video-recorded their encounter as they passed through an airport. It was fascinating to see them take the trouble to meet in this impromptu way. Both were very popular and outspoken vlogging personalities from the United States. As early adopters, they both joined YouTube in March 2006, about six months prior to their meet-up video. Renetto (officially known as

Paul Robinett) was a white, forty-year old man who reportedly owned a candle shop. His videos each regularly garnered thousands of views. He had 38,596 subscribers as of June 2018. Boh3m3 (officially known as Ben Going) was a white man in his early twenties who had quit his job as a waiter at the time of the video. As of July 2018, his videos had earned thousands of views each, and he had 27,874 subscribers.

Renetto and boh3m3 enjoyed vlogging about their observations of YouTube. In the video renetto interviews boh3m3, inviting him to reveal inside information about himself. They chat, discuss aspects of YouTube participation, compare their teeth and types of baldness, and discuss boh3m3's film idea. Having just met, they say they will not hug as they part, but they conclude with a friendly handshake and boh3m3's comic impression of renetto's odd, squeaky-voiced persona from YouTube (which in boh3m3's voice sounds more like actor Adam Sandler). Their historical video demonstrated early on that YouTube sociality could not be contained online and that it was important to record meet-up events and post them on YouTube for others to enjoy.

Meet-up videos are now an important YouTube genre, as most video makers tend to record their activities when gathering in person. Many of the videos focus on noncelebrities—demonstrating how gatherings evidenced a democratized tone. In terms of the corpus of fifty meet-up videos drawn for this analysis, thirty-five, or 70 percent, contained images of people just hanging out. Some videos do not incorporate natural sound but simply depict images of people talking while an added music soundtrack plays. Fourteen, or 28 percent, of the videos mentioned specific benefits of meeting up, such as having fun, learning about the work of YouTubers whom they had not yet watched, enjoying specific moments (such as watching a funny chef during a restaurant dinner), meeting people "in the flesh," and networking. Six videos, or 12 percent, of the corpus referenced difficulties in meeting up, including having car trouble, enduring bad weather, incurring too much expense, and dealing with awkward timing (such as attending while dealing with personal family tragedies).

The videos exhibited similar mediated and temporal trajectories that were cyclically repeated across events. Typically, meet-ups originated with videos advertising them. Pre-meet-up videos (seven videos, or 14 percent, of the corpus) aimed to whip up support and help disseminate logistical information. During the gathering people recorded videos of the event and their interactions (thirty-five videos, or 70 percent). Video creators found it pleasurable to interact through video, with people sometimes interviewing each other on camera. Videos also appeared that offered reflective thoughts after attendees returned home (eight videos, or 16 percent). Videos recorded at gatherings helped those who were unable to attend to partially experience them and helped those who attended to remember their experiences.

Temporally speaking, most videos (70 percent) in the corpus exhibited a "presentist" focus in that the videos concentrated on recording events as they occurred. The videos' presentist energy illustrates the importance of recording moments and taking advantage of video-blogging modalities as a crucial aspect of participation. This finding disturbs the online-offline binary by suggesting that people did not attend a gathering to seek a supposedly pure, unmediated space. Meeting up included recording and sharing representations of interaction, thus showing how sociality was interwoven in mediated ways within YouTube's larger mediascape.

In post-event reflection videos, video makers vlogged about their observations or analyses of events. These reflections usually included expressing enthusiasm for the event and a wish to attend future gatherings, thus establishing a *chronotopic chain of desire* for meeting up. Despite the popular press stereotype that emphasizes YouTube's wacky viral fare, thoughtful video blogs in the sample also depicted video makers intelligently reflecting on and making sense of events they had experienced.

An introspective video on meet-ups was posted on August 12, 2008, by musoSF (his YouTube channel name), who converses with his friend anakin1814 (his YouTube channel name). MusoSF was a white man from San Francisco whose love for music was clear. His videos were often vlogs in which he sang songs or offered musical birthday greetings. He also vlogged about serious topics such as reflections on YouTube and gay marriage. In a nostalgic video about growing up in the 1970s, he expresses an urge to bring back the word "dynamite." His videos see hundreds of views each, with a few earning several thousand views. As of June 2018, he had 1,722 subscribers. At the time of their video, musoSF and anakin1814 had both been participating on YouTube for about two years.

Entitled *Pillow Talk 1: 888 Toronto Meet-up*, this video was the first of a multipart series of videos posted alternately on each of their channels. It was filmed while musoSF and anakin1814 sat in a bed after the event was over. They said that many of the most interesting conversations at the Toronto gathering happened at night as people chatted and hung out in their hotel rooms. Given that they enjoyed social experiences, they expressed frustration over video makers who played up their celebrity. The choice of setting for their retrospective reflection suggested that it was socially inappropriate to wield a camera in a slumber party atmosphere while such quiet, private gatherings were occurring. Still, they felt it important to recreate key events by mimicking what it feels like to gather behind the scenes and talk quietly with other YouTubers during a crowded meet-up.

The *Pillow Talk* video illustrates how emplacement includes subtle interactions beyond the umbrella idea of gathering in a single "place." Hotel lobbies and shared hotel suites where people socialized were neither completely public nor private. On one level their interaction in shared hotel rooms was relatively more public than when each YouTuber was alone, completely away from other video makers. On the other hand, they were relatively more private than when they hung out with hundreds of other YouTubers in a public park. These details illustrate nuanced dynamics of emplacement in which the public and private do not function as a rigid binary. Rather, they are more productively understood as a fractal relation that splinters off to smaller and smaller (as well as larger and larger) interactional units that nevertheless retain a comparative sense of public and private social activity.[44]

Thirty-three, or 66 percent, of the videos contained modest footage of friends talking or experiencing relaxed forms of hanging out. These images echo what anthropologist Richard Chalfen labeled "home mode" images, which are photographs and home movies that focus on interpersonal relationships and themes. Excluding advanced amateurs from his study of US media making in the 1960s-1970s, Chalfen found that home mode media exhibited content and aesthetics that were distinct from other genres such as educational or feature films.[45] Home mode media were created for the viewership of private individuals, such as family members. Scholars often dismiss home mode footage as banal. It is often criticized for reinforcing capitalist, patriarchal family hierarchies, such as when fathers film a new family car or record their children opening expensive holiday gifts.[46] Mediated acts in past eras put males in control of family images and reinforced the father figure as the successful head of the household.

In contrast, media and communication scholar Maria Pini found that contemporary home mode footage exhibits important functions for creating social unity, continuity, and stability among family members who are separated by time and space.[47] Comments posted to YouTube meet-up videos suggest that such videos enable viewers to "re-embody that place and time, and return to that moment" of shared experience.[48] In addition, home mode video has now broadened to include not only biological families but "families we choose."[49] Videos that solidify relationships now appear across a broad social landscape, including people from work, neighborhoods, clubs, and many other social configurations.[50]

Examining commentary posted to the meet-up videos in the corpus reveals how YouTube sociality became emplaced and created shared temporal histories. If commenters had attended the meet-ups, their posts emphasized how the footage brought back memories, thus evoking new conceptions of home mode media that aim to close the temporal and spatial distances between their attendance at a gathering and their subsequent memories.[51] On a post to a San Diego meet-up video, one commenter stated: "Good to meet [you]—it's so fun to relive the day through your clips. Hopefully we'll do another one of these at some point." This commenter introduces a chronotopic desire for future meetings. YouTubers also emotionally connected to events, as one commenter stated in response to a video posted about a New York City meet-up: "awesome video man. wow tears up. i miss it so much. i was in this video 4 times hehe yay. look for the bright yellow jersey hehe." The commenter injects visibility for himself but also emphasizes how much he misses gathering with YouTube participants.

Temporally speaking, a significant proportion (34 percent) of the videos referenced chronotopic orientations, such as anticipating attending a meet-up the next year or remembering or comparing it to prior meet-ups. Even if they had recorded meet-up footage, YouTubers expressed appreciation for seeing the event from another video maker's point of view. These findings illustrate how YouTubers interested in sociality invited increased, more democratized participation, as multiple points of view were valued. For example, a commenter to a Philadelphia meet-up video notes that they intend to post their footage of the event. The video maker replies: "Can't wait to see the events from your camera's point of view. Was great meeting you too! If Illuminatta and I ever get the Long Island gathering going you gotta come up for that." The video maker expressed interest in appreciating other people's renderings of events of the same meet-up and suggests a rendezvous on Long Island, thus creating chronotopic anticipation for future sociality.

If commenters had not attended a meet-up, they often expressed gratitude for being able to experience it through posted videos. For example, in response to GeneticBlend's video *NYC Gathering 777*, a viewer whose channel name is bnessel1973 stated: "I'm so friggin jealous. That looked like an amazing time! Post all the stuff you got, PLEASE! I need to see all of what I missed. Look forward to meeting you face to face, brother." The plea to post more videos simultaneously references a desire to experience the place-based, in-person event and emphasizes a desire to meet "face to face," which all contribute to a larger, interwoven mediascape. Meet-up videos exhibited a vitality that even prompted some commenters to feel that they had experienced events vicariously. Posting to a video depicting a meet-up in Santa Monica, one commenter noted: "I have not been to a single one of them there gathering yet I feel like I have been to all of them. I'm tired. Lol."

With cameras constantly recording and emplacing YouTube, notions of an online-offline binary are severely challenged. YouTubers used meet-up videos in ways that temporally and chronotopically framed their interaction, including anticipating getting together, enjoying collective mediated moments, and reflecting on past events to create anticipation for new cycles of meeting up. For some YouTubers, it was possible to keep the cycles going in person and through videos. Conversely, some YouTube participants encountered participatory frictions when trying to involve multiple modalities in the YouTube mediascape. Viewers did not need to attend gatherings to feel that they were part of YouTube sociality—but many felt deeply grateful if they could.

PARTICIPATORY FUNGIBILITIES AND FRICTIONS

YouTube participants enjoyed—and indeed often maximized—multiple modalities within an interactive mediascape. The term "modality" connotes various characteristics across computer-mediated scholarship, but here it refers to alternative types of interpersonal interaction through specific sensory media.[52] It is not analytically robust to limit the term "modality" to basic categories such as "online" versus "offline" behavior because numerous modalities are apparent within each type, and YouTubers traveled across them in nuanced ways. For example, YouTube offers several modalities, including the ability to post videos, offer text comments, and engage in direct messaging. It is beyond the scope of the study to examine all modalities on video-sharing platforms or all modalities available during a gathering. The point here is merely to note that modalities are multiple and that each one offers sensorial and participatory advantages for YouTubers seeking sociality.

Rather than engage in binaries, it is more productive to speak of degree of intensity and type of mediation across modalities. For anthropologists John Postill and Sarah Pink, intensities refer to the degree of sociality one exercises through media, such as ranging from executing a simple "like" on a Facebook page to engaging in person.[53] The present study is concerned with how social behavior interacts with technical modalities; thus, intensities here refer to the amount of mediation one employs to achieve social ends. For example, a person who attends a meet-up and records only a few moments is exhibiting less mediated intensity than someone who carries the camera around at all times and tries to record as much as possible. An example might include recording many people at once, as depicted in figure 3.4. Recording a few choice moments exhibits a lower degree of intensity of mediation than recording as many as one can. Type of mediation refers to the device used (such as a smart phone camera versus a video recorder) and the modalities that are employed to interact (such as sending asynchronous video messages versus interacting through a synchronous, live video link).

This section proposes the concept of *participatory fungibility* to understand mediation's role in video sociality. A quintessential example of a fungible item is money, which can be used interchangeably for different purposes. This section analyzes nuanced characteristics of mediated participation that appeared to be fungible across degree of intensity and type of mediation. It is also concerned with understanding which types of mediation encountered frictions. Although there are clearly many categories to discuss, this section will focus on emotional, experiential, and physical characteristics of mediated fungibility.

When YouTubers say that they feel connected to people whom they initially met on YouTube and wish to meet them in person, they are displaying *emotional* fungibility across mediated experience. Emotional fungibility means that relationships and feelings toward others may be felt as equally intense across different types of mediation. When attendees came to meet-ups excited to meet someone they knew from YouTube, they indicated that the feelings they held toward other creators exhibited similar depth, whether they bonded through types of media such as comments or videos or whether they met in person and made media throughout the meet-up together. Their depth of feeling resonated across different types of mediated interaction.

However, not all encounters were equally fungible for creators across different types of media modalities. For instance, interviewees described feeling dissatisfied with the YouTube platform's asynchronous aspect and began seeking more "presentist" media, such as live video chats that enabled people to synchronously connect with YouTube friends. For these video makers, YouTube was not *experientially* fungible to other digital media that offered the presentist, synchronous focused that they desired.[54] Experiential fungibility refers to whether people feel a sense of interchangeably equivalent sensory contact when using various types of mediation. In order to interact with their preferred type of sensory modality with other YouTubers, they left the site, at least for a time, to go onto a live chat service called Stickam. Although both sites are digitally mediated and exist within a YouTube mediascape, the activities were not, to these YouTubers, always experientially interchangeable.

Even though YouTubers articulated the belief that commenting was *emotionally* fungible to making videos in terms of how people felt connected to others, not all creators treated the two activities as *experientially* fungible. For example, if commenting and making videos were accepted as experientially fungible, why would YouTubers strongly encourage people to expand their participation from commenting to making their own videos? People often inspired others to expand their modalities of participation. Despite their idealistic rhetoric about equivalence, some YouTubers felt it important to encourage people at the margins to experience YouTube by sharing their own videos.

Sensorially speaking, YouTubers also referenced touch as an important quality available at in-person gatherings. For example, I interviewed DaleATL2 (his YouTube account name), a white man in his forties who stressed that meeting up offered sensory advantages, such as touch and smell, that were simply not present in digital environments. Receiving a few hundred to several thousands of views on each of his videos, he vlogged about places he visited with his family. He also posted comedic vlogs and movie parodies. He had been on the site for about a year and four months when I interviewed him at the SouthTube meet-up in 2007. As of June 2018, he had 2,404 subscribers. DaleATL2 told me that gatherings were important because they facilitated a range of senses:

FIGURE 3.6. YouTubers embracing each other in Hollywood, Philadelphia, and San Francisco, January 19, 2008, July 12, 2008, and February 23, 2008. Photographs by Patricia G. Lange.

> I would equate it to the pen pals of old, but on steroids. Because no longer are you only communicating on paper, you're communicating both visually and auditorially and you've got all the— except for the sense of smell, and touch, and that's what the touch is for [gestures around toward the gathering], this is the touch and smell. You're getting all the senses together.

DaleATL2 saw pen pal letter writing practices as similar but not experientially fungible to making videos because the latter offer visual and auditory sensory experience. In turn, he did not characterize video making as experientially fungible to gatherings because videos lack "touch" and "smell." He appreciated the incorporation of "all the senses" in a way that enlivened his YouTube experience.

The sensuality of touch seemed to be an important part of the meet-up experience for numerous attendees as they interacted together. Indeed, footage recorded for my vlogs and my ethnographic film *Hey Watch This!* (2013) is filled with images of people hugging, shaking hands, and enjoying embodied connections with their fellow YouTubers in co-located places (figure 3.6).

Note that assessments about fungibility are ultimately personal. Some people might not feel experiential fungibility between video-mediated and in-person encounters due to specific characteristics (such as smell), which are not present in all modalities. Yet, degrees of fungibility must be examined in each case. It is possible to experience one type of fungibility but not necessarily all types. For example, just because one does not achieve *experiential* fungibility between videos and gatherings (because they cannot touch people in a video) does not mean that using media lacks *emotional* resonance to other video makers. In these cases they feel emotional but not experiential fungibility across different types of interactive modalities.

Conversely, for those YouTubers for whom touch is unimportant, they may actually accept videos and meet-ups as experientially fungible. In early internet decades it was often assumed that lack of certain sensory cues in digital media meant that people could not bond emotionally. But online participants and researchers quickly demonstrated that this is obviously not true. People may bond quite deeply over media.

In some cases experiential characteristics may be related. Some people may emotionally bond more easily, for instance, through experiential sense of touch. For other people, such as me, touch is not a particularly crucial requirement for bonding with friends. I am not a "hugger," as they say. The ability to hug or smell someone is not necessarily part of my calculus for experiential fungibility, which demonstrates that despite binaries that smuggle in the ethical assessment that in-person interactions are always superior, in fact fungibilities cannot be determined in a universalized way across all people and contexts. Although it is beyond the scope of this project, future studies might investigate how different types of media fungibility may relate to and influence other forms. The goal here is simply to identify and analyze nuanced differences and how they challenge crude online-offline binaries. Mediation is imbricated in daily life, but it is important to remain sensitive to varied engagements with different mediated modalities.

A final dimension may be termed physical or mobile fungibility, which refers to how easily people are able to physically access types of interaction. A person who has no computer would find it difficult to interact in an exclusively mediated way. Indeed, physical access to the internet is not always easily achieved. Conversely, a person who cannot afford to attend a meet-up would not be able to physically meet others in person. A person who could just as easily interact with people through a computer as through travel to meet-ups would arguably be enjoying physical fungibility between media types. Such a person would no doubt have access to considerable resources. Lack of *physical* fungibility does not imply that mediated interaction lacks *emotional* fungibility. It is possible to feel emotional connections to people across media types without being able to access each modality equally. What is considered fungible varies across individuals and different modalities of participation.

Among YouTubers, participatory frictions occurred. It was not always possible to move seamlessly across different types of mediation. While recognizing that the internet represents a "way of life," we must also acknowledge limitations and ruptures of access. Information studies and history scholar Paul Edwards coined the term "data friction" to examine how movement of data may be impeded. Writing in the context of global warming research, "data friction," according to Edwards, "refers to the costs in time, energy, and attention required to collect, check, store, move, receive, and access data."[55] Whenever data move, friction influences and indeed may "impede" movement. In social systems, Edwards contends, frictions may include "conflict" or "disagreements."

YouTubers cited numerous forms of friction that challenged their ability to physically attend meet-ups or to access mediated forms of interaction. For instance, some

YouTubers did not save their video files and used the site as storage. When the corporate entity of YouTube deliberately or inadvertently deleted a video, their physical access to their own mediation was impeded or even destroyed if they lacked a backup. Losing one's own videos exemplifies experiencing data friction—one that caused some YouTubers considerable distress. The videos were not physically fungible across their own personal computer as well as the public platform of YouTube.

Traveling to gatherings included many challenges such as family obligations, limited finances, getting time off work, shyness, and facing fears of meeting people initially known from the internet. For example, one woman I talked to, whom I refer to as Jane (a researcher-assigned pseudonym), said that it was not easy for her family to understand why she wanted to attend gatherings. Jane was a white woman and mother of young children who often vlogged about family moments such as a baby learning to walk and child haircuts. She also sent birthday greetings and recorded comedic skits. Her videos typically received a couple of hundred views each, although a few saw a thousand views. As of June 2018, she had 134 subscribers.

Jane had been participating on YouTube for nearly a year and a half when I interviewed her at the Toronto gathering in 2008. Jane's family's concerns reiterate common binary conceptualizations in discourse about networked interaction. She noted that as a returning student, it was also difficult to take time to attend gatherings. She stated:

> My husband has slowly become more open to our going [to a gathering]. He came with me to Philly, um, and met some people and kind of became more comfortable with the idea of meeting up with "internet people." So that's only been a recent thing, so financially it's not been an issue; it's more been a social issue and a timing issue that only recently [I've] been able to do.

The friction Jane experienced involved social issues, specifically convincing her family that it was important for her to meet up with YouTube friends. The marginalization of YouTubers is exhibited in that, to members of Jane's family, it was initially odd for her to meet up with them.

Paradigms of sociality collided when family members operating within an outdated online-offline binary could not understand why she might wish to socialize with people whom she initially encountered in a mediated way. Her family's discomfort with her desire to meet up with "internet people" reflects a common suspicion of becoming close to those whom one originally met via the internet. For some people, the sequential aspect of meeting people in person first is an important part of a friendship trajectory. YouTubers did not share this temporal and sequential line of reasoning, which reflected a more contemporary acceptance of the interthreadedness of mediated life. Although Jane did not have a problem with finances, she referenced time constraints as a returning student. Jane had to work through these social and temporal frictions to attend gatherings.

Many people whom I interviewed earned modest incomes in fields such as clerical work, grocery store inventory control, and temp work. It was not surprising that people experienced participatory frictions when traveling to gatherings. Most interviewees told me that they preferred attending meet-ups close to their home due to costs and travel time. As a California resident, I found it far easier to attend in-state meet-ups. Another YouTuber who lived in the Los Angeles area seemed to be going to the same California-based meet-ups that I was attending. Given his interest in YouTube sociality, it is perhaps not surprising that he appeared at meet-ups in Hollywood, San Francisco, San Diego, and Santa Monica—all of which are relatively accessible for California residents.

However, attending meet-ups was not easy for all YouTubers. At the meet-up in Toronto in 2008, I asked an interviewee named myloflex (his YouTube channel name) whether he found it "easy" to attend meet-ups in terms of finances and time off work. Myloflex was an Asian-Canadian man in his late twenties whose videos included experimental short films, cooking videos, videos about his health, and meet-up footage. The view counts on each of his videos are extremely varied, ranging from a few dozen to several thousand. As of June 2018, he had 320 subscribers. When I interviewed him in Toronto, he had been participating on the site for just over two years. In answer to whether it was easy to attend meet-ups, myloflex explained:

> Not really. Honestly, um. The one in New York a year ago was—was very, very difficult. [The hotel], flight, um, here I'm a little more local, so it is easier, but getting the time off wasn't easy. I had to work a lot of straight days to get this weekend off. And the drive is just, a commute's a commute in Toronto, so.

He said that despite these difficulties he chose to come anyway because it was "fun" and because one could reconnect with people. He stated an interest in seeing them again "one year around," thus referencing a desire for cyclical, chronotopic sociality—as seen in reunions. Like many attendees, he appreciated an ability to meet up with YouTube friends and to catch up on their lives. Myloflex's story suggests the sacrifices that YouTubers were willing to make for sociality. Going to such lengths visibly demonstrated the personal importance of participating with other YouTubers.

Comments on videos posted after meet-ups also reiterated the difficulties of meeting up in person. In comments on a video posted about the Midwest Gathering in Minneapolis, commenters expressed regret that they could not attend but emphasized a desire to attend convenient meet-ups in the future. One commenter stated: "i wish i was there. if there is one in sf i will go." Another commenter echoed these sentiments: "aww man, i got to wait for another NYC one cause i live in nyc." Reacting to a video posted about the New York City meet-up, a commenter stated:

> I would love to go to a YouTube gathering, but with the kids and finances it's just not doable at this point in my life (unless there is ever one in MA ;). Although I am afraid I would be really shy, as I am in real life. On the other hand, it would be so cool to get to hang out with other youtubers! This was a neat look into the past!

The commenter discusses how parenting responsibilities, finances, and social shyness complicate attendance at meet-ups but suggests that a local meet-up might be possible and that it would be desirable to meet other YouTubers interested in sociality.

Because meet-ups were difficult to attend, they were all the more important to YouTube participants. Mediation of different types and degrees of intensity are part of life for YouTubers in this socially inspired group. At the same time, it is important to recognize individuals' asymmetrical, material affordances. Acknowledging these challenges and the financial and scheduling sacrifices that YouTubers made underscores the emotional depth that people in this social group expressed for one another. Although meeting up on YouTube may have felt emotionally fungible to meeting up and recording people in person, such occurrences were not necessarily experientially or physically fungible. Although it was not feasible to go to every meet-up that one wished to attend, YouTubers often expressed deep regret and sadness at not being able to go, and they articulated a chronotopic desire to do so when possible in the future.

When we examine forms of fungibility, it becomes clear that no single experience "defines" what it means to participate using a rubric known as YouTube. Video makers sought to engage with multiple modalities and degrees of mediation to interact with other YouTubers. YouTube as a concept inflected in-person interaction—people were attending a *YouTube* gathering, after all. The case study of socially motivated YouTubers shows that mediation of many types and degrees constituted the YouTube experience. What was crucial was keeping them open, accessible, and democratized in order to solidify co-created and collaborative sociality.

TEMPORAL EMPLACEMENT

YouTube sociality reveals that binaries of online-offline conceptualizations are flawed. YouTubers used multiple types of modalities to interact, yet their modalities were deeply intertwined. During a gathering a place often became a YouTube place, as people recorded their activities with varying degrees of intensity. Studying emplacement and its orienting concepts of communitas, reunions, and chronotopes revealed YouTubers' idealistic conception of its welcoming, collective, and inclusive atmosphere. People posted meet-up videos such that place framed YouTube participation. YouTubers planned, experienced, and remembered place-based interaction. Taking into account concepts of emotional, experiential, and physical fungibility, we see that YouTubers often made sacrifices in terms of time, finances, and social conflict to engage with other people from the site. Video makers expressed emotional fungibility in finding meaning from a variety of different types and degrees of mediated modalities.

No two YouTube experiences were exactly the same, but they all interwove modalities across time and space to create a larger aspiration to democratized sociality that suggests more of a mediascape rather than a single website. YouTubers engaged in personal and collective forms of chronotopic emplacement that revealed the importance of interacting and marking these events through media and across time. YouTube participants conceptually created chronotopic chains of interaction and anticipatory desire that deeply influenced video makers' sociality as they temporally co-created a sense of shared history that brought them closer together. YouTube gatherings and their resulting videos emplaced interactivity by infusing feelings of past, present, and future mediated experiences that were at times inseparable.

4

SYNCING UP THROUGH RECIPROCITY

If you do someone a favor, do you secretly expect one in return? If someone does you a favor, should they expect payback from you? Or should people give freely, with no strings attached? Does the quality of the favor matter? YouTubers in the study believe that it does. According to populist notions about the "law of reciprocity," people are intrinsically inclined to return a favor. On social media, creators are expected to reciprocate attention that they receive from viewers and commenters by responding personally. Social media experts often wax rhapsodic about engaging in reciprocity—or mutual exchange of things—to maintain strong relationships and enjoy success. Of course, one must not feign interest but rather show true "regard" for the other person.[1]

Yet what exactly constitutes regard? Economic historian Avner Offer defined "regard" as "an attitude of approbation," or a sense of approval or appreciation that people express when they pay close attention to someone.[2] In this model attention is a scarce life resource, so the granting of one's regard becomes a carefully considered gift. Anthropologists are keenly aware, however, that reciprocities take many forms, some of them accompanied by warm and mutual regard and some of them quite self-serving.

This chapter analyzes whether sincere forms of reciprocity are possible in the commercialized, social media environment of YouTube. To display sincere regard means showing genuine curiosity or interest in someone's work rather than feigning attention only to drive up one's own traffic. YouTubers believed in democratized

DOI: 10.5876/9781607329558.c004

media, but within limits. A creator had to demonstrate sincere interest in making videos and encouraging meaningful sociality to receive reciprocal attention.

This chapter demonstrates that despite fears of rampant self-centeredness in media, in fact positive, interpersonal forms of reciprocity are alive and well online. YouTubers' sociality demonstrably involved media reciprocities that bolstered interaction. However, the chapter will also show—contra many pundits—that in certain cases YouTubers believed it was better to withhold reciprocity to improve the sincerity of interactions and the quality of YouTube. The chapter will argue that strategic withholdings of reciprocity—similar to cases in the anthropological record—were sometimes just as important as bestowing it for creating a meaningful environment for sharing the self through media.

Reciprocity is considered to be the cornerstone of society. Anthropologists have studied this concept for over a hundred years. Anthropologist Mary Douglas famously asserted that with respect to small-scale communities, "The cycling gift system is the society."[3] Yet observers worry that media makers focus on themselves, thus challenging the vitality of reciprocity in contemporary social media environments. This chapter shows that reciprocity remains a key aspect of digitally mediated sociality.

In Lefebvrian terms this chapter analyzes how the "growth phase" of social phenomena intensified and how YouTubers deepened their connections to each other through forms of reciprocity. Enacting mediated reciprocity was one way in which socially motivated YouTubers grew closer and invited connections to a wider social circle that prompted feelings of being in a community, as discussed in the next chapter. In the video idiom of YouTube, participants could execute reciprocal support by paying attention to each other's work, including taking the time to watch videos and post comments. Lefebvre urged attention to temporalities and to the way in which consideration to time reveals cultural values. This chapter analyzes such sensitivities, including, for instance, the recognition that taking the time to watch an entire video or respond to comments in a timely way sacrificed one's own life time, which shows social support for a video maker.

Lefebvre maintained that a crucial element of rhythm analysis concerned examining repetition and its functions. Actions that are ritualistically repeated reveal salient beliefs within a culture. This chapter examines how decisions to bestow reciprocity were carefully considered and were systematically repeated across different participants over time. Consistently reciprocating attention offered repeated opportunities for building a sense of mutual connection and sociality.

Notably, although reciprocities may strengthen communal bonds, anthropologists have also observed many negative forms of reciprocity in numerous cultural contexts across time and space. Reciprocity is at times a contested practice. It is not the participatory panacea that many pundits and some scholars assume that it is. It is not reducible to a guaranteed formula or law as characterized by social media consultants.[4]

The chapter will begin with a methodological discussion describing how I engaged in varied levels of reciprocal engagement across two vlogs to understand reciprocity's effects. It will then provide scholarly contextualization of how reciprocity has been applied in social media in general and how it might be conceptualized in the video-sharing environment of YouTube. The chapter focuses on analyzing multiple forms of video-related reciprocities, and it will examine the criteria that YouTube participants used to determine when to bestow it and when to withhold their attention and regard. Understanding these calculations provides insight into the interpersonal dynamics of video sharing. The chapter concludes by drawing on the ethnographic findings to engage in a broader philosophical consideration of classical anthropological ideas about reciprocity as well as its origins and categorizations. This chapter analyzes multiple forms of reciprocity on YouTube to illustrate—and challenge—what is known about reciprocity's roots, motivations, and effects.

ANTHROVLOG VERSUS ANTHROVLOG

Anthropological research often involves comparing different groups to observe subtle cultural characteristics. For the study, I maintained two versions of my video blog (vlog)—both called AnthroVlog. I used the different versions to see how interaction might change when I varied my intensity of participation and levels of reciprocity. I maintained one version of AnthroVlog on YouTube and one on a blog-hosting site called WordPress, a common platform used by early vloggers. A group whom I refer to as first-generation video bloggers began sharing their work *prior* to YouTube's emergence, preferring blog-hosting sites.[5] Early vloggers provided inspiration and models for vlogging to YouTubers. Popular comedic creator Mark Day (40,000 subscribers) directly credited one early vlogger—Ze Frank—as a key video-making influence.[6] After YouTube launched, several first-generation vloggers whom I interviewed were slow to join the site or even avoided it. Video-sharing sites exhibit technical, commercial, and participatory parameters that influence the reading of videos. For early vloggers, YouTube was characterized by poor quality, hostility, and lack of control over one's media. A common strategy was to post videos to video-hosting sites such as blip.tv and cross-link them to vlogs on WordPress. Because I wanted to compare vlogging experiences both within and outside of YouTube, I too established a version of my vlog on WordPress and crossed-linked my videos from blip.tv.

My behavior was similar across AnthroVlog (YouTube) and AnthroVlog (WordPress). For both vlogs I attended video-themed events, interviewed video makers, and created videos. However, I engaged in a key participatory variation. I was socially conservative when participating online within first-generation, video-blogging circles on the WordPress version of AnthroVlog. I spent time in person with first-generation vloggers by attending in-home tutorials, parties, and other events where this group gathered in Los Angeles and San Francisco. However, I posted very few comments to other people's videos. I exhibited a much quieter approach in comparison to my YouTube participation. Within the WordPress-based vlogging environment, I uploaded videos, but I did not engage in forms of *media* reciprocities as they did.

In contrast, on YouTube I was highly active and responsive to the media reciprocities that appeared between socially oriented YouTubers. I commented on other people's videos and took care to answer comments posted to my videos. An example of an exchange of comments is the one below from my video entitled *Video Reciprocity*, posted on February 27, 2008. The video had garnered 15,986 views as of July 2018. As part of my "open field notes" series of videos on YouTube, this video included a compilation of prototypical interview responses from attendees at a San Francisco gathering. Interviewees were asked to share their views on YouTube reciprocities. Sample questions included the following: (1) If someone comments on your videos, do you feel a need to comment on their videos? (2) Do you owe your subscribers anything in particular? (3) If someone subscribes to you or "friends" you (in the social media sense), do you typically subscribe or "friend" them back? When the video was created, YouTube had a friending feature in which YouTubers could accept a friend request, and a hard-coded link was established between the accounts. In 2011 the feature was eliminated; subscription and friend lists were merged.[7]

In the immediate aftermath of the video's posting, I answered many comments on the video, taking care to reply to the content rather than to offer only generic thanks for commenting. The following illustrates how I responded to commenters to my video. In this exchange ShortbusMooner lends her opinion to the video's discussion on reciprocity:

> Some people think that you have to sub back to them, if they sub to you, but I don't play like that. You have to earn my interest. But I do always return the comment favor. I also don't friend just anyone—there's so many that are just bulletin hogs! LOL!
>
> AnthroVlog: Bulletin hog. *grin* I hadn't heard that term. Thanks for alerting me.

ShortbusMooner disagrees with the view that when someone subscribes to your channel, you should automatically subscribe back. Yet she believes in bestowing reciprocity in terms of comments posted to her videos. Her actions indicate a generalized, repeated pattern of support whenever she receives a "comment favor." When she posted her comment, the friending feature was active and YouTubers might receive "bulletins" about their YouTube friends' activities. She notes that one has to be careful about friending just anyone, lest they become "bulletin hogs" who inordinately saturate one's feed with their announcements. In her comment ShortbusMooner explained an insider or emic term, and I thank her for sharing this information.

Reciprocities sometimes traveled across different modalities of interaction. For example, during a meet-up in Santa Monica, a viewer of AnthroVlog whom I did not know introduced himself and said that he had watched my videos and enjoyed them. It was a casual and sincere comment, the timbre of which prompted me to check out his videos and leave a comment when I returned home. I felt the need to reciprocate his regard, even though I was not necessarily interested in the video themes he preferred. I found this exchange enlightening because I viscerally felt a need to respond, even though we did not share the exact same interests in content.

Activity on my videos on AnthroVlog (YouTube) was more intensive than interaction on AnthroVlog (WordPress). Although vloggers from the WordPress crowd were interactive with each other on their vlogs and with me during in-person activities, my WordPress vlog was quiet unless I started opening up and posting comments to other people's videos. I eventually abandoned my AnthroVlog on WordPress in 2009, in part due to lack of activity. In 2013 the video-hosting site blip.tv began pulling unprofitable videos from its site.[8] My videos were also deleted, rendering my vlog a dead thing—even as an archival site. Ironically, in line with the vlogger's ideal of keeping a vlog outside of the Google/YouTube machine to secure more control over one's work, moving off of YouTube ultimately yielded far less control over my WordPress vlog. Subsequent remarks about AnthroVlog in this chapter thus refer solely to my channel on YouTube.

The experiment proved quite fruitful ethnographically. Both vlogs were equally "public" in terms of their global accessibility. I often posted identical videos to both sites. Despite these similarities, nuances in reciprocal attention were revealed in text comments, view counts, and participatory interactions. Commenting on videos often prompted others to reciprocate more intensively than when I interacted with them only during meet-ups. In-person interaction is assumed to be a gold standard for achieving maximally close types of interpersonal bonding, but it was insufficient in this media milieu. Achieving intensive forms of sociality resulted from engaging in a combination of different modalities of video reciprocity. In these mediated groups one needed to engage with media to feel fully integrated socially. In terms of reciprocity, the experiment proved eye-opening. The more I gave, the more I got.

RECIPROCITY IN DIGITAL MEDIA

Reciprocity has captured the attention of digital media scholars over the past several decades. Writing from a sociological perspective, Peter Kollock examined online communities based on computer-programming discussion groups and observed a general disposition among members to behave reciprocally.[9] For instance, online participants contributed public goods such as providing information or assistance. Motivations for helping included the expectation of receiving assistance from group members at a later date as well as building one's own reputation. People might feel a personal sense of "efficacy" by impacting their environment.[10] These examples are premised on the low cost of contributing to the group (it is easy to post a message) and on "identity persistence." If people cannot track who has contributed, it is difficult to reciprocate.

Emotional reciprocities also appear in digital media. In a study of therapeutic environments, therapists' self-disclosures often prompted their clients to open up, thus increasing opportunities for meaningful communication.[11] Similarly, a study of women vloggers that I conducted suggested that when women shared personal thoughts about civic concerns through videos, commenters tended to respond by discussing important issues. It was not only through words but also by connecting with someone's face in a direct camera-address vlog that prompted people to open up about concerns they shared with the vlogger.[12] In her research on social network sites, technology and social media researcher danah boyd observed a "spirit of reciprocity" among teens who felt that if someone was "nice enough" to provide commentary, one had to be "nice" and respond back.[13]

In contrast to examining general inclinations toward reciprocity, researchers who are engaged in large-scale studies of social media measure reciprocity in a specific way. Reciprocity is frequently calculated as a proportion of users who follow each other back using the hard-coded links of a social media service. For instance, researchers studying Tumblr, a blog-based platform, measured reciprocity as "the likelihood that if user *a* follows user *b*, then *b* also follows *a*."[14] Researchers compared Tumblr to Twitter, a microblogging site in which messages ("tweets") were at that time limited to 140 characters. They found that on Twitter 22 percent of participants had reciprocal links compared with 30 percent on Tumblr and 3 percent in the blogosphere in general.[15] YouTubers in the present study did not define reciprocity in terms of following another video maker's account when friending was still active. Instead, they engaged in behaviors such as comment and viewership reciprocity.

Communication scholar Etienne Pelaprat and sociologist Barry Brown studied reciprocities in online discussion forums, gaming, and social networks. They argue that reciprocity is crucial to many types of digital interaction, specifically because it encourages people to "recognize" others and to "share in social life."[16] Describing dynamics that closely resemble the practices observed on YouTube, Pelaprat and Brown state that opportunities for expressing reciprocity become sites of "encounter." Exchanging recognition within such encounters invites online participants into potential relationships. Reciprocating by answering questions in an online discussion forum or sharing personal experiences on a social media site may indicate a desire "to encounter, engage, and be-with."[17] Pelaprat and Brown observed that online query sites often provide answers to people's questions. Answers frequently evolved into a reciprocal, conversational exchange. According to Pelaprat and Brown, posting one's status on a social media site is not a narcissistic act but rather an "offer for others to respond" because participants wish to "express a desire to live life with others through forms of giving and exchange."[18]

An obvious gesture of reciprocity appears at the end of many YouTube videos. People often say, "Thanks for watching!" They express gratitude to their audience for taking the time to watch their video. On the surface, a repeated, ritualistic way of ending a video may appear to mimic standard broadcasting tropes; professional television shows often end with a standardized thanks to their mass viewing audience. Although some video makers offer generic thanks, YouTubers interested in sociality felt and expressed sincere gratitude to people who watched their videos.

Within a limited "attention economy"[19] consisting of professional and amateur video creators, viewers must choose which works to watch. For socially sensitive video makers, when a viewer watches a video, an attentional debt is often created. Video comments and interview remarks reveal that creators often redress these attentional forms of debt by acknowledging their viewers' regard, at least in terms of a polite thanks, but sometimes by doing even more; video creators in turn comment on or watch their viewers' work, engaging in patterns of video reciprocity. Extrapolating from a definition of reciprocity proposed by sociologist Alvin Gouldner,[20] video reciprocity is defined here as a behavior, belief, or ideal in which something is given deliberately and interpersonally to another person in response to a prior video-related event. For example, an event may be a comment on a video. A creator may see the comment and in turn watch and comment on their viewer's video.

Video makers thanked not only their viewers at the end of videos but also often thanked text commenters within the comment section and sometimes engaged in discussions with them. Comments became moments of "encounter," to use Pelaprat and Brown's term. Video makers also created and exchanged video footage for collaborative projects. When asked whether they "owed" anything to viewers who took the time to watch their work, most interviewees were reluctant to identify such reciprocal practices as "obligations." Nevertheless, they repeatedly and systematically engaged in video reciprocity to invite or maintain sociality. Of course, what constituted a meaningful video that deserved attention was subjective and was adjudicated by each YouTube participant's personal interests and preferences. As a rule, however, video reciprocity remained important for establishing social connections through media.

RECIPROCITY IN VIDEO-SHARING CONTEXTS

Video reciprocities include interactional forms of exchange and acknowledgment of reciprocal feelings through video.[21] Interactional moves create a kind of debt with respect to regard, and this attentional debt ideally yields repayment. For example, people may believe that they owe a person thanks after receiving a compliment. A person has bestowed a "gift" of regard through a compliment, and that attention has created a momentary, attentional asymmetry between the two parties. In many US cultural contexts, staring back blankly after being paid a compliment would seem odd. It is customary to ritually reciprocate a compliment with thanks. An expression of regard might prompt a generic expression of thanks, but it is not necessarily less sincere because it is a widely accepted and repeated form. Similarly, if someone watches a YouTuber's video, the creator may feel it necessary to provide thanks. Regard is inevitably a scarce resource. One has only so much time to grant other people attention during one's lifetime.[22] Viewers who watch a video use part of their scarce life resources, and this "sacrifice" should be acknowledged.

Researchers have identified multiple categories of reciprocities. They may be "homeomorphic"[23] in that things of a similar kind are exchanged. An example in a video-sharing context might include subscribing to someone's channel when someone has subscribed to yours. Subscribing to a YouTube channel was free and meant being alerted (such as through email) when a video maker had posted a new video. To subscribe, one simply pressed a Subscribe button located under every video as well as on a video maker's channel page. From a commercial perspective, the subscription feature attempts to lure people back to the site through notifications of new videos that may interest viewers who had subscribed to particular video makers. At first glance it would seem that homeomorphic, or ostensibly similar things in the form of mutual subscriptions, are exchanged.

Reciprocities may also be "heteromorphic" in that dissimilar things are exchanged.[24] For example, when I returned from the SouthTube meet-up, I subscribed to the channels of many of the attendees whom I met. The site enables people with YouTube accounts to comment publicly on a video maker's channel page under a Discussion tab. These comments are visible to all viewers, with or without accounts. Upon returning from SouthTube and subscribing to numerous attendees' channels, I noticed several comments posted to my channel's Discussion page. Out of sixty comments posted, fifteen thanked me for subscribing, which represents 25 percent of the comments. People demonstrated public gratitude for the favor. Examples included "Thanks so much for the subscription," "Thanks for subscribing!," and "Thanks for the subby!" These are examples of repeated, patterned heteromorphic forms of reciprocity in that they return my favor of a *subscription* to their channel with a *comment of thanks* on mine. Similar expressions of gratitude for subscriptions repeatedly appear on other video makers' Discussion pages, and they in turn may offer reciprocal promises for the regard. For example, one YouTuber called The Turner Based Gamer received numerous thanks for his subscriptions on his channel's Discussion page. One creator stated: "Many thanks for the subscription. I'll try my best to keep things interesting for you :)." This comment potentially launches a new cycle of reciprocity through the video maker's promises to deliver interesting content in response to receiving The Turner Based Gamer's subscription.

Video reciprocity on YouTube exhibited temporal dimensions. YouTubers displayed *temporal sensitivities* to acts of viewership. Temporal sensitivities are defined as acknowledgments of the timing of video events and their socio-temporal impacts. Temporal sensitivities include noting how long a viewer watches a video, whether viewers watch regularly over time, and whether reciprocal responses are posted quickly.[25] Creators appreciated it when someone watched an entire video, thus giving of their time and exhibiting sincere appreciation for the work. A well-known trick was to watch the first part of a video and comment so that it would seem as though the viewer took the time to watch the video. Viewers could save time and appear to be social. YouTubers might evaluate comments in terms of whether they demonstrated knowledge of something occurring *late* in the video, which suggested that a viewer actually watched the entire work.

A video maker and author named Kevin Nalty (whose YouTube channel name is nalts) addresses temporal sensitivities in a comedic video called *YouTube Etiquette*, which he posted on July 12, 2007. An early adopter of the site, nalts had been participating for a year and half when he posted this video. Nalts was a white man in his late thirties who created humorous videos and vlogs. His oeuvre aimed to garner mass appeal. He often created video pranks such as nose-picking in public or having a relative pretend to pass gas in a library. He also posted funny vlogs with his wife and family. His prank videos were quite popular, each often amassing millions of views. As of June 2018, he had 236,739 subscribers, which indexes a mass audience following. A professional marketer, Nalty also wrote a book called *Beyond Viral: How to Attract Customers, Promote Your Brand, and Make Money with Online Video* (2010). Nalts worked the site in multiple ways for revenue. Providing advice at a conference in 2012, he emphasized that money from advertisements was usually modest. More profit could be gained from product sponsorships, such as when a YouTuber is paid to make a video about a product.[26] Nalts also worked the merchandise angle (colloquially called "merch") by selling T-shirts, hats, mugs, magnets, mouse pads, stuffed animals, and clocks on CafePress, an online retailer founded in 1999.

In my observation, nalts was a friendly and personable character who appeared to enjoy participating in the social side of YouTube at meet-ups. Interviewees reported attending private gatherings at his house. One family told me they intended to surprise him by arriving at his house in nalts merch such as T-shirts. He exhibited keen understanding of the informal social rules of participation as well as the business side.

In his comedic video *YouTube Etiquette*, nalts states that it is socially important to watch people's videos, which presents a problem because they can be "insufferable"—especially when they are "8-minute vlogs." He proposes a viewing strategy that he dubs "the nalts ¾ rule." He says that he plays a video in its entirety but he'll "walk away from the desk so that [he] doesn't have to endure it." When he returns he skips to about the three-fourths mark of the video's time index. He comments on something in that section, thus "leaving the impression that [he'd] watched the whole video." He also advises viewers to scan the video maker's collection and find something mentioned across videos, such as a beloved pet. He suggests making a comment about it. The comment will give the impression, he assures viewers, that one is a "regular watcher" and has attended to the creator's work *over time.*

His video humorously and parodically emphasizes the idea that truly engaged YouTube participation meant giving of one's time to watch an entire video as a way of fostering sociality between the viewer and the creator. The video reveals how attentional and temporal sensitivities are important for boosting sociality. On YouTube, attempts to create social encounters by providing sincere gifts of time, attention, and critique were often met with an urge to reciprocate. Insincere attempts at reciprocity were challenged, rejected, or ridiculed.

Many early anthropological studies of reciprocity focused on small-scale communities in which the market works differently than it does in large-scale capitalistic societies. Studying perceptions of reciprocity in contemporary video-sharing cultures thus assists the anthropological project of analyzing reciprocity's role in digitally mediated sociality. Rather than assuming that reciprocity inevitably promotes connection, it is treated here as a phenomenon to be investigated and explained.[27] This chapter analyzes the degree to which video reciprocity—and its withholding—were perceived as necessary for promoting interactive participation, preserving video quality, and creating a social atmosphere on the site.

VIDEO RECIPROCITIES ON YOUTUBE

Video reciprocities exhibited several dimensions, including responding to comments on videos, reciprocal watching of videos, and willingness to share video footage in communal ways. When a video was posted among YouTubers, an interactive chain was often launched in which viewers' comments appeared in reaction to a video and then video makers responded to prior text comments with comments of their own. Each interaction exhibited its own dynamic of reciprocity and provided insight into video-sharing cultures.

In popular accounts and scholarly works, anxiety exits that contemporary social media environments solely breed narcissism and feelings of entitlement to the point where "reciprocity gets diminished and life gets a little harder and more isolated for everyone."[28] In this model only positive forms of reciprocity are acknowledged. The claim is that many people in the United States are losing warm, interconnected feelings. The fear is that "reciprocity is the glue that binds society together, and entitlement dissolves that glue."[29]

Despite widespread anxiety that sincere reciprocity is not possible in a commercialized, digital milieu, the data revealed that numerous forms of reciprocity existed between socially active YouTubers. In addition, although the popular imagination defines reciprocity in a singular way, in fact, the anthropological record identifies several types of reciprocity. These included balanced forms in which assessments are made to return relatively similar types of attention and regard. Also apparent were generalized forms in which artifacts such as video footage were shared without an immediate expectation of a return favor.

Reciprocity is a broad term, with nuances that are often elided in populist accounts. Contra the notion that reciprocities are only warm and interpersonally enriching, the anthropological record has long analyzed reciprocities that instrumentally attempt to achieve a return on a reciprocal investment. Anthropologists have additionally observed negative reciprocities that attempt to gain something for nothing. The present data showed that YouTubers accepted certain forms of instrumental reciprocities, which could include sincere sociality. However, most interviewees detected and staunchly rejected self-centered, negative, and harmful forms of reciprocity that threatened the creative and social atmosphere of YouTube. The study argues that reciprocity exists in contemporary digital environments. However, per the anthropological record, maintaining positive reciprocity required repeated, ongoing negotiations to foster meaningful, interpersonal connections through media.

Comment Reciprocity

Comment reciprocity refers to feeling motivated to respond to text comments posted on videos, thus returning the favor of regard that commenters bestowed on a video maker. Many interviewees felt a strong urge to at least attend to the comments posted to their videos, especially if they were interesting, personally appealing, or emotional. Reciprocities and general viewership on YouTube often exhibited patterned temporality. In interviews with me and in their own videos, YouTubers said that most videos are watched within two days. Thus, their *pace of receptive vitality* is reasonably brief. Similarly, on AnthroVlog most text comments posted to my videos typically arrived within a few days. As of 2010, 50 percent of most videos' views are reportedly accumulated six days after a video is posted.[30] Video makers interested in engagement tended to respond quickly to text comments that appeared on their videos, and they displayed temporal sensitivity by apologizing if they took too long to reciprocate.

Comments have particular tempi. It is challenging to articulate what it feels like to receive emotional and responsive commentary in nearly real time after posting a video. When comments appeared just after I posted a video, I felt an emotional impact that the flatness of text cannot convey—even when a comment had a time stamp noting that it was posted only a day ago. It is not just that the comments appeared, but that they appeared *quickly*, indexing an attentive audience that exhibits active enthusiasm for one's work.

An encounter in which a debt is repaid in a direct and relatively timely way has been referred to in the anthropological literature as "balanced reciprocity."[31] An adequate repayment follows a gift—in this case, of attention—within a socially acceptable time window. Timing is a key factor. To receive a reciprocal comment a year later may not have the same impact; indeed it might not be noticed.

Even interviewees who insisted that reciprocity was not obligatory nevertheless responded to numerous comments on their videos, especially the emotional ones. At times video makers responded to and discussed the content of a comment. In other cases video makers responded to a text comment with simple but heartfelt acknowledgments, such as "Thanks so much for watching," "I really appreciate it," or simply "Thank you." The participatory and interactive platform of YouTube facilitated resolution of attentional debt by allowing people to acknowledge a comment or offer thanks.

In a revealing case study, I interviewed a YouTuber named bnessel1973 at a meet-up in Toronto in 2008. Bnessel1973 is his YouTube channel name; he refers to himself as Brian in his videos. At the time of the interview he had been on YouTube for nearly two years. Bnessel1973 was a white man and father in his mid-thirties who posted vlogs about family moments and comedic skits involving humorous characters he created. He was working on a film script and was open to professionalizing his media work. In one genre of his videos, he cuts back and forth between comedic personae he portrays, thus engaging his characters in humorous dialogues. His videos typically see 1,000 to 2,000 views each. As of June 2018, he had 2,445 subscribers. By 2018 his interests had changed, and he referenced becoming a nutritionist and body-builder.

YouTube creators frequently recalled how their participation began and evolved. Brian's version of this genre was called *My YouTube Story*. It was posted on August 25,

SYNCING UP THROUGH RECIPROCITY

2007, and as of May 2015 it had received more than 71,000 views and 471 comments. In the video Brian recalls how his autobiographical trajectory on YouTube began with weight loss videos and quickly proceeded to include footage of his children. He also recounts the disturbing news that he lost his baby boy to SIDS (sudden infant death syndrome). He explains how he used YouTube in comedic ways to reconnect with his former self. His humorous videos helped him find joy again in life, even though he missed his son "every single day." Bnessel1973 received many supportive comments that exuded emotio-temporal dynamics. Comments have rhythms, and the waves of energy that a video creator might feel in reading them are often difficult to appreciate when viewing them weeks later as static text.

Commenters to the video included people with whom Brian socialized at gatherings and privately. Commenters included several of the people profiled in this book, such as Jane (a researcher-assigned pseudonym), Jill Hanner (her official name and YouTube name), and musoSF, DaleATL2, K8oBlog, WpgPeanut, and nbwulf (all YouTube names). Comments sometimes arrived from those who connected with the video from having experienced a similar loss, such as Jane, as well as from those who had not encountered such tragedy but wished to extend their support. Under the right circumstances, asynchronously posted comments could feel "live," especially in the immediate moments after a video was posted. The liveness of comments could also prompt an urge to return the support one receives through them.

Many of the commenters reached out to Brian with supportive messages. The following exchanges alternatively illustrate content-based and emotional reciprocities. In the first example a commenter called LindaSVorhies identifies herself as a person who has also lost a child. The content of her post expresses encouragement to Brian to "have courage" even after such a tragedy:

> LindaSVorhies: Wow! I just clicked on this video because of the photo of the beautiful baby—never thinking it would be this lovely and heartbreaking and hopeful piece. I talked today with a friend who is another one of us—those who have lost a child. We worried about how our husbands have coped with the loss and the grief. How wonderful that you found this creative way to heal yourself and to help others, too. Have courage—life does go on and Life really is Good!

> bnessel1973: I appreciate you sharing this with me. I've found there is comfort in hearing other people's stories about their journey. It lets you know you're not alone, and that there is still life after loss. Thank you so much.

As in therapeutic environments, Brian's decision to open up prompted viewers to reciprocate vulnerability and share their sense of loss. In his reply to LindaSVorhies, Brian reciprocates her emotional outreach by expressing appreciation that she shared her experiences with him. By showing vulnerability, he exhibited "mutuality"[32] with others who endured similar experiences. He discusses the benefit of hearing similar stories from others who have suffered to avoid feeling "alone" and to experience a sense of "life" after a significant loss. Bnessel1973 found comfort in reciprocally hearing other people's experiences of loss and extended his own gratitude for kindness expressed through comments.

This example exhibits reciprocity in terms of comment content and the importance of receiving and providing support to others who have endured loss. In contrast, the next two examples illustrate how reciprocity plays out not in terms of content or the events that are discussed but rather in feelings for the other person. For example, WpgPeanut thanks Brian for his contribution to her corner of YouTube, and, in turn, Brian tells WpgPeanut how he feels about her.

> WpgPeanut: I could have not said it better myself . . . you are a wonderful person that has made me cry and laugh on many [occasions] and I thank you for being a part of my youtube.
>
> bnessel1973: And I hope you know I think the world of you. Truly.

This exchange exhibits what economic anthropologist Marshall Sahlins called "balanced reciprocity," which aims to reciprocate with the "customary equivalent of the thing received and without delay."[33] Ideally, reciprocal comments are posted relatively quickly and exhibit roughly equivalent qualities, such as in how bnessel1973 and WpgPeanut display mutual admiration. In the following example Brian's sister also posts a comment that Brian returns, but in a way that does not strive to achieve content balance or parity as much as it reveals his general regard for his sister.

> SuziNess1968: Brian, I am so proud of you. I've watched you, video by video, since the very first day you started your YouTube adventure. [Your nephew] signs on three times a day just to see if Uncle Brian is on "cause he might be posting something!"— Today, watching this, shows EVERYBODY what I already knew: You are amazing! And I know I'm your sister, but I think I speak for MANY when I say WE LOVE YOU—and Thank YOU—for just being you.
>
> bnessel1973: I was going to make a long comment, but you know how much I love you and how much we appreciate everything you've done for us. I couldn't have made it without you.

This exchange illustrates what Sahlins called "generalized reciprocity," which does not necessarily strive for balance but simply provides regard in a way that is not "stipulated by time, quantity, or quality."[34] In this case Brian notes that he intended to make a lengthy comment, perhaps because his sister's comment was several lines long. Ultimately he feels that it is unnecessary because his sister is aware of how much he appreciates her love for and support of him and his family. It is apparently less important for Brian to match length of content than it is to simply show his gratitude through a posted message directed lovingly to her.

Reciprocity through commentary might orient to content, such as in the comments that share in the pain of loss, as well as to interpersonal regard. They also suggest a patterned tendency among socially motivated YouTube participants to reciprocate regard. Repeated, ritualized reciprocity bolsters these creators' values of making social connections through video. Bnessel1973's video on his YouTube journey received 471 comments. Notably, he posted over 100 comments that responded to people who reached out to him. This means that he responded directly to over 20 percent of the commentary he received. This is a high return rate on commentary and shows a tendency to acknowledge those who engaged in meaningful commentary on his video. The data demonstrate that despite fears that we are losing reciprocity, in fact for socially motivated YouTube participants, interactional reciprocity is consistent and warmly personal.

Participatory temporal sensitivities were well illustrated by NorCalCorsello (his YouTube channel name), a man whom I interviewed at a meet-up in San Francisco in 2008. He had been on the site for over a year. Generally receiving a few hundred to sometimes a thousand views for each of his videos, NorCalCorsello was a white man in his mid-thirties who enjoyed vlogging on topics such as resuming skateboarding after a long hiatus. He also vlogged on current issues of the day, including high-speed train proposals, globalization, and border patrol. As of June 2018, he had 619 subscribers. Responding to whether he would comment back when someone commented on one of his videos, NorCalCorsello stated:

> I do just because I like the interaction and I feel if someone's taken the time to look at what I've done and actually put in a comment, then I'm gonna see who they are and what it is they have to say as well. So I don't know if it's a "have to" as [it is] just because if they took the time, I want to take the time.

Note that NorCalCorsello bases his calculus around time. If someone "took the time" to comment, he felt motivated to reciprocate by donating his time. He proceeded to learn more about them and check out their work. NorCalCorsello articulates Peralta and Brown's argument that reciprocity serves as an opening volley in a potentially ongoing encounter. Reciprocity functioned to initiate a dialogue.

Interaction was highly valued across interviewees; yet they were often inclined to respond more interactively if a comment was interesting or inspiring. Reciprocity was selectively bestowed according to merit. Interviewees described themselves as "picky" with regard to the extent they would comment back. If interviewees sensed that a video maker simply wished to promote a channel and gain viewers without displaying a genuine interest in interacting, then they were disinclined to comment back.

Writing from the perspective of new media studies, Geert Lovink expresses skepticism about the value of comments. He argues that commenting constitutes "a necessary yet wasted human compulsion" and that their sheer volume means that we do not care about comment content.[35] Creators are assumed to be more concerned about the impact of commenting in terms of their commercial advantages. Voluminous comments index popularity and the potential for monetization of videos through advertisements. However, precisely because commenting is time-consuming, people who took the time to comment interpersonally tended to invite sociality. Commenting was not wasted on the people who valued it. Yet mutual regard was not automatic; comment systems were used to test and sometimes establish further channels of sociality through forms of reciprocal attention.

Visual Reciprocity

Pundits often see reciprocity in warm and mutual terms. Yet, commensurate with the anthropological record, the present data revealed reciprocities that were based on calculations of potential returns and benefits. One form of reciprocity involved mutual viewing of videos, sometimes accompanied by pledges of mutual subscriptions, a practice known as "sub for sub." By activating the structural feature of subscriptions, it was possible to visually display a mutual commitment to viewership.[36]

On the surface, it would seem that mutual obligations to subscribe did not exist. In interviews most respondents said they felt no obligation to subscribe to the channel of someone who had subscribed to theirs. This viewpoint resembles patterns on Twitter, in which there is generally no presumed obligation to engage in mutual following. Media scholars Marwick and boyd state that on Twitter, "There is no technical requirement of reciprocity, and often, no social expectation of such."[37] Since subscribing to someone's channel on YouTube meant being alerted to new videos, interviewees did not want to be alerted about new videos that were of poor quality or exhibited content that they were not interested in watching. The quality of the content influenced individual assessments to reciprocate.

Nevertheless, some YouTubers attempted to use "sub for sub" as a strategy to gain more views. Invoking sub for sub, a creator might subscribe to another video maker's channel with the understanding that the person receiving the subscription would feel reciprocally obligated to subscribe back. The hope was that mutual subscriptions would encourage both video makers to watch each other's content, provide channel visibility through increased subscriptions, and drive up viewership for each other's work—potentially boosting monetization opportunities.

Although most interviewees and video makers in the study eschewed this practice, a few creators saw this as a clever strategy for mutual promotion of each other's work. For instance, one interviewee, a white woman, homemaker, and mother in her early thirties named spricket24 (her YouTube channel name) supported the practice. Receiving tens of thousands of views on each of her videos, she said she would readily contemplate a professional media career. She vlogged in humorous ways about family life and meet-ups as well as topics such as voting, sex in the dark, how she quit her job, and an iPad Christmas debacle. She opened the spricket24 account in March 2008, three months before I interviewed her in Minneapolis. As of June 2018, she had amassed 44,824 subscribers.

Spricket24 took pride in "pioneering" the sub for sub practice, as she believed it was a good way of building a following. However, she admitted that the social aspect became more difficult as her audience grew. During her interview I asked her about the practice of sub for sub. Spricket24 replied:

> I would like to say that I pioneered that. I have a video from when I first started
> where I was, like, if you sub to me, I'm gonna sub to you. But after I reached 3,000,
> I couldn't keep up! So I think it's cool that people are still doing sub for sub. And
> I think that as long as you post videos that you are proud to post and you're happy
> about them, and it's not, like, filled with hate speech or it doesn't hurt anybody else,
> then sub for sub is great.

Although she felt it was a viable strategy, she also believed that videos should have merit, insofar as one is "happy" with them as a creator and they are not "hurting" others. Contrary to fears of self-centeredness overtaking opportunities for sociality in a mediated community, the data show that even some sub for sub supporters had creative and participatory limits and refused to reciprocate if the videos were of low quality or hurtful. Videos needed to exhibit a baseline of attention-worthy content to merit visual reciprocity.

One video I encountered from outside the study promoted the strategy. A video maker named Ontus (his YouTube channel name) was a white man who posted a video entitled *sub4sub?* on YouTube on March 28, 2008. He characterizes the practice as "brilliant" and "awesome" because, if executed widely, it could provide a "launch pad" of subscribers and facilitate meeting new people. He saw his subscription count rise from 73 to over 200 by deploying this practice. However, even within an assessment that privileged viewing metrics and increasing followers, Ontus also references the benefit of new social encounters as important.

Ontus implicitly supports what scholars label "instrumental" forms of reciprocity, in which the gift giver seeks to gain something by manipulating interpersonal relations in a way that does not preclude sociality.[38] Such "instrumental" gifts become a "quasi-commodity" because each party seeks to engage in the transaction for personal gain.[39] Anthropologist and Chinese studies scholar Yunxiang Yan argues that instrumental gifts, which aim to achieve "utilitarian ends," can be distinguished from expressive gifts, which are "ends in and of themselves" and thus cement long-term relationships.[40] Although reciprocity is often characterized as warm and interpersonal compared to cold and impersonal capitalist exchange, sociologist Marcel Mauss observed that reciprocity frequently cements economic as well as political relationships in societies based on reciprocal exchange.[41]

YouTubers tolerated simultaneous instrumentality and sociality as long as the social interaction seemed sincere and not feigned solely to obtain views. According to Yan, instrumental giving may exist in a "grey area" between a commodified transaction and a gift meant to propagate social relations. Fueling this tension was the fact that the mechanisms that video makers and viewers used to express interpersonal interest were also used for commercial purposes within YouTube's attention economy. Comments, likes, and subscriptions could all be used for inviting sociality, for assessing monetization potential, or for multiple purposes.

The site's design features, in combination with varied user goals, create what researchers have called "context collapse." Communication and media studies scholar Alice Marwick and technology and social media researcher danah boyd argue that context collapse occurs when social media technologies "collapse multiple audiences into single contexts."[42] Similarly, anthropologist Michael Wesch describes this dynamic as "an infinite number of contexts collapsing upon one another into that single moment of recording."[43] Most interviewees sought reciprocities that yielded feelings of "mutuality,"[44] or similar ways of using YouTube for social interaction. When context collapse complicated these preferences, conflict ensued. Peralta and Brown's argument about reciprocity revolves around how "relations of reciprocal recognition resist institutionalisation."[45] Yet it becomes complicated to resist institutional control amid deliberately orchestrated context collapse. The YouTube engine encouraged monetization through social mechanisms.

YouTubers had to determine motivations when the same features could be used for multiple purposes. According to interviewees, it is possible to assess the sincerity level of those who promote their work, based on the quality of comments and overall interactions over time. Creators who invoked reciprocity exclusively for their own gain—such as to increase view counts on their videos while only pretending to care about the YouTube community—would be read as insincere. For instance, generic text messages posted on videos such as "Have a nice day!"—accompanied by the winking emoticon ;-)—could cause skepticism. These comments do not reveal knowledge or appreciation of specific video content. In comparison, heartfelt interactions typically included interpersonally meaningful details about one's videos or recollections of mutual experiences at meet-ups. Interactions were interpreted as sincere as long as they were perceived as interested in getting to know creators through their video content.

Generic comments would be especially suspect when left in the same form across many videos. Viewers might detect instances in which basic messages were probably posted by a representative of a famous YouTuber or even an automated software program known as a "bot." A celebrity YouTuber officially known as Lisa Donovan (her YouTube Channel name is LisaNova) reportedly deployed a bot to leave automated comments on each of her subscriber's profile pages during a two-week period.[46] According to viral video expert Kevin Nalty, the action faced deep backlash in the YouTube community, whose members classified the comments as spam.[47] He recalled that she even made a public apology for the spam bot.

Invoking a common (and frequently flawed) argument about the ease of identity manipulation in online milieus, researchers on narcissism fault the cover of the internet and social media as enabling viewer manipulation. Online participants strategically promote only their best selves to gain attention. Yet, paradoxically, narcissism scholars also report that viewers can easily detect problematic overpromotion using clues such as (1) content of postings (e.g., salacious nudity, achievement-oriented announcements, excessive partying); (2) orders of magnitude of friends they have; and (3) types of email names they use.[48] Clearly narcissists could not hide behind a facade of being their "best" selves because they were easily identified as narcissists! These identifications suggest that attempts at online identity posing, aggressive self-promotion, and negative interaction behaviors have limits and become difficult when interaction is anticipated to continue over time.[49] Members of social groups can identify obvious violations of local media-sharing norms. Yet viewer agency is often ignored in laments about narcissism.

Viewers detected reciprocity manipulations, and the attention spammer could receive public social sanctions. Indeed, the LisaNova spam debacle lasted merely two weeks and reportedly ended with a public apology. Scholars who decry the loss of reciprocity often focus on the alleged perpetrators rather than acknowledging the agency of online participants who can detect and actively resist blatant stunts. While attempted manipulations will likely continue, community members will correspondingly deal with them on a collective level as they deem necessary.

Eschewing Visual Reciprocity

Aside from the exceptions discussed in the previous section, most interviewees saw sub for sub as self-promotional. The practice was perceived as insincere because requestors seemed to be engaging in a social exchange but were actually sweetening their viewing metrics at the expense of sociality. This was especially true of a more devious form of the sub for sub practice in which the requestor unsubscribed after locking in a reciprocal subscription. This was done to inflate their *comparative* subscription counts. By immediately unsubscribing, only the requestor gains an additional subscriber from the deal. A video maker may not notice what has happened and may continue subscribing to the sub for sub requestor. This is a competitive practice that ultimately helps one video maker at the expense of another.

The devious form of sub for sub requests that benefited only the requester may be anthropologically categorized as "negative reciprocity." Sahlins defined negative reciprocity as an "attempt to get something for nothing with impunity."[50] Scholars and pundits who demand increased reciprocity need to consider the anthropological insight that negative and highly competitive forms of reciprocity also exist. These forms are understandably concerning to those who track complications to achieving sociality on social media. Negative reciprocities were generally not tolerated among YouTubers seeking to maintain sociality.

Numerous videos on YouTube decry even mutual forms of sub for sub in which both parties adhere to the deal. Even successful professionals who monetize their content are suspicious of the practice. For example, Roberto Blake (his YouTube channel name and official name) criticizes the practice in a video called *Why YouTube Sub4Sub Is Bad*, which he posted on March 20, 2015. An experienced YouTuber, he joined the site about six years prior to posting this video. Blake is a professional media maker and graphic designer in his early thirties who is sponsored, which means he promotes products within the content of his videos. He earns money from advertisements on his videos, which focus on educating and motivating creative professionals. Characterizing himself as a "black nerd," his content is targeted at widespread YouTube audiences through topics such as providing tips on growing a channel quickly, vlogging on creative thoughts, net neutrality, product reviews, personal branding, graphic design, and making money through sponsorships. He also posts an occasional vlog about personal issues, such as needing to take a YouTube break and dealing with haters. Blake's videos typically receive several thousand views each. As of June 2018, he had amassed 315,116 subscribers.

In his video on sub for sub, he argues that subscriptions do not guarantee viewers and thus do not grow one's audience. He elects to refrain from ranting, given that he believes that people using sub for sub are typically younger, gaming-oriented, or inexperienced with the online entertainment space. Part of the problem, Blake argues, is that the YouTube service examines a variety of metrics in addition to subscriptions, such as watch time over a specific time interval, user engagement (such as commenting), and view-to-subscriber ratios. If the ratios are off, high subscriber numbers will not guarantee monetization. For example, if an account has many subscribers but only a few views for each video, then the videos will be ranked lower and perceived as less relevant in terms of content.

Blake also offers philosophical reasons for eschewing sub for sub. Subscriptions add value to viewers because they will be alerted to personally interesting content. But a viewer who is only engaging in a "quid pro quo" behavior is not really interested in the content and will not likely engage with the creator over time. Ultimately, he argues that sub for sub is a type of bribe and a meaningless quick fix. He warns viewers that those who "hijack" his comments with these requests are banned, and he deletes sub for sub requests. Based on his success, he persuasively argues that creators should earn subscriptions by providing value to viewers and garnering relationships rather than "begging" for attention.

Mutual attentional agreements like sub for sub appear on other social media and are reportedly received with similar suspicion.[51] In a study of social media sites by boyd, interviewees noted that people sometimes posted comments on other people's media for self gain. They wished to attract attention to their own work.[52] On Instagram the practice occurs through hashtag manipulation. Creators use hashtags (the octothorpe or pound sign symbol #) to post key words to their images so that viewers may locate content of interest to them, as in #smile or #food. Invoking the sub for sub principle using Instagram terminology, people affix hashtags such as #likeforlike, #like4like, or #follow4follow to their photographs so that others interested in this practice will "like" their images. The expectation is that their photographs will be "liked" or that their account will be mutually "followed" back. "Likes" constitute a key metric that Instagram tracks to gauge popularity and engagement. On Instagram the practice is often used for self-promotion without necessarily attending to media content.[53] People who engage in this practice are labeled "like hunters" who use these hashtags to gain views in order to achieve micro-celebrity status.[54] The practice is not widely accepted. Indeed, writing from a graphic design perspective, Eric Andren observes that such hashtags are commonly blacklisted on the site.[55]

Sub for sub requests often upset socially motivated YouTubers, as explained by an interviewee named musoSF (his YouTube channel name), whom I interviewed at a gathering in Minneapolis in 2008. He had been participating on the site for about two years. MusoSF was a white man from San Francisco (whom I estimated to be in his thirties to early forties). In his videos he sings songs and vlogs about contemporary topics such as gay marriage, socially oriented material, and reflections on YouTube meet-ups. His videos typically receive a few hundred views each, with a few in the thousands. He had 1,722 subscribers as of June 2018. Notably, he objected to being reduced to subscriber numbers in terms of how people viewed him and his work. In response to a question about his views on sub for sub, musoSF stated:

In my case, that—that just pisses me off because I . . . that's not what it's about for me. It's not about, let's try to [have that], that number, that—that statistic of, I've got the most subscribers or I've got more subscribers than you. That actually conflicts with the whole friendship aspect. It's like, it's not a competition, it's making friends, and some of my friends have a lot more subscribers than I have and they probably always will. And some of my friends have fewer than I have and some of them have changed and we've swapped places. And so, yeah, so that annoys me 'cause that's not why I'm there, it's not why my friends are there, and so I just either ignore those things or delete 'em. They bug me.

MusoSF expressed frustration over video creators' attempts at using sub for sub to commoditize their work at the expense of the interpersonal, friendship aspects of YouTube.

Bids for reciprocal viewership could also disrupt people's preferred temporal rhythms of interaction and discovery of new content. Attending to interactional rhythms often reveals important clues about cultural dynamics and how and when videos were appropriately identified as worth watching. The timing and pace of encountering other video makers was viewed as important to WpgPeanut (her YouTube channel name), whom I interviewed at the gathering in Minneapolis in 2008. WpgPeanut was a white woman with children who was very active in the social aspect of YouTube. She participated both online and offline with several YouTubers whom I interviewed for the study. Although she later deleted her account, she rejoined YouTube in 2017.

On her reopened channel, she posts videos apparently made several years ago (such as birthday greetings to a friend from YouTube) as well as new videos of her children, comedic videos of her singing to friends, and vlogs on subjects such as a computer virus. Videos on her new account typically receive a few dozen views. As of July 2018, she had one subscriber, most likely because she had deleted her account. In her interview she said she typically deleted sub for sub requests because she wished to discover videos of interest in her own time rather than be told what to watch instantaneously. WpgPeanut stated:

> I'm gonna watch what I'm gonna watch. Not because you're going to tell me to watch. If I find you later down the road and I like you, then I'll subscribe then.

WpgPeanut's remarks imply a preference for a particular "internal"[56] rhythm for encountering videos spontaneously and deciding whether to make connections with other video makers. By proposing an immediate interactional rhythm, sub for sub requesters were arguably trying to force a pace "external"[57] to WpgPeanut's organic viewing practices. Attempts to rush this external rhythm of discovering videos and making social connections to someone with a different internal rhythm create what Lefebvre refers to as "arrhythmia" or a pathological rhythm that reflects underlying problems.[58] Such arrhythmias represented an interpersonal rhythmic rupture and were met with a withholding of WpgPeanut's regard.

Contrary to scholars and pundits who maintain that reciprocity is a participatory "law," the present data jibe with revisions in the anthropological record in which withholding reciprocity is at times just as important as is bestowing it to promote an interactive atmosphere. Maintaining social connections within the creative space of YouTube required explicit denial of even mutual, reciprocal sub for sub requests from makers of poor-quality videos. Interviewees generally took both their participation and creative reputation seriously and did not wish to promote bad videos. In contrast to scholars who feel that reciprocity is the key to maintaining sociality, the data show that strategic withholdings were often crucial for maintaining creativity and sociality on the site.[59]

Inalienable Forms of Exchange

In separate studies anthropologists Annette Weiner and Maurice Godelier focused on different communities, but both concluded that what is withheld from circulation is often just as crucial to societal maintenance as that which is shared.[60] For example, Godelier contends that withholding symbolic items such as crown jewels and government constitutions from everyday circulation is important for sustaining group identification.[61] Weiner argues that some objects have an "inalienable" quality, which means that they "are imbued with the intrinsic and ineffable identities of their owners" and are thus "not easy to give away."[62]

Although these scholars were referring to objects, similar observations may be made about human attention and the technical factors that index it. In digital realms technical features such as subscriptions and comments may exhibit inalienable qualities. Opinions or comments about a video are issued from particular individuals and are not necessarily interchangeable, even if the comments are similar or even identical in content. Praise from a close relative who calls one's work a "terrific video" is not necessarily interchangeable with the same feedback from a stranger who is a successful professional video maker. For example, I was delighted when I received a compliment from popular YouTuber nickynik (his YouTube channel name) on my featured video on community.

Nickynik was a white man in his early forties whom I had interviewed in New York City in 2007 after he had been participating on the site for nearly a year. He garnered a following on YouTube through content targeted at mass audiences such as featuring pranks, stunts, a video journal on a movie he wished to make, and vlogs with YouTube celebrities. Each of his videos saw tens of thousands of views. As of June 2018, he had 15,475 subscribers. He posted a compliment to the Discussion page of my AnthroVlog channel, calling my video "excellent." He noted that it was a "big deal" to get a video featured on the front page of YouTube and that my work was deservedly being recognized. In a Lefebvrian vein, he attended to the timing of his compliment by apologizing for "not seeing it sooner." He encouraged me to "keep up the great work" in the future. Knowing that a YouTube celebrity had recognized my work was admittedly gratifying. His comment held a different meaning for me than one from a family member who might feel obligated to provide support by posting an encouraging comment.

Pelaprat and Brown make a similar observation in their study of reciprocity in contemporary digital media environments. They state that the objects being exchanged "stand in for the person giving or reciprocating. Hence they cannot be the same, for they have to be tied to the identity of the person in the exchange."[63] In addition, the value of what is exchanged is inherently "ambiguous." This ambiguity is key, they argue, because it prevents an accurate accounting of giving and receiving, which invites perpetuating cycles of interactional exchange.

The present study contributes to the anthropological record by demonstrating that the classical categorization of so-called "homeomorphic" gifts—or exchange of similar things—are actually only ever "heteromorphic" in the digital environment of YouTube. At first it might seem that sub for sub represents a homeomorphic type of reciprocity since the practice involves exchanging the same technologically conceptual thing—video subscriptions. Yet each subscription originates from an individual, which makes them inherently different. For example, when a person using the practice purely for monetization makes a request to someone who sees it as a gateway to sociality, their goals are not in sync. Some people will follow up and watch and support the creators to whose channels they subscribe; others subscribe in name only and do not watch any videos. Some creators are knowledgeable about technical aspects of video making while others are not. Their support through subscriptions exhibits different meanings and ramifications.

What constituted the interpersonal value of a subscription differed across individuals. Although most interviewees said they could spot and avoid insincere requests, bids for attention through comments and subscriptions might prompt an exploration of that video maker's videos or channel page. For example, in response to a question about subscribing to the channel of someone who had subscribed to his, NorCalCorsello noted that although he did not always automatically return a subscription, he "usually" subscribed back. His assessment was ritualistically repeated across offers in a way that highlighted YouTube participants' belief in encouraging encounters and connections. He stated that a subscription to his videos would at least prompt him to examine his new subscriber's YouTube channel. If that person created "unoriginal work" or the channel was merely a list of the subscriber's favorite videos, he would be disinclined to subscribe back. To subscribe back to such a channel would mean getting announcements about bad videos or no announcements at all if the person was not making original videos, thus rendering a "subscription" pointless.

Subscriptions differed in value according to the requestor's participation. The subscription might prompt an initial favor of attention, but ultimately videos had to exhibit content that merited attention over time. What qualified as earning attention might differ across media makers. It might relate to mutual interests or willingness to exchange personal self-expressions through grassroots video blogging. Whatever the calculus, a subscription's value depended on the requestor's participatory intentions.

The data demonstrated that subscriptions were never equivalent because they originated from different individuals, thus exhibiting inalienable qualities. When a creator received a request to subscribe, it was common to investigate the requestor's work. A central aspect of the calculus revolved around assessing the participation of the people motivating technologized features such as subscriptions, which ultimately varied in meaning according to the goals, output, and intentions of the individual video maker who made the request.

Patterned Reciprocity

Interviewees' comments suggested that a repeated pattern of attentional reciprocity existed on YouTube, even beyond the social group under study. A description of this pattern surfaced in an interviewee's description of so-called cheaters on the site. An interviewee named robtran (his YouTube channel name) was a white man in his early forties. He created film parodies and vlogged about current events and personal observations. He enjoyed practicing his filmmaking skills on YouTube. Receiving hundreds of views on each of his videos, he had 416 subscribers as of June 2018. He had been participating on the site for about a year and a half when I interviewed him in 2008 at a meet-up in San Francisco.

Robtran explained that "cheaters" used both bots and human-centric methods to gain attention. He became frustrated when people mindlessly subscribed to many creators. This strategy perversely worked because YouTubers often exhibited a willingness to return subscriptions as a "courtesy" to others. He characterized mass-subscribing to large numbers of people as a form of "cheating" because he believed that the practice artificially inflated viewing metrics and thus deserved redressing by YouTube staff. Robtran stated:

The unsophisticated way of [cheating], is to simply go through and spend X number of hours a week or a day going through and randomly subscribing to as many people as you possibly can every day. So you have thousands and thousands and thousands of subscriptions. Well, let's say you have 8,000 subscriptions; you're bound to have at least 1,500 or 2,000 people subscribe back to you because a lot of people do it as a courtesy. If you subscribe to them, they'll automatically subscribe back, just to be nice, you know. [What's] happening is YouTube is partnering these people. And they're ignoring the whole cheater issue.

Robtran identifies an underlying pattern of reciprocity that has been observed generally on social media.[64] Whether or not this behavior contextually constitutes "cheating" is arguably interpretive. Clearly, robtran's negative judgment of the practice echoed those of social YouTubers, and his assessment of YouTube "partnering" sub for subbers in the early years contrasts with Roberto Blake's observation years later that high subscriptions alone were insufficient to sustain monetization. In robtran's view, a significant number of YouTubers reciprocated a new subscription as a courtesy, even if they did not know their new subscriber. The strategy partly worked because a certain percentage of people automatically subscribed back, "just to be nice."

Critics concerned about video-fueled narcissism might argue that although returning such subscriptions may appear to emerge from "courtesy," people are actually in it for themselves. Social media features such as friending appear to be "inherently competitive."[65] However, if selfishness and competition were the only driving factors of subscribing to other people's channels, there would be no logical incentive to *subscribe back*. Receiving a new subscriber means that the other person has already agreed to be alerted when new videos are posted. If one has already secured ongoing attention, why would one need to return the favor?

A self-centered, competitive behavior—which was not practiced by interviewees— was to collect asymmetrical, unreturned subscriptions to demonstrate one's competitively higher popularity compared with that of other video makers. An analogy is seen in Twitter, in which people may "follow" another Twitter user and be alerted to their latest tweets. In the Twitter-verse, popular account holders may be "followed" by many Twitter users, but they may follow only a very few back.[66] It is a social media status symbol to be "followed" on Twitter or "subscribed to" on YouTube by many people without following or subscribing back. By locking in a new subscriber, attention of at least one kind is secured. If monetization or self-centered attention are key goals, it is arguably more advantageous to have many more subscribers than other people do. Thus, it would not be in one's instrumental interest to subscribe back.

FIGURE 4.1. YouTubers juggle together at a meet-up in San Francisco on February 23, 2008. Screenshot by Patricia G. Lange from *Hey Watch This! Sharing the Self through Media* (2013).

Of course, it is also possible that multiple desires are at work in a given encounter. People may wish to enact a courtesy and may hope that the mutual subscription will increase interest in their work. Reciprocity, while often idealized in scholarship and public discourses, may also emerge from a desire to ensure one's long-term interests through acts of mutual exchange. Video makers tried to gauge others' intentions in terms of mutual bids of regard. When an interaction was perceived as sincerely interested in sociality or exhibited creative merit, interlocutors intensified interaction.

Forms of attention such as comments and subscriptions did not always prompt unilateral reciprocity, but they represented invitational "encounters," to use Pelaprat and Brown's term. People whom I interviewed often sought ways to pull in new YouTube participants or lurkers. Contrary to the concerns expressed in narcissism discourses, interviewees said they might subscribe to others' channels as a subtle way of encouraging newcomers to upload videos with their own point of view.

Participatory invitations and acceptance exhibited a cyclical, interactional pattern. Like the jugglers at a meet-up in San Francisco (figure 4.1), video makers worked in tandem to produce and share videos and promote interaction on the site, effectively creating something greater than that which each creator alone could achieve.

The image of the jugglers serves as a metaphor for patterned forms of socially motivated video exchange. Sharing a video is like tossing a ball in the air to another person, who might catch it and toss another back. Or they might toss commentary back and forth. To stop tossing or providing attention is to interrupt YouTube's cycle of interactivity. Patterned forms of interactional reciprocity were thus an important mechanism for making the site compelling for sociality.

Sharing Footage

YouTubers interested in sociality defied pundits' fears of lack of reciprocity by sharing footage and making heartfelt video collaborations. Scholars define generalized forms of reciprocity as those that involve a bestowal of a gift or assistance motivated by a spirit of sharing rather than expecting something directly in compensation.[67] Immediate exchange is not expected, but it is implied that the attentional gift might be honored in some fashion at an indeterminate future date, such as children caring for aging parents. In generalized reciprocity within video sharing, receiving a return gift of attention rested "on a diffuse obligation to reciprocate when necessary to the donor and/or possible for the recipient."[68]

Video practices exhibiting generalized reciprocal sharing included contributing time or footage or both to create collaboration videos, or what YouTubers referred to as "collabs." It was not uncommon for people to request footage from fellow video makers to create collab videos in which individual recordings were compiled into one video message. Common collab themes included birthday greetings and charitable pleas.

In one video a video maker whose YouTube channel name was DaleATL2 thanked people who had compiled a set of birthday greetings into a video for him. Receiving hundreds and sometimes tens of thousands of views for each of his videos, he had 2,404 subscribers as of June 2018. DaleATL2 was a white man in his early forties with young children. He typically created comedic videos and vlogs of his family on adventures such as attending fairs and parades. He also created a music video promoting a SouthTube meet-up in Georgia.

One video—entitled *You People Are CRAZY (and GREAT)!!! Thank You So Much!*— was posted on May 21, 2008, two years after he had begun participating on the site. The video provides thanks and recognition for the people who contributed footage for the birthday video sent to him. In the text description of his video, DaleATL2 lists the contributors to his birthday collab and thanks them for "taking the time to edit this wonderful video together." He promotes the birthday video's contributors by displaying links to their YouTube channel names so that interested viewers may check out their videos. Included on the list are people profiled in this book, including bnessel1973 and GeneticBlend (their YouTube names).

DaleATL2 is genuinely moved by his friends' work, which he acknowledges as time-consuming. As the present temporal analysis argues, taking the time to do something difficult for someone else yields a visible, personal sacrifice. DaleATL2 recognizes particular individuals in his "thank you" video, which resembles an award speech. He praises specific contributions that helped make his birthday video special. The birthday video functioned as an attentional gift that DaleATL2 honored through his reciprocal video of gratitude. He states in his video:

I am blown away. You guys, all my friends, [were] so giving of their time just to put something together. I mean, birthday videos on YouTube are a dime a dozen, and everybody who knows everybody is doing birthday videos for everybody, and it takes so much time just to live your normal life, much less take some time out to [be] creative just for one other person, and for you guys to do that for me blows me away. I don't feel like I "delerve" [sic] it. Even though you say that I do. I did have a great "dane" [sic], it was a great dane back when it happened a month or so ago, however long ago my birthday was. Doesn't matter. Because today feels like my birthday. All over again.

Knowing the time and effort it takes to collect and edit footage into a video made the gift of attention that much more touching for DaleATL2. He acknowledged the contributions and friendships that motivated the gift. He noted that it takes time to live one's "normal life," much less to go to these lengths for one person. Even though his birthday passed weeks ago, he stated that the birthday video was a gift that kept on giving; the day he received the video felt like his birthday "all over again."

In addition to praising people's contributions in the text description and in his speech within the video, DaleATL2 makes an interesting visual editing choice of his own. As he thanks people, the lower right corner of the screen contains an inset box that incorporates images from the original birthday video (which I could not view because it was marked as private). The split-screen technique creates a visual tribute to the video that was created in his honor. Private footage from the original birthday video is incorporated into his public thank-you video, which shows the fluidity with which private material can easily become public. By incorporating this footage, attention is physically split between DaleATL2 and the images of the birthday video's creators. DaleATL2 edits the video so that he literally shares the screen with those whom he felt he owed a debt of thanks. His choice to showcase his birthday collaborators reads as a touching tribute to their thoughtfulness, time, and hard work.

Collabs were also created on YouTube to promote special causes or exchange civic messages. An example is the video entitled *Angelcheeks*, which was posted on February 27, 2008, by bnessel1973. Between its initial posting and July 2018, the *Angelcheeks* video received 83,416 views. The video begins with cute baby pictures of the video maker's son, whom the viewer quickly learns has passed away from SIDS. At a meet-up in Toronto in 2008, bnessel1973 told me that after his son died, his family had to deal not only with the emotional fallout from his passing but also with numerous unexpected expenses that fortunately, they were able to handle. However, they encountered other families who were not as financially prepared to deal with the counseling and funereal expenses emerging from a child's passing. They were moved by the plight of these families and established a charitable organization, the Angelcheeks Foundation, to assist families who have lost a child under two years of age. The foundation provides information about SIDS and life insurance and offers opportunities to network with other families who have experienced similar tragedies.

The *Angelcheeks* video is a collab in which more than twenty individuals contributed special messages promoting the foundation and its goals. Video contributors included many people who were part of the friendship group of YouTubers whom I studied, including (as listed by their YouTube names): DaleATL2, GeneticBlend, musoSF, kenrg, WpgPeanut, OhCurt, and nalts. Each contributor recorded a few words with their face in medium close-ups. Taken together, their segments provided information about how the foundation aimed to preserve the "memory," "dignity," and "spirit" of deceased children by helping families deal with medical, counseling, and funeral costs for their loved ones. The video also provided information such as Center for Disease Control statistics about SIDS as well as a link to the foundation's website, which invited donations and provided information about SIDS prevention.

Similar to DaleATL2's approach in his thank-you video, bnessel1973 also recognizes individuals who participated in the collab. He provides a screenshot of each video maker and a subtitle of their name on the image. He also thanks YouTuber CyndieRae, who provided the video's music. As an image of her singing and playing a keyboard appears, a subtitle extends thanks to her "For writing and performing the most beautiful song I've ever heard." Video contributors to the *Angelcheeks* video enjoy varying levels of YouTube popularity. While some boast several million views on their videos, others see a modest few hundred. YouTubers were clearly not chosen because of their metrical popularity but because they wished to support a friend in need.

Friends' time and effort were graciously acknowledged, and each person received a "shout-out" or positive mention of their YouTube channel name. A shout-out using a YouTube channel name enables viewers to check out the contributor's videos by accessing the channel page on the site. In the description of the video, bnessel1973 states, "My eternal gratitude to everyone who was a part of this video. You will forever have a piece of my heart. My family thanks you." A kind of interactional debt arguably manifested when people gave their time to participate in the *Angelcheeks* video, and that debt was addressed through multiple forms of mediated thanks both within the video and in the accompanying text description. Heteromorphic reciprocity is enacted through thanks, public recognition, and shout-outs to the accounts of YouTube participants, which exhibited a form that was different from the video footage that contributors originally provided. In his way, bnessel1973 ultimately addressed each individual's gift of donating footage to the collab.

In the video-sharing culture of YouTube, generalized reciprocity also took the form of providing footage of an event without necessarily expecting direct sharing of footage in return. For example, I was recording a YouTube meet-up in Hollywood in 2008 when an interviewee named OhCurt (his YouTube channel name) took comfort in the fact that I was recording, freeing him from operating a camera himself. Typically receiving hundreds and sometimes thousands of views for each of his videos, OhCurt was a white man whose vlogs included varied themes, such as expressions of his personal opinions on YouTube culture, discussions about being gay, and humorous observations of life. He had joined YouTube about five months prior to our interaction (using his OhCurt account—he reportedly had a different prior account). As of January 2009, he had 2,648 subscribers. His OhCurt account had been deleted as of June 2018. As I panned the camera around the attendees at the Hollywood meet-up, I eventually trained the camera on him, prompting the following exchange:

OHCURT: See, the thing is, I know you're shooting footage. If I post nothing on my channel, we're still covered.

PATRICIA: Maybe. You trust me that much? There's been mistakes. (laughs)

OHCURT: That's true. And I actually thought I was recording in Atlanta, when it turns out, I had hit the Stop button.

PATRICIA: Oh yeah?

OHCURT: Some of that footage was very confusing.

PATRICIA: It happens.

OHCURT: Yes.

OhCurt's reaction demonstrates interactional reciprocity in a way that invites sociality. OhCurt and I jokingly reminded each other that people's media were not necessarily reliable. After I initiated vulnerability by admitting to prior mistakes, OhCurt socially reciprocated by pointing out a time when he had made recording errors. Such reciprocal admissions of mediated vulnerability created an encounter that served to momentarily equalize us socially. It reciprocally emphasized our "mutuality" rather than reinforcing a hierarchy in which one person appears definitively more capable with a camera.

OhCurt was clearly more of an expert than I was. His well-executed videos received many more views than mine. Nevertheless, he was gracious, and his act of reciprocal media vulnerability served to move us toward sociality rather than technical competition. In my book *Kids on YouTube* (2014), I discuss how people perform technical affiliation to beliefs or practices assumed to be associated with technical cultures.[69] Often the goal in such technical performances is to showcase one's own prowess by revealing what one knows or what one has achieved through technical activities. The key is to demonstrate comparatively superior knowledge or skills. By admitting to technical mistakes, OhCurt levels the social field and does not reiterate his (considerably greater) technical expertise. His remarks resist interactional competitiveness and performance of technical ability, and the effect was to foster a feeling of sociality.

This exchange also illustrates how generalized reciprocity was enacted through sharing footage. Since someone would likely be recording something interesting in this heavily mediated milieu, he did not have to record footage himself. Because other people were operating cameras, the events and memories were appropriately "covered."

A willingness to share footage is another way to demonstrate an interest in participating in a video-sharing culture. My communal participation was put to the test when a YouTuber asked me to share footage that he saw me recording at an event in Toronto. He asked me to share this footage, given that he was unable to record it. Regrettably, I felt I should decline because I did not want my footage to circulate widely online before I could review it and create and distribute my own visual ethnographic statement. In this moment of *reciprocus interruptus*, I was arguably displaying an outsider perspective to socially oriented YouTubers. They apparently shared footage more freely, such as for collabs. My withholding highlighted the fact that video sharing, conducted in a spirit of interpersonal giving, was seen as a common practice among socially driven participation on YouTube.

Expressing Gratitude for External Support

Contrary to fears of losing reciprocity in digital realms, YouTubers clearly supported fellow video makers who were in need. In hard times such as illnesses, YouTubers might receive aid in the form of donations. In turn they may express the need to reciprocate that regard in videos by thanking those who helped them. YouTubers might use the video platform to respond to external support they received outside of YouTube. For example, an interviewee named ZenArcher (his YouTube channel name; he also used the nickname "Po") was a white man in his early fifties who was a very popular early vlogger on YouTube. He joined a year and a half before I interviewed him at SouthTube in 2007. Recognized as a vlogging pioneer who helped shape the standard of vlogs on the site, he was inspirational to many people. Appearing on camera in his charming, signature cowboy hat, ZenArcher's video blogs were down-to-earth views of his life and memories. He discussed many subjects, including religion, ethics, life choices, and memories of near-death experiences, such as nearly dying while drag racing. Tributes characterized him as a master storyteller with a personality that radiated empathy, vulnerability, and a willingness to handle confrontational issues, such as incarceration without legal representation.[70] He was surprised and delighted when his video explaining YouTube's terms of service to another video maker was featured on the YouTube home page, which brought in many new viewers and subscribers. Each of his videos received several hundred to thousands of views. He had 3,124 subscribers as of June 2018.

ZenArcher posted a video entitled *Crisis Avoided—THANK YOU* on July 29, 2014. Videos leading up to it revealed serious health issues that were troubling him, including heart problems and two forms of cancer. The video thanks people who sent money and helped him survive a crisis that included a struggle to pay rent. He opens the video with an admission. He states: "I should have made this video days and days ago but the truth of the matter is, I just couldn't." He explained that the pain in his hands complicated his ability to make videos.

The point of his video was to thank the people who had helped him. He admits not actually knowing the identity of all those who had donated to his cause. Using first names, he extends thanks, stating: "I'm humbled by the way that you came forward to help me when I needed it the most." He expresses gratitude and explains that the money was used to help pay rent, buy gas, obtain medicines, and make his doctor's appointments. Even though he appears to be gravely ill (YouTubers reference his eventual passing in February 2015), he nevertheless feels motivated to reciprocate the regard he received by thanking everyone. Notably, he attends to the temporality of the reciprocity by apologizing for his lateness, stating, "I'm humbled by it and I'm sorry that I didn't say so sooner." ZenArcher exhibited temporal sensitivity by acknowledging the importance of bestowing reciprocity quickly. At the end of his video he says in an emotional voice: "I'm sorry it took so long for this to get there and again, thank you." It is heartening to see that he received help from fellow YouTubers, yet deeply poignant to see how someone who is suffering expresses the need to extend gratitude and reciprocity for the assistance he received. It is heartbreaking to see how much it meant to him to be mindful of extending reciprocal thanks in a timely way.

THE ROOTS OF RECIPROCITY

Engaging in a visual research project on YouTube facilitated interrogation of core anthropological concepts, such as the origins and dynamics of reciprocity. At times the origins of reciprocity and the substance of what was actually reciprocated were difficult to pinpoint, an observation that is consistent with findings in the anthropological record of past societies. Seeing a comment such as "thanks for this video" posted to a video seemed to suggest that the comment was providing thanks for a gift that was given in the form of a video. The video appeared to be prompting heteromorphic reciprocal interaction in the form of thanks.

Yet precise origins of reciprocity have been critiqued as rather illusive. Actions that seem to immediately reciprocate a prior event may actually have their emotional roots in interactions that are not necessarily visible, especially since they occur atemporally. When people exchange gifts, typically feelings of regard for the other person accompany this interaction. As a result, within an exchange it can be difficult to disentangle exactly *what* is being reciprocated: a feeling, an object, a manifestation of a prior relationship, or some combination.[71] For instance, if someone gives me a birthday present and I give them a birthday gift later, is my gift motivated solely by the prior birthday present or simply because I like the person (or both)? Temporally speaking, it may be tempting to evaluate reciprocal encounters immediately after an exchange.

Anthropologists recognize and analyze long-term, patterned cycles of reciprocity. They have observed that "gift-inducing reciprocity" is often "intermingled" with "liking reciprocity," whereby the latter concept emphasizes mutual feelings of interpersonal regard that persist over time.[72] For example, as mentioned above, at a meetup in Santa Monica a YouTuber told me that he had watched my AnthroVlog videos and enjoyed them. After the gathering I looked at his channel page on YouTube and watched and commented on one of his videos. To observers outside of our encounter, it would seem that my comment stemmed from my reaction to the video itself and that I was reciprocating attention based on the video. Yet, as a YouTube participant, I knew full well that I was not invested in the video's subject. However, I did feel motivated to watch at least one video and comment on it, simply because he had paid attention to my work and had introduced himself to me in person. It did not feel sufficient to thank him for watching my videos at the gathering. It seemed appropriate to address my feelings of gratitude by attending to his work in a mediated way. The reciprocity that I expressed displayed my appreciation for his underlying *regard*. The root of my reciprocal act of attention was not visible in my text comment on the video.

Pinpointing the origins and meanings of reciprocal acts is not straightforward. In fact, as philosopher and sociologist Georg Simmel astutely observed decades ago, the feeling of gratitude for a received gift often emerges not from the act of receiving a particular item but rather more fundamentally from gratitude over "the mere existence of a person" whom we appreciate the opportunity to "experience" in encounters or relationships over time.[73] Teasing apart the origins of video reciprocities can be challenging or even impossible. Gratitude is not just expressed for an object such as a video coming into the world but rather reflects deeper appreciation for specific histories of interaction or even *qualities* about a person that we are grateful to experience.

When a video retains relevance, comments may continue to be posted over time, as happened in bnessel1973's case. Even though his video *My YouTube Story* was posted years ago, people provided commentary detailing their responses for several years afterward. That he continued to receive comments long after it was posted indicates its emotional force and underscores the importance of attending to temporalities of video-sharing practices, as Lefebvre urged.

Comments do not necessarily reciprocate gratitude only to the video but also illustrate how people appreciated bnessel1973's personal qualities and gifts to the world. Many commenters responded to bnessel1973's presence rather than to the video. Comments were directed at him and the way he bravely faced adversity. He was characterized as "amazing," a "hero," "special," "wonderful," deserving of "respect," a "great guy," and possessing an "infectious" spirit. Commenters called him "the real deal," "the funniest guy on YouTube," and "an inspiration to anyone who's ever endured such a tragic loss."

People felt "honored" to meet him or get to know him. One viewer stated:

> It is nice to see you do videos like this. It is hard at the same time. I'm grateful to know you and your family. You all are truly special people.

Another viewer stated:

> You are hysterically funny and imaginative, yet also human, warm and generous. You and [your wife] are very special people and I have felt truly uplifted after watching your videos. So thank you!

One commenter noted that a whole "sub-community" was springing up around him and his work. In an interview one woman told me that she connected to this social group in part because she too had lost a child and had made a video about it.

Reacting to bnessel1973's video, she posted the following comment: "You seem so much farther along on your journey than I am on mine, but I know that it's never an entirely linear one so I'll keep plugging away. I hope that your friends, your family and your outlet of YouTube continue to help heal you. Thank you again for sharing so much."

Commenters sometimes thanked bnessel1973 for "being here" in the world or in *their* "YouTube." Another commenter thanked him "for being part of their [life]." As Brian's sister commented, "Thank YOU—for just being you." These remarks illustrate how comments display gratitude for the opportunity to experience a *person* and not just a video. Commenters admired aspects of his character that were positive or inspirational. The comments showed that viewers were grateful to interact with Brian in their corner of YouTube and in their world more generally.

The research demonstrated that interactions formed a larger series of practices that were not easily emotionally teased apart as they traveled across modalities. What seemed like a reciprocal act that reacted to something specific (such as a video or comment) could actually be responding to something outside of the interaction itself, such as gratitude that the person existed. Of course, the commentary might also bundle gratitude for the person and the material item simultaneously in that they are inseparably bound together. Teasing apart such nuances may not always be possible or desirable, but their dynamics become clearer when scholars move beyond analyzing videos as single texts and attend to processes of video sharing over time, including interwoven comments, videos, and interview remarks. In YouTube's "mediascape,"[74] analyzing a video-sharing culture requires exploring interactions and practices that include multiple forms of reciprocity, both specific and generalized.

RECIPROCITY: AN INSIDER'S VIEW

Contra the naysayers, positive forms of reciprocity were frequently enacted among socially motivated creators. YouTubers exhibited generalized, balanced, and instrumental forms of reciprocity. For example, generalized forms of reciprocity[75] included sharing footage in ways that did not rely on finely calibrated calculations to satisfy a specific prior, attentional debt. As expressed in interactions, videos, and comments, YouTubers counted on footage of interactions to be freely shared so that people who were participating in events could later enjoy the footage online, even if they were unable to record the moments themselves. The study contributes to the anthropological record by showing how positive forms of reciprocity played an important role in social encounters in digital milieus in ways that challenge discourses of video-centric self-centeredness. People attended to commenters, and they co-created videos for other people for a range of causes, including raising awareness about civic concerns and helping people in need.

Lefebvre urged an examination of how temporalities reveal important cultural dynamics. On YouTube, not only was reciprocity important; attentional debt also exhibited a temporal dimension. Temporal sensitivities were exhibited, for instance, through the creators' belief that videos took time to watch and should be attended to in full in order for viewers to show sincere and engaged forms of regard. In addition, YouTubers believed that reciprocity in the form of thanks should be addressed quickly, within a few days or even hours of a posted video or comment, to ensure recognition of YouTubers' mutual regard. Lefebvre also noted that rhythmic dynamics reveal and therefore demand analyses of ritualized forms of repetition. YouTubers interested in sociality demonstrated repeated and patterned forms of reciprocity in terms of reciprocating regard when comments were posted to videos. Creators perceived these moments of regard as possible encounters for strengthening social connections. As discussed in the next chapter, such connections might even build to yield a "peak" of sociality through achieving a sense of community on the site.

Although some scholars see reciprocity as a panacea for achieving sociality, in fact, commensurate with the anthropological record and given recent critiques of the concept, many forms of reciprocity exist, some of them negative. The present research revealed that withholdings of attention amid insincere or competitively negative forms of reciprocity were also important for maintaining an appropriately interactive atmosphere on YouTube. Scholarly concerns about narcissism inordinately focus attention on media creators while ignoring analyses of viewers' agency in bestowing attention. Yet the present study demonstrated that viewers are not simply passive recipients of self-centered material; in fact they make conscious decisions about whom they will watch and under what circumstances. They carefully considered the personal and social impact of bestowing reciprocity. When interviewees received undeserved requests for attention, such as in the practice of subscription for subscription, they typically withheld their regard. Video makers preferred to deny attention to substandard work by a smaller proportion of video makers who seemed to be in it for themselves. Withholding perceived undeserved reciprocities appeared to be as important as bestowing positive video reciprocity for encouraging sociality and maintaining creative integrity on the site.

The present discussion about reciprocity in one mediascape not only illustrates one set of practices on a particular site but also aims to stimulate scholarly and classroom discussions about how reciprocity plays out in digital milieus. Much work remains on investigating the nuances of reciprocity across and within particular social media sites. Questions of interest include: What forms of reciprocity occur on social media? What are the norms of reciprocity for a site as a whole or for particular social groups that use it? What happens in an interpersonal sense when such norms are ignored or transgressed? Does media quality play a role? If so, how is quality defined? Under what circumstances are reciprocities accepted or withheld, and how do participants determine reciprocal motivations? What are the ultimate effects of engaging with reciprocities on a particular site? A key factor concerns analyzing to what extent media makers have control over their media and commensurate reciprocities in hybrid socio-commercial environments that collapse motivations within specific technical features.

By engaging across different groups, the study provided key insights about cross-modal participation and its effects on reciprocity. My experimental AnthroVlog/AnthroVlog debacle demonstrated the importance of involving multiple modalities when fostering sociality through media. It was insufficient to participate in person as I did with vloggers outside of YouTube. Contrary to assumptions that in-person interaction promotes the highest level of interpersonal engagement, in fact, to be perceived as social amid a media-oriented group, one had to engage and participate at least in part through *media* by posting comments and interacting online.

The present case study simultaneously draws on and yet also updates the anthropological record. As has been observed in anthropology in the past, certain gifts exhibit an inalienable quality. Even if YouTubers exchange the same category of gift, such as a subscription, they do so as unique individuals with inalienable qualities that are imbued within the gift. Although it has been stated that only some gifts exhibit inalienability, in this digital milieu most forms of apparently similar types of technologically encoded gifts of attention are arguably never precisely equivalent. They emerge from different people with individual personalities, investments in sociality, and interpersonal goals. The study supplements the anthropological record by showing how inalienability systematically appears in a broad way in a digital-sharing milieu. The findings challenge the general feasibility of the category of the homeomorphic gift in realms where technical features collapse multiple motivations, each originating from different individuals.

The study also reinforced the sociological contention that pinpointing the precise roots of reciprocity is illusive. A text comment that appears to directly display appreciation for a single video may emerge from a much larger spirit of gratitude that a video maker simply exists in the world and is willing to share their point of view through video. At root, appreciative commentary about single videos or even video makers may be grounded more fundamentally by a basic feeling of gratitude for the medium of video itself. Expressions of gratitude imply appreciation for what videos and their creators might accomplish socially, civically, and educationally when personal expression is freely and interpersonally exchanged.

5

WHAT DEFINES A COMMUNITY?

One of the first YouTubers I met was a white woman in her early forties whose YouTube channel name was ShortbusMooner. During her interview in the peaceful setting of a public park, she eloquently and staunchly described YouTube as a community—a cornerstone concept in anthropology. As she spoke, she gestured toward the meet-up we were attending in Marietta, Georgia, as proof that YouTubers formed a community. ShortbusMooner strongly believed that people cared about others and helped them in hard times. She recalled how YouTubers rallied around people who had been seriously ill and had campaigned to support them. She observed that if everyone was "anonymous and didn't care about each other, then those things wouldn't happen." In one of her videos, ShortbusMooner argued that YouTube was not one community but many diverse communities, a position echoed by several interviewees.

Most meet-up interviewees—including those with varying levels of popularity on the site—felt that YouTube was a community, in part through shared interests such as social forms of video sharing. In contrast, YouTubers outside of the study held diverse views. Some commenters saw the site as merely a "platform" or a "business" that amounted to little more than an "opinion poll" or "marketing strategy." These conflicting perspectives invite reflection on what constitutes community within commercialized milieus. For example, are YouTubers' inventing new ideas about community or do their conceptualizations resemble those in the anthropological record? What is the function of community on YouTube? How does it work

DOI: 10.5876/9781607329558.c005

and what are its limitations? What are its temporal dimensions? What are the characteristics people use to determine whether a community has formed?

In terms of the Lefebvrian mode of analysis, this chapter examines how people reach a "peak" of sociality such that they believe that YouTube functions as a community, or may become one under the right circumstances. The previous chapters discussed growth phases of social intensification that for some YouTube participants supported traditional notions of the community concept. In temporal terms, an important aspect of building community includes experiencing shared happenings—often through media—that occur contemporaneously. For example, videos that appear on the first page of YouTube could help viewers share cultural content and promote a sense of togetherness.

Lefebvre noted that rhythmic patterns might be linear or cyclical. On YouTube the development of sociality took both forms. Groups such as the one analyzed in this book experienced a linear trajectory that began by spending time together using various modes of interaction. They then strengthened social bonds through forms of reciprocity, formed a sense of community, and experienced eventual decline in intensity of interaction, as discussed in the next chapter. The community phenomenon exhibited a cyclical quality. As new groups arrived, their videos suggest that they too began interacting socially and exploring whether YouTube could function as a community within their social circles.

Clearly, not all YouTubers experienced the site as a community at the same time, with many people never seeing the site in this way. Lefebvre identified "arrhythmias" as multiple rhythms that conflict in discomforting ways. As YouTubers, interviewees took the time to build toward community while other YouTube participants were only beginning to understand its possibilities. Mass audiences engage with the site as a broadcast medium. For them, a tangible community will quite likely never materialize. Different paces of community acceptance resulted in participatory arrhythmias that yielded complications for its widespread uptake and arguably contributed to its eventual decline as a social milieu for the people studied in this book. The next chapter will explore the end of the Lefebvrian trajectory of YouTube participation that moved from birth/beginning, as marked by arrival to the site, to death/end, as people left, passed away, or decreased intensive participation.

In contrast to mass viewing audiences, most interviewees did feel emotionally close to others and felt that YouTube sociality exhibited important community dynamics. Since community formation through media is a sociological fact,[1] I initially wondered why people kept revisiting this question in interviews with me and in their own videos. The answer lies partly in the term's ambiguity and because, as this chapter argues, it is through discourse in videos, commentary, and ongoing collective participation that community is created and maintained.

As new media generations appear, they may not automatically consider themselves to be part of a community, so it is a process rather than a concrete category. It is unsurprising that so many digital ethnographies—especially those that deal with a new medium—inevitably include people's reflections on the relevance of community for their social collective. Discussions of community cyclically recur across mediated groups that are attempting to make sense of their developing social formations. The chapter calls for retaining the conceptual rubric of community but not to secure a restricted and potentially elitist definition. It draws on an engagement with public anthropology to advocate retaining the idea of community as a proxy term for a collective project that involves online participants of different contributory levels to continually shape its social parameters.

The chapter opens with a discussion of the multiple lines of ethnographic evidence that were used to analyze perceptions of community. Next it revisits how the term has been conceptualized in the anthropological literature and in digital scholarship. The chapter then analyzes interviewees' responses to questions about the meaning of community. Responses were compiled in a video entitled *What Defines a Community?*, which was posted as part of my open video field notes series on AnthroVlog. The chapter critically interrogates YouTubers' notions of community in light of the anthropological record and its revisions.

The chapter then analyzes commentary from viewers who interpellated themselves into the study by posting comments to my video, which investigated numerous and nuanced parameters of community on YouTube. To interpellate the self into discourse means to identify oneself and one's interests as subjects of the discussion.[2] Far more interesting than their determination of YouTube's community status were their criteria for assessment and the ways in which their interactivity with the video's content and with other commenters provided clues about the feasibility of public engagements with anthropology. Standard reactions to diverse and sometimes hostile commentary often include faulting anonymity as the culprit. This chapter tackles this debate head-on by demonstrating that productive commentary largely came from YouTubers unknown to me. Foreclosing anonymous content thus threatens to preclude meaningful engagement in networked spaces. Such a finding suggests that dealing with anonymous others is important for sharing information and accomplishing civic goals. The chapter completes its examination of the ethnographic data by analyzing how YouTubers address community in their own videos, demonstrating that the topic of community continues to exhibit vitality—and controversy—among YouTubers.

Drawing on examples from prior projects as well as the present effort, the chapter addresses the question of whether public forms of anthropology can shed analytical light on theoretical concepts such as community. The answer is a qualified yes, as long as participatory expectations are well managed. Publics should be provided with adequate resources to contribute effectively, and parameters of interaction must be appropriately crafted.

The chapter concludes by engaging in a theoretical reflection on community that asserts that the term is best understood as processual rather than categorical. It is not yet time to dismiss the notion of community in anthropological and ethnographic research on media. Even if individual scholars choose to do so, it will emically reappear as new cycles of interaction are launched and discussed in new media. The concept should be retained and its processes of negotiation should be critically examined in each case. In considering community dynamics over time, it is clear that collaborative efforts will be required to determine whether specific instantiations and ideals of community may be collectively realized.

ANALYZING MULTIPLE LINES OF EVIDENCE

This chapter draws on three main lines of evidence to analyze community. The first source of evidence is a compilation of video-recorded interviews that I conducted at a SouthTube meet-up in Marietta, Georgia, in September 2007. The compilation video that I created and posted is called *What Defines a Community?* The second line of evidence is an analysis of a random sample of text comments that were posted to my compilation video as of June 2009. The third line of evidence involves analyzing representative case studies of videos that YouTubers made on the topic of community in 2014.

What Defines a Community? is a six-minute video consisting of video-recorded responses from seven out of a total of thirteen interviewees whom I spoke with at the gathering. We discussed many subjects, but the compilation video includes only remarks about community. The video principally argues that for many interviewees, YouTube fostered community. At the same time, their narratives contain fascinating and important nuances about community that echo diverse perspectives on its meaning in the scholarly record. A key aesthetic choice was to include only interview remarks rather than provide an expository voiceover by the researcher. A central goal of the video was to invite audiences to reflect on their own views of community by hearing the nuances and diversity in the narratives. Interview footage for the video was chosen as representative of the interviewees at the gathering and across the project. Interviewees' criteria for adjudicating YouTube's community status varied widely, ranging from patterns of consistent, mutual aid to inevitable drama and conflict. For interviewees, YouTube was more than just a website: it represented an outlook of acceptance and interactivity through video sharing.

The video intersperses interview footage (figure 5.1) with observational images of attendees hanging out, having a picnic, making videos of one another, and taking

FIGURE 5.1. YouTubers discuss their views at a SouthTube meet-up in Georgia, on September 23, 2007. Screenshot by Patricia G. Lange from *What Defines a Community?* (2007).

FIGURE 5.2. A YouTuber photographs people hanging out at SouthTube, a meet-up attended by people of multiple generations, in Georgia on September 23, 2007. Screenshot by Patricia G. Lange from *What Defines a Community?* (2007).

photographs (figure 5.2). The images depict the beautiful natural park that served as the setting for a technologically driven social group ranging from children to older people who gathered based on their shared interests in YouTube and video. On average, each video interview lasted about ten minutes. As YouTubers, we stayed close to the action; the noise of the meet-up is often heard in the background.

YouTube editors featured *What Defines a Community?* on the site's welcome page for several days in early October 2007, where it garnered more than 1 million views and 1,906 comments. Editors likely selected my video because it was a popular topic on the site and because YouTube has historically highlighted self-referential material.[3] My video's featured status provided an opportunity to test how a video created within an anthropological framework with a group of YouTube enthusiasts might be received among a larger swath of heterogeneous viewers. Although commentary ranged from pointless critique to thought-provoking engagement, constructive interactivity was highly visible.

To study viewers' reactions to the video for the second line of analysis, I drew a random sample of 100 comments from the 1,906 posted comments. I numbered each comment from 1 to 1,906 and then used a random-number generator to select 100 of these comments. I sought to obtain a representative sample of the entire corpus of comments in order to analyze them according to levels of engagement with the video. The analysis of comments revealed the diversity of opinions on the subject as well as the opportunities and challenges for sharing anthropological material through connected learning models.

Drawing on scholarship from anthropology, sociology, and game design, Boellstorff and his colleagues argue in their book, *Ethnography and Virtual Worlds,* that "descriptive" quantitative information may be necessary for uncovering patterns in digital ethnography studies.[4] By collecting a random sample from a larger number of voices, ethnographic work may reach a broader swath of opinions than only those from a delineated ethnographic study. Analysis of text commentary from a heterogeneous group supplements information from interviewees who attended gatherings and were thus invested in the topic.

Media anthropologist Gabriele de Seta argues that ethnographic participation in digital environments lies on a spectrum from watching interaction to exhibiting a more "active presence" that "extends in different dimensions according to the platforms used, the devices at hand, software availability, access to connectivity in time and space, as well as the social circles and practices one participates in."[5] The meaning of the term "participation" in digital ethnography is often taken for granted, de Seta argues, although it connotes numerous levels of interactive intensity. By participating as a video maker rather than a lurker, I was able to experience—but also tasked with—dealing with a broad array of reactions to the video's contemplations on the prospects for achieving community.

De Seta's point underscores the importance of acknowledging the shifting boundaries and connotations of digital participation in a single study over time. Numerous technical and social features shape the possibilities for making videos and participating in mediated groups. For example, I edited my video at a YouTube editor's request so that it could be featured. The original version contained footage of an interview with a YouTube employee. However, because YouTube had a policy of not featuring staff members in front-page content, the editors requested that I remove this footage and repost the video. I acquiesced because I wanted to see, from a research perspective, what would happen if my video appeared on the "front page of YouTube." I left both versions of *What Defines a Community?* on YouTube using the same title. However, it was the abridged video that was featured and is discussed here.

As comments were being posted, I elected not to moderate them. When comments exceeded more than a few dozen, it became tedious and time-consuming to moderate each one, let alone reciprocate by responding. According to new media theorist and activist Geert Lovink, "Writers, editors, and moderators play a vital role in establishing a culture of frequent commenting."[6] The difficulty of dealing with a high volume of responses suggests that we are not understanding commentary as much as gaining a general impression of it. As Lovink observed, "Instead of a close reading, we practice intuitive scanning."[7] To address the challenges raised by scale, this analysis engaged in a close reading of a representative sample. At an indeterminate time between June 2014 and June 2018, comments were edited and many were removed. I do not recall receiving an explanation about why only 552 comments were left on the video as of June 2018.[8]

My decision to forgo comment moderation caused confusion among my viewers. Friends from video-blogging circles urged me to delete hurtful and threatening comments. Although I was tempted to do so, moderating comments risked changing the outcome of the research. Overmoderation might privilege my personal predilections and foreclose forthright debate about the acceptability of diverse forms of public commentary. How could discussions about what is appropriate occur if the researcher's judgment influenced which potentially controversial commentary was removed? Artificially sanitizing the data risked depicting a false picture of positive participation.

The decision to leave distasteful commentary yielded methodological and theoretical insights. Ultimately any choice about comment moderation (removing or retaining comments) potentially influences the data *creation* as well as collection. To the extent that abusive commentary may be compared to graffiti or subversive public messages, leaving such commentary possibly attracted additional offensive commentary and should arguably be removed.[9] The graffiti effect refers to the idea that comment "vandalism" tends to attract like-minded remarks. Therefore, leaving hurtful commentary may have biased the data in a negative direction. Of course, comment moderation, like graffiti removal, does not guarantee freedom from subversive postings.[10] A freshly cleaned, blank slate is known to prompt hurtful messages. Because some people have fun writing words that wound, inappropriate commentary will likely never disappear, despite efforts to improve participatory, digital literacies.

No position of pure neutrality exists with respect to comment moderation on public research sites. De Seta argues that investigations of problematic behaviors such as trolling tend to fall on specific axes; researchers display either endorsement or critique.[11] According to de Seta, some scholars attempt to contextualize antisocial behavior while others denounce unethical communicative practices. In his work on trolling, de Seta takes a more dialogical approach, which includes involving commentary, even of the distasteful variety. In part, the goal is to invite social media users' own interpretations, a position similar to that taken in this analysis.

Rather than remove comments (including those I found ethically and personally objectionable), the goal was to leave them up for examination beyond a single researcher's interpretation. The exercise revealed that any comment-wrangling choice inevitably had ramifications on what constituted the data itself.

The third line of evidence involved analyzing representative case studies of videos in which YouTubers address the subject themselves. This line of analysis revealed that YouTubers have mixed feelings about its prospects. Taking the three lines of evidence together, it is clear that community remains an important topic on the site and that YouTubers' diverse narratives echo prior theoretical rubrics of community. The most pertinent model for this analysis is that of Benedict Anderson's idea of imagined community. YouTubers bonded ideationally and through participation in shared media. Video makers spent considerable energy pondering the question of what defines a community, often in ways that closely resemble theoretical scrutiny in the anthropological record.

RECONSIDERATIONS OF COMMUNITY

The concept of community is notoriously difficult to analyze. Anthropologist Anthony Cohen noted that the term "community" "has proved to be highly resistant to satisfactory definition in anthropology and sociology."[12] YouTubers' wide diversity of opinions on community is perhaps not surprising, given that scholars have spent a hundred years contemplating its meaning. Early analyses privileged place as community's most common criterion.[13] The communities that anthropologists studied were typically distinctive, small, homogeneous, and self-sufficient. Yet scholars have acknowledged that "no real community is perfectly so."[14] Studies of urban settings, diaspora, and reconsiderations of anthropology as a field science have problematized place as the locus of community.[15] Group members typically use this term when they believe they have "something in common" and that this something "distinguishes" them from people in other groups.[16] Under this rubric community is relational because it opposes attributes in one group to those of another. For example, YouTubers saw themselves as different from friends and family who did not share their interests in making videos, accomplishing sociality through media, or participating on YouTube.

In their comments on *What Defines a Community?* people sometimes had difficulty accepting mediated groups as true communities. Sociologists Barry Wellman and Milena Gulia argue that people who refuse to accept the possibility of online community "are confusing the pastoralist myth of community for the reality."[17] They argue that "community ties are already geographically dispersed, sparsely knit, connected heavily by telecommunications [and] specialized in content."[18]

Approaching the subject from an anthropological perspective, Vered Amit argues that more recent studies of contemporary communities show that they are "situationally limited," "ephemeral," and "episodic," yet community relationships "nonetheless facilitate the development of a much appreciated sense of belonging."[19] It is arguably the case that "*all communities are virtual communities*" (emphasis original)[20] if the term "virtual communities" connotes people who mutually identify with particular interests rather than being physically co-located. The term "virtual" is often used to refer to mediated, "dispersed" interaction but is (mis)interpreted to mean not quite "real." In fact, communities have actually never existed as the idealized tropes that linger in the popular imagination. Amit argues that community is not a locally bound entity but rather an "idea or quality of sociality" that privileges collective identities.[21]

Benedict Anderson's idea of "imagined communities" powerfully reconceptualized the concept of community and serves as a useful rubric for understanding networked communities. It has been applied to the study of numerous realms, including groups on YouTube and Twitter.[22] Imagined communities are not "imaginary" or fictional but are rather internally "imagined" because its members "never know most of their fellow members, meet them, or even hear of them, yet in the minds of each lives the image of their communion."[23] Imagined communities are formed among dispersed, mass audiences.[24] According to Anderson, people feel loyal to a collective partly through mediated practices that promote hegemonic, nationalist agendas. For instance, ritualized media practices such as reading national newspapers across the United States every morning "simultaneously" and "sequentially" created a communal collective with shared experiences and ideas.[25] People may never meet fellow Americans, but through media they are aware of common experiences and loyalties.

Engaging in ritualized media such as reading the morning newspaper in standard, national languages is a key aspect of Anderson's rubric. These rituals enabled people to simultaneously access information about events and thus feel a collective sense of moving through historical moments together. Temporally speaking, the fact that a newspaper's contents reached obsolescence on the "morrow of its printing" did not hinder but rather played a crucial role in helping members of the imagined community ideationally envision other people who would be reading it simultaneously, receiving similar information, and seeing themselves as part of an experiential collective at a specific moment in time. Critics of Anderson's concept urge an exploration of how communities are formed not just through mental "ideation,"[26] which alone does not account for intensive commitment such as dying for one's country, but through interactions and shared experiences that address infrastructural complications posed by various stakeholders.[27]

Anderson's analysis focused on media rituals such as reading newspapers. The number of Americans who read physical newspapers is declining. Still, 50 percent of Americans between the ages of eighteen and twenty-nine and 49 percent between thirty and forty-nine access news articles online, suggesting that people still wish to obtain information from collective sources, although increasingly in digital form.[28] Offering mass content is a key way of establishing temporal media rituals that create a collective. Having human editors curate videos for the welcome page enabled YouTube viewers to engage in cultural content available to everyone on the site. Although human editors at least partly curated aspects of YouTube's front-page content in 2007,[29] the site changed its welcome page layout several times between 2009 and 2013. Using algorithms, individual welcome pages foregrounded material that viewers would likely watch on the basis of their viewing patterns.[30] The "front page of YouTube" became different for each user. As of 2018, it focused on recommendations to keep people tuned in rather than videos to encourage collective viewing experiences, the way readers experienced newspapers—or prior iterations of YouTube.

Featuring vernacular videos to broad audiences at a single moment in time was one way that YouTubers shared media experiences that facilitated community formation. Drawing on Lefebvre's temporal analysis, it is clear that sharing moments at the same time fostered a sense of communal experience. For example, six years after my video had been posted, one viewer left a comment that intertwined our mediated histories with that of YouTube. Trebuchet1221 stated: "This was one of the first videos I can remember watching on youtube, I recall seeing this featured on the front page back in 2007 after I uploaded my first video. Man this brings me back."

Despite frequent layout changes, YouTubers connected through video. Vloggers who believe that YouTube is a community "see themselves as a group of people brought together by their shared interest in authoring video blogs; they interact with each other through different tools, both on-site and through back-channels, and create a unique culture comprised of linguistic terms and gestures."[31] According to information studies scholars Dana Rotman and Jennifer Preece, discussions about YouTube's community might originate "from a comment, reflection or question video-posted by one of the more popular vloggers who reflected upon the nature of the YouTube community. Response videos and comments continued these discussions over a prolonged period of time."[32] Media and communication scholars Stuart Cunningham and David Craig note that social media entertainment may also be characterized as "communitainment," which incorporates social media, communication, and interactivity as well as "an ethos of community (an ecology where fans, subscribers, and supporters directly constitute the communities that trigger the sustainability of content creator careers)."[33]

At this point, community is as much fantasy as social science. As Cohen argued, "Community exists in the minds of its members, and should not be confused with geographic or sociographic assertions of 'fact.'"[34] In studying digital communities, communication studies scholar Howard Rheingold similarly observed that, "Community is a matter of emotions as well as a thing of reason and data."[35] Researchers have observed many YouTube articulations about community, in part because of a connection creators make to others who share an interest in making YouTube videos.[36] As communication scholar Michael Strangelove observed, "Amateur online video practices bring strangers together and often turn them into friends."[37] Despite its contested status, the concept of community "retains connotations of interpersonal warmth, shared interests, and loyalty."[38]

Whether or not YouTube functions as a "true" community is less fruitful to adjudicate given its shifting and heterogeneous populations. A more interesting task is exploring the criteria that groups use to make their determination and the ways in which they express their ideals. Inspired by anthropologist Mary Douglas, Strangelove argues that "it is this very process of debate that constitutes a community and perpetuates its very existence."[39] Examining opinions about community is facilitated by YouTube's discursive environment, in which "there is much reflection on the norms and ideals of the community."[40] Community is discursive terrain and an ideal that will continue to be debated in mediated groups because it is a cyclical, recurring phenomenon. Each new group that meets on a digital site and bonds through mediated, shared experiences negotiates its status over time.

INTERVIEWEES ANALYZE PROSPECTS
FOR COMMUNITY ON YOUTUBE

Interviewees' responses about whether YouTube was or could be a community constitute the first line of evidence discussed in this chapter. Notably, interviewees used criteria that mapped closely to those in the updated scholarly record. However, contrary to more common characterizations that emphasize homogeneity as central, people whom I interviewed did not always see community as delineated only by cultural sameness or even mutual regard. Notably, several interviewees cited diversity, conflict, and separate groups of friends operating in parallel in their discussion of what defined a community.

ShortbusMooner, the YouTuber whose opinions on community opened this chapter, based her assessment on multifaceted criteria, including willingness to meet up, mutual helping, drama and conflict, and multiple community groups. ShortbusMooner joined about a year prior to her SouthTube interview. She vlogged about concerts and YouTube meet-ups she attended as well as sunsets, a friend's new drum set, cats, gardens, and facts about herself. Her videos see a few hundred to a thousand views. She had 404 subscribers as of June 2018.[41]

ShortbusMooner's privileging of meet-ups as important underscores that it is crucial to experience *co-temporal* social interactions, which facilitate emotionally driven identities of belonging.[42] She also cites traditional ideas of helping others. At the same time, she also observed the "inevitable drama" on YouTube that she avoids but that is nevertheless part of collective sociality.

Similar to ShortbusMooner, DaleATL2 (his YouTube channel name) also accepted multiple types of participation as important. He optimistically felt that it was tolerance of *diversity* that demonstrated that YouTube was a community. DaleATL2 was a white man from the South in his early forties who had been on YouTube for a year and four months when I interviewed him. He created humorous vlogs with his family as well as movie parodies and vlogs of places he visited. Most of his videos garner hundreds of views each, although many see thousands of views. As of June 2018, he had 2,404 subscribers. DaleATL2 lists aspects of diversity such as race, religion, and sexual orientation as key factors in shaping YouTube's community. He stated:

> If you've gotten video of this whole event, you have seen a cross section of society
> that goes from race, creed, religion, sexual orientation, you name it. And it's all
> right here at this event. And that to me is the definition of community, but better.
> Because you've got people getting past the stereotypes and seeing people as people, as
> individuals.

Narratives also contained conflicting criteria that accepted oppositional factors as facilitating group sociality. Such portrayals in effect underscore DaleATL2's perhaps idealistic observations about YouTube diversity. For example, an interviewee named proudyke (her YouTube channel name) was a white woman in her late forties who had been on YouTube for just over a year at the time of her interview. She posted vlogs, political videos, and tribute videos to family members and celebrities who had passed away. Her view counts vary from less than a hundred each to a few with a thousand, such as those featuring a political figure or a YouTube celebrity. She had 333 subscribers as of June 2018.

Proudyke initially states that it is "cohesiveness" and "camaraderie" that constitutes community on YouTube. Yet she also accepts "haters" as community members given that YouTube represents a "microcosm" of a society. She addresses naysayers who do not believe that digital sites can foster deep levels of connection, calling YouTube a "real" community. Interviewees generally defined haters as people who post pointlessly mean-spirited, inarticulate, or harsh criticism, such as "this sucks," or cruel comments unrelated to the video, such as "go die."[43] For proudyke, even haters are part of the community, even if their commentary is discomforting. Although harassing behavior should be addressed, scholars argue that community participants nevertheless bond over the shared experience of dealing with haters and trolls.[44]

Narratives also contained descriptions of interconnected YouTube groups. Interviewees who saw YouTube's community this way included ZenArcher and lemonette (their YouTube channel names). ZenArcher was a white man in his early fifties who pioneered vlogging on YouTube by recounting his philosophies on life, often dealing with topics such as religion, ethics, and life choices. Each of his videos received several hundred to thousands of views. As of June 2108, he had 3,124 subscribers. Having joined the site a year and a half before our interview in 2007, he was very active in the social side of YouTube. Several tribute videos of him appeared after he reportedly passed away in 2015.

ZenArcher surprised some commenters when he stated that he knew many YouTubers better than he knew his own neighbors. For ZenArcher, YouTube's social circles resembled groups in one's local community, which creates a sense of community on the site. Larger groups often divided into smaller, interconnected circles of friends and acquaintances. Like proudyke, ZenArcher referenced the microcosm aspect of YouTube. In terms of interconnected groups, he explained how he traveled between them:

> [YouTube] is a community in every way that your city is a community. There are kids
> that are running around with skateboards jumping on park benches. It's at YouTube.
> There is, uh, political people at YouTube. There are the Paris Hiltons and the Jamie
> Kennedys that entertain because it's their business and they're there. And none of it
> hurts YouTube. It all helps YouTube because it is a community just like the city that
> you live in. So when you go out in the city and you see an old woman having trouble
> putting groceries in her car, that's at YouTube. When you see somebody that's acting
> up and having a good time, that's at YouTube. It is a community, and there are little
> circles, like in your community you have your group of friends and somebody else
> has their group of friends, and you have a friend that goes between, that happens at
> YouTube. There are little circles. I don't belong to any one of those circles, but I'm one
> who travels between those circles. And that's what community's all about.

Lemonette similarly believed YouTube was a community, but that it included many social groups. Lemonette was a white woman in her early fifties from the South who made comedic vlogs, often from her car. Her videos regularly saw several thousand views each, and she had an impressive following among vloggers, boasting 5,828 subscribers as of June 2018. I interviewed her about a year after she had joined the site. The idea of community had limits, she believed, given that "not everybody wants to join in." She noted that at least "they can still have their say and their show can't get canceled." Her view is perhaps optimistic. YouTubers certainly reported receiving strikes against their account as well as suspensions and deletions for posting copyrighted material. But her point is well taken. If people followed the terms of service as interpreted by YouTube, they had a platform to share their voice and interact.

Not everyone whom I interviewed agreed that YouTube, or even the social groups that I was studying, formed a community. Across the study a few interviewees mentioned intensive self-promotion as a primary reason that people attended gatherings rather than to achieve sincere sociality. Yet these voices tended to be the minority. For most interviewees, sharing an interest in videos, engaging in cotemporal "shared happenings" such as attending meet-ups, collectively viewing and commenting on videos, collaborating on video projects, and hanging out socially were crucial activities for achieving community formation.

COMMENTERS WEIGH IN

Commenters who posted to my video revealed an interest in or at least curiosity about networked community. An analysis of these comments serves as the second line of evidence discussed in this chapter. Writing from the perspective of conducting anthropological research through digital ethnography, Pink and her colleagues propose the term "stakeholder ethnography" to characterize the practice of involving partners in research who are interested in similar issues but who "are not versed in the existing anthropological concepts that are commonly used to refer to such complex sets of relationships or with the debates underpinning them."[45] Stakeholders exhibit concerns similar to those of researchers, or at least demonstrate a willingness to collaboratively explore them.

Commenters interpellated themselves into the research as proposed stakeholders when they shared their views on how YouTube exhibits or complicates community formation.[46] Pink and her colleagues' ideas might be productively combined with the notion of "para-ethnography" as advanced by anthropologists Douglas Holmes and George Marcus. Para-ethnography is inquiry in which the proposed subjects of ethnography are engaged in similar intellectual work as that being conducted by the researcher. Although research participants are not aware of traditional anthropological theories, para-ethnography invites them to be "epistemic partners" with researchers to achieve a "common analytical exchange."[47] Drawing on the Malinowskian tradition of anthropology, para-ethnography invokes the "native point of view" while also recognizing ambiguities in the ethnographic encounter. Para-ethnography is meaningful for digitally based ethnographic projects because it is concerned with "analytical engagements" that examine "formations of culture that are not fully contingent on convention, tradition, and the past, but rather, constitute future-oriented cognitive practices that can generate novel configurations of meaning and action."[48] Para-ethnography in this context is concerned with identifying future possibilities of community formation through discourse-based analysis.

The random sample of 100 comments revealed three principal forms of engagement. They included videos that interacted with: (1) the video's content; (2) the video maker; and (3) other commenters. In addition to interactivity, other analytical categories included hating, spamming, profanity, whether the commenter posted more than one comment, and whether the comment appeared in an interactive comment thread (defined as two or more comments that include responses to others on the same topic).

Interactivity to content is defined as discussing information, ideas, or events in the video. The following is an example of a comment that is interactive to the video's content: "Its [*sic*] not a community as much as an online forum is. While it does allow for interaction, it doesn't cater for this as much as a forum. Youtube is more a platform to broadcast. IMO." In this case the commenter disagrees with the main findings of the video but responds to the main topic of the video. Comments that qualify as *interactive to the video maker* respond directly to the creator. Examples include "Check your headroom on interviews" or "CONGRATS PATRICIA!!!!!!!" While the former comment provides advice on how I should improve my technique, the latter comment shows support for my achievement of being featured.

A comment that is *interactive to another commenter* directly addresses another commenter or the substance of their post. For example, one commenter expressed confusion about why my video was anthropological, stating: "I think there is a [misunderstanding] here, an anthropology is the science of study of ancient [civilization], how they live, how they socialize or engage to each other." Another commenter exhibited interactivity with this commenter by offering to correct this impression: "The misunderstanding is yours. Anthropology studies human beings in all times and places doing all kinds of things. There are anthropologists studying Mcdonald's [*sic*] employee culture and fashion and memes and current practices of female genital mutilation etc." Commenters sometimes interacted with each other by discussing material within and surrounding the context of the video.

Comments could be interactive in more than one way, as in the following comment by fredrika27. The comment not only addresses the topic of the video but responds to another commenter. It also tacitly provides support to the video maker.

TABLE 5.1. Major Categories in the Random Sample of 100 Comments

Category	Number of Comments
Constructive commentary that addressed video content	36
Hater commentary	26
Commentary that addressed the video's quality or execution	18
Commentary that constructively addressed another commenter (on and off the video topic)	14
Commentary that unconstructively addressed another commenter	12
Interactively indeterminate	11
Commentary that addressed the video maker	8
Spam	8

Note: Comments could be coded in more than one category; therefore, the total is more than 100.

> What is your problem? This person happens to be undertaking serious research and asking legitimate questions. As a Youtuber, I take offense at your allegation. I have a BA, two MAs and a PhD. I've done research in the US, Germany and Kenya. Much [of] my research has been done in the internet community and helped people better understand their world.

The commenter is interactive to another commenter and analyzes the merits of my work. The comment responds to the content of the video by talking about research on the internet community. The commenter contributes to the creation of a "para-ethnography," by revealing personal background information such as educational achievement and experience conducting research on several internet communities.

In general, the commentary exhibited more interactivity (36 percent) than hate (26 percent). Given YouTube's reputation for problematic commentary, the random sample unsurprisingly included numerous hater comments containing pointlessly harsh criticism or profanity, such as "this is the most horrible video I have ever seen" and "what the fuck . . ." Hater comments also included sexualized or misogynist insults such as "What defines a community? a team of women working together to suck cock n balls. that's teamwork. especially when everyone is lending a helping hand. scrutum!" According to communication studies scholar Joseph Reagle, who engaged in a detailed study of online commentary, offensive remarks often reveal an intensely gendered dimension.[49]

Conversely, 36 percent of the random sample contained constructive commentary, which was defined as interacting with the video content without containing hate (see table 5.1 for a list of major categories).

The sample also contained a fair amount of spam (8 percent), such as chain-letter-type comments and solicitations to watch unrelated videos. Indecipherable comments were those that were acontextualized, rendering precise categorization difficult. An example of an indeterminate comment would be "Why are people so ignorant?" I surmised that this comment was targeted at other commenters. However, without further details, this comment could technically be addressing the interviewees within the video or the filmmaker herself.

Assessments of YouTube's Prospects for Community

Commenters in the sample expressed a more diverse assessment of whether YouTube was a community than did interviewees at meet-ups. Six commenters believed that YouTube was or could be a community, while two said it was partially a community. Eight commenters said it was not, while fifteen commenters did not weigh in using definitive judgments and were thus "neutral" comments. Twenty-one comments used the word "community," and an additional ten comments discussed dimensions of community without using the term. Some commenters solely weighed in with their opinion, such as the remark "It's a big community!!!" or "Youtube has none of the definitions of community. Sorry," while others rhetorically justified their view. For example, a comment by maggothon provided context for his opinion: "I [agree] timur ılenk, I have found such a community on YouTube and it has been a positive experience for me. I have made friends in several different countries as well as other parts of this country, we '[communicate], gather around ideas' and so on just as you said. I love it." Maggothon's comment is actually a response to another commenter called timurılenk. Over an interactive thread of four comments to each other, they agreed that YouTube was a community that was geographically dispersed and had facilitated friendship connections internationally. In this exchange the comment displayed two forms of interactivity. One form was related to the content of the video, and the other to another commenter.

Timurılenk's comment did not appear in the random sample and thus was not counted in the final tallies, but it is provided here for context. Timurılenk followed maggothon's comment with the following reply: "[YouTube] is world wide community giving everybody [possibility] to [exchange] the thoughts about something, to communicate world wide. People communicate, gathering around ideas, get organised about [ideas], influence on others by commenting or [posting] videos." In an earlier post Timurılenk expressed the belief that YouTube did not control comments and that this lack of censorship facilitates bridging differences in cultures, countries, and "even religions," thus echoing interviewees' notions of diversity as a defining characteristic of community. This comment thread is interesting not only because it shows how a video might stimulate reflection on a scholarly subject but also because it suggests the potential for spurring discussion between viewers themselves, yielding connected forms of learning. Rather than functioning pedantically, dialogic videos seek to stimulate reflection and discussion as commenters explore their truth.

Commenters might interact with video content by disagreeing with the interviewees' beliefs. A commenter named ShrinerMcbitey disagreed that YouTube was a community and stated:

> I'm sorry, but you are pathetic if this is your "community." One person commented he knew you tube better than his neighbors. . . . umm yeah thats [*sic*] a problem. And that's not what "community is all [about]." The internet in general may connect people who otherwise would not have, in [general] though electronic communication is bad communication. Remember communication is 85% non verbal.

ShrinerMcbitey not only disagrees that YouTube is a community but also judges people who believe that it is, calling them "pathetic." Particularly distressing to this commenter was ZenArcher's statement that he could know YouTubers more than his own neighbors. ShrinerMcbitey's objections echo earlier anthropological models of community as rooted to place. To the extent that interactivity is important, such comments are productive because they explore dimensions of the issue even if they disagree with content. Constructive comments may include justification for a person's views and may invite additional reflection.

Articulating a position and marshaling evidence to defend it are important steps for exploring civic issues. These comments suggest the potential for open, public discussions. Yet they also suggest that work is required to draw out viewers who wish to weigh in but may need participatory encouragement or development of rhetorical skills to craft arguments that bolster their positions.

Fifteen commenters engaged with the topic in a way that was "neutral"; they did not explicitly state whether they regarded YouTube as a community. An example of a neutral comment is the following post by danbergam: "A community is given by the interaction between human beings. The more is the sincere effort spent by each one of its members, the more that community is accomplished." The comment is weighted more toward exploring a definition for the term rather than expressing a direct opinion about the YouTube community. It is possible that viewers may try to infer from the comment whether YouTube resonates as a community. For example, viewers who believed that YouTube did offer the means to interact in "sincere" ways might infer that this definition qualified YouTube as a community.

In another neutral comment a poster named Fatpandas provided three scholarly citations for its definition:

A community is:

A collection of interdependent people who share a common residential locality and some feeling of belonging (Edgar, Earle and Flop, 1993)

or

Any social category or aggregate that [has] a shared sense of membership (Water and Cook, 1993)

or

set of independent and interacting members with a common identity and common fate with a set of ethics governing relationships. (Klessig, 1996)

Fatpandas' comment is constructive not only because it provides definitions but because it offers scholarly citations from sources that explore the meaning and application of the community concept. Such participation resembles "para-ethnography," in which researchers work alongside other experts or epistemological stakeholders in an investigative terrain.

In this case Fatpandas wrote themselves into the research project by sharing citations of potentially enlightening scholarly works. The first citation, which likely references Edgar, Earle, and Fopp's sociological work *Introduction to Australian Society* (1993), emphasizes residence and belonging as key criteria. The second citation, which may refer to Waters and Crook's *Sociology One: Principles of Sociological Analysis for Australians* (1993), emphasizes a shared sense of membership. This is constructive commentary because it widens the scope of knowledge sharing. Rather than only drawing on personal experiences, Fatpandas provides information that invites other commenters to consider multiple scholarly perspectives. Neutral comments that share key information are arguably just as important as expressions of clear-cut positions for expanding para-ethnographies. Rather than weighing in with views that are definitive but not well supported, neutral comments invite consideration of multiple dimensions of complex sociological concepts.

Criteria for Defining Community

A key goal for this exercise was to identify criteria that YouTubers used to assess community. Although no particular characteristic received a critical mass of agreement, four commenters said that some sense of sameness in terms of identity was important. In contrast, one commenter pointed out that diversity was an integral characteristic. While two commenters claimed that geography was important, three said that it was not. Four commenters noted that being able to communicate online was insufficient for guaranteeing community formation. Interestingly, Lennyfoshenny, a commenter who said that communities like

YouTube are being created because they bring together people from "different social situations," also noted that YouTubers "share many traits in common." It is the combination of both diversity and sameness that leads to feelings of closeness. Lennyfoshenny stated:

> In my opinion, a community does not have to be based on geographical location. I believe a community is where a tight bond between people is formed that includes people from all sorts of different social situations. Due to globalization today, people from across the world share many different traits in common, which is why communities like youtube are becoming far more easily created.

Definitional elements of community also included helping others, feeling a sense of safety, understanding one's social responsibility, knowing one's neighbors, feeling an intensive bond, exhibiting a "collective consciousness" (which echoes the posthuman discussion developed in chapter 6), and using similar forms of media. STEELPOT1's comment is particularly interesting because it evokes scholarly notions of "imagined community" that orient around mediated interaction and knowledge circulation that are temporally in sync. STEELPOT1 argued:

> [Community] . . . a microcosm, fraction of society. Entire United States is built of [these] "microcosms" based on geographical locations. Major town or county surrounded by locals. All watch the same weather, news, read the same paper etc.

In STEELPOT1's model, a community is a "fraction of society" that is based on geography. In line with Lefebvre's call to parse temporal influences, this answer echoes Anderson, whose analysis includes accessing and watching "the same weather" and "news" and reading "the same paper" at the same time in order to reinforce communal experiences.[50]

Critics of the imagined community concept suggest that it overemphasizes homogeneity, ignores the role of conflict, and pays insufficient attention to how institutional, political, and economic forces shape community.[51] Notably, themes of conflict and contestation appeared in the comments. A few argued that the authoritarian and economic forces that undergird YouTube complicate achieving genuine community. In one such comment, PresOfWeb noted:

> Youtube is a dictatorship. [Its] members don't establish the guidelines. Youtube is a business; it forces us to view ads for [its] sponsored videos. Youtube is a monopoly, buying out the competition.

PresOfWeb observed that participants do not establish their own guidelines and that strictures established by the corporate entity of YouTube are implemented for commercialization and profit. For some commenters, the word "community" could also connote a frivolous, banal, or insincere quality.[52] Commenters complained that celebrities on the site merely simulate an interest in fostering a community to self-promote. Maggothon stated:

> Anthrovlog: i agree. the word "commune" refers to the desire to "talk over" or "discuss" and "community" as a group of people having a common interest and being in the same vicinity is not a requirement. the level of commitment is what you are hearing here. these folks are more interested in dissing one another, you or the people on the film and that would not be a community, as they correctly state they are in it for the entertainment or to just make "comments." To be continued

Notably, maggothon reiterates the importance of community's rhetorical aspects by citing the importance of "communing" and "discussing" its parameters. Such a position echoes this chapter's main argument about the centrality of participation and discourse to create and sustain community. In a "meta" way, maggothon emphasizes the importance of ongoing dialogue by noting that the discussion is "to be continued."

Constructive Interactivity

Comments coded as constructive in this analysis included attributes such as offering a sincere reaction, justifying an opinion, critiquing the material discussed within the video, or adding information. More than one-third of the comments in the random sample addressed central content in the video, such as anthropology, community, or sociality. Interactivity among commenters suggests that under the right circumstances, networked dialogue through the circulation of visual research may be a productive exercise.

Interactivity also occurred between commenters who discussed themes in the video. Even strongly worded interactions could be intellectually productive, as in the following thread:

> blaggabloogy: Bottom Line . . . Youtube is a corporate entity established for the sole means of turning a profit. You guys are buying into this shit hook, line, and sinker.

> rabidzebu32: so true

> cavwondagainsti69: Um, as if every community isn't in some way a capitalist center, with excess as its agenda? face it. [Random sample comment #1]

> blaggabloogy: Some communities, not ALL. The Youtube "community" is simply in existence as the result of a corporate entity trying to make money. It was NOT established with the belief that it would—in any way—benefit its members. Good point

though. I just don't like the way they try to market the whole "Youtube" community facade. It's so phony. But, don't get me wrong, I'm all for Capitalism. Just get off the "community" ploy.

Cavwondagainsti69's comment is the one that appeared in the random sample, and it is clearly interactively posted in response to blaggabloogy's comment that YouTube is a "corporate entity." Blaggabloogy states that it is misguided to believe that community could emerge from a commercialized platform. Even worse, to believe that YouTube could be a community is to buy into a corporate agenda that uses such interpersonal rhetoric to lure in consumers who will watch videos, thereby justifying advertising and marketing tactics. Cavwondagainsti69 takes issue with this comment by stating that every community is entrenched in capitalism, thus challenging the idea that a corporate platform cannot promote community because of its commercial goals. Whether one agrees or disagrees with these strongly worded contentions, clearly commenters engaged with each another on relevant issues. This exchange is consistent with Julie Uldam and Tina Askanius's research findings on contentious climate debates on YouTube. Writing from the perspective of business and communicative theory, they found that even "hostile" exchanges could lead to "reciprocity" and "dialogue."[53]

In addition to interactivity as assessed in terms of engagement with video content or with other commenters, an additional category of interactivity included direct responses to the video maker. Eight percent of the comments included a remark addressed to me and were either positive (two comments) or negative (six comments) in their assessments of my approach or ability. For example, one commenter negatively stated, "this isn't funny at all. nice try but better luck next time," whereas another (from someone whom I had met previously in the video blogging community) said, "congrats, this is awesome!!!"

Commenters not only reflected on content; they also explored nuanced dimensions of intellectual concepts with other people, much the way students in a seminar might debate issues among themselves after being prompted by an instructor. In addition, just as classroom discussions exhibit tangents and heated exchanges, similar behaviors appeared in the video's commentary. Education is an ongoing process. Involving heterogeneous audiences in discussions about complex social science concepts will take time, patience, and cultivation of constructive self-expression.

Arrhythmic Acceptance

The random sample revealed that commenters experienced prospects for community at different rates, producing participatory arrhythmias, or what Lefebvre saw as multiple conflicting and discomforting rhythms. The interviewees and a few commenters clearly saw evidence that YouTube was a community or at least contained social support and interconnections that could facilitate it on the site. For instance, maggothon's comment above noted that he had "made friends in several different countries as well as other parts of this country." The experience had been "positive" for him, enabling him to "communicate" and to "gather around ideas."

Alternatively, some commenters in the random sample were only just learning that people were interacting on the site in this way. Building social closeness takes time, and comments revealed that YouTube participants were experiencing asymmetrical, arrhythmic knowledge of YouTube as a community. While some commenters such as ghostinvestigator began opening their minds to the possibility of achieving it after seeing the case study in the video, others remained skeptical. Ghostinvestigator exemplified a more positive reaction to community's prospects:

> I think this is great! With all the negativity that goes on in the internet world it's awesome to see people actually coming together for good. :)

Similarly, a commenter named garthward expressed more conservatism but acknowledged that aspects of a "global village" may exist, even if participants achieve awareness of it at different rates. The commenter discourages readers from becoming "obsessed," which also indicates trepidation with its acceptance: "Well . . . don't get obsessed with YT but it does delineate some aspects of the global village and collective consciousness even if some of us aren't aware of it yet." Commenters also exhibited skepticism about the feasibility of internet sociality given concerns about safety, as demonstrated in the comment from nitrofreakmanho:

> that was kind of weird . . . I never knew there was a Youtube gathering . . . what if some freak that you "think" you know shows up and then a kid goes missing . . . don't get me wrong, I think Youtube is great but this is different.

Commenters and interviewees did not accept the possibility of community at the same rate. They exhibited an arrhythmic pace of acceptance of community, which arguably limits its intensity to members of social groups that simultaneously experience an ethos of community. Commensurate with Lefebvre's and Anderson's analyses, the simultaneity of acceptance emerged as a factor in facilitating YouTube community. As the YouTube case shows, websites tend to exhibit relatively short cycles of intensive participation (roughly three to five years) before people in specific social groups move on, sometimes to newer, cooler sites. This implies that asymmetrical temporal acceptance of community on websites complicates widespread and possibly sustained uptake in sociality. While a few commenters expressed openness and interest in sociality once they encountered it through the video, others acknowledged its possibilities but were not ready to embrace it fully because of their concerns. *What Defines a Community?* appeared to a mass audience who exhibited diverse interpretations, some of them accepting of its content. Other commenters engaged in adversarial or even unintended readings of its ethnographic findings.

Aberrant Readings

When sharing their work, visual anthropologists are concerned with how audiences will receive the material. Particularly disturbing are scenarios in which viewers engage in what Peruvian filmmaker and visual anthropologist Wilton Martínez calls "aberrant readings" of films. Aberrant readings contradict a filmmaker's communicative intentions and only "reinforce stereotypes of otherness."[54] It is safe to say that comments such as "BOO dorks! old fat people!" constitute aberrant readings of *What Defines a Community?* Such comments reference images in the video, but not in meaningful or respectful ways. They refer to people in the video but reinforce negative ageist and weightist stereotypes. My video intended to visually depict people of diverse groups who explored well-articulated thoughts about community.

One solution is to provide fuller context for ethnographic videos. Pink argues that "a limitation of anthropological film is that it lacks the cultural contextualization and theoretical explicitness that are sometimes necessary to promote cross-cultural understanding."[55] One approach involves using the technical features of video-platforms including accompanying text, video lectures, or digital annotations that could be overlaid on videos.

However, using such tools does not guarantee their use or *their* adequate interpretation.[56] Anthropologist Peter Wogan observed that students may respond in playful or disrespectful ways to uncomfortable material, even when viewing high-quality ethnographic films *in serious classroom settings*. Wogan studied classroom reactions to classical visual ethnographies. He observed that abruptly incongruous juxtapositions of images influenced interpretation. Unexpected images, such as an indigenous man wearing a tin-can headpiece, prompted responses such as laughter—even when students were prepared to experience visual, cultural differences.[57]

Providing too much classroom mentorship or information in visual works may also complicate student exploration of nuanced material. Wogan argues that "we should recognize our capacity as instructors to fill in filmic gaps that trouble us, and we should allow students to wrestle with complexities."[58] Dialogical approaches carry risk as they may reinforce stereotypes. However, it is also true that avoiding dealing with offensive stereotypes does nothing to dispel them. An argument exits that through diversity in discussion, insight may one day be achieved.

UNMASKING ANONYMITY'S ROLE IN DISCOURSE

A central debate in discourses about the effectiveness of networked knowledge exchange concerns the role of anonymity.[59] Specifically, it is believed that the assumed anonymity of interactants is largely responsible for problematic behaviors, such as posting mean-spirited or even threatening comments. These concerns prompt an investigation into what extent anonymity influenced the timbre of discourse in the present study. Notably, being anonymous online does not create commenters' prior rampant racism, homophobia, sexism, or other prejudices; those who engage in hurtful discourse at root likely already hold these biases or at least exhibit a willingness to perpetuate them online. People bring prior interaction patterns to digital milieus, as renowned linguist and communication scholar Susan Herring observed. She studied gendered forms of aggressive argumentation and personal attacks, or "flaming," in an online professional linguistics forum in the 1990s.[60] She found that males exhibited more aggressive styles and were easily identified as men by community members, even when they pretended to be women. Elaborate identity ruses are increasingly difficult to maintain *over time*.

People post anonymously online every day without spouting hate simply because they can (try to) do so anonymously. For instance, in a study of politically themed Usenet groups discussing inflammatory subjects such as gun control and racism, communication scholar Zizi Papacharissi found that anonymity used for impoliteness was not the norm, thus dismantling the technologically deterministic view of mediated anonymity as inevitably problematic.[61] Discussants in the study often apologized or expressed regret when discussions veered out of control.

Numerous studies demonstrate that anonymity is not the leading offender in many contexts. Writing from the field of political communication, Myiah Hutchens and her colleagues drew on surveys of undergraduates and people who frequent political blogs to analyze flaming intentions, where flaming is defined as hurtful personal attacks. Within the student sample they found that "contrary to prior research, anonymity was not a significant predictor of flaming intention."[62] Instead, the researchers noted that individuals tended to respond with hostility when their *political beliefs were challenged*. For the study on blog users, anonymity only increased people's disposition to flame when their views received indirect challenges. The researchers concluded that local norms in digital environments significantly shaped flaming behaviors. Types of activity (such as intense political discussions) and media dispositions (such as seeing flaming as acceptable) were more predictive of flaming than anonymity.

Conversely, in the present random sample, most of the constructive, interactive comments came from commenters who were anonymous to me. All but two of the constructive comments came from posters whom I had never (knowingly) met. Just because commenters were anonymous to me does not guarantee that I was anonymous to them—indeed anonymity works two ways. Given that the majority of *positive* commentary came from *anonymous* posters, it becomes difficult to support the claim that anonymity is the main culprit behind degraded online interaction. Why do concerned citizens never propose that anonymity should be *encouraged*, whenever *anonymous positive* discourse appears? Reversing the standard proposition reveals the problematics of focusing on anonymity rather than dealing with underlying societal prejudices and creating useful pedagogical strategies that could improve participatory literacies.

When aggressive commentary meets standard definitions of harassment, it should be dealt with accordingly, involving legal entities as necessary. However, in many gray areas one person's "hater" comment is another person's blunt critique. A harsh comment for some might seem to others to be a legitimate means of self-expression and knowledge exchange. Consider whether the following comment posted by truesign constitutes hating:

> horse [biscuits]!! its [*sic*] just video made by people who want to get noticed or
> become famous most of the videos are lame if it got rid of the crap it might be some-
> thing but right now it crap.too many idiots no content. sad sad sad.[63]

Truesign's comment is strongly (and awkwardly) worded and contains the word "crap" twice. YouTube is seen as "lame" and exhibiting "no content" because it is filled with "too many idiots." The comment echoes often-heard popular and scholarly claims that people use YouTube and tropes of community to "get noticed or become famous." Assessing hater commentary can be subjective, and opinions may change according to who is posting, viewing, or coding the commentary.[64] Yet categorizations are crucial given that appropriate solutions depend on understanding the types of violations that cause individuals harm.

Anonymity is often conflated with accountability, which are two different concepts. The argument goes that because online interaction is anonymous, it is mean-spirited and will meet with no consequences. Precisely speaking, this is an overgeneralization. It is possible to be anonymous in terms of withholding personal information from one's general audience, yet still have one's comments blocked by a fellow YouTuber. One's account might be closed for violating the terms of service. One can be relatively anonymous but still experience consequences. Conversely, criminal acts occurring in person, such as illegal police brutality, may result in no legal consequences, even when perpetrators' identities are known and widely publicized.

When individuals exhibit persistent, identifiable behaviors across the same account names or nicknames online, they become *pseudonymous* rather than completely anonymous.[65] Over time it may become relevant and desirable for administrators to marshal resources to trace and block pseudonymous users' IP addresses. In some cases, "digital detective work" such as issuing subpoenas to obtain IP addresses from website operators and service providers have identified harassers.[66] Administrators may complicate perpetrators' ability to be repeat offenders.[67] It is important to analytically tease apart anonymity—or rather pseudonymity—from accountability. Although there is a relationship, they are not isomorphic.

Even when measures are introduced to ostensibly reduce anonymity, comment cordiality does not automatically improve. Reagle discusses an initiative in which the social media platform of Google+ was integrated into YouTube in 2013, yet was quickly removed in 2015 due to uproar from users.[68] The idea behind the integration was to reduce anonymity, since comments would be linked to an "identifiable Google+ profile" with a user's supposed official name.[69] A result of this integration was that trolls and spammers continued their work. Further, the move alienated many legitimate social media users who had "relied on pseudonymity for safety" due to unfortunate circumstances, such as being harassed by stalkers.[70]

Hundreds of thousands of users reportedly signed petitions in protest,[71] and YouTube cofounder Jawed Karim angrily wondered, "Why the fuck do I need a google+ account to comment on a video?"[72] Online participation includes a balance of features and functionality, including protecting privacy. People may not wish to be forced into interaction that is mandated to reduce anonymity. Ostensibly such moves are about improving commentary, but they arguably facilitate more targeted advertising. Reducing anonymity is often pitched for cordiality but is used by corporations to track consistent consumer patterns.

Removing (assumed) anonymity is not necessarily an acceptable solution in all civic contexts. Lovink argues that people may fight for a "right to anonymity."[73] For example, journalists have maintained a right to protect anonymous sources so that the weak can expose corruption among the powerful. Lovink provides an interesting thought experiment by asking, what would happen if all of our voting decisions were made public? It is one thing to disclose information about our politics on social media voluntarily; it is quite another to have our voting record immediately available for coworkers and employers to judge our professional merit on the basis of our politics. A certain amount of anonymity is healthy in particular contexts.

Despite the fact that online anonymity has now been "effectively destroyed" through technological tracing mechanisms, Lovink argues that "the vast majority of the internet population still considers the internet a free-for-all playground where you can say anything you like."[74] In a study of social media across the world, anthropologist Daniel Miller and his colleagues concluded that "with regard to social media, the issue of anonymity has reversed into a concern over lack of privacy."[75] Although the prevailing folk assumption is that harassment is always anonymous, in fact people routinely reveal their prejudices and biases using their official names. Examples abound in which people nonanonymously engage in incendiary online interaction,[76] with offenders of violent threats sometimes having a traceable, public history of violence offline as well.[77] As Reagle observes, people may be surprised to learn that "embarrassing" and "nasty" comments are frequently "made in the open and beyond the cover of anonymity."[78]

If we apply a temporal lens, it is clear that anonymity is not a steady state. It can be reduced or removed in particular circumstances. Whether people in a given encounter will work to reduce mutual anonymity depends upon whether it is *relevant* to do so, whether they have a strong enough *desire* to go through the process, and whether they have the appropriate *resources* to track down a commenter's identity information. For example, how much does one need to know the official name or home address of a commenter who contributes interesting critiques or who provides anonymous help through a digital service? There is no relevance or desire to obtain this information in casual discourse. In the case of harassment, it is obviously relevant and desirable to track down perpetrators and bring them to justice.

Over time, one's interlocutors become more familiar as they exhibit behavioral patterns using the same pseudonym. Identifiable traits include consistent speech habits, preferred modes of interaction, and repeated engagement with specific discussion topics.[79] In my video I noted two cases of hater commenters that provided clues about their personality, even though I did not know them personally. Leaving such digital footprints means that even the most secretive anonymous interactants—even hackers—may end up being publicly identified,[80] especially when, as I suggest, *there is sufficient relevance, resources, and desire to do so.*

All of the hater commenters were anonymous to me in that I had never knowingly met them. Two commenters—microwavefishsticks and teddieppl77—exhibited hate and behavioral regularities across their comments. Their commentary was similar in that it was filled with mean-spirited forms of hate and prejudices. Microwavefishsticks appeared twice in the random sample with this kind of commentary:

> The best communities are the ones with every asshole on the planet coming together. Jews, blacks, mexicans, racists, homos, whites, haters, lovers, retards, scholars, assholes, truck drivers, circus freeks [*sic*]. This is just a bunch of fat boring white trash telling everyone they should be like them.
>
> Fuck you

Similarly, teddieppl77 also appeared twice in the random sample, contributing this comment: "See no one likes to look at fat ppl. If you are fat I want you to know that, I am one of the ppl that laugh at you as you jiggle by."

Examining their commentary in the random sample yields a prediction that their commentary across the entire corpus of comments posted to the video would contain similarly hateful and prejudiced comments. These predictions were confirmed. In the entire corpus of 1,906 comments posted to the video, microwavefishsticks contributed a total of 43 comments, of which 40 (93 percent) qualified as hater commentary because it contained profanity, misogyny, and other prejudices. This behavior pattern was remarkably consistent across this commenter's participation in the video discussion. Although I do not know the person's official name, I know that microwavefishsticks posts hater messages in a public forum and that their commentary formed at least 2 percent of the total comments.

Examining the commentary of teddieppl77 yielded a similar result. Teddieppl77 contributed a total of 101 comments to the video, of which 83 percent were hater comments; 42 percent of his remarks commented on weight. Teddieppl77's commentary was also remarkably consistent, often engaging in petty battles with other commenters and routinely expressing a rejection of "fat people." Elsewhere teddieppl77 claims to be an "Aussie." Although I do not "know" these posters, their behavior patterns were consistent across the entire corpus of comments, which provided identification clues.[81]

A crucial question is, how did anonymity impact constructive commentary? Although haters were anonymous to me, so too were the people who contributed positive commentary. Anonymity was not a useful predictor of problematic commentary in the random sample. In fact, anonymous posters were the key drivers of constructive commentary in the discourse. Such findings complicate the mythos that anonymity is principally the problem in galvanizing support for public anthropology and stakeholder-driven "para-ethnographies."

The flip side of the assumption that anonymity creates agonism is that knowing one's interlocutors guarantees in-depth dialogue. Yet the study results did not confirm this assumption. Very few of my online acquaintances posted comments. I personally knew two commenters from the random sample who posted comments. I greatly appreciated their support, but the comments did not advance the discussion by engaging with content. One comment came from an acquaintance whom I had met in the video blogging community outside of YouTube; it read: "congrats, this is awesome!!!" Presumably the congratulations had to do with being featured on the YouTube welcome page. The other was a comment from someone whom I had interviewed in San Francisco. This comment was part of a thread in which the commenter argued with another commenter who had posted insulting remarks.

Although I appreciated that the commenter tackled a hater in my defense, the comment did not engage with the video's content. The reality is that knowing the identities of commenters did not guarantee their interactive engagement with the video's central subject.

Conversely, identities are not fully revealed, even in person. When interacting with others, what we know (or what we think we know) about people only has a *probabilistic* likelihood of being correct.[82] We may assume we know people when we meet them in person, but our confidence may be misplaced through interpretive arrogance or because a situation is complicated. Consider the Olympian Bruce Jenner, a transgender female. For years, people who interacted with her in person (including her most intimate family members) assumed she saw herself as a man.[83] These observers may have felt 100 percent sure that their assessment was correct. These same people would have been 100 percent wrong. Her childhood experiences, lifelong cross-dressing, and transition to being a woman called Caitlyn suggest, as was demonstrated in sociological research back in the 1960s,[84] that our assumptions about people *in person* are nowhere near foolproof.

This study argues that it is time to move beyond the obsession with anonymity for understanding online dynamics.[85] Anonymity, or at least partial anonymity, is part of daily life. When we engage in civic discussions, we need rhetorical skills to persuade publics who are largely unknown to us.[86] Further, it can be just as important for digital ethnographic research to cultivate "weak ties," as discussed by sociologist Mark Granovetter.[87] Weak ties may exhibit a low investment in time and energy with an ethnographer or within a specific ethnographic project, but such participants nevertheless help the ethnographer cultivate information from a "vast knowledge space."[88]

Unless we are content to persuade only our close family and friends about important social issues, we will need to connect with and convince people largely unknown to us regarding issues of civic concern. Notably, more research is needed to understand how anonymity encourages people to speak out, particularly on sensitive or controversial topics. It is also important to focus on supporting those who are being harmed rather than only on transgressors.[89] We need to refocus the dialogue away from overemphasis on anonymity, which in any event is becoming difficult to guarantee in digital spaces and is a poor predictor of commentary's usefulness. We need to intensify peer mentorship and deploy social and technical solutions that redirect public dialogue in productive directions.

EXPECTATIONS FOR COMMENTARY AND NEXT STEPS

Much has been written about the paucity of engagement with serious topics on YouTube. Researchers have understandably expressed skepticism about the prospects for online information sharing and sincere discussion on video sites, especially given their propensity to exhibit hurtful and off-topic commentary.[90] I share concerns about whether it makes sense to try these dialogic, public engagements. However, assessments of online commentary are often limited to structural considerations, often without considering key factors that may influence a video's reception, such as whether the content actually addresses viewers' concerns. For example, one study examined commentary on a public service announcement posted to YouTube, which aimed to discourage teens from smoking marijuana.[91] The study focused on ludic comments that did not appear to take the warning seriously. Although the study acknowledged some of the positive commentary and debate that the video generated, it ultimately concluded that YouTube's playful atmosphere forecloses the entire site from having any prospects for public deliberation.

Notably, the study did not consider additional factors, such as whether teens find this topic necessary for a public service announcement. Nearly half of the US population now supports legalization of marijuana for recreational use.[92] Studies criticizing YouTube's potential often focus on the negative comments in a "glass half empty" way rather than building on the engaged participation that frequently appears in research studies of commentary.

The present findings exhibit patterns more similar to those in a study investigating the prospects for civic engagement on YouTube in the environmental realm. In an analysis of comments posted to a climate change activism video called *War on Capitalism*, researchers noted that approximately 30 percent of the comments were isolated rather than threaded and 20 percent contained abusive language such as "I hope you fucking die!"[93] However, the researchers observed that most of the commentary appeared within threads of conversation; even some of the hostile comments engaged in reciprocal dialogue. Researchers discounted concerns about the site's structural limitations, such as the limited numbers of characters allowed in individual postings, principally because they observed workarounds that bypassed these limits. Social media participants might break their posts into several comments to relay their point.[94] The researchers concluded that, although the discussions did not conform to idealized Habermasian debate, such comments served a civic function. Even hostility could lead to reciprocal and interactive engagement.

Pundits have observed that when one engages large publics with *any kind* of material, one usually encounters the "30 percent rule": roughly 30 percent of the viewers will love the work, 30 percent will hate it, and about 30 percent will be indifferent.[95] Intriguingly, the numbers presented by the *War on Capitalism* comment study and the present analysis show a breakdown that is not far from these heuristics in terms of content interactivity (36 percent) and hatery (26 percent). Whether such observations are consistent across diverse sets of video commentary is an empirical question. The point is that one should probably expect to receive large numbers of detractors when engaging with very large and disparate public audiences. Notably, at least some proportion of commenters will also likely engage with the material, other YouTube participants, the video maker, or all of these.

One solution involves taking active steps to redress hate speech. Writing from the perspective of improving internet safety, journalist Courtney Radsch investigated female journalists' responses to online misogyny.[96] While some women responded by "letting it go," others took active approaches that included taking screenshots and reporting abuse (the "name and shame" approach). Documenting and publicly shaming abusers helped some female journalists to deal with harassment on personal as well as professional levels. In one instance an Australian journalist discovered that her harassers on Facebook were children. She accessed their mothers' profiles and sent them screenshots of their children's posts. She even received an apology letter from one of the children. Radsch offers solutions for changing commenter behavior. An example might include having people go through training programs before being allowed on social media. She proposes "shifting cultural norms so that such attacks become unacceptable."[97] Radsch's "multifaceted" solutions and analytical energy focus on recognizing and changing participatory problems.

Comment moderation has been a long-standing tactic in online environments, as was illustrated by the reflections of one attendee at a New York City gathering in 2007. He officially refers to himself as Mike Street on YouTube; he is the creator of the blog GreasyGuide.com as well as *Smart Brown Voices*, a podcast that invites listeners to "Learn from Successful Black and Latino Startup Founders, Entrepreneurs, Activists, Marketers and Creatives."

Mike Street was a black man approximately in his late twenties. His videos included vlogs, interviews with black celebrities, gaming content, and social issues, such as tax hikes and voting. As of July 2018, he had 571 subscribers and his videos often garner thousands of views each. A very early adopter, he joined YouTube in December 2005, just as it became available to the public. Characterized on his podcast as a "social media nerd" and "technology activist," he had served as a community manager for online sites. A decade later he worked in social media, marketing, and media consulting.

Mike felt that YouTube should increase its vigilance in removing inappropriate commentary. In my vlog *YouTube Your Way*, posted on October 2, 2007, his interview responses articulated the often-heard criticism of YouTube as a "free-for-all."[98] He believed the site should provide a more participatory atmosphere, at a minimum using automated "filters" to deal with unacceptably inappropriate commentary. Mike believed it was important to keep a site's tone positive. His practice was to remove any comment that was "sexist, racist, or homophobic." He stressed that people should express their opinion—until they cross a participatory line.

Several solutions have been suggested to deal with YouTube's problematic commentary. One proposal involves reputation systems that rate commenters to reduce negative behavior patterns. YouTube instituted a commenter rating system that enabled viewers to rate a comment as thumbs up or down. The system identifies "top comments," ostensibly to prioritize those that achieve high ratings and numerous comment responses. However, the up-down comment rating is perceived as a rather crude mechanism. Similar to Mike Street's suggestion, in 2013 YouTube instituted a "blacklisting" feature that enabled creators to review posts with certain words before they were posted.[99] In 2016 YouTube instituted mechanisms such as moderators and algorithms to detect inappropriate comments and to hold them for review.[100] Identifying a convenient formula for dealing with these issues will be difficult. Decisions about how to deal with haters vary by situation and individual disposition, and a valid choice may be to take a break or cease interaction when hate-filled commentary becomes overwhelming.

A more extreme solution involves disabling commentary altogether. In examining online discourse from a communication studies perspective, Joseph Reagle observed patterned cycles of comment inclusion and exclusion. Prominent bloggers, fed up with comment abuse, disabled comment features on their sites. However, after protests from viewers, comments became re-enabled along with technical or social features to deal with negative commentary. This approach is said to be like "cultivating a garden" in that if the weeds are pruned, "flowers will begin to grow."[101] Reagle's observations are particularly interesting, as they illustrate what Lefebvre identified as important, cyclical behavior that reveals cultural patterns and values. Digital sites see initial enthusiasm and growth of comments, and then face decline and death when comments are disabled. In answer to his book's final question about whether commentary is ultimately worth it, Reagle concluded, "Comment is a characteristic of contemporary life," and given that commentary is here to stay, "we must find ways to use it effectively."[102] To improve the quality of interactivity, he advocates cultivating "comment communities," in part by reading, acknowledging, and finding ways to deal with the comments "at the bottom of the Web."

YOUTUBERS' VIDEO MEDITATIONS ON COMMUNITY

If we apply Lefebvre's rubric, it is clear that YouTube's community operated in linear and cyclical ways, depending on levels of analysis under study. It functioned in a linear sense when examined at the scale of analysis within a particular group. Participation developed and intensified over the course of a couple of years in a linear trajectory from inception to decline. Yet it was also apparent that community took on a cyclical quality when analyzed across the website. As newcomers arrived, some of them began to use the site interactively in their social circles and explored possibilities for achieving community.

Community continues to be a popular topic on YouTube. In June 2018 a search for the term "YouTube community" revealed tens of thousands of videos. In addition to interviews and comments, the third line of evidence examined in this chapter concerns analyzing how YouTubers discuss community in their own videos. When they speculate on its prospects, they are arguably conceptualizing YouTube as a perceived social space rather than only a website or service. Videos that address the topic reveal disagreements between supporters and skeptics. Opinions are expressed again as new media generations appear on YouTube. In a video entitled *Little Youtube #community*, a white transgender video maker in her early twenties whose YouTube channel name was OneTakeAsh referenced the gratitude she felt toward popular video makers who supported her when she was a "little YouTuber" with a mere 200 subscribers.[103] As of June 2018, she had 435,617 subscribers. OneTakeAsh's videos regularly saw several thousand views each. She vlogs on subjects such as gender, white male privilege, contemplating top surgery, and her relationships. Her video about YouTube community was posted on August 10, 2014, nearly five years after she joined the site.

In the video she reveals that when her channel amassed 10,000 subscribers, she felt deeply appreciative of those popular YouTubers who had helped her. She also sought to do "collabs" with "little Youtubers" who demonstrated a genuine interest in community. She characterized the work of many "big YouTubers" as predictable, formulaic, less interesting, and less authentic to watch. YouTubers, including young people like herself, expressed interest in collaborating in social ways and cultivating lesser-known voices.

Conversely, videos on the site also explore complications for engaging with a community. In a video posted on December 13, 2014, called *THE YOUTUBE COMMUNITY SUCKS!?*, a popular YouTuber whose channel name is BRITTNEYLEESAUNDERS (also her official name) admits that it would be great if the site were more "tight knit" and more people were "friends." At the time of the video's posting, she had been participating on the site for over three years. Brittney was an Australian woman in her early twenties whose videos revolved around subjects such as makeup, answering viewers' questions about her, Australians trying foods, and YouTube characteristics. Her topics appear to garner widespread viewership and monetization. In one video she notes that she would be open to acting professionally. Her videos typically saw hundreds of thousands of views each. As of June 2018, she had over 1 million subscribers. Brittney argues that people are embroiled in a "competition" for attention and, presumably, advertising revenue from ads placed on videos. She describes a tension that surfaces on platforms that simultaneously encourage sociality and self-promotion.

Videos such as these prototypically reflect the discourse that YouTubers engage in when trying to make sense of their mediated social formation. Videos on community continue to appear from YouTubers of different eras. Over a decade after the site's launch, creators are still discussing prospects for community on YouTube. The recurrence of discussions about community demonstrates that the concept remains open to negotiation as each media generation arrives and must collectively assess its merits and possibilities as a meaningful interactive frame.

LEARNING BY GOING "VIRAL"

Lessons for the future may be drawn from the present exercise as well as past experiments with YouTube pedagogy. Participating on YouTube as a video maker, sharing one's research publicly, and collecting data through commentary are exercises that lie at the intersection of research and experimental pedagogy. Lessons learned from varied levels of participation across different projects must be examined to see how attempts at public pedagogy might be shaped. Sites that follow video traffic maintain that educational videos rank among the top ten most popular videos on YouTube. Key to their success is serving children and college students, providing up-to-date information, and grappling with complex issues.[104]

Efforts to share research with the people that one studies using visual means is part of a long scholarly tradition in visual anthropology. Anthropologist Jean Rouch posited the idea of a "shared anthropology" that would include screening one's work with community insiders with whom a researcher hoped to engage.[105] However, creating *digital* materials while drawing on visual anthropology insights is still a relatively new field. Anthropologist Sarah Pink argues that "although the number of practitioners of this type of digital visual anthropology is steadily increasing, as yet it is the domain of a narrow group."[106]

Pink highlights early pioneers working at the intersection of digital and visual anthropology.[107] She references the work of Peter Biella, Napoleon Chagnon, and Gary Seaman, who created the Yanomamö Interactive CD-ROM project in 1997, as well as the visual anthropology of Jay Ruby, who established a website and welcomed contributions from the people in his ethnographic study of Oak Park, Illinois. In 2018, anthropologist Robert Lemelson and a team at the University of California, Los Angeles (UCLA) released *Tajen: Interactive*, a web documentary that uses multiple senses to explore ritual and emotional aspects of contemporary Balinese cockfighting, thus supplementing Clifford Geertz's classic work.[108]

Numerous educational videos have appeared on YouTube from countless institutions. Notable examples are the videos from the *Why We Post* (2016–2018) global social media project run by anthropologist Daniel Miller at University College London (UCL). However, the UCL researchers do not study YouTube; they use it to post information about their research results about other media.[109] The present work showed advantages and challenges of collecting data by discussing the same site on which one is participating. Collecting data as well as sharing anthropological research enabled forms of "para-ethnography" in which stakeholders were interpellated into a collective discussion that drew on multiple levels and types of expertise rather than only on those of the professor or facilitator.

Media scholar Alexandra Juhasz launched a well-publicized experiment by teaching a class called *Learning from YouTube* directly on the site in 2007. All of the students' assignments were constructed as YouTube videos or comments. Class sessions were recorded and posted to the site, and a press release was issued, thus opening the classroom to the general public.[110] Such exercises take on a self-reflexive quality. The course and the experience of learning online morphed into the mediated phenomena that the class was exploring.[111]

Similar to the present study, Juhasz reports that the scale of commentary was exhausting to deal with and students were mocked. Ultimately, the poor quality of videos and comments, lack of technical features to link materials to the discussion, commercial influences, and time demands on the students and the professor led Juhasz to conclude, "YouTube is not made for higher education, nor should it be."[112] Collectively, our studies suggest that scale is a crucial factor. Aiming for more circumspect audiences may be easier to handle in terms of tailoring content and dealing with feedback. Clearly, teaching directly on YouTube exhibits considerable challenges. Individual educators must decide how much they will tackle, and it is a legitimate decision to forgo public engagement.

Notably, Juhasz also observed that students learned from the experiment, including crucial meta-lessons about what and how students learn, especially within the parameters of specific technical infrastructures. By participating on YouTube despite its challenges, it is possible to understand how people learn by exchanging commentary, not only with the video maker/scholar but with other commenters. Future video-sharing platforms might address these limitations by being more nimble in providing access to information as a connected exchange is unfolding. Commenters in the present study at times invoked scholarly sources to support their arguments, suggesting that access to informational links could raise the bar in interactive discussions.

Anthropologist Michael Wesch also participated in experimental video pedagogy by posting an original video of his, called *The Machine Is Us/ing Us*, on March 8,

2007. The video went "viral" and had accumulated over 1.7 million views as of June 2018. The video argues that "with no code to learn, any person can create and organize information and thus, 'teach the machine.' In turn, the machine uses people to create links between different information streams and between its users."[113] In addition, Wesch launched a highly lauded Digital Ethnography project, which includes videos, lectures, and publications to explore the relationships between culture, technology, and education.

Wesch learned much from his digital experiences that might help craft future approaches.[114] He discovered that it was possible for an academic without professional training in filmmaking to collaborate with others and to reach millions of people. He learned that it was possible not only to reach fellow anthropologists but also to cross disciplinary boundaries. Despite the fact that the experience was generally positive, Wesch remains circumspect about unbridled use of technology in the classroom. Recent works focus on thinking more fundamentally about the relationship between teachers and students. According to Wesch, "The real secret of great teaching" and a "force more powerful and disruptive than any technology" is "love."[115]

Similar in spirit to the present study, Wesch advocates creating what Parker J. Palmer has called a "community of truth,"[116] in which the professor is not the final authority of objective facts in more interpretive fields but rather students and teachers interactively and dynamically collaborate in an ongoing search for knowledge to foster "openness to the world, to each other, and to difference."[117] While continuing to explore digital tools, Wesch's work focuses on interpersonal, pedagogical philosophies for inspiration. Models based on communities of truth are appealing for pedagogical experimentation as researchers, educators, and the general public may work together to create shared environments that facilitate interaction and information exchange.

Not all participation can be fully controlled, as when one's work goes viral. Even when networked projects are designed to scale, they always have the potential to reach—for better or worse—far larger audiences, as Wesch and I experienced. Approaching the topic from an information studies perspective, Karine Nahon and Jeff Hemsley argue that quality and professional training are not necessarily benchmarks for virality if a work has salience or personal emotional resonance for people sharing it.[118] The term "viral" connotes an artifact's rapid spread and reach across a critical mass of individual viewers and varied networks. Nahon and Hemsley define virality as "a social information flow process where many people simultaneously forward a specific information item, over a short period of time, within their social networks, and where the message spreads beyond their own [social] networks to different, often distant networks, resulting in a sharp acceleration in the number of people who are exposed to the message."[119] Some scholars object to this term because the definition of "viral" is variable and carries a connotation of illness. Writing from the perspective of media studies, Jenkins, Ford, and Green prefer the term "spreadable."[120]

What Defines a Community? received many more views and comments within a few days than did any of my other videos. Whether the views were generated in a top-down "broadcast" way because people watched it as soon as they encountered it on YouTube's welcome page or whether it received a viral "bottom-up" surge from rapid sharing is impossible to know. YouTube was not yet collecting information on sharing metrics at the time of the video. Nahon and Hemsley argue that it is difficult to achieve a wide audience through top-down promotion alone,[121] suggesting that my video saw at least some views through bottom-up sharing.

Nahon and Hemsley state that artifacts such as videos may constitute an individual viral event but that a particular discourse may also go viral, giving rise to "viral topics."[122] In viral topics, subjects of interest become part of a larger "mediated conversation" with many different artifacts playing a role. The subject of community received a great deal of attention on the site. My video was clearly part of a larger viral topic of interest—one that provided a prime opportunity to engage with a broader public while collecting data.

In contrast to previous, bold experimentation, my project modestly aimed to see if publicly circulating a scholarly video or "open video field note" and sharing findings-in-progress might stimulate discussion about classical anthropological concepts as they applied in mediated environments. Instead of considering traditional and online educational forms as oppositional, this approach is commensurate with discovering new ways to create more open classroom connections in which learning may occur in fluid ways such that researchers and audiences work toward creating a knowledge-based, ethically grounded "community of truth."[123]

Creating connections not only imparts information about content through videos, but as Juhasz demonstrated, students may viscerally experience meta-lessons about how they learn in technologized ways. In line with de Seta's dialogical approach, discourse posted to any single video should be considered merely an opening volley in a series of exchanges between scholars and audiences. Rather than adjudicate a definitive answer to the query on what defines a community, this chapter argued that it is far more productive to keep asking the question.

COMMUNITY AS PROCESSUAL

Most interviewees believed that under the right circumstances, YouTube could facilitate community—often in spite of its commercialized infrastructure. YouTubers' reasons for envisioning the site as a potential springboard for community were broad and diverse. This project adds to the anthropological record by investigating how their definitions mapped to scholarly conceptions. Drawing from ethnographic data, the study found that community was discursively perceived as a process, one that must be negotiated through discourse as well as through participation in co-temporally shared moments of interaction. Processes of community building stem from discussing and debating what constitutes meaningful community in specific milieus.

YouTube is often dismissed as incapable of offering meaningful interaction, and vernacular videos and comments are judged harshly. In fact, there are videos of high quality on the site that are not necessarily made by professionals. Part of the problem involves finding videos that are not being promoted or featured on YouTube but that have meaning to audiences even if their quality is not at the highest standard. Michael Newman, a scholar in journalism and mass communication, argues, "No longer is professionalism assumed to be the norm and standard of quality. The notion that do-it-yourself amateurism can stand on equal ground with media industry professionalism signals a democratic challenge to hierarchies of aesthetic value."[124] In her research on viral music videos, film and media studies scholar Carol Vernallis, who is often dismayed by the site's video quality, also observes that many of her students create impressive videos, even using modest tools, and they receive upward of 1,000 views.[125] Vernallis's findings suggest that creative energies could be harnessed for establishing connected forms of learning through grassroots media—as long as the topic sparked meaningful engagement.

A thriving discourse of community continues to appear in YouTube videos and comments.[126] My video served as a form of "para-ethnography" in which viewers interpellated themselves as stakeholders into a discussion about community formation. Videos and other artifacts offer moments of reflection on topics that require ongoing negotiation. Although researchers have long known that communities can spring from digital milieus, it is not a given that a particular group of creators operating within a specific combination of techno-cultural circumstances will agree that the platform inspires that level of bonding.

If community is processual, then it will require spaces and platforms to negotiate its development and maintenance. Wesch's references to "communities of truth" are appealing in this context because they collaboratively involve students in identifying high-quality material that students might create. Participating in video-sharing sites will likely require more energy rather than disengagement or comment closures. As a future blueprint, designers and automated algorithms might deploy ways of identifying comments that productively contribute to discourse and build on them.

The title of this chapter has a double meaning in that it refers to the title of my video and to the underlying theoretical inquiry that inspired it. Students often wonder why scholars try to define intellectually slippery terms such as "community." If the term has so many connotations, surely a conclusive definition cannot be achieved in a few classroom sessions in a semester or even across a particular scholar's career. Indeed, even within anthropology, scholars such as John Postill tend to reject the term, citing its connotations of homogeneity, elision of conflict, and lack of dynamism as key factors in its uncertain usefulness for scholarship on mediation.[127] John Postill and Sarah Pink draw on the work of fellow anthropologists Nigel Rapport and Vered Amit to argue that many of the situations they study in digital contexts "are neither communities nor networks—they are hybrid forms of sociality through which the ethnographer and their research participants gain variously mediated senses of contextual fellowship."[128]

Yet numerous arguments exist that it is important to retain the concept of "community" where applicable for intellectual and practical reasons. First, it is important to avoid complacency and exercise the mind by discussing and debating historically important terms. Second, not all terms are interchangeable with community. Amit argues that the egocentric bias of personal networks does not necessarily guarantee the formation of warm, interpersonal, and interconnected feelings of reciprocity, sharing, and responsibility that the term community at root connotes.[129] Third, the term community is clearly emotionally laden and continues to resonate with people other than scholars, as evidenced by the fact that so many YouTubers discuss it passionately in their videos and comments as well as in research interviews.

A term that continues to widely resonate emotionally is worthy of study. As Amit suggests, community must still "mean" something, as it offers "substantive referents for a sufficient number of people or it wouldn't continue to be enlisted for so many causes."[130] Finally, from a practical perspective, such communities—which have also been called "communities of sentiment" or "communities of interest"—have civic possibilities.[131] Explicitly or latently, they may move individuals from experiencing "shared imagination to collective action."[132] Given that so much of human sociality has moved to mediated sites that contain political and commercial agendas, it is imperative that discussions about sociality and the desired platforms that are required to support it are recognized and encouraged. Groups of people who perceive themselves to be creating communities may be mobilized for important causes that aim to improve equality and social justice.

Conversely, it is important not to overly idealize the term. Communities can also be stifling and limiting, and therefore their support must always be subject to the will of those who wish to participate within their parameters.[133] Rapport argues that

a notion of cultural holism needs to be replaced with a "processual view of culture," as something in the making, existing in its use, whereby social milieux are neither internally coherent (and prone to addition) nor clearly bounded. Inasmuch as community exists it is a matter of an ongoing negotiating of commonality, working through division and disagreement, risking divergence as much as sharing, and likely to mobilize fracture and severance as much as belonging.[134]

In the popular imagination community connotes a warm and embracing environment. But individual experiences show, as did those of YouTubers, that working through division and controversy is an active process that requires investment from stakeholders to make community viable.

Taking a Lefebvrian view, my study revealed community dynamics to be linear when seen at the scale of analysis of the social group under study, and cyclical when viewed from the perspective of the website, in which discourses of community appear in waves over time. The reason community appears in so many digital ethnographies—and will likely continue to do so—is partly because as each social formation on a new medium finds itself growing closer, it is faced with the possibility of social bonding, potentially to the point of achieving community. A key part of this bonding often includes experiencing shared happenings at the same time, especially through media. Yet not all participants are able to accept or even recognize the possibilities of community at the same time. Thus, the process requires using discourse to grapple with whether community is an appropriate characterization of participants' experiences. While interviewees largely had arrived at a moment of acceptance, commenters displayed diverse and even suspicious views about its desirability. Lefebvre's model provides insight into the temporal dynamics of this process. His categorization of arrhythmic participation manifested on YouTube as people came to understand the presence of community at different participatory rates. Maintaining intensely diverse views on community's feasibility at different times complicated its widespread and sustained uptake on YouTube.

Discourse takes a central position as groups work toward achieving what they believe to be a form of community. Recognizing these recurring patterns facilitates open discussion about how collective digital scholarship should proceed, and calls for collaborative projects in which scholars assist stakeholders, where appropriate, in productively engaging in discourse required to achieve their social goals. If community is more of a rhetorical and participatory process than a bounded entity, creating platforms that enable discussion of formative communal groups and their infrastructural requirements will be of vital importance.

The study's findings suggest that community is a process, not a static element, in which people negotiate its parameters and decide whether they will continue to participate in a communal configuration. Lovink points out that a major problem with online commentary is that "there is a widespread unwillingness to reach consensus and to come to a conclusion in a debate."[135] To some extent this may indeed be a problem in forums grappling with pressing issues requiring much-needed solutions. But in terms of community, it is arguably the case that arriving at a definitive answer may be more isolating and disenfranchising than allowing a space for the discussion to continue. The anthropological concept of community retains vitality, but it will only persist as a mediated, social formation to the extent that people want it—and have an appropriate forum to discuss what it is or could be.

6

PORTALS TO THE POSTHUMAN

At an internet research conference, a speaker asked attendees to reflect on all the ways we generate and create digital data, including online accounts, emails, and social media. Glancing around the room, I saw many stunned expressions—including my own. Suddenly vast seas of digital pieces of our lives danced before our eyes. The question brought to life the realization that we are being digitized in ways far beyond our knowledge or control. People are creating digital footprints in the form of countless representations in photographs, videos, and interactions. Together, these make up one's digital legacy. These alternative versions of ourselves, or "alters,"[1] may live on in a posthuman realm. They may exist indefinitely beyond the human life cycle and invite other people to judge, interact with, and make sense of partial dimensions of our personhood.

The staggering number of our digital details invites us to ask, just how important is our mediated legacy? What are the consequences of leaving representations of ourselves online in perpetuity, even after we leave a site? Who (or what) should control our representations: humans or algorithms? Or, perhaps realistically, some combination? As our digital lives increase exponentially, these questions take on urgency, whether or not we are ready to acknowledge them as important life questions. It may seem as though we are only participating in ephemeral social media in daily life. Yet creating and sharing media influences who we are. We want people to think that we are clever, politically active, funny, or technically competent. Whether a video is an earnest vlog or a hilarious video of a cat dashing around with

DOI: 10.5876/9781607329558.c006

a tissue box on its head, connotations about a video maker's legacy become available for others to *assume* and judge.

This chapter addresses the phase of the Lefebvrian cycle involving decline and the end of a participatory trajectory. Video makers may leave YouTube through digital migration, lack of interest, or passing away. This chapter analyzes the end of participating on YouTube within a social group as its members experienced it amid interactive, commercial, and technological choices and parameters. A central goal of the chapter is to examine the impact of individuals' digital legacies. The next chapter supplements the Lefebvrian rubric by analyzing the idea of participatory rebirth. It addresses how YouTubers' concerns about monetization reveal what a renewed video-sharing site might look like.

From its inception, a video is highly influenced by many factors, some of them beyond our influence. Key elements include the viewing desires of our potential audiences, the technical parameters of the platform we post on, and the socio-cultural expectations of online video. Once a video is posted, we no longer have control over its uses and interpretation,[2] an observation that Plato similarly made about writing's independence from its author that may be generalized to different forms of media.[3] Practically speaking, we forfeit aspects of individual agency or choice about how our self-expressions and representations will be viewed or consumed in the present and in unimaginably distant futures. Indeed, it is through the process of making and sharing a video that our "selves" are created, questioning the stability of identity.[4]

Examining ethnographic data from video-sharing cultures prompts the question of how our humanity—the locus of traditional anthropological study—is being influenced by engaging in technical acts such as making videos. Our exogenous, mediated representations may vanish given ever-changing media formats—or they may exist in perpetuity. These combined representations evoke the idea of the "posthuman," in which a person's subjectivity may move beyond a particular body in ways that challenge the assumed existence of a stable, singular, autonomous, agentive self.[5] The posthuman has many connotations, but it often refers to the idea that human identity is no longer contained in a body but may exist in representational form in ways that influence unknowably large numbers of people. In turn, others shape who we believe we are or wish to become. In one of the posthuman's myriad conceptualizations, a singular super consciousness emerges. In another version the posthuman constitutes a collective or hive that contains the disparate thoughts of many, such that individual identities become connectively incorporated.[6] This chapter focuses on the latter vision, in which we can access a multiplicity of voices on a broad scale through YouTube.

Some scholars reject the posthuman as broad conjecture that disregards the human spirit. Others see it as forthcoming but still far away—the stuff of science fiction. This chapter argues that YouTube is already a site of the posthuman for individuals and at the level of the site itself—provided that the concept is viewed as a feeling tone or rubric for experiencing media rather than as a label for individual bodies or identities.

The chapter begins by situating its argument with regard to prior conceptions about what constitutes the posthuman. It draws on illustrative posthuman characteristics to analyze how configurations of people, algorithms, and media combine to alternatively threaten individual identities and provide a comforting connection to a collectivity from which one is never abandoned. The chapter analyzes how people react when confronted with the identification challenges of the posthuman, particularly when techno-social interactions complicate fantasies of agentive participation and representational control in video cultures. An example includes mean-spirited remix videos in which one's work is changed in ways that contradict one's intended message and self-perception. A further example includes how algorithms on YouTube aggressively promote such offensive videos. These characteristics combine to function as violative alters that challenge one's sense of personhood and cast doubt on the practical viability of achieving comprehensive digital literacies in media-sharing cultures. The posthuman experience on YouTube invites consideration of participation's connotations and implications, not just on a particular site but across media ecologies.

The chapter then examines how interviewees visualize the trajectory of their digital legacies after they pass away. Their narratives orient to their media's purpose and projected temporal engagements. While some interviewees envisioned a permanent legacy to provide comfort to mourners, others saw themselves as unimportant in a vast world and believed their media should be rather quickly deleted. Such stories echo the connective aspect of the posthuman as well as feelings of being merely one voice in a much larger social field.

Next, the chapter calls on interviewees' narratives of departure within media ecologies to propose new analytical concepts for characterizing digital migration patterns. In some cases creators left the site, but they retained its social framework when interacting with YouTubers on other social media, enacting a conceptual migration. Stories of digital migration illustrate how the posthuman collective on YouTube reacts when members disappear without explanation. Those left behind may become distressed if they have supported creators over time.

The ethnographic data provides a foundation for the chapter's conclusion, which analyzes whether a "post-YouTube" exists. In crucial ways YouTube itself exhibits signs of being a posthuman entity. We tend to think of websites as monolithic, but sites also have alters that are mutable, unpredictable, and expansionist. Alternative versions of a concept of YouTube travel beyond a website in multiple incarnations. In fact, various ideals of what should constitute YouTube travel within and across mediascapes, all with their own technological features and participatory expectations.

The chapter probes the idea of the posthuman to critically examine the ramifications of having uncertain control over one's mediated legacy. The argument is not that we should surrender control but rather the opposite. If we wish to preserve the human element of the posthuman, we must be vigilant as to how technologized parameters such as algorithms are deployed to shape the content and context of media creation. A posthuman mediascape may not yet be a universal reality, but the YouTube case enables media makers to gaze through its portals to begin parsing its parameters and effects in the present and in perpetuity.

ON POSTHUMANISM

YouTube resembles the type of posthuman rubric that facilitates a heterogeneous collective. It contains representations of the thoughts of large swaths of people who can provide content and access seemingly infinite amounts of information and media. Not only can we connect to myriad voices, we can also experience different versions of ourselves over time and across contexts. Alters may refer to visual representations such as videos[7] but also to subtle sets of information such as data-driven behavior patterns tracked over time, which may be aggregated into bundles. Alters vary temporally. We may see a video that we made as a child and another that we created as an adult. These videos exist for a time in temporal simultaneity. Time plays a significant role in how we deal with posthuman experiences, thus encouraging a focus on temporality, or different cultural ways of experiencing time.[8]

The posthuman is a controversial concept. By definition, anthropologists study humankind. As anthropologists who study social media usage, Miller and his colleagues underscore the fact that they are not studying "posthuman" entities but rather human beings who have "attained" more capabilities through technology. They state, "We propose a theory of attainment to oppose the idea that with new digital technologies we have either lost some essential element of being human or become post-human. We have simply attained a new set of capacities that, like the skills involved in driving a car, are quickly accepted as ordinarily human."[9] As an anthropologist, I too study humans, however technologically integrated they may be. Humans have been incorporating exogenous components to advance their capabilities for millennia. I share researchers' concerns about breathless overgeneralizations about the death of humanity.

The argument here is not that we must study individuals as fully realized posthuman entities. Yet it is difficult to claim that it is only attainment or augmentation of controlled skill sets that emerge when YouTubers interact. For example, people must deal with how others appropriate their videos. They must contend with large-scale algorithmic search filters that ignore unprofitable videos, thus complicating an ability for all types of creators to be heard. To extrapolate from the car-driving analogy, imagine a driver behind the wheel of a dystopic autonomous vehicle with a control system that has been hacked, locking the driver out of the means of preventing a collision. Within a posthuman YouTube paradigm, individuals may not only experience augmentation; in some cases they may lose control entirely over their own image. These challenges have consequences that merit critical investigation.

The concept of the posthuman may also appear troublesome because long before it came into fashion, scholars from numerous disciplines explored similar issues, including questioning the boundary between the self, technology, and others. Scholars have challenged the idea that a person has a stable identity throughout the life course or across contexts. The vast literature on performative identity shows that there is no stable, authentic core self that somehow can be represented in a video. Identities are marshaled for particular contexts, and we hold various degrees of allegiance to specific performances. For the anthropologist, the very idea of culture as a collection of norms, behaviors, and values that exist prior to the existence of human beings creates a kind of collective, distributed consciousness. When one is born into a culture, one does not necessarily feel a sense of open-ended choice about who to be and how to act—at least not initially. Notions of an agentic, individual self also differ cross-culturally. What constitutes a "human" has been changing for millennia, such that anthropology involves studies of human-machine and other combinatory cyborg entities that construct humanity.[10]

Posthuman, fluid identity positionings that function across uncertain boundaries between a person and other people and material objects have been widely studied in disciplines such as poststructuralism, postmodernism, feminism, queer theory, science and technology studies, cyborg studies, and actor-network theory.[11] The idea of a stable and autonomous self is arguably a recent intellectual invention that privileges people who have historically had the "wealth, power, and leisure to conceptualize themselves as autonomous beings exercising their will through individual agency and choice."[12] The liberal, agentive self is something of a fiction. In actuality, we have always been "posthuman,"[13] if the term refers not to antihuman or nonhuman beings but rather to humans who must continually work through other-inflected proposals for personhood that emerge from a combination of technologies, cultures, and configurations of human bodies.

Despite these thoughtful critiques, the "posthuman" is a useful construct for studying video-making anthropologically because it reveals how people work through what they believe to be their mediated self, in part by complying with or raging against the posthuman's blatant challenges to it. Whether posthuman beings exist is not at issue here. What is important is that conceptually the idea of the "posthuman" bundles metaphors about embodiment, heterogeneity, distributed and collective "intelligence," algorithmic living, egocentric border confusion, and machine-influenced subjectivity, thus facilitating meaningful analysis of representational and mediated experiences.

If identity is a fiction, it has been useful for constructing personal coherence and meaning in one's life trajectory. If "identity construction makes connections between who we are, how we imagine ourselves, and how we want others to see us,"[14] then it is important to understand how individuals react when they are confronted by glimpses into the posthuman that challenge their ideal sense of self as they interact with collective others through technologized media. People may not always recognize their imbrication in a posthuman condition until they are tangibly confronted with it. Yet points of tension emerge when people experience disturbing versions of posthuman circumstances.

Of particular interest is analyzing how posthuman forms take shape in socially inflected, digital idioms. Anthropology is well suited to apply its lessons to media environments to see how notions of what is "human" are constructed.[15] The posthuman may unfold differently across social media sites and platforms and across individuals. Various milieus should be explored if we are to envision a history of future possibilities that are accommodating to the human spirit. Indeed, "the best possible time to contest for what the posthuman means is now, before the trains of thought it embodies have been laid down so firmly that it would take dynamite to change them."[16] Among future generations, posthuman inflections of identity will be naturalized as digital life ways, beyond question or critique.

Being human today means making, participating in, being unknowingly recorded on, or being affected by media. When confronted with the posthuman as viewed through mediated portals, individuals may understandably be reluctant to move through that doorway. Yet in moments of "contact and collision" with posthumanity,[17] a wide range of fascinating, hopeful, and disturbing interrelations between humans and technology may be startlingly revealed.

NET REVERBERATIONS

The posthuman has a "collective, heterogeneous quality" that evokes the idea of "distributed cognition."[18] Information is dispersed not only across individuals but also in the technological parameters and platforms in which one's imaged and imagined self is located. For instance, when a video is created and posted to YouTube, the video's ontology or source of life is partly shaped by the platform, which exhibits specific technical, cultural, social, and participatory parameters that lie outside of the video creator's mind. To take a simple but illustrative example, crafting a video that is under fifteen minutes simply because a video-sharing platform restricts videos to a fifteen-minute limit, or because YouTube viewers will not likely have the patience for long videos, orients individual "self" expression to a peculiar and sometimes unpredictable combination of factors that include human and technological elements.

Human ingenuity is seemingly limitless, and workarounds are routinely created. For example, before 2010, YouTube users who were not partners were not permitted to upload videos that exceeded ten minutes.[19] Video makers became partners when they gained sufficient views and agreed to have advertisements placed on their videos. Partners subsequently shared ad revenue with the site. Only popular creators were invited to be partners in 2007. By 2012 it became possible to monetize single videos.[20] Partners were allowed to create videos longer than ten minutes.

Video makers worked around the ten-minute limit by breaking up a long video into ten-minute installments. Still, this workaround shapes the video to the technical parameters of its destination rather than individual creative choice. Whether one's videos were broadcast in full or in awkward ten-minute chunks became a reputational marker in which aspects of technical and participatory identities could be hypothesized by viewers who understood these hierarchical constraints.[21] Status could be read temporally. A creator who could broadcast a video in its entirety was most likely a partner and therefore exhibited high commercial status and value to the site. Of course sites change, and so do their parameters. In 2010 the time limit was increased to fifteen minutes for user-compliant accounts.[22] Numerous separate yet interconnected or even competing parameters influence how one's participatory reputation is crafted and interpreted. By posting a video or comment, YouTube participants are partially "writing themselves and others" into the public eye through sets of reputational clues.[23]

Analyzing the posthuman may require exploring points of contention and ways in which people manage or resist being pressured into this condition. The following discussion will focus on a case study of an individual whom I will refer to using his YouTube channel name of robtran. His experiential window into the posthuman was emotionally disturbing due to a combination of techno-cultural and interactive parameters that complicated his YouTube participation. If one vision of the posthuman represents a "hive" mind, it is especially fitting to focus on a single individual and his confrontation with collective forces that challenged his interpretation of agentive personhood.

Robtran was a white man in his early forties who often vlogged about current events and personal views. He also created parodic videos and posted a tribute video to a famous broadcaster. His videos typically receive hundreds of views each. As of June 2018, he had a few hundred subscribers. He had been participating on

YouTube for about a year and a half when I interviewed him in San Francisco in 2008. Expressing an interest in making films, he said that he appreciated the opportunity to practice his filmmaking skills on YouTube.

During his interview robtran spoke about his unsuccessful attempts to engage with what others believed was a YouTube community. He had difficulty negotiating a favorable mediated reputation that accurately reflected his beliefs. Choices made by algorithms and other YouTubers in the collective not only went against the grain but were violative of his self-perception, including the persona he was trying to project on YouTube.

Violative Alters

In order to understand robtran's experience, it is helpful to invoke one particular vision of the posthuman. N. Katherine Hayles, a scholar in postmodern literary criticism, calls on science fiction novels to viscerally illustrate how posthuman experiences such as those of robtran may unfold.[24] In her seminal work on elucidating posthumanism, she invokes Greg Bear's novel *Blood Music* (1985) to describe how the body may be radically absorbed via technical mutations into a distributed collective. In the story a researcher swallows intelligent biochips that he invented, believing he can later retrieve them. The biochips evolve out of his control until each achieves human levels of intelligence. These cells take over the inventor's body, which is reformed into a kind of goo. A consultant named Michael Bernard also becomes infected. Bernard flees to an isolation ward to reduce the risk of spreading the infection.

Notably, the original biochips mutate and form their own collective consciousness and agenda, quite beyond the goals of their original inventor. Eventually Bernard is also taken over by these cells or beings. While he transforms into intelligent goo, he begins to engage in a dialogue with the cells, thus hearing "music" in his own blood. As his body is being engulfed by the exogenous cells, he learns that, to them, he is now a "cluster" of cells that were "chosen to re-integrate with BERNARD."[25] Bernard protests and tells the intelligent cells that he, in fact, is Bernard. The cells ominously answer, "There are many BERNARD." Each copy of him functions as a new version of a concept called BERNARD. The book eerily and effectively uses the convention of capital letters to indicate not an original entity but a concept or idea of a person that can be copied yet subtly altered across iterations.

In this posthuman vision, an autonomous, singular, agentive self does not function apart from an unknown quantity of alters. In crucial ways the alters echo but never exactly replicate the person that was once called Bernard. In *Blood Music* the cells believe that this absorption, which creates many BERNARDs, is the price one must pay to achieve integration into an intelligent collective that offers much more than a singular being ever could. It offers substantial "augmentation." One has access to countless data, and, importantly, one is never alone. Human identity and physical form are less significant than are seamless communion and immortality.

Existing as an alter in a posthuman condition may "augment" or increase capabilities and possibilities for humans in ways that are neither inherently positive nor negative.[26] Joining a collective such as YouTube expands the possibilities for gaining information, connection, and self-expression. Writing from the perspective of experimental digital media studies, Beth Coleman also explored augmentation, which connotes incorporating additions to networked subjects that interrelate technology and an imagined sense of self, one that may vary contextually. However, augmentation is only one part of the story. While it may afford possibilities for self-expression for some people, it creates emotional distress for others when they feel unfairly manipulated by their environment or the collective. Indeed, Coleman acknowledges that "augmentation" can be used for manipulation and coercion as well as for individual good.[27]

Robtran's experience exhibits a struggle with exogenously created "alters" that combine within a posthuman environment. Numerous ROBTRANs arguably exist on YouTube in the form of remixed parodies of his videos, but many of them conflict with and even violate his preferred sense of performative personhood in deeply disturbing ways. In studying robtran's narrative, one finds several similarities between his experiences and those of the fictional Bernard/BERNARDs.

Although participating on YouTube started off as fun for him, robtran wound up dealing with an anti-fan base of "haters" who created obscene and unkind remixes of his videos. Robtran explained his participatory trajectory:

> It started off as a lot of fun in August and early September of last year, and then starting in mid-, late September for reasons I can't understand, and I—I'm not going to try, I attracted the attention of a coterie of about twenty or thirty people, based in Scotland and Belgium, who hate me [laughs]. They make obscene video responses. They take my videos off of YouTube and mash them up. For example, I made a video about anti-Semitism, which was of course against it, and they took it, mashed it up so that I was saying, like, "I hate Jews" and titled it "Robtran Hates Jews." And, see, with YouTube if you type in "robtran" what you see, before you see any of my videos, is one after another of these mash-up hater videos, that these people produced. There's about thirty of them altogether. They even formed a group called the "blobtrain" that is dedicated to hating me and harassing me.

In robtran's case, a group of troublesome video makers remixed his videos and distorted his ideas in deeply insulting ways. Notably, not all of robtran's videos received such treatment. Other YouTubers profiled in this study, such as ItalianStallionette and kenrg, commented on his videos. In one comment ItalianStallionette called robtran a "kind soul," and in another kenrg thanked him for his tribute video to a famous broadcaster saying, "That was a great tribute and history of a great broadcaster. Thanks."

Yet the treatment robtran received from the mash-up video creators disturbed him. Terms for people who engage in such irritating behavior have varied across sites and over time. YouTubers referred to such troublemakers as "haters," or people who post mean-spirited criticisms or pointless insults. In the 1990s people posting aggressively mean comments were called "flamers." Communication studies scholar and critic Howard Rheingold defined flames as "outbursts of angry personal attacks."[28] According to anthropologist Tom Boellstorff, in the online environment of Second Life and in some gaming cultures, individuals causing distress are referred to as "griefers."[29] Although important and nuanced differences between these groups merit further study, the behavior exhibited against robtran appears to map most closely with YouTubers' definition of "haters" and what scholars and pundits call "trolls."[30]

According to communication and digital technologies scholar Whitney Phillips, not everyone who causes trouble online self-identifies as a troll, and it is not clear whether the people who targeted robtran considered themselves to be so. Even self-identifying trolls display diverse characteristics. While some trolls claim they have ethical limits, others do not. Some trolling is innocuous while others meet a legal standard of harassment. Trolls may engage in one-time incidents or maintain a routine practice of provocation. What seems to be consistent across robtran's tormenters and the "sub-cultural" or "self-identifying" trolls that Phillips studied is that they seem to be motivated by doing it for the "lulz," which means laughing at someone and deriving pleasure from their distress.[31] Trolls of this type wish to show that public displays of political conviction should be called out and mocked. Phillips keenly observes that this stance is ironic given that they are enacting their own strongly held convictions through trolling. Of interest to trolls is proving that one should not hold or publicly exhibit forms of "ideological rigidity."[32]

Under the posthuman rubric, these hater mash-up videos function as "alters" or alternative versions of robtran's representation. These alters disregard robtran's values and ideas of social justice. Words were literally put in his mouth. His videos were hacked to contort his criticism of anti-Semitism, making it appear that he himself was anti-Semitic. Robtran's experiences seriously call into question the notion of achieving advantageous "augmentation" by being able to make videos. These events also challenge certain connotations of "participatory cultures" that emphasize active decision-making about how one's media will be created and circulated.

These violative alters were not of robtran's making and cannot be easily removed (if ever) from internet or YouTube collectives. Robtran may certainly produce alternative images and accounts of himself and his ideas, but the violative alters may lurk in ways that not only distort his sentiments and beliefs but create unwelcome mutations that challenge his ability to project a consistent, self-affirming public identity. In a sense, these haters also add to the participatory space of YouTube by introducing interpersonal and processual conflicts.

The mash-ups' aesthetic features revealed them to be obvious mockery rather than authentic statements of robtran's beliefs. Hater videos that parodied robtran were typically technologically modest and transmitted a single image (say, that of a Scottish flag) while bagpipe music played and slow-scrolling text accused him of "slandering" the Scottish people and "offending" their honor. Yet I saw robtran issue no such insults in any of his videos. Such simplistic production values and accusations did not impress. It is hardly intelligent to use basic video-making techniques to insult or wildly accuse a video maker in mean-spirited ways. These incidents challenge the posthuman notion of a collective "intelligence," given that these haters' goals included cyberbullying and abusing a person's image and public persona. Violative mock-ups produced a posthuman feeling tone in which alters were created of robtran that he could not control but nevertheless remain part of a widely accessible YouTube collective.

Algorithmic Anxiety

Equally disturbing for robtran was the fact that the site's search engine parameters increased the visibility of these distorted alters. Analyzing posthuman dynamics on social media sites includes examining the interrelated aspects of technical platforms and participatory practices. Robtran described how the search algorithm promoted these violative alters to the top of search lists for his YouTube channel name. In some cases he claimed that these video alters appeared on search lists *before* his original work. As long as viewers kept watching them, YouTube's search engine placed them ever higher on search lists sorted by view counts. Such participatory distortions are likely to mount in the near term, as algorithms are becoming part of everyday life across numerous contexts.[33]

Searches that I conducted by "upload date" pushed his comparatively older videos further down the list, given that he had not uploaded a video since 2012. Searching by upload date returned more recent video titles such as *Down with Robtran* and *War on Robtran* to the top of the list. A search using the "view count" filter returned two videos at the top from robtran, and the rest were from other people. The collective viewing of these videos over time influences how the search engine prioritizes results. As more people watch the trolls' videos, the more likely they will appear at the top of search lists that sort videos by view counts. A bundle of technical and human-centered practices combined to yield a listing in which robtran's voice feels drowned out by the ROBTRANs created by haters and trolls.[34]

Our stories became algorithmically entangled due to the mechanics of recommendation lists, which aim to return material that viewers would likely wish to watch. Since I did watch several robtran hater views to conduct this analysis, the algorithm kept returning similar videos as recommendations for me through my AnthroVlog account. Yet I watched them only because they upset my ethnographic interviewee, not because I had any organic interest in watching unimaginative videos that featured basic text scrolls of silly insults. I resented the algorithm's skewed profile of my viewing habits, which created an inauthentic alter for me. As far as the algorithm was concerned, AnthroVlog (or ANTHROVLOG, to use posthuman nomenclature) preferred to watch insulting videos (multiple times), which is partly true but mostly not. This algorithmically constructed profile did not conform to my self-perception as a knowledgeable, aesthetically discerning, socially supportive, and technically savvy viewer.

Robtran also expressed disquietude over an obscene video that he said his haters had made and linked to his channel name. In this video (which I could not locate) a man apparently mimed oral sex for several minutes. When a video is proposed for viewing by the Google recommendation system, the video is indexed with a small, representative thumbnail image taken from the video. Robtran's concern was that this offensive video, which he saw listed next to his video in the recommendation list, would not contain any hints of its offensive content in the thumbnail image or video description. He worried that friends and family looking for his videos might inadvertently click on the obscene one because it referenced him. Robtran explained:

> Now because the little thumbnail that comes with [the obscene video] doesn't really look like that, I can't allow my grandmother, my niece, my sister, or my mother to look at my YouTube channel, [to] look at my videos because when you run a search of my name or even if I were to send them a direct link to my channel page, if they looked at a video, the first thing they're going to see on the right panel is that guy going [mimes oral sex motions] like this for three minutes. You can just imagine my grandmother going, "Oh look, somebody likes Robby," and then clicking on that, but not knowing any better, and having a heart attack!

Robtran faced intense anxiety when his work was linked to a hater video that was obscene and offensive. He feared that people searching for him might find and watch the other video first and be exposed to its repugnant contents, quite against his and presumably many viewers' wishes. Of course one can immediately stop watching, but the damage may be done. There are some images, however fleeting, that one cannot unsee.

Much public discourse criticizes young people's ostensibly foolish choices about what they post, suggesting that youth lack proper digital literacies. While developing media skills is undeniably important, it is also clear that even innocent videos may be used in unfortunate ways. Creators do not have control over a site's algorithms, which may promote disturbing alters of their work. Communication scholar Michael Strangelove makes the point that we live in a historical moment in which so much fakery and simulation abounds that people long to project an aura of authenticity, order, and stability about themselves. He argues that confessional video blogs and autobiography are popular because they offer the allure of projecting an authentic self. He quotes Karen Wright, who, writing in *Psychology Today*, observed, "Amid a clutter of counterfeits, the core self is struggling to assert itself."[35] Even if identity is ultimately a fiction, many people would nevertheless empathize with robtran's frustration. In his case the problem is not rampant narcissism through making too many videos. Rather, the predominance of disturbing alters strongly suggests that he should make *even more* videos that reflect his social sensitivity, in part to drown out the counterfeit versions that have accrued online and that are algorithmically privileged in search engines.[36]

Robtran told me that he had repeatedly yet unsuccessfully requested that YouTube staff remove these videos. He equated them with harassment, but YouTube apparently did not. In YouTube's policies users are warned that "not everything that's mean or insulting is hate speech." Yet hate speech is not permitted.[37] According to YouTube, "Hate speech refers to content that promotes violence or hatred against individuals or groups based on certain attributes, such as: race or ethnic origin, religion, disability, gender, age, veteran status, and sexual orientation/gender identity." The policies against harassment and cyberbullying state, "We take this issue seriously and will remove comments, videos or posts where the main aim is to maliciously harass or attack another user. However, at YouTube we understand the value of free expression, so please understand that not all negative or mean videos and comments will be removed."[38]

YouTube has provided creators with an "augmented" capability to make and share videos.[39] But one group's successful augmentation compromised robtran's self-expression. Uneven abilities result in *asymmetrical augmentation*, which occurs when one party or set of individuals is given access to capabilities, yet similar or other capabilities are simultaneously withheld or reduced for other people. The haters' augmented ability to express their humor was facilitated by the site and its technical features, such as search engines and recommendation algorithms. Conversely, robtran's self-expression was compromised. Asymmetrical augmentation may considerably detract from a video maker's enjoyment or even basic ability to engage in media sharing. As long as these videos are watched, the viewing algorithms smugly march on, promoting these videos and associating them with ROBTRAN even as robtran rages against their attempts to mar his preferred projection of public identity.

Manipulating Reputation Systems

YouTubers identified problems with reputation systems, which enable people to evaluate the usefulness of media such as videos and comments. From the first rating onward, voting on video quality creates one reputational index for the creator or the media that is rated or both. When I began studying YouTube, it offered a rating system of 1 (Poor) to 5 (Awesome!) stars that enabled people to record their assessment of videos.[40] Yet when most people rated something, they reportedly gave it either one or five stars rather than the intermediate ratings.[41] By 2010 and continuing in 2018, the site offers only a "thumbs up" or "thumbs down" rating system for videos and comments. At the time of robtran's interview, the site still had the five-star system.

YouTubers quickly learned that reputation systems could be used tactically. For example, in ethnographic interviews that I conducted for my book *Kids on YouTube* (2014), young people said that their rivals on YouTube might rate their videos poorly. In this way, competitors could maintain a relatively higher viewing reputation.[42] An occasional one-star rating would not necessarily affect a video that was also rated favorably by many viewers and friends. However, a collective strategy of many people weighing in or using automated bots to rate videos could influence a video's assessment and, by extension, the reputation of the video maker. Automated methods violate the site's terms of use, but they routinely occur. When they are detected, view counts may be removed. In a high-profile case, the Universal music label was stripped of nearly 1 billion allegedly fake views.[43]

Reputational manipulation became more personally challenging for robtran when he made a video for a sick child that was continually one-starred in a harassing way. A video maker whose YouTube channel name was SadieDammit (now known as SimplySadie) posted a video on December 6, 2006, called *The Hugs for Jacey Campaign*. The video invited viewers to make video responses that sent good wishes or virtual "hugs" to a ten-year old girl named Jacey who was in the hospital battling leukemia and whose mother had posted videos that alerted SadieDammit to her story. Robtran felt moved by this plea and made his own supportive video. He said that it felt "really good" to send good wishes to Jacey and that her mom had commented by thanking him and telling him that Jacey had liked the video. Unfortunately, his haters rated the video poorly until it finally accumulated an average rating of one star (Poor) in the YouTube system. Robtran explained his concern:

The haters started one-starring this video. And they one-starred it down to one star. And I was afraid that people were going to look at that and think, "Oh my God, this has one star and it's from a Hugs for Jacey Campaign." You know, that's what it says, "Re: Hugs for Jacey Campaign." They're gonna think "God, what did that asshole say to her? I mean what kind of an ogre is this guy to—" Because people see one star and they assume, it's got to be awful. So, at the time I had about thirty to forty subscribers. I asked them, please, I told them the whole story in a video, and I said please come and five-star that back up to the level, and then once it's up to five stars, I'll turn off the ratings, right? Nobody answered the call. Nobody. Sadie, eventually, well, I subscribe to SadieDammit, and she came, and I asked her, like much later, and she did it of course. But nobody else did. Not a single other person. And I was totally shocked by that. I mean, and I've had people say, "Well, you take this stuff too seriously." It's like, well yeah, it's stuff I've worked on. And in this particular case it's something I had a certain emotional investment in, and why can't you can't you dig that, dude? Why can't you understand that?

The episode upset robtran because some people assess videos—and, by association, the abilities and commitment of video makers—by examining rating systems. Although experienced users are suspicious of rating systems for these reasons, robtran was nevertheless concerned about being perceived as a "hater" rather than as someone supporting a person who was suffering. On such a sensitive topic, viewers might see a single-star rating and avoid the video, believing it contained insensitive or hurtful commentary about Jacey, the subject of the video. The episode was doubly traumatic because he reached out for community assistance and asked viewers to rate his video highly as a countermeasure. Yet he received little help in driving the rating back up to levels that would publicly display his sincere support for a community member in need.

The Needs of the Collective

Robtran's narratives also contained positive glimmers of a posthuman condition that emphasizes personal connection and support. Given his negative experiences, robtran contemplated leaving YouTube altogether. He created an angry farewell video only to be persuaded to remain by viewers whom he characterized as "saner heads" who urged him to stay. These "saner heads" arguably functioned in a posthuman way to draw him back into a collective that felt richer amid broad participation. YouTubers who encouraged him to remain needed him to continue contributing to the site, to make the collective experience more diverse and interesting.

Interconnected yet competing energies produced anxieties for robtran and others who felt that their media making was out of control. Posthuman rubrics often include a vision of an agentive self being absorbed into an intelligent collective that includes many voices. Most synonyms for the word "intelligence," including judgment, reasoning, understanding, or cleverness, do not apply to the haters' output that threatened robtran's sense of mediated self. On the other hand, "saner heads" in the collective encouraged robtran to stay connected.

Perhaps it would be more productive to refer to such posthuman constructs as collective forces in a more Latourian vein.[44] When bundled together, collective forces produce significant effects that sometimes augment but at other times challenge an individual's desire to express the self in technologized realms. Collective forces include humans with intelligence and consciousness as well as technologically driven entities lacking consciousness (so far), such as search algorithms. These forces create conditions in which an individual feels pulled toward absorption into a larger human-material configuration, for better or for worse. Given that they impact individuals who join—or become absorbed in—mediated milieus, collective forces must be taken seriously, whatever their origin. Some collective forces invited robtran to remain in the collective while others alienated him by threatening his sense of self. As long as the goals of collective forces remain in tension, Hayles is correct to refer to *Blood Music*'s blissful vision of absorbative posthumanism as "improbably idealized."[45]

Posthuman Tremendum

In addition to the novel *Blood Music*, Hayles also drew inspiration from a novel called *Terminal Games* (1994) by Cole Perriman.[46] In this science fiction story, a detective explains that humans experience a feeling called "tremendum" when they encounter death, specifically when they see a dead body. According to the *Encyclopedia Britannica*, "tremendum" is a feeling that combines a sense of mystery, fascination, and repulsion. Metaphorically peering through posthuman portals may evoke a feeling of posthuman tremendum in which one encounters a constellation of forces that influence one's idealized personhood but are not easily manipulated by individuals. Human agency is to be recognized and respected. Yet, practically speaking, it can be difficult to orchestrate all of the factors—such as algorithmically identified alters—that produce a collective. Creators arguably felt a sense of posthuman tremendum when they experienced a combined sense of mystery and repulsion that emerged from the impact of forces operating outside of yet influencing construction of the self.

Anthropological research in technical realms will continue to include studies of intersecting, parallel, and confrontational sets of collective forces that integrate or reject individual nodes into a collective. It is not precisely accurate to say that a video expresses a preexisting person in part because people's identities are mutable and because identity is worked out through practices such as mediation. Processes of video creation and distribution crucially influence identification.[47] Understanding posthuman tremendum requires exploring individual experiences and concerns that emerge within and across complex, temporally fraught, mediated landscapes—both now and in the future.

DIGITAL LEGACIES

Life has a particular rhythm, punctuated by a beginning and an end. Technically speaking, one becomes "posthuman" after death. Even the earliest media enabled people to continue past their life cycle, at least in terms of perpetuating their thoughts and productivity through creative works and images. Online videos extend a person's representational life and challenge the boundaries between a sense of self and alters that may exist in perpetuity. After creators pass away, their media—which obviously can never be the sum total of their lives—take on existences of their own. Nevertheless, people often have definitive ideas about how they would like to craft their digital legacies. Interviews demonstrate that YouTubers had specific—often temporally oriented—visions for how to shape their posthuman identities.

Scholars have analyzed tensions that occur when people represent themselves or someone else through media.[48] Biography and autobiography are essentially linked, as it is not possible to tell one's own story without relating those of others.[49] Studies of biography and autobiography show that even during willing collaborations between biographers and subjects, many factors, including asymmetrical professional agendas, anxieties about fidelity to the historical record, and searches for authenticity in self-expression, become fraught with ethical dilemmas.[50] Such tensions result in media skirmishes or clashes between creators and users of media in everyday vlogs.[51] Family and friends may not always agree on how a person should be depicted.

Representations of desired legacies are becoming increasingly important areas for scholarly fields devoted to understanding mediated self-exploration. Scholars participating in the Death Online Research Network promote the study of how digital media are playing a key role in life experiences such as death and grief.[52] A central goal involves analyzing how cultural notions of identity change amid the vast creation and circulation of media representations. Internet studies scholars Tama Leaver and Tim Highfield researched what they characterize as the "ends of identity," namely birth and death. Leaver and Highfield see these experiences as particularly vulnerable moments given that the subjects of media do not have agency to shape their representations or to choose how those representations should be circulated. They explore how "individuals use visual social media when sharing information about others who cannot speak or interact for themselves: the latter shape the content (and may appear within it), and are responsible for the meaning drawn from it, yet are not directly or explicitly participating."[53]

Although Leaver and Highfield pinpoint the "ends" of identity as especially revealing, their contribution invites general exploration about what it means to deal with representations that are created without one's knowledge, in ways that frame possible interpretations of identity now and in the future. As national governments and corporations push toward a "real name web," aspects of one's identity and others' representations of it may live on indefinitely through digital mechanisms such as keyword tagging and algorithmic links. Their data suggest that in the posthuman sense, death is not truly the "end" of identity. If identity is performative and worked out on a social stage, as argued by renowned sociologist Erving Goffman,[54] then Leaver and Highfield rightly ask, "Who builds the stage, and how will the performance be remembered?"[55]

Living under a posthuman rubric entails confrontation with such issues on a potentially massive scale for ordinary people who might not otherwise have a public persona. These tensions are intertwined with known and unknowable technical manipulations that have not existed to the same extent in previous eras. For example, contested celebrity biographies or paparazzi invasions are par for the course for public figures,[56] but the availability of video cameras combined with the ease and openness of online distribution and interaction creates mediated contestations for individuals who would not otherwise find themselves in the public eye. Notably, individuals who create public diaries and web pages for particular audiences have also witnessed struggles over authenticity and privacy.[57]

Posthuman tendencies observed on the social media site Facebook frequently also apply to YouTube. As a researcher of autobiography and digital life narratives, Laurie McNeill observed that "the close embrace of the corporate, technological, and autobiographical enables the software to play a significant role in directing who users imagine themselves to be."[58] Viewers obviously generate their own interpretations, despite what viewing algorithms return. Nevertheless, anxieties will likely persist and may even become exacerbated, even as policies are privately and legally negotiated.

Communication scholars Dorthe Refslund Christensen and Stine Gotved of the Death Online Research Network describe how digital death has become domesticated and how mediatization—or media logics, economics, and structures—influence societal practices around digital death and expressions of grief.[59] Christensen and Gotved distinguish between using digital media to "move on" versus "keeping hold."[60] While the former emphasizes coping with loss, the latter is about reintegrating into society but in a way that establishes "continuing bonds" with the deceased. In the latter model, scholarship focuses on how grieving is not a stage or phase but rather a continuous media ritual.

Anxieties emerge when social media structures, technologies, and services do not map to human coping strategies. For example, one person whom I interviewed pointed out a common anxiety about digital legacies: not all services have policies that respect the wishes of the deceased or their families in terms of the videos, comments, and profile pages that a person leaves behind. A YouTuber with the channel name PrincessDiana161 was a grandmother whom I interviewed in Philadelphia in 2008 about a year and a half after she joined YouTube. A fiercely proud New Yorker, her media reference growing up in Spanish Harlem and working with Mitú, a Latino-based media brand and digital network. Each receiving thousands of views, most of her videos involve cooking themes in which she leads viewers through recipes in lively and humorous ways. As of July 2018, she had 66,208 subscribers. She participated heavily in the social side of YouTube at meet-ups and on the site. For example, she enjoyed responding to "tagging" videos in which she is tagged by another YouTuber to reveal personal facts.

PrincessDiana161 was pained to learn that a family who had lost a son in Iraq did not have access to recent pictures of him and thus could not continue to bond through media. The social media site MySpace reportedly deleted his account after his death. In her interview she stated:

> MySpace deletes accounts from people that are deceased. Which is a terrible thing because recently my daughter's friend died in Iraq and [his] family, the only thing they had was the MySpace account to remember him by, as far as, you know, recent stuff that he had done. And as soon as he died they deleted the account. Let's hope YouTube never does that. You know?

Leaver states that social media policies with regard to digital death are often "minimal" and "blunt."[61] Services may allow a user's profile to convert to a "memorial" page. MySpace policies enabled family to delete or preserve a profile as long as accurate documentation of death and family connection could be provided.[62] Such policy changes are commensurate with those of services that allow material to be deleted or remain according to the user's wishes. For example, Facebook users may determine the status of their profile after death by designating a "legacy contact" who would manage the account.[63] However, legacy contacts have limited abilities. They are reportedly able to write posts and respond to friend requests, but they cannot see private messages, delete photographs, or delete the whole account.

Google established a similar policy by which users could decide whether to delete some or all of their data after certain periods of time or alternatively, name heirs to be "inactive account managers."[64] YouTube's policy reportedly requires a death certificate and documents that give account managers power of attorney over the YouTube account. To obtain legal control of the account, applicants must send YouTube their legal name and contact information, including a verifiable email address, and relevant documents.[65]

Personal or familial preferences about the dispensation of media will likely continue amid uncertainty over social media policies and even legal conflict.[66] Leaver recommends that services enable one's heirs to "curate" a deceased relative's content "posthumously."[67] He notes that many people handle such decisions in an ad hoc way by leaving their account passwords with immediate family members. However, he argues that the obvious growing demand for managing online digital legacies will necessitate more concrete "policies and practices" that "provide more fine-grained control over the digital legacies."[68]

Tensions about media legacies are not new, but emerging configurations of human and technologized collective forces may combine to impact one's imagined legacy in ways that conjure the posthuman. For example, when one passes away, the collective energies of one's heirs may conflict with the needs of commercial entities. Heirs may wish to delete popular videos or accounts that still draw eyeballs to a site that wishes to keep them, thus bringing collective forces into ongoing tension. People and other media-driven entities may exhibit a particular type of polyrhythmia, what Lefebvre termed "arrhythmia" or pathologically incompatible rhythms.[69] Participatory arrhythmias result over conflicting media ideologies, to use Gershon's term, about the appropriate temporality of media's existence.[70] While some entities wish to see the media live on indefinitely, others have reasons to discontinue them, thus creating temporally driven conflict.

A person is arguably doubly "posthuman" after death, in part because one no longer takes human form and because our heavily mediated lifestyles mean that our alters live on in myriad forms. Social media engines are even using extractions of media fragments to simulate a contemporary online presence through eerily accurate visual facsimiles.[71] Within heavily mediated idioms, one cannot, practically speaking, guarantee a particular legacy. Yet this does not preclude a fundamental human wish to try.

Points of "contact and collision" between human and posthuman experiences became visible when YouTubers were invited to reflect on their desired mediated futures. While recording my ethnographic film *Hey Watch This!* (2013), several interviewees spoke of battling serious illnesses such as cancers, a temporary inability to walk, and kidney transplants. I learned at a gathering in Philadelphia that some YouTubers had been discussing this theme; thus, it had emerged as an emic, or group insider, issue for them. I asked interviewees if they had reflected on the dispensation of their digital media after they passed away. This line of inquiry was emotionally difficult to discuss, as it confronted all of us with our finitude. Yet interviewees earnestly and frankly engaged in contemplating these matters in fascinating ways. While some interviewees were caught off guard, a few had clearly contemplated this question. One interviewee had created a video to post on YouTube in the event of his passing.

In surveying the literature on research about cultural rituals of death, Christensen and Gotved analyze not only lifestyles but "deathstyles" of online participants. Deathstyle is defined as "the ways in which we perform practices around death."[72] At issue here are digital deathstyles and the ways in which they are handled on multiple levels through videos. Interviewees revealed a surprisingly wide set of attitudes about how their video content should be curated or positioned for a community—and also temporally in terms of how long after their death they imagined their video-mediated legacy to persist. When reflecting on their media's dispensation and future impact, interviewees frequently considered the wishes of other people, such as family, friends, and their mediated communities.

In general, interviewees' answers sorted into three categories. In terms of the dispensation of their YouTube accounts, interviewees preferred to (1) have the videos removed just after they passed away; (2) keep the videos but for a limited length of time or have them curated for content or both; (3) leave the videos up as they were for posterity to let others judge and process them in their own way. Many interviewees wanted their media to remain at least for a while in order to showcase different dimension of their personality or to comfort friends, family, and community members. Interviewees illustrated a common contemporary pattern in which people work through grief by visiting social media profile pages, web pages, videos, and sites that contain images of loved ones.[73]

In terms of temporality, these interviews facilitated a *pre-posthuman* investigation of interviewees' visions of their future mediated selves. The answers exhibit a patina of futility because controlling one's image is difficult at this historical moment of heavily mediated humanity. Interview narratives about digital legacies do not yield predictions about mediated futures as much as they disclose human desires within a mediated present. Anxieties that emerge reveal how our data becomes privileged over our personhood, a classic characteristic of the posthuman condition. As digital media scholar Grant Bollmer explains, "The anxieties of disconnection suggest a larger fear that humans are gradually becoming insignificant in the face of technological networks because data matter more than people."[74] Perhaps ironically, the futility of one's wishes inevitably brings human dimensions to the fore. Exploring human desires is an area in which anthropology is well suited to bring marginalized humans—who are colliding with posthumanity—back into focus.

"I'm Not Anyone Important. Who's Gonna Sit There and Cry over Me?"

When analyzing how death is handled, Christensen and Gotved argue that three categories of expression are often apparent: an individual sense of loss; a sense of how a community mourns and commemorates its members; and cultural mourning for people whom survivors may not know personally but whose death has significance (such as political figures or victims of a tragedy in the news).[75] Notably, interviewees often oriented around the community level when discussing their envisioned digital deathstyle on YouTube. I interviewed a white man who requested that I refer to him by his nickname of Thor. He felt it important to have a video that alerted the community to what had happened in the event of his passing. His channel on YouTube exhibited a prolific output of comedically inflected video blogs, tutorials on how to use drones and quadcopters, product review videos on devices such as cameras, and vlogs of events and places he had visited. His videos had several hundred to a thousand views each. He had 12,630 subscribers as of June 2018. Attending several meet-ups, he was clearly interested in participating in the social side of YouTube. By the time of his interview in Philadelphia in 2008, he had been participating on YouTube for nearly two years. I asked him if he had considered what would happen to his videos and his YouTube account after his death.

> THOR: I would probably like it to, uh, be up just for a little while and then take it down. I'm not anyone important. Who's going to sit there and cry over me? I'm just another person in this world. It doesn't matter. I have a video already set for it that my brother knows to upload if something happens to me, and after a couple of weeks, the account goes away.
>
> PATRICIA: And what—what is the video that your brother is set to upload?
>
> THOR: The video just says that, you know, if you're looking at this video now, something happened to me. I died. Somehow, some way, I died. And, you know, thanks for everything, I had a good time here, and, and, you know, there's not much I can say but you know [that's] the way it is.

Clearly he had contemplated these issues long before the ethnographic interview. He had prepared a video that his brother knew to upload. He described its contents as expressing gratitude to the people who had made YouTube an enjoyable experience. He preferred that the video only remain for "a couple of weeks." Challenging societal fears about narcissism, he did not wish to have his account remain in perpetuity as a monument to his existence. Interestingly, service providers of social media sites are now acknowledging users' more specific temporal wishes with respect to the dispensation of their digital alters. Sites are now offering the choice of keeping an account open for three, six, nine, or twelve months after one's passing.[76] Thor crafted his envisioned digital legacy not only around his immediate family and loved ones but also toward fellow YouTubers who he acknowledged might wish to know what had happened and how he had perceived his time on the site.

Thor's answer was poignant. He eventually wanted his account taken down because he was not "anyone important." If anything were to illustrate the more negative reading of posthuman sentiment, this would be it. A human individual and his contributions feel insignificant compared with the vast swath of past, present, and future humanity. Yet he was an important person who made a difference to people on YouTube through his videos and his participation.

Thor was not alone in questioning his social legacy. I interviewed a young white woman in Philadelphia just over two years after she joined the site. She asked to be referred to in this study by the name of Veronica. As of July 2018, she had forty-four subscribers. Her video content included mostly vlogs on subjects such as going to college, experiencing a car accident, and debating the greatest athletes of all time. She also posted meet-up videos and footage from places she visited. Her videos each generally garner anywhere from a few dozen to a few thousand views, including one about a meet-up in Philadelphia. She too expressed a wish for her videos to remain, but only for a while. In terms of her digital legacy, she thought it would be interesting to leave up her account so that others could post videos about their memories of her. She stated:

> I would actually want someone to probably continue it. And—well, not even continue it for a long period of time. But I would want someone to post a video of how their—people that know me to post videos on what they remember about me. And things like that. And kind of it be archived, that if people want to see. Because it has raw emotion on it. And I don't think that you get to see that a lot. Like, a lot of people don't want to open up. And things like that. And I would want to know what people thought about those few videos that I did post and what they did mean to people. So, if it meant anything to anybody. Or if it really showed who I was.

Veronica wondered whether her videos had meaning to others or whether they had revealed who she truly was. She expressed a posthuman desire to see how others react to her passing. She observed that people are generally hesitant to open up emotionally in US culture, a sentiment echoed by other interviewees, and she wondered whether leaving her videos up would help people share their "raw emotions." In this way, Veronica articulated an idea of making death more visible to enable people to publicly explore emotions, an idea that has been observed in research on digital memorialization.

Cultural sociologist and digital communication scholar Stine Gotved observed that death is often invisible or culturally downplayed. She contemplates the possibility that desires for posthumous representation and memorializing on social media may increase the visibility of dealing with life-cycle issues by closing "the gap between public exposure and private sequestration" that is common in many cultures today.[77] Gotved points out that although much has been written about using media to facilitate the grieving process by continuing bonds with the deceased, forging such bonds is not the only dynamic that researchers have observed in digital memorialization. In Veronica's vision, the media she leaves behind would offer an opportunity for people to experience "raw emotions," which she believed to be a rare occurrence for many people in the United States. Her media are not only about establishing continuing bonds but also about inviting social and cultural change in handling life-cycle endings through her digital legacy.

Veronica stated that she "would want to know what people thought about those few videos that [she] did post." Her turn of phrase is interesting because technically after her passing she would not be able to "know" anything. Yet she hoped her videos and others' memorials could be archived and accessible. She envisioned a space that invited others to contemplate her life and more fully experience their own emotions. In this sense Veronica, as well as Thor, crafted digital deathstyles that accommodated community forms of mourning.

Both Thor and Veronica seemed uncertain about their mediated value to other people, but they handled their doubt in different ways. Thor desired a clean break by having videos deleted relatively quickly. In contrast, Veronica envisioned an archive of memorial videos to her, in part to explore the loyalties and emotions of those whom she left behind.

Representational Curation

Leaving a channel up was not sufficient for some interviewees in terms of shaping their digital legacies. One respondent, whose official name was Ryan Basilio and whose YouTube channel was thetalesend, spoke about having loved ones curate his YouTube channel. The goal was for them to prune away unimportant videos that did not contribute to his self-perception as an engaged member of the YouTube community and society in general.

Sadly, Ryan passed away from cancer in May 2012.[78] He was a twenty-nine-year old man of Filipino descent who joined YouTube in 2006, about six months after YouTube formally opened, which makes him an early adopter of the site. His videos were largely direct-camera-address video blogs in which he explored a variety of interesting subjects, including political news events, gay rights, movie reviews, his illness, how to make better videos, his haters, and how YouTube had changed since its inception. Each of his videos received thousands of views, and as of June 2018, he had 1,936 subscribers. Ryan was kind and always willing to help me with my project. He was a friendly person who participated in the social side of YouTube. Even after he became ill, he still took the time to provide tips to others to help them improve their videos and increase the quality of participation on the site.

In an interview in San Francisco, he talked about expending less energy on YouTube and spending more time on a separate live-streaming video site. Over time we became Facebook friends and mutual Twitter followers. At a meet-up in Santa Monica in 2009, about three years after he joined the site, I asked him, as I was asking others, what should happen to his account should he pass away. Looking back, his remarks take on a special poignancy. His comments indicated a change in his perspective since our conversation a year earlier due to health challenges. Ryan said:

> Um, I mean, before I think I answered this that, like, I didn't care, it could just stay up. But, um, since I had the whole—I almost died twice this year—situation happen, um, I think I would like someone to first, uh, delete most of my videos, keep the videos that they think are good, sentimental, something like that. Um, of course I'd have to get someone also to know my password, things like that for me, but, um, I mean it's—it's just like Facebook pages or, uh, YouTube pages where people have died. It just kind of keeps living on. [I] would just like to—because there's a lot of frivolous videos on there. And a lot of people do put frivolous videos on there. And it's just me responding to people, and things like that.
>
> But I would like, at least, I mean to—to know who I am. [To] be that person who does [the social media] thing, the person who talks about the issues of their time and things like that. I would like that preserved at least. So that other people would know what kind of a person I am. Even if it is edited that way, I just want them to know what—what I believed in. What I was doing at that time.

Ryan expressed an interest in having his account maintained, but after the removal of "frivolous" videos in which he ephemerally responded to other people. He articulates Leaver's idea of having an ability to curate his own representation, which Leaver anticipates will be a far more common demand on social media services in the future.[79] Ryan said he wanted those videos to remain in which he discussed important issues of the day.

Ryan envisioned his voice continuing after his death, showing who he was as a person and how he contributed to civically engaged discourse. In addition to his YouTube vlogs, he was also an iReporter for the CNN.com website, in which citizens sent in video, audio, or image files to report news of interest. After his passing, many of his videos remained on YouTube. As of June 2018, his account included not only serious videos but more comical work, such as a twenty-second video depicting an extreme close-up of him flaring his nostrils. His channel page description remains written in the present tense, with an invitation to contact him via his email account.

All of this information provides evidence of who he was—from a certain point of view. Each video, as well as all the information on his channel page, and the account as a whole represent posthuman "alters." Ryan wished that others might see him as a civically engaged and caring person, and people who knew him saw him that way. His interview serves as a poignant portal into the human desire to shape one's legacies, not only for immediate friends and family but for other people over time and across generations to appreciate one's life and civic contribution.

Generational Knowledge

Whereas some interviews desired eventual removal or curation of videos to shape future reception of digital legacies, others felt it important to leave images behind that showed nuanced dimensions of personhood, including their foibles and social sides. For instance, PrincessDiana161 stated in her interview that, as a grandmother, she would want her YouTube account to remain. She envisioned her digital legacy as one that humanized the figure of a grandmother on the internet for her heirs to enjoy and maintain connections to bond with her. Her hope for a digital legacy that facilitated family ties is a common motivation for retaining media.[80] When I asked why she wanted to keep her account open, she stated: "Just for my granddaughter, you know. I would like her to continue—as she gets older. I want her to be able to see grandmommy makin' a fool of herself on the internet!"

Similarly, a man whom I met at several meet-ups whose YouTube channel name was nbwulf also expressed a desire for his videos to remain so that his children could see different sides of him that were not necessarily revealed in daily family life. Most of the people whom I interviewed were early adopters of the site, and nbwulf was no exception. Nbwulf was a white man and father whose account lists him as joining in April 2006. I interviewed him three years later at a Santa Monica gathering in 2009. As of June 2018, he had 229 subscribers.

Nbwulf's early vlogs were varied, often showing creative aesthetics and other types of content, such as one in which he slowly comes into focus and reveals a delighted facial expression. As of July 2018, only two videos remained on his account. His two remaining videos each received a few thousand views. Those who try to judge his productivity at a point in time are thus not given the whole picture.

In the two remaining videos, footage is generated from a camera mounted on a motorcycle, giving the viewer a feeling of a "ride along" with him. The videos are often sped-up with visual effects and accompanying music.

Although only two videos remain, during our interview in Santa Monica he said he originally envisioned leaving his videos up for his children to enjoy:

> I'd want [my channel] left up. I think that, you know, if something did happen to me, I'm kind of glad that I did get involved with YouTube because there's all these videos and vlogs and things that I've made that my kids can see. You know, and it's like, you know, they can see another side of me where I was interacting with my friends, and interacting with the community, and just talking about life. And, you know, so they can see some of these videos that, [without] YouTube or a site like [it], [I] would have never shot in the first place. [So it's] similar to back in the day when people would really write detailed diaries. And then you have something to leave behind when people find these later in life and you can really kind of learn more about the personality of a person that you never really saw when you lived with them every single day. Um, so I'd want it—I'd want it left up.

Notably, nbwulf references the predigital paper diary format as analogous to the idea of leaving videos behind that show a side of a person that even close intimates might not see in daily life. Nbwulf made many friends by participating on the site. It is perhaps not surprising that the videos he made with adult friends would have different content and themes than those that he would prefer to experience with his children. He talked about how these sides of himself (or in posthuman terms, "alters") might never have emerged without YouTube or a site like it to encourage particular kinds of mediated self-expression. Aspects of nbwulf's identity were collaboratively created in part through YouTube participation.

Nbwulf's analysis is eloquent and perceptive. He describes how he has mediated himself within the parameters of a particular site, which attracted specific kinds of collective social forces. Who he now is, and who his kids will see, depends upon the fact that he made videos within a specific context. Nbwulf's narrative exemplifies a temporal orientation to his digital legacy. Although his videos express adult ideas and interactions not always meant for children, they could be shared as kids matured into adults. They would then appreciate nuanced dimensions of their parent's character, humor, and social life. In this way a closeness and intimacy that may not have been accessible during in-person interaction could become sharable. Nbwulf's narrative displays an external focus toward his videos' effects on his children. Interviewees often exhibited an outward focus that considered the influence of their media on other YouTubers and the potential impact of their video legacy on their loved ones' feelings and wishes.

Community Support

Online memorials offer a source of comfort to people who are grieving.[81] Interviewees spoke about how YouTube channels and videos served as sites of memorial for people who were mourning lost friends and relatives. In Ryan's case his Facebook page reads, "Remembering Ryan Basilio," and posts show family and friends celebrating his life and expressing their grief. People think about him and mourn him publicly. Posts around his birthday are particularly moving and communicate people's sense of loss and regret that Ryan tragically passed away at such a young age.

The sudden aspect of people passing is jarring and upsetting. One interviewee talked with sensitivity about the value of YouTube videos as not only sites of individual memorials but as a means of dealing with communal grief. Susan (a researcher-assigned pseudonym) was a white woman whom I surmised to be in her thirties. I interviewed her at a meet-up in Philadelphia in 2008, about two years after she had joined the site. Typically, each of her videos received a few hundred to thousands of views. In a video in 2009, she observed that she had some 3,300 subscribers. We spoke about a range of subjects, including her perception of participatory dynamics on YouTube. She was deeply religious and very proud of videos she had made in which she had expressed her faith.

In response to a question about what should happen to her account should she pass away, Susan emphasized the videos' ability to facilitate community mourning. When YouTube friends of hers had passed away, she felt comforted by connecting with them through their videos and account pages. She said:

> That's a really good question because [in] some of my early videos I shared my personal faith a great deal and I would definitely want those on there. They're not there currently, um, because a glitch happened and I lost all my videos. But, um, I shared my faith and I think that was very important. [Those] are the best videos I've ever made. And I would want those out there. If I were to die, I would really want the videos to remain. Not as a testimony to who I am but as a member of a community. There have been a few deaths in our community. Um, a couple that I was very close to. One was FreeWingz and he died of a massive heart attack very unexpectedly at the age of thirty-three. And I'm subscribed to him and he's subscribed to me and there's no way on God's green earth I'll ever unsubscribe from him. And I visit his page as a memorial. And so, not that I would necessarily want people visiting my page, but I think that certain people I've grown closer to might want to.

Susan emphasized how YouTube pages and videos might facilitate handling grief within a community of friends. She describes how she lost friends on the site, such as a man of Vietnamese descent named FreeWingz (his YouTube channel name) who suffered from polio and whom Susan recalls dying of a heart attack in his thirties. She remained devoted to keeping their technical links alive, for example, through the feature of YouTube subscriptions.

FreeWingz vlogged and created clever special-effects videos, typically garnering thousands of views for each of his videos. He joined in 2006, seven months after YouTube opened to the public. His subscriber count was modest, listed as 217 as of June 2018. In one video entitled *VLog to GOD—PART ONE—(The Voices of Creation)*, FreeWingz records a message to God in which he confesses that he has not created vlogs lately. His mind goes blank and he loses his voice. He tells God he loves Him and asks for help in gaining inspiration for another vlog. Comedically, a majestic voice off camera begins calling his name and soft music plays. FreeWingz presses his face to the lens and asks who the being is and how this being got into his camcorder. The video ends with a black title card and white writing saying, "coming soon. VLog to GOD—PART TWO—(Walking with Satan)." His humor and creativity are touching and apt for the YouTube environment, in which life and afterlife may be viewed through a lens. His work invites viewers to empathetically connect with his life and the challenges he faced.

Susan's wish to stay connected to FreeWingz illustrates how a combination of emotional, social, and technological collective forces create posthumanity. Susan wished to preserve technologized links between her and friends who had passed away. She confirms that "there's no way on God's green earth I'll ever unsubscribe from him," exhibiting a more positive, collective form of the posthuman that emphasizes eternal connection. Susan said that she sometimes visits FreeWingz's page as a memorial, much the way one would pay one's respects to deceased loved ones by visiting their tombstones at a cemetery. She expressed an interest in keeping her videos up, not for her own legacy but as an acknowledgment of others' need to connect, pay respects, and mourn by interacting and maintaining "continuing bonds" through images left behind on YouTube.

Susan and her friend FreeWingz remained linked not just generally through media but through the feature of a video subscription that implies a live link between a viewer and video maker. Temporality becomes elided in the posthuman collective. The idea behind subscriptions connotes the potential for receiving alerts about new, forthcoming material. Of course, there will be no new videos from FreeWingz himself. The account might produce new material, such as memorials, if others maintain the account and are granted an ability to post on it. Even though FreeWingz will not be posting new videos, the feature nevertheless shapes the parameters of the quality and type of memorial interaction that may occur between viewers and the deceased. Rhythmically speaking, it fuses a present temporality to a past friendship dynamic. Future studies of posthuman memorials should consider how posthuman configurations take shape through temporally asymmetrical, experiential features and the interactive expectations and resulting emotional impact that those features suggest. It is powerful and perhaps comforting to believe a live link exists through an ongoing feature such as a subscription, even though the person has passed away.

A pattern emerged to suggest that participants often crafted their legacies in anticipation of how *other* people might feel about the continuation of their media. Some YouTubers focused on having their site maintained for community purposes. Others advocated maintaining it only for a short period of time or deleting it altogether, as maintaining their legacy seemed unimportant. Not all interviewees shared the idea that videos should remain to keep their legacy alive. Perhaps individuals who feel insignificant deserve even more attention as their alters continue to thrive and inspire others within a posthuman, mediated ecology. In the future an important role for anthropologists and visual ethnographers will be to create alters that highlight the marginalized, human aspect of individual voices that may become lost amid mediated swaths of posthumanity.

DIGITAL MIGRATION

Lefebvre asserted that the media "day" never ended and in fact had "neither beginning nor end."[82] Nevertheless, YouTube's viewing and participatory cycles apparently parallel human rhythms of work and play. For example, viewership on YouTube peaks in the afternoon in the United States during weekdays and in the late morning on weekends (Eastern Standard Time).[83] Highly trafficked viewing windows correspond to the times when people have free time outside of work and school. Research suggests that viewing times vary according to the device that is used,[84] but in general viewership peaks on the weekends, with a low point beginning on Monday.

Websites are also impacted by human usage, suggesting a posthuman link between humans and technology. Interviewees say that websites such as YouTube do not last particularly long. Their narratives and ethnographic observations indicated that perhaps the most intensive use for this social crowd occurred over a three-year period (although for some the cycle was slightly longer at five years). Over time, YouTube's intensity of usage cooled for those creators and video bloggers who migrated to other sites such as Facebook and Twitter.[85] I define *digital migration* as a transfer of intensity of participation to a different online site or service in response to changing user preferences, desires, and platform modifications. Three types of digital migration occurred on YouTube: radical migration, conceptual migration, and in-migration.

In *radical migration* people basically stop using a particular medium and migrate completely to another service without much consideration of the earlier site. A person's account on that site may be deleted or left open to atrophy. The second type of migration is more subtle. It constitutes a *conceptual migration*, in which people may cease or vastly reduce their usage of a site; yet it nevertheless serves as an orienting social context that influences people's interaction on other sites. For example, a person might abandon YouTube but provide a link to the social media site they are currently using to keep social connections to YouTubers. Continuing to engage with YouTube friends on another site constitutes a conceptual migration that brings the former framework to a different site. Although not exhibiting the traumatic and emotional rupture of diasporic people's violent separation from a homeland, conceptual migrations similarly bring meaningful identifications of prior sites to sociality experienced in new digital milieus.[86] People who stopped using YouTube but continued to meet up with people whom they thought of as "YouTube friends" on other sites were enacting this type of conceptual digital migration. For example, Thor's Twitter account description reads: "I suck More so you can suck Less . . . Sucking at Youtube Since 2006." Clearly his persona on Twitter orients toward YouTube, such that Twitter becomes a means to express a YouTube-inflected persona and related social connections.

A third type of digital migration is *in-migration*, in which people remain on the same site, in this case YouTube, but switch intensity of participation to a different YouTube channel that they create. A new channel page that updates one's video catalogue may more accurately reflect current interests. I went through an in-migration when I switched accounts from an experimental channel I started in May 2006 to AnthroVlog, which I launched in May 2007. I opened the earlier account because I wanted to learn to vlog, but I did not widely publicize my initial efforts. After switching to AnthroVlog, I left my prior channel open but stopped using it. YouTubers might delete an old account and start anew, or they might keep both channels alive. In-migration implies that they divert intensity of participation to a new channel. At times YouTubers do not necessarily decrease intensity on old channels but rather engage in more *expansive* video making, in which they participate across multiple accounts that serve different purposes. This is an additive approach rather than a migration away from something.

Online participants might migrate when a social media site lost its cool factor or became less community oriented. At a meet-up in Santa Monica in 2009, I interviewed a documentary filmmaker called K8oBlog (her YouTube channel name) who discussed her views on YouTube's changing focus away from sociality. K8oBlog was a white woman in her late twenties who had been participating on the site for about three years. Her videos each typically received thousands of views. As of June 2018, she had 13,343 subscribers. She vlogged on an array of topics: having a bad hair cut, discussing her film, trips to the dentist, and going to events such as

YouTube gatherings and the film festival South by Southwest. She enjoyed the social aspects of the site and cited commercial saturation as a key reason why she believed YouTube's popularity was waning. K8oBlog stated:

> I think [YouTube is] on its way out [nods head]. I mean, you know, MySpace had its time, uh, Facebook might be on its way out as well. Twitter will be, you know, I mean. That's what's interesting, like websites, they don't last very long. Yeah, I think YouTube is on its way out. I think it's because it became so corporate and there's so much about advertising that I think a lot [of] people are turned off. And maybe just the novelty of it has kind of worn away.

K8oBlog and other interviewees intuitively identify an online rhythm of websites and how they work. They gain momentum, in part, because they are "novel." They have their "time" and then people lose interest and migrate to other sites after a few years. K8oBlog talked about migrating to Twitter. For K8oBlog, Twitter helped her keep connected to the YouTube community, thus enacting a conceptual migration. She used Twitter to promote her documentary by alerting her Twitter followers to screenings of her film. She also appreciated observing Twitter users as they discussed her film during a screening. Conceptual migration does not mean that her Twitter feed is filled only with YouTubers. It simply indicates a preference to interact with a recognizable group of YouTube friends on a platform other than YouTube while retaining its conceptual and social connotations.

A video blogger from outside of YouTube alerted me to Twitter and suggested that I obtain an account, which I did in 2009. I began following YouTubers on Twitter. Many of the people whom I met at gatherings and who enjoyed YouTube sociality began using it too. In some cases Twitter became another way of sharing YouTube videos, as it was possible to post links to videos in its brief messages. One creator who vlogged outside of YouTube said that it was easier to keep in close contact with vlogging friends via Twitter rather than through video blogs, which felt like static video-hosting web pages rather than interactive platforms. Over time I began following other colleagues and Twitter accounts of interest, but a visible contingent of YouTubers still forms a large part of my contact list on Twitter. Personally, I still think of this group as "YouTubers" rather than "Twitter friends," even though technically they are both.

While K8oBlog described a significant decrease in intensity of her YouTube usage, other YouTubers talked about Twitter as simply being an additional service to use. Nbwulf, for example, enjoyed the social aspect of YouTube and told me that his Twitter participation was just an addition to his YouTube participation rather than a direct replacement. In response to a question about whether he had migrated to Twitter, he stated, "Some people might see it as a migration because of the lack of activity on YouTube, but it's not." Nbwulf eventually removed most of his YouTube videos and simply left contact information on his YouTube channel that referenced a Twitter account name and a gaming contact. Providing information about the Twitter account suggests that it had become a key way for him to communicate with YouTube-centric and other friends. Prior to his decrease in video productivity, nbwulf insisted that the move did not represent a full-fledged migration. This dissonance between his video output and his image of continued YouTube participation bolsters the argument that YouTube retained social vitality and that his migration conceptually retained a notion of YouTube even off the site.

The posthuman collective evidenced distress when YouTubers suddenly migrated away or their account went quiet through a disruption in the posting of new videos. Learning that someone had deleted or abandoned a channel prompted questions of concern from those left behind. Supporters might take active steps to locate a YouTuber's social media destination(s) to discern their status. Such digital detective work might be conducted to relieve anxiety or at least confirm that a YouTuber was alive and well.

Feelings of concern about missing YouTubers were well articulated in a video entitled *Disappearing YouTubers*, which was posted on July 9, 2017, by Tony Huynh, a popular video maker who was known more widely by his YouTube channel name, thewinekone. A very early adopter who joined when YouTube had just opened to the public in mid-December 2005, he had participated on the site for over eleven years when he posted this video. Thewinekone was an Asian-Canadian man in his mid-thirties whom I observed at a gathering in Toronto. He had amassed a following due to his humorous vlogs on subjects such as trolls, pick-up lines, singing songs, snow days, being stalked for his YouTube fame, problems with rude movie goers, and critiques of bad YouTube vlogs. Each of his videos received thousands and sometimes even tens of thousands of views. As of June 2018, he had 120,203 subscribers.

Disappearing YouTubers documents the discomfort people feel when creators stop posting videos and the active steps that viewers and supporters take to locate them. Viewers may experience genuine concern if social media links have disappeared or life updates have ceased, suggesting potentially difficult times—or even death. In the video thewinekone states:

> I hate when YouTubers disappear for a long time and I'm stuck wondering, where
> the hell did they go? So then I have to resort to looking up their Twitter, Instagram,
> Snapchat, Facebook—all their social media, just to see what they're up to and that in
> turn makes me feel like a creepy cyber-stalker. More so than I already am. The worst
> is when I found out that they haven't posted *anything* on social media so I'm stuck
> wondering, what the hell happened to them? Was there a life-changing moment
> for them and they had to ditch the internet? Or did they just not feel like posting

anything? Or did they actually die? I mean, you never know with some of them, especially the ones that don't share much about their personal life. Like, who would I even have to look for to find out if they're doing okay? And sometimes they pop up out of the blue with no explanation, no update as to what has been going on. It's like I've invested so much time, months, maybe even years, in watching you, supporting you, following you, and you don't even tell me what's been going on with your life? You act like everything's completely normal and you haven't been gone for half a year. That's weird.

In a posthuman configuration those left behind in the collective may feel a sense of loss or discomforting disconnection when people pass away or leave the site without explanation. I experienced these feelings when a YouTuber whom I had hung out with at gatherings deleted his YouTube account and severed other social media links. People may simply change creative direction or may be dealing with serious problems, as reportedly happened to thewinekone himself—a fact that perhaps motivated his concern about others. According to his Wikipedia page, he took a break from YouTube in 2014 due to an "undisclosed illness" but retains a "cult-like" following despite his slow upload schedule of one video every few months.[87]

Notably, his narrative exhibits a strong temporal orientation. He discusses anxieties arising from concern for other people as well as from his and others' need to be informed given that they had attended to another person's work *over time*. In his video thewinekone emphasizes the temporal sacrifice one makes for other video makers, including the "months, maybe even years" that he has spent paying attention to them through their media. He implies that the personal investment of his scarce life resource to someone else's work reciprocally merits an update where possible. People may exhibit asymmetrical allegiances to the posthuman collective, which for some may be rooted in temporal contributions that support individuals to keep them connected.

IS THERE A POST-YOUTUBE?

Ethnographic data from video sharing invites philosophical reflection on the posthuman status of technologized devices and services. Websites do not stand alone but are embedded in competing and interconnected media ecologies within which people interact. Even during YouTube's height, YouTubers had always expanded their sociality to multiple modalities while still seeing YouTube as an orienting framework for sociality. For example, several interviewees noted that they used a live video chat site called Stickam to connect with other YouTubers.[88] Many interviewees met with "YouTube friends" on Stickam.

One interviewee, whose YouTube channel name was anakin1814, posted a video on March 15, 2008, called *YouTube Community: Season 2*, in which he reflected on his media behavior as situated within a larger media ecology. A white man in his mid-thirties, anakin1814 vlogged in ways that were often thoughtful and personal rather than aimed at widely accessible comedic or viral fare. He sensitively vlogged about a wide variety of topics, including art, guilty pleasures, YouTube community issues, birthday greetings, the environment, and music. Although a few videos saw a thousand views, most of his videos received a few hundred views. As of June 2018, he had 2,490 subscribers. At the time of this video, anakin1814 had been on YouTube for about two years. He discussed how YouTube was used not in isolation but rather along with other social media sites. Despite the number of sites in which he participated, he described how YouTube retained a special importance within his personal media ecology. In his video he stated:

> So many of the relationships I have on here that have extended now into Facebook and Twitter and Skype and Stickam and Yahoo IM and MySpace. It's all about a community. And it seems like YouTube, though, is the mother ship; it's the portal and all these other things are conduits. You know, I was a MySpacer before I was ever on YouTube, and the amount of friends I have on there is changing; it's all more of a place to collect my internet friends now and some real-life friends.

Anakin1814 used multiple media, such as the live video-streaming service Stickam, to engage with YouTubers. Media scholars Jean Burgess and Joshua Green also observed that Stickam functioned as a "supplement" or "plug-in" to YouTube early on.[89] For YouTubers whom I interviewed, it similarly functioned as an additive *satellite* site to YouTube. Its use did not constitute a radical migration but rather expansively extended interactions and relationships that originated through YouTube. In other cases or over time, social media sites replaced YouTube as it cooled in popularity. After experiments with live streaming concerts, sports, and interviews, YouTube offered a live video-streaming option in 2011,[90] which some pundits argued contributed to Stickam's eventual demise in 2013.[91] Nevertheless, for anakin1814, YouTube functioned as the "mother ship" or the orienting "portal" that provided a gateway to his other "internet friends." Even though he used many different sites, the concept of YouTube anchored his conceptualization of his internet-based, media ecology.

Websites, like people, exhibit existential cycles. People are born, live, and die, and so do websites in a sense. Websites are created, people use them, intensity reaches a peak, and eventually people go away or websites change with regard to their usage. Some websites actually "die" if they are shut down, as happened with sites such as blip.tv or Stickam.[92] Sites may also effectively die when people leave or stop using them.

Sites may remain technically open but be "dead" because they are irrelevant, as reportedly happened with MySpace.[93] Indeed, one pundit has even used the term "MySpace dead" to talk about a certain type of website death, which means the site is still up but is not widely used or considered relevant, even though it was used by many people between 2005 and 2009, perhaps even the majority of US teens.[94] The concept of digital deathstyle may be applied to understand not just human processes of death but also nuances in different trajectories of website usage, intensity, decline, and demise. If a site's operators are clever, they may find ways to adapt amid changing media styles. An attempt was made on MySpace to reposition itself for musicians, who formed a key initial demographic for the site.[95] If a site cannot maintain active usage, it may die or remain only nominally open, effectively becoming "MySpace dead."

Alternatively, groups of people may migrate to other sites in ways that conceptually retain the idea and sociality of the original site in which they interacted, as was the case for several YouTubers in this study. In this way YouTube lives on in a "post-YouTube mediascape,"[96] in which its social connotations migrate to different social media. Although many interviewees now gather on other social media sites, they interact as YouTubers through their conceptual migration. They share YouTube videos and discuss YouTube-related topics on Twitter and Facebook.

Through multiple trajectories of usage, a site called YouTube has given rise to numerous YOUTUBE alters. Here capital letters are used to distinguish between a website that everyone "knows about" through a singular, monolithic narrative, to a concept depicting the multiplicity of versions of the site in a way that visually echoes the literary connotation from posthuman fiction. The original YOUTUBE in which interviewees posted communicative videos continues for some, while for others it is more of a social framework or even a future ideal. A contingent of YouTubers interacts via Twitter, thus creating a YOUTUBE alter on Twitter. To talk about YouTube as a single site elides its complexity and varied trajectories of usage over time, as well as different versions of YOUTUBE, past and present. Drawing inspiration from posthuman fiction helps envision myriad conceptual YOUTUBE alters that can never be identical but nevertheless connote key nuances and dimensions of use.

One may apply similar lessons from reflections on how "the Internet" is often treated as a singular entity to rethink and recognize multiple conceptions of YouTube. Indeed, as I have pointed out elsewhere, "Frameworks that treat 'the computer' and 'the Internet' as singular entities that are distinct from other realms potentially smuggle in a researcher's prior assumptions about what these entities connote to them, what capabilities they offer, what limitations they have, and what people experience when using them."[97] As media studies scholar Kevin Driscoll and information science researcher Camille Paloque-Berges argue, "The Internet has always been multiple," and thus histories of particular forms of usage are required to understand its sociological and technical trajectories.[98] One may make a similar argument about YouTube, which from its inception enabled numerous pathways of usage, including notions of community, revenue, performance, sharing, and uncertain digital legacies as well as multiple levels of social intensity. In line with the findings of Driscoll and Paloque-Berges, many histories of YouTube are required to understand its impact. Driscoll and Paloque-Berges encourage scholars to "find and document hidden histories, obscure sources, and less visible networks" and to recognize how sites exhibit "uncertain or inconsistent temporalities."[99]

As newcomers arrive, they too may find a niche for expressing vernacular voices that create new YOUTUBE alters. Indeed, new groups invoke community rhetoric that calls forth aspects of identity or shared interests when participating on the site. For instance, Asian and Asian American video makers are active on YouTube in part through popular channels run by Ryan Higa (whose YouTube channel is nigahiga), Kevin Wu (whose YouTube name was KevJumba), and Christine Gambito (known on YouTube as HappySlip, whom I interviewed for this study). This activity has given rise to what scholars characterize as the "Asian/Asian-American YouTube community."[100] Scholars studying trans and queer populations have also noted how vloggers have bonded through participation on the site and have recently observed an active "trans YouTube community."[101] Researchers have observed that people with mental illnesses, such as bipolar disorder, turn to YouTube to create communities, find support, and establish connection by sharing their experiences.[102]

YouTube has spawned a "protoindustry" of what communication and media scholars Stuart Cunningham and David Craig characterize as "social media entertainment" or "communitainment," which draws on the technical and networking affordances of social media to produce mass forms of entertainment.[103] Characterized by innovative content and "nontraditional media ownership," such approaches offer opportunities for alternative voices to find a platform. For Cunningham and Craig, communitainment involves intensive interactivity and content but is also "driven by an ethos of community" that sets the genre apart from traditional media. Examples appear in the many communities on YouTube that revolve around common interests such as gaming. For example, many kids enjoy watching older teens navigate the sandbox creation game of Minecraft through multiple genres, one of which includes "Let's Play" videos. These videos provide comedic commentary as a player moves through a game. Scholars refer to groups on YouTube who bond through the game as the "Minecraft YouTube community," which has fostered collaborative learning.[104] Communitainment typically depends on combining aspects of entertainment, such as gaming, with unique communicative commentary from creators as well as interaction between video makers and audiences.

As they migrate, interactants are all creating and experiencing "post-YouTube" alters via other sites, platforms, and subgroups on the site. A kaleidoscope of YOUTUBES now potentially reconceives its original meaning both within the site and across digital realms. Each of these, as Driscoll and Paloque-Berges suggest, should be examined as important alternative narratives that challenge the typical representation of a single website marching toward what is often portrayed as a teleological trajectory of monetization, professionalism, and what interviewees characterize as a systematic stifling of the vernacular.

Clashes with the posthuman may take many forms, some of them encouraging, some of them distressing. As people in media-making environments see themselves drowning in a sea of alters, anthropologists and visual ethnographers will quite likely feel a responsibility to bring visibility to those who see themselves as unimportant or who become lost in the media shuffle. Anthropologists and ethnographers have always been attuned to raising awareness about marginalized voices. In this case the problem is not video narcissism but rather its opposite: a profoundly anxious feeling of being inhumanely ignored or, perhaps even worse, distressingly distorted in media. Video creators' poignant, emotional, civic, and funny videos are antidotes for the disorienting feeling of posthuman tremendum. By the same token, perhaps it will be a posthuman collective that ultimately provides reassurance and connection. In response to creators' laments about who will cry over them, perhaps it is time for anthropologists to cry—and laugh—a little.

7

LIVING WITH ARRHYTHMIA

PROSPECTS FOR RENEWAL

A well-known adage declares that "old soldiers never die; they just fade away." The same may be said of YouTubers. A YouTuber's presence may remain long after the intensity of the person's participation has faded into the ether. Videos and their commensurate potential for interactivity linger on—perhaps asymptotically. Engagement with a video's half-life approaches but may never reach zero. Some day, somewhere, a viewer might watch the video and then comment on it or share the link or both. When YouTubers take a break, it is sometimes difficult to determine whether their absence is permanent or just a temporary hiatus from which they will return in force. It is interesting to watch people who have not vlogged in a while regain their footing. One video maker struggled to remember his signature taglines and chuckled to himself when he remembered how to sign on and off.

An advantage of longitudinal research approaches is that they deepen understanding of media use by analyzing the evolution of participation and the video genres that appear in reaction to change, both personally and on specific sites. An example of a genre that contextualizes individual participation trajectories is the *return video*, in which a video maker has taken a hiatus from posting videos (ranging from few weeks to a few years), and then returns to record a statement that fulfills a social purpose. Return videos deserve study in their own right, particularly for their aesthetics and social meaning. They contain important temporal elements, such as accounting for a past absence and updating viewers on future plans. Video makers often begin by apologizing or explaining why an account has atrophied. Next, they

DOI: 10.5876/9781607329558.c007

catch the viewer up on what is happening currently in their lives. Return videos end in varied ways. For some, the return is brief and the video serves as a final good-bye. For example, one YouTuber posted a return video stating that his time on YouTube had become less intense ironically because of the opportunities he had received and the people whom he met and now socialized with through the site. In his video this creator says that due to his gratitude to YouTube for what he has achieved personally and professionally, he will never officially close his account. He nostalgically admits that he misses "the old YouTube" and he signs off, thanking his audience for watching. Deliberately leaving his account open invites the asymptotic possibility of future engagement with his work.

As a YouTuber in a specific media generation, he found meaning in the concept of YouTube in part due to a cohort of friends who met and traveled on a video adventure together. He and his YouTube friends constitute a media generation, which may include people of many different ages. Early vloggers on YouTube of the same media generation included people in their teens and twenties and older, including people in their seventies. Media generations are not defined as much by age as by the mediated parameters—including features and other people—that they encounter when making videos and socializing. The idea of "the old YouTube" is intertwined with a social group.

A return video may acknowledge support that a video maker has received. For example, one YouTuber posted a video in 2012 after a three-year hiatus. He opens by saying that he "never expected to make another video for this channel," but he felt the need to thank the YouTube friends who had supported him by promoting his books on health. He is "blown away" by the fact that the friends he made online years ago can still be counted on to help him, and he felt that the easiest way to thank the YouTube crowd was to make a video.

Return videos may conclude with a reassurance that one has not really left YouTube as well as a promise to post new material. For example, one interviewee returned to say that he needed a break to reflect a bit, explore other interests, and get some work done. He hoped that his viewers had not forgotten him because he is "back," even though he admitted that his pace would be slower. He said he would post three or four times a week instead of five or six. Another video maker posted a video in 2014 after not posting since 2012. She was in her twenties when I interviewed her in 2009. In her return video in 2014, she is in her mid-thirties. She catches viewers up on her professional achievement of making a film and her change in personal status; she is now married. She turns toward the future, stating: "I'm going to try to make videos now. But, like, just in one take, 'cause who the hell would want to edit anything?" At the end of the video she seems uncertain if she will continue posting videos.

Lefebvre's approach urges analytical attention to temporal trajectories and change.[1] Observed parameters of video sharing invite theoretical supplementation to Lefebvre's rubric. Specifically, this chapter will discuss the prospects for and dynamics of rebirth or renewal. It extends beyond studying traditional linear trajectories that move from birth/beginning to death/end and calls on ethnographic data to analyze interstices between cycles—real and envisioned. It analyzes the possibility of renewing vitality in video sharing by highlighting characteristics and features that are meaningful to socially inspired creators. As new media generations appear, they too will launch new cycles of participation, some of them coexisting with those of veterans on the site. Similar to marriage vows that must tacitly be renewed every day as one chooses whether to continue a relationship, so too must YouTubers decide whether to end participation or to remain and under which circumstances it will be acceptable to do so.

The purpose of this chapter is to analyze how socially oriented YouTubers responded to several of the site's major monetization changes in ways that highlight how they conceptualized an ideal of YouTube. What constitutes interviewees' notion of "the old YouTube" did not precisely exist in the way that they conceived of it—as evidenced by the details discussed in this chapter. YouTube's monetization trajectory was a continuous process that began very early in its life cycle. The argument is not that socialization is incompatible with monetization; indeed, several interviewees were YouTube partners, which means they received a share of profits from ads associated with their videos. Advertisements include several forms such as pre-roll ads, overlay ads, and display ads. Unskippable pre-roll ads play in their entirety in the viewing window before a viewer may view a video. Skippable pre-roll ads allow viewers to hit a Skip Ad button and watch the video after the advertisement plays for a few seconds. Overlay ads run on the bottom of a video as it plays. Display ads appear to the right of the video or above the video suggestion list. Although several YouTubers in the study were interested in both monetization and sociality, it is clear that the site's commercial choices strained interviewees' perception of social opportunities on the site.

The chapter addresses numerous events that ushered in tensions during the study period, including a move toward commercial video-streaming services, revenue-sharing partnerships, prioritization of popular creators, the rise of networks, monetization of meet-ups, algorithmic impacts on extremism and video quality, and burnout. In each case the chapter outlines the changes, provides ethnographic data showing video makers' reactions, and analyzes how the responses reveal YouTubers' ideals for video sharing.

The vision of a socially oriented site includes democratized media sharing that requires active attention and shaping in light of tensions resulting from other participants, monetization pressures, and video makers' own creative cycles. Although monetization and socialization may theoretically coexist in hybrid environments, the choices made at times in the YouTube case show discomforting misalignments in the pace of operation between humans and the corporate entity of YouTube. Temporalities—both human and machine—influence the meaning of mediated interaction. When multiple rhythms conflict, they may result in distressing temporally asymmetrical experiences that Lefebvre termed "arrhythmias." Arrhythmias occur at multiple levels. For example, they may occur between video makers and the operations of a platform or between video makers and viewers. Human creators cannot always keep pace with the rapid demands of audiences and algorithms.

Given that a permanent state of arrhythmia is likely to persist in hybrid commercial and social video-sharing environments for the foreseeable future, it is crucial to analyze YouTubers' reactions to changes in their media ecologies. Of particular importance is examining how specific changes conflicted with what YouTubers believed video-sharing sites should accomplish. Critically interrogating these changes, resulting arrhythmias, and interactive effects aims to prompt future discussion about solutions that visualize new or renewed creative spaces that achieve what socially motivated YouTubers imagined and desired.

YOUTUBE'S EVER-CHANGING LANDSCAPE

Between its public launch in December 2005 and 2018, the YouTube platform underwent continual change. Keeping pace with all the nuanced ways in which features were changing—each with various levels of visibility to users—was extremely difficult. This situation has been characterized as "permanently beta," or the feeling of constantly being in test mode when using technology and experiencing flux as companies make product changes in response to the commercial environment.[2] YouTube participants sometimes noticed changes before an official announcement had been made. In other cases YouTubers thought they were operating in a particular mediated environment that had already changed—without their awareness.

The rapid pace of change was discomforting and difficult to follow, representing a kind of arrhythmia between the tempo of the site and what YouTubers could process. Rapid change rendered it difficult to contextualize how alterations impacted the environment for social video sharing. YouTubers reacted in diverse ways to specific changes. For instance, in 2006 YouTube had a "friending" feature similar to that of other social media sites in which people could make a friend request to another YouTuber. If the request was accepted, a hard-coded link between them was established on the site. YouTube "friends" could send out "bulletins" or updates on their activities to each other. However, many interviewees did not particularly care for this feature and characterized the bulletins as spam.

YouTube eliminated social media friending, but it retained subscriptions (lists of channels that one wishes to be alerted about new video postings), basically merging both lists on a user's channel in 2011.[3] In contrast to interviewees in the study, many commenters on YouTube's user forums were quite annoyed that YouTube had eliminated friending. YouTube's staff explained the rationale for the merge by citing confusion between the friend and subscription lists. An alternative explanation is that the march toward monetization played a role in how the site's features and layout were framed. The change signaled that YouTube's parent entity, Google, privileged the connotation of paying for content over that of being a social media friend. Even though subscriptions to individual video makers were still free as of 2018, paid subscription services that removed ads and offered exclusive content were also introduced in 2014–2015.

Internet entrepreneur and marketing expert Gary Vaynerchuk reportedly coined the expression, "If content is king, context is God," thus updating or even challenging Bill Gates's observation about the priority of online content.[4] Vaynerchuk defines context as "the circumstances and facts that surround a situation." Of course the importance of context has long been explored by anthropologists, linguists, and other scholars. Unstated and rapid contextual changes represented problems for users (and scholars) who were trying to make sense of the circumstances under which YouTubers were interacting and participating on the site, particularly in terms of the media logics, financial environment, and structures that influence interaction.[5] Operating under changing but undisclosed circumstances can be disconcerting. Many of the changes that this chapter describes revolve around how monetization impacted interviewees and their interactions as they continued to use YouTube for self-expression and sociality.

Morphing into a Streaming Service

YouTube's business model appeared to drive toward offering video-streaming services. For example, YouTube rebranded a music service called YouTube Music Key (launched in 2014) into YouTube Red in October 2015.[6] In 2017 YouTube launched a service called YouTube TV, a video streaming service costing $35 per month and aiming to compete with established video-streaming services such as Hulu and PlaystationVUE.[7] YouTube TV offers what is available on broadcast television stations plus sports, news, and special cable entertainment programs.

YouTube Red was a subscription service costing $10 per month that allowed viewers to watch content on the site without advertisements, offered offline viewing, and enabled viewers to play content such as music in the background of other apps. It also provided original programming content from YouTube stars such as Joey Graceffa (his official name and YouTube channel), a white American actor and singer in his twenties who is known for vlogging and gaming themes. Graceffa joined in 2009, and as of June 2018, he had more than 8 million subscribers. Original content was also offered from Smosh, the YouTube channel of two white American comedians in their early thirties, officially known as Ian Andrew Hecox and Daniel Anthony Padilla. They are known for their comedy sketch and gaming videos and are YouTube veterans, having joined when the site was still in beta phase in November 2005.[8] As of June 2018, Smosh had 23 million subscribers.

Just as YouTube Red was being introduced, complaints were appearing that the service would not likely succeed and could adversely affect creators. Reviews of YouTube Red were uneven, with one pundit arguing that eliminating brief ads was not worth the price, especially given YouTube's announcement to eliminate unskippable ads in 2018.[9] Other creators reportedly had not yet heard of the changes; as one Twitter user stated: "It worries me that as a YouTube creator I have no idea what 'YouTube Red' is, or how it will affect my channel, beyond what's in the media."[10] Informational lags exemplify arrhythmias or misalignments in participatory rhythms between video makers and site operations. Although YouTube sometimes announced changes on their blog, creators complained about YouTube's lack of timely communication. Features changed quickly and reportedly without warning or contextualization, thus complicating creators' ability to respond to the site's new parameters.

A video maker who discussed YouTube's commercial changes was Chris Sanders (his official name and YouTube channel name), a black man in his early thirties who was an early adopter of the site, having joined in May 2006. He had been participating on YouTube for over nine years when he posted a video entitled *4 Reasons YOUTUBE RED IS GOING TO FAIL | Rant* on October 21, 2015. On his YouTube page he described himself as a motivational speaker, anime fan, and nerd "hoping to inspire others through the promotion of nerd culture and positive thinking." His videos receive thousands of views each, with a few seeing tens of thousands of views. As of June 2018, he had 61,455 subscribers—a significant following.

Sanders believed that being able to listen to videos while multitasking should be a basic feature of a free YouTube. Further, he argued that the landscape of viewing competition is so saturated that most young people will simply find something else to watch if they encounter content behind a YouTube paywall. Some viewers may see these paid services as a way to support their favorite creators. But in Sanders's view, subscription fees would likely be split between all the creators that a person subscribed to, such that each creator would effectively receive less revenue than that generated from ads on videos or related merchandise. In his video Sanders stated that for creators, this business model "lowers our revenue and then in turn, and I'll be really honest here, makes some people not want to do YouTube."

The pace of YouTube's rebranding presented arrhythmic challenges for people tracking the latest changes, with one journalist complaining: "YouTube has branded and re-branded its feature so many times that it is hard at times to understand what is what and how is it different from the previous one."[11] Illustrating his lament, YouTube scrapped YouTube Red in 2018 and rebranded it as YouTube Premium, charging $11.99 per month for new members.[12] It promised ad-free viewing, an ability to listen to music in the background, original content, and access to downloading YouTube videos. In May 2018 YouTube introduced YouTube Music, which offered access to listening to music, finding recommendations, and experiencing playlists (curated groups of songs). The basic service was ad-supported while YouTube Music Premium was ad-free but cost $9.99/month.[13] One reviewer complained that although YouTube's music catalogue is vast, the service omits key metadata and includes crowd-sourced, inaccurate information about music, artists, and song chronologies.[14]

YouTubers do not necessarily accept these services, citing concerns about lack of control for creators and viewers. Some commenters feel they are already funding their favorite YouTubers through sites such as Patreon, a crowd-funding service started in 2013. Patreon allows supporters—or "patrons"—to donate funds to creators on a one-time or recurring basis.[15] By donating to creators, some viewers feel that they should not have to doubly pay for premium viewing services on YouTube. Further, some creators do not necessarily want to participate in ad programs, and video makers fear that services such as YouTube Premium threaten creator control over distribution of funds. An example of eschewing ads is found in the vlogbrothers channel on YouTube, which is run by two white American brothers whose official names are John Green (forty years old) and Hank Green (thirty-eight years old), both apparently multimillionaires.[16] The Green brothers reportedly did not originally run ads. Even when they eventually did, they donated ad profits to charity.[17] Concerns exist that paid subscription programs will vastly reduce creator control over monetization choices, benefit only the top creators, and negatively impact participation in the YouTube community. Monetization changes that reduce control and complicate interaction were perceived as threatening to socially oriented—and even some professional—participants.

Tensions between Monetization and Socialization

Sharing profits through a partnership program may function as a kind of mutual reciprocity between YouTube (which provides the platform) and the creators (who provide content). Each entity ostensibly benefits from the other. Yet it is video makers who bring viewers to the site through their hard work and creativity. However, tensions emerged after the initial launch of the partner program in 2007, which video makers said created social hierarchies on the site and constituted a "rough issue" for some interviewees. YouTube has frequently revised its partnership rules. Originally limited in 2007 to a select group of invitees with high view counts and subscriptions, the site expanded late in 2007 to allow anyone with sufficient views and terms of service compliance to *apply* for the program.[18] In 2012 YouTube expanded the program to allow anyone to click a button and authorize Google to place ads, even on single, popular videos—a move that invited criticism from those who previously had to apply to the program and await authorization.[19] Resentments between partners from older media generations and those who could monetize immediately yielded arrhythmic, participatory conflict. The situation created temporal unevenness as prior partners had to wait and be evaluated while others could instantly achieve single-video monetization. Participants are not always aware of their options. A team of creators attending VidCon 2016 noted that they only realized they could monetize their work after one of their videos had already gone viral; thus, they missed out on potentially significant ad revenue.

In some cases tension ensued because people wanted partnership but were not popular enough according to YouTube metrics to receive it. Others felt that the program created social hierarchies that divided YouTubers and put a strain on interpersonal sociality. Critics believed it provided too much support to creators whose videos received many views but who were not necessarily perceived as having the technical or creative skills to merit increased visibility or compensation.

Tensions worsened as the partnership program expanded and individual profit potential became more competitive. Revenues are estimated to be quickly declining for smaller video makers as there are now more than a million people in the program.[20] Although official statistics are not provided, content creators claim that YouTube takes about 45 percent of the ad revenue from a partnership, sometimes rendering the actual ad revenue stream quite modest.[21]

The drive to monetization at times yielded unfortunate interactive dynamics. In his video *A Rant Response for Renetto . . .* , which was posted on August 16, 2009, OhCurt (his YouTube channel name) expressed frustration about YouTube's increasingly commercial atmosphere. At the time of the video, OhCurt had been participating on YouTube for at least two years (although he mentions having a prior account that he had deleted). OhCurt was a white man who vlogged about themes such as YouTube culture, being gay, and humorous observations of life. Each of his videos typically received hundreds of views, with his more popular videos garnering thousands of views. Although his account had been deleted by June 2018, he had 2,648 subscribers as of January 2009.

OhCurt participated socially at meet-ups and in his videos. He was also a YouTube partner—which he said garnered him very little profit. He expressed concerns about monetization's impact on the site's sociality. In a post on his blog outside of YouTube, he expressed the wish that Google would spend more resources to engage with the YouTube community. In *A Rant Response for Renetto . . .* , OhCurt stated that in the past people had responded to each other thoughtfully through comments and videos, but interactivity declined when monetization metrics encouraged video makers to aggressively exhort viewers to "Rate! Comment! Subscribe!" at the end of every video. OhCurt felt this practice was detrimental to the site's social atmosphere.

Concerns over monetization's impacts on video-making creativity and quality have been part of the conversation since the site's inception. Indeed, such discourse is as old as art and commerce. An interviewee whose YouTube name was thetalesend posted a video on June 16, 2011, titled *I hate what youtube has become*, which he characterized as a "rant." He said he began migrating to other sites once YouTube began focusing in earnest on commercialization. Thetalesend (whose official name was Ryan Basilio) was a Filipino male in his mid-twenties who often vlogged about socially conscious topics such as gay rights and the importance of voting. His videos each garnered several thousand views, and he had 1,936 subscribers as of June 2018. He noted that he was happy that 150 to 200 of his subscribers watched him consistently. When I interviewed him for the second time in Santa Monica in 2009, he had been participating on the site for about three years.

In *I hate what youtube has become*, thetalesend said he had observed an increase in mean-spirited videos capturing unfortunate life moments, interpersonal sniping, and envy, all of which combined to poison YouTube's social atmosphere. The problems emerged in 2008, he argued, when people began launching accusations that certain people did not deserve to be partnered and were cheating to achieve success on the site. He was disappointed that YouTube was resembling commercial video-streaming sites rather than serving as a venue for "normal" people to put up their own messages and form a sense of community.

In an interview for my ethnographic film *Hey Watch This!* (2013), Ryan said he believed that in its more heavily commercialized instantiation, YouTube could no longer realistically promote community. In answer to my question of where YouTube was headed from a social perspective, he stated:

> YouTube is still gonna go strong. But it's not going to be mainly from user-generated content. It's gotten more commercial, you've seen all the ads, pop up a lot more. As

a community-based, kind of social media thing YouTube is pretty much done. But as a place for people to find interesting videos and videos that may be promoted by YouTube, it's not gone yet. But it may be. Someone is bound to make a service that is more user-friendly and whenever someone finds or adopts that area people will move on. It's like the rest of the internet. We had MySpace and now we have Facebook. No one's on MySpace anymore and now we have Twitter, so. Whoever gives the next best step, that's who's going to go on. That's just the way the internet is.

His prediction about YouTube creating streaming services proved correct. Although he felt that YouTube would continue, he believed that its commercial emphasis had destroyed its prospects as a community-based social platform—a contention that may or may not bear out for future media generations. He believed that some day a more "user-friendly" site might materialize. Sadly thetalesend passed away in 2012, before his ideal could take shape. It is especially moving that he envisioned a place where vernacular voices could be continued, given the fact that he himself—even as a partner—used YouTube to reflect on important matters of the day.

In 2017 YouTube updated its rules to require that creators achieve 10,000 combined lifetime views on their channel before they could activate monetization.[22] In 2018 YouTube began requiring a channel to have at least 1,000 subscribers as well as 4,000 hours of watch time in the past twelve months for the creator to participate in ad-revenue sharing.[23] Part of the motivation for the tightened rules stemmed from concerns that more than 50,000 ostensibly family-friendly channels had reportedly posted inappropriate content such as terrorist materials, hate speech, and sexualized images of children.[24] In addition, the site announced plans to hire human editors to moderate content and train algorithms to detect inappropriate videos, all in an effort to make YouTube a more ad-friendly atmosphere.

Monetization is not necessarily incompatible with socialization. Several YouTubers interested in sociality ran ads on their videos. Anthropologists are also well aware that the human spirit finds workarounds to facilitate sociality, even within restrictive, commercialized regimes. At the same time, YouTube's corporate decisions created tensions, which will likely spur new video-sharing approaches. Given its critical mass of videos and viewership, it is not likely that new sites will initially compete directly with YouTube. Rather, the landscape may see the emergence of niche-based, socially supported, and thematically circumscribed sites that can manage scale and interaction more effectively, whether or not monetization is a primary goal. Conversely, concerns remain that thematically targeted sites may complicate the diversity, discourse, and debate that characterized YouTube's initial environment.

Catering to Larger Creators

YouTube steadily targeted their services to support larger and more popular creators—who often became popular after starting modestly and building an audience through grassroots efforts. Privileging mature creators does not take into account the temporal need to support creators at the beginning of their video-making trajectory. Congregating resources in the hands of top creators risks ignoring the cultivation of new voices who exhibit monetization potential. A sustainable model would likely require supporting creators across multiple points on the temporal spectrum of development.

In 2012 YouTube introduced new resources for top creators in the form of several production-based YouTube Spaces, including facilities in London, New York, and Los Angeles as well as Sao Paulo, Tokyo, Mumbai, Paris, Berlin, and Toronto. In 2018 YouTube launched a YouTube Space in Dubai.[25] The purpose behind these creator spaces is to provide successful YouTube participants with "high end audio, visual and editing equipment in addition to training programs, workshops and courses."[26] These facilities are large-scale. The YouTube Space in Los Angeles is 41,000 square feet. The facility launched in Canada is 3,500 square feet and provides select participants with free equipment, such as lights, cameras, and microphones.[27]

To use the recording space and participate in workshops, users must have at least 10,000 subscribers. Established mainstream actors who have YouTube channels, such as Amy Poehler and Rainn Wilson, have used this space. The top twenty-five YouTubers invited into the Los Angeles Space when it opened boasted tens of thousands to hundreds of thousands of subscribers.[28] Reports indicate that although the space is free, creators must cover key expenses such as actors, crew, and costumes, resulting in even popular YouTube stars feeling underpaid.[29]

Complimentary use of such creator spaces are largely out of reach for YouTubers with a more modest social following. YouTube does provide resources via its online Creator Academy, which includes videos on topics such as starting a channel, working toward monetization, understanding analytics, and developing production skills. Weighting resources to established creators, however, represents an arrhythmic pattern, as this creates tensions with smaller creators at the beginning of their video-making trajectories and risks ignoring support for future media generations on the site.

The Rise of Multi-Channel Networks

Monetization also gave rise to controversial entities called multi-channel networks (MCNs), also called multi-platform networks, or simply networks. YouTubers complain that networks take their profit but offer little in return. Multi-channel networks are independent entities that are not owned, endorsed, nor affiliated with Google or its YouTube division. Acting as a middleman between YouTubers and YouTube, networks promise to promote channels, derive content, manage digital rights and monetization, and develop audiences in return for a share of a YouTube channel's profits.[30] Each network assists multiple YouTube channels, sometimes focusing on a theme such as the Machinima MCN, which manages several gaming channels. Networks have broadened their business strategy to become multi-platform networks as some support work posted on other social media such as Instagram. Reports indicate that even the names "multi-channel" and "multi-platform" are misleading, as some networks pre-date YouTube channel support and others have pivoted to represent lucrative combinations of entertainment businesses such as production companies, talent firms, and social-video enterprises.[31]

One of the first, largest, and best-known networks is Maker Studios, which was founded in 2009 in Culver City, California, by popular YouTube star Lisa Donovan (her YouTube channel name is LisaNova), her brother Ben Donovan, and Lisa Donovan's then fiancé Danny Zappin, along with YouTubers Shay Carl Butler (known professionally and on his YouTube channel as Shay Carl), Kassem Gharaibeh, and Philip DeFranco (formerly known on YouTube as sxephil).[32] As of 2014, Maker Studios boasted 4.5 billion monthly views from videos generated across thousands of channels that the company represented.[33] Maker Studios represented top YouTube performers, including channels with millions of subscribers.[34] Disney purchased Maker Studios for $500 million in 2014.[35] A few months later Lisa and Ben Donovan left the company; Zappin had already departed under bitter circumstances, claiming he was forced out in 2013.[36]

Networks are controversial on YouTube. Creators complained that they did not receive timely support from networks to assist them with their projects—yet the networks took substantial profits. Several years after the Disney acquisition, in 2017 it was announced that many YouTubers were being let go. The announcement was met with relief from those creators who reported that Maker Studios collected as much as a quarter of their earnings, yet were allegedly unresponsive when contacted for help and never provided useful developmental and marketing services.[37]

In general, interviewees did not discuss networks or Maker Studios in their videos. An exception is a video maker who asked that I refer to him in the study by his nickname, Thor. I interviewed Thor at a meet-up in New York City in 2007. He was a white man whom I surmised to be in his late thirties or early forties and who had joined the site in October 2006. His videos focus on product reviews and demos on devices such as cameras, drones, and quadcopters. He also vlogged about visiting people and places. His videos—which run ads—each receive several hundred to a thousand views. He had 12,630 subscribers as of June 2018. Thor is an example of a

YouTuber who collects revenue through ads but who also makes videos emphasizing sociality and friendships.

Thor posted a vlog called *Visiting Maker Studios Los Angeles California* on April 15, 2012, in which he toured the facility. He trains the camera on himself and his surroundings, video-blogging style, and interviews Lisa Donovan, Ben Donovan, and Danny Zappin. Thor exhibits an easy sense of engagement with them given that he had met them early in YouTube's life cycle. As he puts it, he has known them "forever" and is very "proud" of their success. He truly knew them when, as they say. As the video opens, pulsing music plays as he pans the camera around numerous individuals hard at work at their computers. Zappin gives him a tour and points out different groups, such as producers and animators, and areas of the facility including prop storage and production studios.

During the tour Thor mugs to the camera saying, "This is like a *real* business." Thor asks questions about the purpose of networks and how they work—anticipating his audience's curiosity. He asks Zappin whether networks such as Maker Studios will be the "death" of solo YouTubers. Zappin explains that the YouTube environment changed drastically between 2005 and 2012. He recalls that when Lisa Donovan was among the twenty video makers on YouTube with the most subscriptions, she had 700 subscriptions. By 2012, he says, networks became advantageous because it took at least 1 million subscribers to achieve top-100 most subscribed-to status. Zappin tries to position Maker Studios as focused on creating content as well as monetization, in contrast to networks that concentrate on profit. Notably, the lucrative Disney buyout shows Maker Studios' successful monetization—or at least an assumption about its future potential.

Thor's framing of his visit arguably sets him apart from the serious businesslike scale and atmosphere of Maker Studios. Thor jokes to some of the studio's writers that he is doing "old school YouTubing" in case they "don't recognize it." Thor surmises that these writers and studio workers must be baffled at how YouTubers of his media generation coped with creating one-camera, self-operated YouTube productions. He ends the video by humbly telling his viewers that he must "get out of their hair." He is touched that they generously took time out for "an old guy" like him. He characterizes their gracious interviews as demonstrating "loyalty, fun, and friends." Notably, although he asks about the future of the solo YouTuber, in fact in prior videos he had experimented with collaborative productions and had already predicted that more large-scale production of content was the direction in which the YouTube platform was headed. Although positive case studies exist,[38] YouTubers complained bitterly about the performance of networks.[39] Thor's video aesthetic and content choices in his vlog sets the social activities of his media generation apart from the large-scale efforts of profit-oriented networks.

Monetizing Meet-Ups

Where profit opportunities exist, businesses will mushroom. As it happens, meeting up makes money. Video blogging and creating YouTube videos are certainly not the first artistic contexts in which commerce draws on models of friendship for success. Sociologist Howard S. Becker, a musician playing piano in Chicago night clubs in the 1940s, discusses tensions between artists and the friends whom they "use" in their work, such as characters in novels or subjects of photography.[40] On YouTube, conflict emerged when individuals profited from sociality in ways that interviewees believed could threaten democratized and accessible interaction.

Commercial organizations began holding large-scale conventions that required a paid ticket to attend and structured the amount of time that might be spent with individual creators. Conventions typically included performances, workshops, parties, and informational panels. They also featured celebrity meet-and-greet events, which one YouTuber described as waiting in line for hours to speak with a YouTube star for five minutes.[41] These included (listed by launch date) Summer in the City (2009, in the United Kingdom), VidCon (2010, based in Anaheim, California), Playlist Live (2011, in Orlando, Florida, and Washington, DC), and FanFest (2013, in Singapore and then expanded to India, Australia, Korea, and Japan, Toronto, and Washington, DC).[42] The YouTube Black FanFest made its debut in 2017 at Howard University in Washington, DC.[43] It was launched partly as a reaction to critiques about YouTube's lack of diversity.[44] In 2016 fifteen large-scale YouTube-themed events took place around the world.[45]

Playlist Live was created by AKT Enterprises, an Orlando-based entertainment and merchandising company that sells products such as T-shirts for musical acts and businesses. Playlist Live events originally launched in 2011 to promote YouTube, and in 2017 attendance was estimated to be 13,000 guests and 500 creators.[46] Like other commercial conventions, it includes celebrity meet-and-greets, panels, workshops, and live performances.

VidCon is held annually at the Anaheim Convention Center, which is very near Disneyland. The event was started by Hank and John Green of the vlogbrothers YouTube channel.[47] In 2017 the event expanded into Europe and Australia.[48] The VidCon I attended in 2016 boasted approximately 25,500 attendees,[49] compared with the estimated 1,400 that reportedly gathered at the first VidCon in 2010.[50] Originally catering to video bloggers, many of whom were on YouTube, VidCon expanded to include other types of videos and social media, with a more central focus on celebrities. One of the biggest themes in 2016 was live streaming. YouTube was still a major sponsor of the event in 2016. In 2018 Viacom acquired VidCon, which remains a stand-alone subsidiary.[51]

Despite visible vocal objections to the commercialized meet-ups, a few inter-viewees did attend these commercial events, in part to boost their professional work. OlgaKay, MysteryGuitarMan, and Thor were among the few interviewees who made videos about their activities at these conventions. In most cases video makers recorded activities and structured content that resonated with their sta-tus on the site. For instance, one of OlgaKay's Playlist Live videos is titled *Playlist LIVE Highlights w/Pillow Fights*, posted on March 30, 2011. It is a compilation of her adventures at Playlist Live, both presenting to the public as a YouTube celebrity and collaborating to produce content with fellow popular video stars.

OlgaKay (her YouTube name and stage name) is a Russian American, white woman in her twenties who had been on the site and successfully monetizing her work for nearly five years before posting this video. Her videos routinely garner tens of thousands views each, with some even reaching hundreds of thousands to a mil-lion views. She had 824,413 subscribers as of June 2018. Part of her success involved crafting videos with widespread appeal: comedic vlogs such as eating pizzas with weird flavors and juggling odd objects like soap and cameras.

Her PlayList Live video shows her speaking on a panel about issues such as deal-ing with haters, which she believes are mostly kids. She found that if you reach out and acknowledge that they are "probably having a bad day," they apologize for their behavior. She also interviews YouTube celebrities and vlogs at a dinner with similarly high-profile YouTubers such as Shay Carl, cofounder of Maker Studios. Dinner guests pass around the camera and vlog into it, often without seeming to know whose camera it is.

One interviewee who frequently recorded his attendance at large-scale commer-cial events was Thor, who made five VidCon videos in 2011. In two videos he does not actually attend VidCon (in 2013 and 2014) but instead gathers with friends. He also made sixteen videos about Playlist Live in Orlando, documenting yearly attendance from 2011 to 2014 and again in 2016. He notes in his videos that he is from Florida, so the fact that he lives relatively near the Playlist Live venue perhaps facilitated frequent attendance.

In his Playlist Live and VidCon videos, Thor walks around with a camera, chats with YouTubers whom he knows from the past, and reports on changes, such as how conventions differ from prior grassroots gatherings. He wears a white T-shirt bearing the YouTube logo and his signature baseball cap worn backwards with the word "Thor" written across it in white letters. He enjoys pranking attendees. At one point he pretends to cut into a multi-hour-long line of fans waiting to see YouTube celebrities such as Jenna Nicole Mourey, a white American actress and comedian in her late twenties who has over 18 million subscribers. Better known by her YouTube channel name of JennaMarbles, she shares comedic thoughts and beauty vlogs. Thor jumps to the head of the JennaMarbles fan line, records fans' exasperated reactions, and then steps out, noting that he is only kidding. In another prank he fools fans into thinking that they are in the wrong line, and they confess that the lines are so long they do not know where they should be.

In keeping with social YouTubers' more democratized outlook, he takes a poly-rhythmic approach to interviewing. He makes a concerted effort to socialize with people exhibiting different temporally based status levels, including event organizers, YouTube celebrities and veterans, and new fans. He interviews people from differ-ent media generations, including old friends and people who have just joined the site. He enjoys helping younger fans meet the YouTube celebrities whom he knows. When YouTubers from his era approach him, they hug, chat, and often recall how they met at a specific meet-up, thus calling up a chronotopic chain of sociality that links their shared history. Thor's interactions echo those I observed earlier at grass-roots meet-ups in which YouTubers treated all participants as important. For instance, one participant at a Minneapolis meet-up took delight in gathering signatures from YouTubers of multiple levels of popularity for his souvenir T-shirt (figure 7.1).

Unlike YouTubers who criticize commercial events, Thor appears to enjoy meet-ing up, on camera at least, even in the large-scale venues. Nevertheless, he often sets himself and his cohort's vlogging activities apart from those he observes at the com-mercialized Playlist Live conventions. For example, in a video entitled *Playlist Live 2013—@shanedawson Hello, @Harto, @JoeyGraceffa*, posted on March 25, 2013, Thor observes YouTube celebrity Joey Graceffa talking to fans outside of the venue on the lawn. Thor remarks that this type of interaction is how it used to be done, when YouTubers did not wait in long lines but more casually greeted fellow video makers—even celebrities—in public settings such as parks.

Although media generations are not necessarily age-bound, Thor frequently uses age-related observations to describe his reactions to Playlist Live dynamics. Often his characterizations exhibit arrhythmias in the sense that he feels temporally out of sync with new YouTubers arriving on the scene. In a video posted in 2013, he says he "feels like a middle-school principal" when vlogging amid a sea of young teens. Thor seems delighted when younger attendees recognize him from YouTube and chat with him for his vlog. On the other hand, he admits that he no longer rec-ognizes the top YouTubers at the event. In a Playlist Live video posted in 2016, he wonders aloud if he is "aging out" of coming to YouTube conventions. He expresses arrhythmic social distance from the teens and the objects of their affection in the commercialized conventions.

In terms of feeling tone, commercial motivations, and sheer volume, events such as VidCon 2016 offered vastly different experiences from the grassroots YouTube meet-ups that I had attended. The energy at VidCon radiated from mobs

FIGURE 7.1. A YouTuber autographs a fellow participant's T-shirt at a gathering in Minneapolis on June 7, 2008. Screenshot by Patricia G. Lange from *Midwest Gathering*, posted on AnthroVlog on June 12, 2008.

of thousands of frenzied fans who came to watch their favorite YouTube stars. Grassroots event organizers whom I interviewed tended to actively discourage the kind of promotional energy that the large-scale, fan-centric events exhibited. Grassroots organizers' rationale was to provide a democratized aura for the gatherings that did not single out the site's top performers but rather felt more inclusive.

It would be inaccurate, however, to assume that as meet-ups grow in size they cannot foster interpersonal forms of community or that grassroots meet-ups displayed no exclusivity or orientation toward celebrities. At VidCon it was possible to find communities of interest if one knew where to look. For example, I attended a panel called "Fighting for a Cause," in which women video creators, including one academic, talked about the challenges they faced in using video to promote causes such as feminism, transgender issues, and exploring Latinx identity.[52] I was very interested in these subjects and video makers, and I felt there were moments when I could connect with other people holding similar video-related interests.

Observers noted that such events could create warm, interpersonal feelings. For instance, during one lunch at VidCon 2016, a young girl told her adult companion at our table that she felt a special "joy" in coming to VidCon. No one would be able to "judge" her, she noted, given that the event was filled with people just like her who liked to watch videos and spend a lot of time at a computer.[53] This rhetoric closely resembled the discourse I heard among socially driven, early adopters. Eleven years after YouTube's launch, people still expressed concerns about being "judged" by others who did not understand their media-making interests. One academic observer who attended VidCon felt that the event was not about video at all but rather about fostering "relationships and communities in a way that no other medium can claim." Further, he stated that people came to VidCon "not to consume content but to commune around it,"[54] suggesting that, for some, VidCon's size did not preclude meaningful sociality.

Despite YouTubers' rhetoric of democratized participation, celebrities attended grassroots gatherings in part to promote themselves. YouTubers are fans as much as they are video makers, and they often greeted YouTube stars at smaller gatherings, sometimes asking for autographs, photographs, and selfies. In the first few years of YouTube, meet-ups exhibited plenty of excited fan energy as YouTube-famous stars mingled to promote their work and expand their social networks. At several gatherings small crowds of fans crowded around select individuals to talk, create videos together, or request photos and autographs. For example, in Minneapolis, Adam Bahner—known more widely by his YouTube channel name of TayZonday—happily greeted fans of his "Chocolate Rain" song, which he sang in a video with the same name. His *Chocolate Rain* video, posted in 2007, went massively viral and caught the attention of mainstream media. By June 2018, he had accrued over 1 million subscribers, and his *Chocolate Rain* video had amassed over 100 million views.

According to a video interview on a website exploring viral video stories, TayZonday grew up in a biracial household (his mother is black and his father is white) and his "Chocolate Rain" song was a statement on racism.[55] His videos, often of him singing songs in his distinctive *basso* voice, typically each garner hundreds of thousands to a million views. He was in his mid-twenties and had been participating on YouTube for about a year at the time of the Minneapolis gathering and his interview with me in 2008. He eventually moved from being a teaching assistant at the University of Minnesota to becoming a media celebrity. In the decade since *Chocolate Rain* went viral, he has been singing, acting, and doing voice work in the entertainment industry. At the Minneapolis gathering, he wore a *Chocolate Rain* T-shirt and was happy to meet and talk with a group of fans who gathered around him.

YouTubers sometimes perceived celebrity performances at gatherings as threatening to democratized participation. Although they were common at commercial events, they sometimes garnered criticism at grassroots meet-ups. For instance, at the gathering at the Science Centre in Toronto, a microphone was set up and several better-known YouTube participants performed songs and bantered with other creators. However, a few interviewees complained to me that such performances threatened the spirit of the event, which was not about self-exhibition or promotion but rather socialization. Although it was pleasurable for some attendees to see YouTube stars perform, others felt that they were out of place in socially motivated contexts.

In contrast, commercial events intensely promote celebrities in a way that some YouTubers felt created social divisions. At VidCon I observed that celebrities were protected as stars with security guards, and access was carefully orchestrated as they were escorted through back entrances to panels and performance stages.[56] For example, I interviewed a Brazilian filmmaker officially known as Joe Penna, whose YouTube channel name is MysteryGuitarMan. At VidCon he headed a panel giving advice to aspiring video creators. He had been on the site for about a year when I interviewed him at a gathering in New York City in 2007. At that time he was a teenager in college and was contemplating changing careers to go into making media professionally. MysteryGuitarMan found fame on YouTube experimenting with video technique and form. He made creative musical videos in which he played unusual instruments, used objects as instruments (such as blowing into bottles), created stop-motion effects, and used split-screen techniques to create the effect of being an entire band playing a song with multiple instruments. As of June 2018, he had 2.7 million subscribers, and each of his videos regularly garnered hundreds of thousands of views.

In 2007, although there was a great deal of fan energy at the gathering he and I attended along with about a thousand others in New York City, most people simply milled around and chatted with their favorite YouTube personalities, often on camera. By 2016, MysteryGuitarMan was a YouTube celebrity and our follow-up encounter at VidCon emerged during an organized meet-and-greet in which fans stood in line to speak with him. Interaction was limited to chatting briefly and perhaps taking a selfie.

When I caught up with Joe in 2016, he was in his late twenties. He had married and started a family. He had parlayed his successful YouTube activities into a professional media career that included making commercials and films. During his talk, he mentioned lean years in which he worked hard and money was scarce, but he ended up achieving life goals such as making films. Although he did not recall his ethnographic interview with me, I reminded him that I was an anthropologist collecting data on YouTubers and that when we last spoke he was contemplating a career change. I asked him what the single greatest factor was in convincing him to change direction and pursue making videos. He said that it was his family's support of his new career plans that helped him decide to professionalize his work.

FIGURE 7.2. Patricia G. Lange and Joe Penna (MysteryGuitarMan), June 24, 2016. Photograph by Joe Penna.

Naturally wanting the full ethnographic fan experience at VidCon, I was pleased that he agreed to pose for a selfie (figure 7.2). Usually I am camera shy. No doubt drawing on years of experience taking fan selfies and using his sense of humor, MysteryGuitarMan put me at ease, even taking several shots for me to choose from. I was grateful to him for participating in my research for my book *Kids on YouTube* (2014), so the image is special to me. Even at a large-scale convention, brief moments of meaningful interaction were enjoyable and created emotional connection to the event. I felt I had a window into the fan experience and appreciated why someone would feel excitement and a sense of connection by talking to a favorite creator.

Lack of vlogs by interviewees on these commercial conventions suggests that YouTubers in this study had either moved on from YouTube or preferred more intimate emplacements of their sociality and community formation. In contrast, many vloggers have created videos about grassroots gatherings that are lovingly crafted and posted to YouTube. Even the larger grassroots meet-ups, such as the one at Toronto's Science Centre, was organized by a YouTuber who worked there. It felt more democratizing in part because it did not require paid admission, enabling anyone to attend.

When VidCon began preparing for its inaugural 2010 launch, YouTubers reacted in diverse ways. Some were concerned that it co-opted YouTubers' grassroots sociality for profit aimed at a select few. Ryan Basilio (whose YouTube channel name was thetalesend) was especially disturbed when the organizers of VidCon began advertising for their event. He feared that it would be an expensive "boondoggle" that would violate the democratizing spirit of meet-ups. In 2009, after being on the site for about three years, he posted three videos vehemently protesting the monetization of sociality in the form of VidCon. Although he acknowledged that the event might not necessarily be bad, he was concerned about its organization and budgeting.

The first video, *Vidcon What a Rip Off*, was posted on December 9, 2009; the second was *Response to Vlog Brothers Vidcon Is a Ripoff!* and was posted on December 10, 2009. In these videos Ryan complained that the admission price was steep. The event was slated to be held in a high-priced Los Angeles neighborhood without access to public transportation. Attendees were meant to stay in an expensive hotel costing $150 per night. Since YouTubers could only afford to attend meet-ups annually, he argued, they should not have to spend so much money to gather with friends. He proposed options such as enabling YouTube creators to attend for free in return for donating their skills, such as playing instruments or singing at concerts.

In Ryan's third video, entitled *What I Have Done So Far to Block Vidcon 2010* and posted on December 11, 2009, he discusses concrete steps he took to legally stop the event. He describes having contacted several government organizations, such as the Los Angeles County Planning Commission and the Beverly Hills City Council, to discuss his concerns about the impact of the event and the likely beneficiaries of its profit. He demands that VidCon organizers be more transparent about their budget.

He received forty-seven comments in total on the videos; seventeen of the comments agreed with his position while eighteen disagreed. Six comments expressed both agreement and disagreement with his point of view. The rest were neutral (three) or indeterminate (three). Those who agreed with Ryan's position cited cost, profits being funneled to a select few, lack of public transportation, and anticipation of crowded events with poor content.

Comments reveal the posthuman, asymptotic aspect of video sharing. The majority of the forty-seven comments (93.6 percent) appeared within the first year after the three videos were posted.[57] However, two comments were posted to his third VidCon video one year later, and one was posted to it four years later. Clearly, the intensity of participation occurred relatively soon, but a few responses appeared much later. Even after Ryan tragically died from an illness in 2012, a commenter (who may or may not have known about Ryan's passing) felt motivated to provide his assessment four years after the video was posted. Ryan had addressed a topic that inspired others to consider and discuss. In 2014 a commenter stated: "The first few years were actually very fun because it was small and intimate, now you just wait in line for hours to pay to take a picture with some online douche." This comment provides a comparative, longitudinal assessment that is relevant to this analysis. Even years later, the comment is greatly appreciated. The comment describes a social arrhythmia in which attendees have to wait a considerable time for an encounter exhibiting little interpersonal quality time with a creator, in contrast to the relaxed temporality, opportunities for engagement, and casual atmosphere of early VidCons and of grassroots meet-ups.

Those who disagreed with Ryan's protest reminded him that this was a convention rather than an informal gathering and that VidCon's ambitious plans to hold concerts and panels would naturally require expensive audio-visual equipment and appropriately large venues. Further, conventions were more about professional networking than having fun. A few commenters outside the study expressed confusion about why the introduction of VidCon was so upsetting to him. Commenters who disagreed with Ryan also noted that traveling to any gathering, even if free, incurred expenses such as travel costs.

Thetalesend responded that, contrary to accusations, he was not protesting to receive an "ego boost"; in fact, his main concern was for "equality" for YouTubers, many of whom cannot afford to attend expensive events. Illustrating his point, videos documenting grassroots meet-ups often depict YouTubers sharing hotel rooms and carpooling to events. Joint travel experiences were often just as important as the actual public event. YouTubers vlogged in their cars, building anticipation by singing, joking, and recording their friendship. For thetalesend, much of the problem revolved around helping a select few profit while not giving back to YouTubers who helped create the site. As one commenter put it: "In these trying times in the world, we need to connect w/people not profit off them!"

The data suggest that large-scale meet-ups can support some measure of sociality, perhaps contrary to the arguments by interviewees. However, YouTubers expressed the view that grassroots gatherings offered more intimately emplaced interactive framings and therefore significant advantages. For some participants, meet-ups should not represent avenues for monetization but should support creative expression and sociality.

YouTube Extremism

YouTube has always been known for its shocking viral fare. However, despite opportunities for simultaneous sociality and commercialization, the addition of formal monetization metrics did yield incentives for creating extreme forms of video content. The site uses automated systems—including algorithms that recommend increasingly outlandish videos—to keep people watching. Reports in 2018 indicate that YouTube's algorithmic learning systems privilege videos that represent extreme positions, conspiracy-theory laden claims, and videos obviously lacking in facts. Yet viewers do not necessarily agree with or enjoy such extremist videos. Algorithmic and human viewership patterns combined at times to incentivize video makers away from doing thoughtful work and toward making videos that were "light on facts but rife with wild speculation."[58] In 2011 thetalesend's video *I hate what youtube has become* observed these trends and noted that YouTube had become a "dangerous place," showcasing inflammatory videos as well as demagoguery.

The rapidity at which algorithms exacerbated the site's extremism has prompted concern. Human tendencies toward viewing the outlandish help train algorithms but are only part of the equation. Experiments with newly opened accounts demonstrate how quickly Google's algorithms recommend increasingly extreme content for new viewers, even with accounts containing a sparse viewing history.[59] Algorithms invite arrhythmic viewing patterns that discourage videos exhibiting measured thoughtfulness or containing ideas cultivated over time. Nor do algorithms appear to take into account human preferences that do not always seek immediate gratification of the extreme variety. These patterns even became too perverse for advertisers, as companies reportedly boycotted YouTube when their products were used to advertise discomforting videos.[60] Algorithmic trends also have political implications when videos return information about political candidates in false, extremist, and asymmetrical ways. Algorithmic incentives for promoting biased videos have civic impacts beyond aesthetics and sociality on the platform.[61] Extremist videos may unduly influence wider voting populations. To counteract such problems, more research is required on algorithmic effects and how they might be trained to return more balanced or well-researched content. Ironically, by repeatedly watching these videos for analysis, researchers risk indirectly contributing to the perpetuation of extreme content. For example, although one researcher clicking on extreme videos for a research project is an algorithmic drop in the bucket, it is also arguably true that, collectively, researchers frequently viewing disturbing videos within an algorithmically organized environment may be creating a *negatively polarizing research effect*. The way in which algorithms are currently being deployed is rapidly creating a field in which thoughtful content is decreasingly offered as even an option, which greatly concerned YouTubers who believed the site should offer timely access to democratized content.

Temporal Padding of Content

Manipulating length of videos is another way in which monetization offered incentives for creators but challenged quality and the viewing experience, thus creating arrhythmias between creators and viewers. When YouTube celebrity and viral video maestro Kevin Nalty published his book *Beyond Viral* (2010), it was practically a truism that brief videos were optimal, given viewers' limited attention spans amid an intensely competitive online viewing environment. Nalty (whose YouTube channel name was nalts) was an early adopter who joined the site in January 2006. He was known for popular comedic and pranking videos, each of which saw millions of views. With 236,739 subscribers as of June 2018, he had clearly mastered the viral formula. In his book Nalty stated that views were "inversely related to the length of videos," which he said should ideally be two to three minutes long.

By 2016, video makers were extolling the advantages of so-called long-form videos (ten minutes or longer). Videos that lasted at least ten minutes or even a few seconds longer were believed to retain viewership for a prolonged period, thus driving up ad revenue.[62] Of course this "ten-minute trick," as pundits refer to it, only works if people actually keep watching. Its impact was assessed by video makers such as Felix Kjellberg, better known by his YouTube channel name of PewDiePie (63 million subscribers), a Swedish YouTube mega star in his twenties who found fame by making vlogs and videos with gaming commentary. It feels a bit ironic to quote criticisms about YouTube quality from PewDiePie, given that he has seen substantial controversy over what critics label his abrasive and anti-Semitic commentary.[63]

Nevertheless, PewDiePie's concerns were widely quoted. He complained that monetization incentives reduce the quality of videos by encouraging time "padding"—sometimes to ridiculous degrees. Examples of what is here termed temporal padding include video makers answering the door or taking a bathroom break but leaving the camera running and not editing these moments out. Such time-based tactics may add thirty seconds to a video's length, tip it over the ten-minute mark for more revenue, and leave viewers staring at uninhabited screens.[64]

These patterns represent participatory arrhythmias because an ideal video length for creators may not be read the same way by viewers, who seek continually robust content within a video, as measured temporally. Tension emerges when people use YouTube to support their livelihood and engage in temporal padding in ways that viewers may feel threaten the quality of individual videos and the site as a whole. Certainly viewers may stop watching or flag bad videos, but these acts impact a creator's need to make a profit, including those who wish to engage simultaneously in monetizing their craft and enjoying human sociality.

Burning Out

Arrhythmias may occur when human creators cannot temporally satisfy demands of audiences, algorithms, and the platform of YouTube.[65] When I began my research in 2006, putting up a video once a week was a standard practice for vernacular vloggers—a grinding pace for me. In 2018, top-performing, professionally oriented YouTubers reported feeling a pressure to post *once per day*. As one pundit put it, "It is strongly believed that YouTube accounts with more than 10,000 subscribers should post daily because YouTube's algorithm favors frequency and engagement."[66]

Participatory arrhythmias may result in creator burnout, a documented problem on the site. OlgaKay, a YouTube celebrity and interviewee, found the constant pace of producing new content challenging; at one point she was posting twenty videos per week.[67] She was worried about slowing her pace lest she "disappear," and she reported in a media interview that her life's activity became oppressively work-related. Party invitations required her to make time calculations about her YouTube work, prompting her to wonder: "Can I film there? . . . If somebody's uncomfortable with me filming I don't think I can go and have fun with you guys because I need content."[68] She took a break and returned by reconceptualizing YouTube as one part of her profit-making activities. She also focused on creating and selling new merchandise, such as her colorful and playful line of Moosh Walks socks. The pace of vlogging required to ramp up and commercialize one's channel was not always compatible with the human pace of maintenance, which represents a participatory arrhythmia across different points in a YouTuber's video-making cycle. The resulting exhaustion created burnout and prompted new income-generating options that were not as temporally aggressive but were humanly sustainable.

Professional media maker Roberto Blake (also his YouTube channel name) posted a return video of the type described in the beginning of this chapter called *WHY I TOOK A BREAK FROM YOUTUBE*. He posted his return video on April 9, 2018. He opens by stating that if you do YouTube "long enough" (he had been on the site for nine years), sooner or later you will make a video about taking a break. Blake's video collectively responds to viewers who were aware of his history of depression and had reached out to him when his pace of participation demonstrably slowed for two months. Perceiving an irregularity between Blake's current and prior video-posting pace, viewers sensed a resulting arrhythmia and expressed concern. Notably, his break was relatively brief. It was the irregular *pace* of posting that caused viewer anxiety. The posthuman collective apparently begins getting nervous when a YouTuber's participatory pace slows without explanation. In this example, arrhythmia occurred at two levels. One type of arrhythmia reflected an irregular pace between Blake's past and current video-posting schedules. The other arrhythmia occurred between Blake and his viewers, who desired a faster video making pace from him than he was able to deliver at that time.

Blake's videos typically receive several thousand views each, and he had amassed 315,116 subscribers as of June 2018. He is a graphic designer in his early thirties who characterizes himself as a "black nerd," given his many technical and creative interests. He earns money from clients and from sponsorships and advertisements on his videos, which include occasional vlogs about personal issues. His content mostly aims to motivate creative professionals, such as by providing mentoring on growing and improving one's channel. In his return video he explains that he was ill for a couple of months with the flu and took a break from YouTube, which he says impacted algorithmic assessment of his performance. He reassures viewers that he is not burned out, although he expresses concern for people on YouTube who are. Diversifying profit-making activities, such as speaking at conferences and mentoring clients, reduced his financial pressures. In his video he explains:

> Doing less content and prioritizing other things, whether it's my health or whether it's the growth of my business, I'll be real with you, that has hurt me a little bit in the YouTube algorithm. I know that and a lot of other creators are experiencing exactly the same thing. And it's not great, it sucks, but you know what? Our supporters, our viewers can always help us beat the algorithm with doing one simple thing, sharing videos that you think deserve more views, that you think deserve support, or that you think can entertain or educate or motivate people. If you want a video to be successful, if you want a YouTuber to be successful, whether they have 1,000 subscribers, 10,000 subscribers, or 100,000 subscribers, then it's down to you making a choice to share those videos with other people that you think will enjoy them as much as you do. And I think that, ultimately, that's a big part of what YouTube is about at its core.

Conflating sociality with the mechanics of viewership and monetization, he notes that supporters—and tacitly members of a posthuman collective—can help "beat the algorithm" by showing support for videos that deserve to be shared. Notably, his discourse democratically encourages support for YouTubers (and potential clients) at various magnitudes of subscription rates. Expressing concern for the many people around him who struggle to maintain an exhausting pace, he advises them: "If you feel like you're burning out, take a break. If you feel like you're sick and you're not up to doing something, if you can put it off and it's not gonna hurt you too much financially, then put it off." His advice for video makers to take breaks when necessary recognizes that algorithmic tempi and human pacing are sometimes arrhythmically out of sync.

Complicating these tensions were changes in the qualifications for partnership. Stricter requirements in 2018 included having 4,000 hours of watch time over the past year. The new rules garnered mixed reactions, with some YouTubers reportedly seeing them as far more demanding, thus rendering it difficult to take breaks. Videos appeared in which YouTubers pleaded with their audiences to at least run their videos in the background in order to preserve adequate watch-time metrics.[69]

Crowd-sourced assistance attempts to address misaligned arrhythmias between the pace set by audiences and algorithms versus what a human can accomplish. It is fascinating to observe Roberto Blake calling on viewers to help "beat the algorithm" and circulate content when a YouTuber needs a hiatus for health reasons. Taking breaks from making videos, diversifying across a variety of money-making activities, and setting time limits on video-creation efforts were all strategies that YouTubers proposed to deal with burnout. YouTubers' experiences also show how the posthuman collective senses subtle variations in video tempi that reveal discomforting arrhythmias between video makers and viewers. Arrhythmias sometimes prompt the posthuman collective to reach out and provide support.

CREATING NEW CONTEXTS OF PARTICIPATION

Writing from the perspective of communication and media scholarship, Cunningham, Craig, and Silver argue that "fall from grace" narratives in which an innocent YouTube becomes compromised by commercialization are not always productive or accurate.[70] It would indeed be incorrect to assume that the early YouTube years (2005–2010) were conflict-free or inherently democratic. As this chapter has demonstrated, even when interviewees say they miss the "old YouTube," numerous problems had existed on the site, including conflicts that were not always related to monetization, such as haters. Interviewees' statements as well as ethnographic observations contradict the existence of an ideal YouTube.

Nevertheless, such contradictions should not be summarily dismissed due to inconsistencies. Statements that emerge from nostalgic remembrance are actually crucial sites of investigation, as they are meaningful to the people who believe in or desire that reality. American literature scholar and oral historian Alessandro Portelli has observed, "The importance of oral testimony may lie not in its adherence to fact, but rather in its departure from it, as imagination, symbolism, and desire emerge."[71] Such idealistic portrayals highlight YouTubers' desires for using video to accomplish equitable sociality.

Cunningham, Craig, and Silver state that rather than equating change with corruption, it is more beneficial to understand how new "screen ecologies" depend on the availability of platforms in which content creators "may be able to exercise a higher level of control over their career trajectories than previous models of professionalizing talent."[72] The key here is control—which YouTubers did not always experience in terms of their media, sociality, or representation in monetized milieus. The degree to which creators can navigate the demands of sociality and commercialization must be studied in each case, but such tensions are likely to persist in hybrid—and arrhythmic—environments for the foreseeable future.[73]

YouTube exhibited tensions early on. At the same time, its initial openness before monetization took root gave the platform a sense of possibility. Strategic changes expanding monetization complicated socially oriented YouTubers' ability to express themselves and connect with others aiming for shared cultural experiences. For example, the 2009 revamping of the site's layout organized the welcome page around personalized content. By 2010 an individual viewer's welcome page featured what was most popular on the site as well as individual recommendations. By 2013 the site resembled the commercial video-streaming service Netflix—YouTube's long-term plan visually realized in readiness for its introduction of streaming services. YouTube had morphed into a personalized, commercially driven service rather than one that encouraged mutual, collective, and shared forms of viewing across the YouTubian community.

Video makers who wish to reincorporate a central dynamic of sociality will need to grapple with the arrhythmias and conflicts documented in this chapter. Providing creative resources at various temporal stages of development, enabling more control over an account and its monetization, and helping creators deal with the pace of content generation to avoid burnout are all strategies that YouTubers felt could ameliorate participatory and creative tensions in a hybrid environment. Whether YouTubers stay on, take a break and return, or migrate away permanently remains to be seen. What is certain is that the narrative of successful monetization of professional content often ignores the role that vernacular video played in laying the foundation for YouTube. Withholding support from trailblazing voices risks ignoring the very forces that created the possibility of monetization at all.

8

CONCLUSION

Thanks for Watching analyzed YouTube sociality. To conduct this research, I became a member of video-mediated, social milieus. Of particular importance was not only watching videos and reading discourse but also participating in the process of media creation as it occurred and as it influenced interactional dynamics. In addition to analyzing video artifacts and observing the ways in which people interacted on YouTube, I also attended gatherings across the United States, camera in hand. I became another voice that contributed to recording a concept of "YouTube" as a state of mind—one that reached beyond the parameters of a website or corporate entity. Rather, it became a feeling tone and organizing framework for sociality with connotations of friendship, fun, and participatory tensions. Participating on YouTube also influenced my scholarship, as I received the personal encouragement to practice video-making skills and create vlogs and an ethnographic film—experiences that deepened my understanding of nuanced video sharing and interaction.

YouTubers' experiences alternatively ratified, expanded, or challenged the extent to which traditional anthropological concepts applied in this digital milieu. In general, most terms apply, although some must be expanded in socially oriented video-making groups. For example, the figure of the chronotope, which collapses the notion of time and place in ways that are meaningful to video makers, helped contextualize how YouTubers created a shared sense of history. This study expanded on this concept by introducing the notion of chronotopic chains of experience. For

DOI: 10.5876/9781607329558.c008

instance, two YouTubers reenacted taking a video selfie in a way that self-consciously echoed the same activity at a prior gathering, thus inter-threading and problematizing binary notions of online and offline interaction. They created a chronotopic chain of interaction that offered emotional connection and intertwined their personal histories with that of YouTube.

In other cases the particular parameters of video mediation invited reconsideration of anthropological critiques of controversial concepts such as posthumanism, participant-observation, community, and reciprocity. Posthuman configurations involving technical and social factors intersect with the limitations of human characteristics to yield experiential rather than strictly corporeal posthuman instantiations. Amid the condition of posthumanity, it is increasingly important to honor individual voices. Attending to nonfamous YouTube participants is especially important given algorithmic implementations that complicate video makers' ability to craft their personal and public video statement. Creators may experience posthuman tremendum, which refers to the feelings of awe and fear of their media being out of control in technologized ways. Posthuman tremendum may be especially acute when one's individual data are recognizably depersonalized and aggregated to fulfill corporate or policy agendas. For all the claims of having narcissistic control over media, people do not always have the control they desire. Given how other video makers may manipulate and drown out one's voice, it may be necessary to give quieter voices far more rather than less attention through media. Conversely, posthuman media collectives may offer a sense of comfort and connection, as individuals in group formations feel a sense of disquietude when a constituent inexplicably disappears from socially integrated configurations.

Critics of participant-observation suggest that it is an outdated and sad oxymoron. The study invited reconsideration of these critiques in light of how interacting with a camera and participating while observing often became a key aspect of YouTube sociality. Skeptics argue that it is not possible to fully participate in sociality if one is engaged in the detached, reflective observation required to analyze behavior. Yet for some video activities, observing through a camera constituted robust and meaningful participation simultaneously; indeed, they constituted the same act. Certainly we must all decide what to mediate and when in terms of ethics and interpersonal sociality. However, for mediated activities such as vlogging, it is not possible to reasonably speak of separating participation and observation. Further, the data show how these critiques risk reifying Cartesian binaries that assert a mind-body split in which it is assumed that one cannot engage both the body and mind simultaneously. As seen in the "playful paparazzi" incident in chapter 2, observing through a camera was an important way in which YouTubers and vloggers bonded by providing supportive attention to the nonfamous and nonstereotypically sexualized media object.

Notions of "community" produced controversy on the site—which is perhaps not surprising given the term's overdetermined meanings in the anthropological record. Clearly, the concept retains widespread rhetorical force as evidenced by several lines of data, including interviewees' remarks, YouTubers' own videos, and the commentary that flooded videos on the subject. Rather than ignoring such a fraught concept, the term community is better conceptualized as processual rather than categorical. It will quite likely remain in flux as long as new media generations arrive and grapple with what the term connotes to them and others whom they encounter. Working through notions of community means that, rather than eschewing anonymity, constituents will need to work with unknown others in order to build coalitions of shared interests and activities. When understood temporally, it is clear that accepting and dealing with initial anonymity is a necessary starting point for launching the processual activity of creating community through discourse.

YouTubers' concept of reciprocity illustrated traditional notions as well as more recent updates in the anthropological record. Contra pundits that decry its loss, the research showed that positive forms of reciprocity are alive and well in certain digital milieu, with many YouTubers engaging in reciprocities that acknowledge their fellow video makers' regard. The study also showed that traditional nuances of reciprocity in the anthropological record—including self-serving and negative types—were also visible on YouTube. At the same time, the study echoed theoretical reworkings of reciprocity, such as the idea that withholding certain forms of reciprocity may be as crucial for community creation and maintenance as bestowing it. The data also challenged traditional anthropological categorizations of homeomorphic versus heteromorphic forms of reciprocity in digital milieus. Drawing on prior anthropological studies, it argued that since the root of reciprocity lies in a gift from a specific person, no two gifts—however functionally similar they appear—truly qualify as homeomorphic. At root, digital forms of reciprocity discussed in the study emerge from different people with particular emotions, intended meanings, and feelings of regard.

The lessons learned about reciprocity and other anthropological concepts serve as a springboard for future discussions of how these rubrics and their temporal frames play out in different social groups on YouTube as well as outside of YouTube on other social media. For example, reports indicate that issues of reciprocity, such as mutual "liking" practices on the photo-sharing site Instagram, garner suspicion, as has happened with YouTube's sub for sub mutual subscription pledges to watch each other's videos. On Instagram, when people begin to "like" photos autonomically (or to use an automated program or "bot" to do so), the reciprocal action and the "like" itself may lose meaning to Instagram users.[1] Timing is also crucial in the way people enact reciprocities on social media. An inadvertent "like" on an Instagram photo posted long ago may give the impression that the "liker" is "stalking" the user or being "creepy."[2]

Lefebvre's temporal focus inspired this research, which aims to produce a "history of the future."[3] As YouTube moved toward commercialization, it is important to remember how some YouTubers used the video-sharing site in more social ways. Although sociality and a monetized art world are not necessarily incompatible among creative professionals, YouTube's choices clearly yielded deep tensions. An often-heard comment when YouTube first launched was that people should not complain about the site's policies given that uploading and sharing videos was "free"—a philosophy that tacitly sees the relationship with YouTube as reciprocal. YouTube provides a platform and creatives supply content, generating profit that benefits everyone. However, YouTube users have since become savvy to the adage "If you're not paying for it; you are the product."[4] In other words, free participation means agreeing to be surveilled so that targeted ads and other commercial goals may be achieved to increase profits for a select few. Case studies are needed that carefully document how people use video sites so that future user-friendly sites might reflect and support vernacular and social forms of media sharing.

Insights gleaned from this study provide important comparative material and lessons for the future as scholars examine new media generations on YouTube and other socially motivated media. Of particular importance will be handling the specific social, commercial, and technological parameters that set the stage for interaction. One solution may be to reintroduce features that facilitated sociality but were unprofitable, such as the video response feature, which provided a link to videos that addressed a prior video. This feature was deleted in 2013 due to the low click-through rate of responses.[5] Although not profitable from a monetization aspect, the move prompted concern among those who felt that video responses encouraged community engagement.[6] Whether design solutions lie in bringing back older features or offering new alternatives depends upon interactive needs.

New Lefebvrian cycles are emerging whose borders are tricky to adjudicate. Questions emerge such as, are the choices and behaviors exhibited from new media generations similar or different to those of other socially oriented groups on YouTube? How do these interactions compare to those on other social media sites? What behaviors carry over as people digitally migrate, and how does interaction adjust to migration patterns? A collective scholarly conversation will be required for comparing different forms of mediation across time and space. Of particular importance is analyzing nuances in video-sharing milieus and understanding participatory trajectories of vernacular work that are often ignored in official accounts of YouTube.

ALTERNATIVE NARRATIVES AND ANTI-MEMORY

YouTube is a vast entity. Each research approach is inevitably a partial view of a site that is massive, constantly changing, and difficult to conceptualize as a whole.[7] It is challenging to identify pockets of meaningful discourse amid a heterogeneous social space that exhibits multiple and sometimes conflicting monetization agendas and digital literacies. Notably, alternative narratives of usage such as those found in thoughtful videos and comments are just as important as popular channels, YouTube celebrities, and viral videos—even if they do not receive splashy attention.

Moving beyond dominant discourses, we see that social media are not stable entities or neutral platforms of interaction. A temporal, long-term view reveals that social media are continually changing and that people use them in various ways across different social groups. There is no pure, stable, or best use of a particular site. For example, in the global, large-scale study of social media run by anthropologist Daniel Miller, researchers note that there is not a real or more authentic "Twitter," just because they observed that English schoolchildren used it for friendly banter and adults used it to exchange information.[8] A key aspect of their research details how use of social media sites varies according to location and demographics. These observations demonstrate the importance of attending closely to partial and emplaced views.

Miller and his colleagues did not focus on YouTube as part of their study of social media. Their understandable rationale was that although individuals as well as companies disseminate messages on the site, YouTube mostly functioned as a "form of public broadcasting."[9] However, to their point about the importance of studying media in different socio-cultural contexts, it is important to remember that although social media sites such as Twitter are now used to broadcast messages, some people still use it socially, as did the children in their study. Similarly, YouTube's broadcast structure has not precluded social uses.

Considering the temporal dimension is crucial for analysis, given that usage frequently changes. Technology and media researcher danah boyd and information studies scholar Nicole Ellison found that social media platforms often start with specific intentions that morph over time; for instance, Cyworld was a Korean discussion forum tool but became a social network site.[10] The social media site Orkut, they point out, began in the United States as an English-language site, yet later Portuguese-speaking Brazilians became the central users. Individual sites also change connotations over time. As Miller and his colleagues state, an early version of Facebook was designed so that male students could rate the attractiveness of female students. The site has changed in usage, but it is fair to ask whether the platform retains its original connotations in terms of participatory ratings that encourage competitive self-presentation. I agree with the conclusion of Miller and his team that "the usage by any one social group is no more authentic than any other."[11] Thus, even a broadcast platform such as YouTube may also facilitate sociality.

Variations in Twitter usage across different countries illustrate how a platform may move from being a social network site to a broadcast medium. Twitter is generally characterized as social media. Yet pundits argued years ago that Twitter had lost (at least among adults) its interactive tone and was mostly used by journalists and experts to disseminate information.[12] Researchers have shown how Twitter shifted to privilege broadcasting messages over conversation. In 2009, merely three years after Twitter was launched,[13] political philosopher Jodi Dean argued that only 5 percent of accounts were responsible for 75 percent of the tweets.[14] These statistics led Dean to conclude that Twitter had become saturated with "super users" and "automated zombies." Similarly, media scholar Jean Burgess analyzed nearly 1 billion tweets from Australia between 2006 and 2015 and concluded that although numerous tweets continue to be posted, "Twitter is becoming less conversational and more like a news platform."[15] Whether these patterns continue over time or within particular social groups is an empirical question—as Miller found in studying its use in England. What is important to acknowledge is that intensity of sociality may change over time within particular social media sites and across different social groups.

Comparative research conducted across countries and different types of social media lead to an intriguing hypothesis. Perhaps social media platforms generally begin life in more social ways, but as they age they morph into broadcast-oriented platforms as participants migrate to cooler sites? Or do groups initially engage socially, experience participatory complications, and then migrate to other sites to maintain social ties? Perhaps such dynamics are not specific to a particular medium but rather indicate a patterned cycle of mediated participation that begins with sociality and ends with broadcasting across particular demographics. Although addressing such hypotheses is beyond the scope of the present study, they prompt additional investigation of the changing timbre of sites over time. Researchers should conduct long-term studies to investigate whether social media have a certain social "shelf life" (arguably three to five years), after which they mostly offer mass broadcasting, or whether different services maintain multiple trajectories of usage according to the needs of new media generations as they arrive to a site. It is vital to study alternative narratives of social media across time and space to avoid overgeneralizing about particular technical platforms and to achieve deeper understanding of mediation patterns.

I believe there are ethical as well as research-oriented obligations to seek out and understand the dynamics of diverse, alternative narratives of usage. Noted visual anthropologist Faye Ginsburg poignantly details how mediated environments facilitate communication among the disabled, such as people with autism.[16] Design is inherently political, as individuals may not always attain equitable access to mediated spaces and activities. Sites should be designed to facilitate identifying pockets of meaningful interaction on YouTube. Complaints that it is difficult to find worthwhile videos risk morphing into elitist discourses that absolve scholars and other experts from seeking out and acknowledging alternative voices. It is not sufficient to decry the difficulty of identifying relevant work. Researchers and designers must actively pursue mechanisms to identify and circulate important messages. We must find ways to "beat the algorithm," as the YouTubers say, when certain algorithms are constructed to excessively privilege harmfully extremist messages. It is an ethical imperative to widen attention to focus on thoughtful voices beyond already-interested parties within particular communities. Under the right circumstances, alternative narratives can be civically powerful. We need to find collective ways to facilitate the design of interfaces that help diverse viewers locate and cooperate with insiders of diverse groups to learn more about their experiences and circulate their message.

Concerns about accommodating diverse media makers will likely intensify over time. "Cultural" practices on the site emerged from numerous trajectories,[17] including drawing on larger cultural formations. When people arrived on YouTube, they brought their own cultural expectations and ideas about what was appropriate to share on the site. The group under study is largely from the United States, a large and heterogeneous country. Diverse norms, expectations, and practices inevitably shaped their participation and influenced video-sharing cultural practices.

The YouTube platform itself was influenced by concepts from commercial structures, which provided the environment that YouTube participants experienced when they arrived. Indeed, YouTubers encountered media syncretism on the site, in which visible mixes or blends of ideas, beliefs, and practices became part of their cultural milieu in the mediated environment of YouTube.[18] Although the term "syncretism" is often used in anthropology to refer to mixed blends of religious practices, it is possible to identify media syncretism on YouTube. The site's design clearly drew on multiple media models to form a new participatory platform. For example, YouTube drew on the idea of a "subscription" model to promote videos. As of June 2018, with the exception of specific, paid ad-free viewing and select-content services, subscriptions to individual video makers were free. Offering free subscriptions aimed to draw viewers back to the site and was thus advantageous for the corporate entity of YouTube as well as for the video maker who received more views. Subscribing viewers arguably benefited by being able to keep up to date on the latest videos of their favorite creators. At the same time, the idea of a "subscription" prepares the way for eventual paid access, which is what occurred on the site.

YouTubers' history of receiving subscriptions for free arguably problematized acceptance of paying for YouTube at all. This is an example of media syncretism, in which older ideas about media use encountered tensions within new parameters of social usage and interaction.

Scholars who study internet histories have observed that the "internet," which was conceived as a "network of networks," has taken on a monolithic connotative history in which a single version of its creation story is reiterated. In fact, the internet has multiple histories, false starts, and ways of usage. Media studies scholar Kevin Driscoll and information science researcher Camille Paloque-Berges argue that it is crucial to uncover and analyze varied technological trajectories. As they state, "The Internet has always been multiple."[19] One may extrapolate from their contention to argue that it is through exploring alternative narratives of usage that one may begin to appreciate everyday experiences, ethical concerns, and future prospects for designing equitable and interactive mediated spaces. Of particular interest for Driscoll and Paloque-Berges is understanding "relations of authority" or, more specifically, "who or what is authorised to be connected" or "who or what is more visible or central than others."[20] They argue that the singular history of the Net takes on a teleological quality that contends that the way "the internet" unfolded is the best way. Keeping alternative historical narratives in play, they argue, helps dismantle notions that the way that things reportedly unfolded were the "fittest" and therefore the only or right way of executing internet networks.

A similar argument may be applied to narratives of YouTube usage. A popular teleological history has taken shape in which it is deemed "inevitable" that a free video-sharing site such as YouTube would become intensely monetized and commercial and that those who are not "fit" enough to run with the pack should be left to atrophy through hard-coded features such as being banned from monetizing one's work unless specific thresholds are reached through creation of ad-friendly content. YouTube promotes and provides significant resources to video makers who achieve celebrity, therefore creating a self-fulfilling prophecy. Of prime importance is preserving alternative narratives that challenge YouTube's teleological story. Its history is one way that worked on a certain level, but other useful participatory trajectories that privilege sociality more centrally could also be respected and accommodated, perhaps through newly designed, alternative platforms.

We must not only remember alternative histories. We must assertively and actively "forget"—or at least de-emphasize—attention on the success stories that dominate singular, teleological narratives. This is especially true when particular histories erase important vernacular voices and interactivity. Of course, the idea is not to literally forget key events. Rather, if we take a page from the post-phenomenologists' book,[21] what is required is a kind of "anti-memory" that sets aside a particular paradigm that was successful in order to achieve a new one.[22] Philosophy of technology scholar Galit Wellner draws on the work of philosopher Gilles Deleuze and psychiatrist and political activist Félix Guattari to argue that "becoming" requires "anti-memory." In other words, "becoming does not return to a fixed past but instead orients toward an unknown future and a redefined past."[23] Wellner explains:

> To start a revolution, the revolutionist needs to break away from the past just as the ancient fish had to forget the sea. In the technological realm, we have seen that the argument that cell phones cannot be used to access the internet had to be rejected in order to develop a cell phone of the third historical variation. In order to become, one needs to forget what one cannot become.[24]

YouTube was enormously successful; it is an online juggernaut of commercial video. We need to suspend our "knowledge" of this trajectory and temporarily "forget" its type of success if we wish to create a "history of the future" in which subsequent pockets of YouTube or new user-friendly sites may be forged with or without monetization. We need to preserve and analyze diverse YouTube alters to understand what might be possible and desirable for future video-sharing practices. Of course we cannot literally "forget" (nor would we wish to) YouTube and its tremendous influence on the cultural zeitgeist. At the same time, however, we need to suspend teleological acceptance of its deliberate choices. Proposed below are research approaches that aim to help construct an anti-memory of success within a particular context to create alternative and possibly transformative opportunities for spectacular new types of socially driven, video-mediated interaction.

A PROPOSED FRAMEWORK FOR RESEARCHING VIDEO-SHARING CULTURES

YouTubers interested in sociality shared their message through videos on a site with particular constraints, conventions, and expectations about video sharing and commenting. When these experiences and norms were taken together, participatory groups on YouTube exhibited cultural patterns. Humorously referring to the site as "YouTubia" playfully showed how YouTubers encouraged sociality. Shared practices included comment and video reciprocity, subscriptions, and collab videos as well as enthusiasm for the site itself. Challenges included dealing with discomforting temporalities of change, haters, asymmetrical access to YouTube's partnership program, and "sub for sub" mutual subscription demands, all of which contributed to distinctive cultural practices of video sharing.

Ethnographic studies of media sites may broaden participation by showing how new groups from different countries, ethnicities, and areas of interest use YouTube to accomplish their own forms of sociality. Examples include groups of people who play Minecraft, a sandbox video game in which people build things using blocky graphics. With more than 42 million videos, Minecraft became the most watched gaming title on YouTube in its history.[25] Teens and young adults with high-profile accounts often record their activities and amusing commentary as they build things on the site. Information is shared, and the resulting social connections have spawned a thriving community.[26] Subsequent generations of imagined communities from groups dealing with transgender issues or mental illness also use the site in multiple ways,[27] and their similarities and differences in comparison with previous groups should be acknowledged and analyzed.

How might sites and the groups that use them be studied ethnographically as new generations of users appear? The following discussion offers suggestions for studying new groups as they interact within parameters that change over time. Based on the lessons learned from YouTube, this section provides proposals for studying video-sharing practices in ways that will quite likely shed analytical light on how people share the self through video and, more generally, through media as new cycles of media generations appear. Notably, media generations are not solely determined by age. Some of the early vloggers on YouTube were middle-aged adults who vlogged alongside twenty-year-olds as they shaped video-sharing conventions.

Although these recommendations originated from video sharing, they might also find use in a wide array of digital media contexts. Of course, it is not always possible to invoke all of these characteristics within a single study, nor will every parameter apply across all types of media research. Different studies will require various approaches and combinations of styles to gain insight. The following characteristics are noted because they were advantageous when studying socially motivated YouTubers. They aim to facilitate a broad range of perspectives on video sharing and other social media cultures across diverse groups and sites.

Emphasize Empathy

A cornerstone of anthropological and ethnographic investigation includes empathizing with other people. Conducting media research empathetically means exploring what media makers aim to express through form, content, and media-sharing practices. It does not mean agreeing with everyone's choices on what to mediate and when. It simply means suspending one's disbelief long enough to ask respectful questions about the meaning of individual practices. At the very least, it involves expressing sincere interest in why people make media, even if artifacts seem technically subpar or feel "boring" to outsiders of the interpretive communities that the media targets.[28]

Far too often, cultural elites dismiss vernacular media that is now part of daily life for many people. Yet everyday video has demonstrably contributed to public culture in fundamental ways. For example, Moran analyzes how vernacular aesthetics are integrated into narrative storytelling in mainstream fiction films.[29] He describes how a shaky home movie in a fiction film can reveal much about a cinematic character. The aesthetics of so-called amateur video are integrated into professional works in ways that have irrevocably contributed to cultural production of media.

In addition, although some cultural critics are filmmakers themselves, it feels as though some of the most virulent critics of vernacular video have never tried to make and share media with a global public. While I do not believe that every critic should be a media-making expert, a little appreciation is in order. Making media is hard work! Those of us involved in academic video blogging can attest to the complexity, time intensiveness, and the vulnerable state one experiences when sharing ideas-in-progress with the world through video.[30]

Experimental psychologists argue that achieving empathy is a choice. Even the most disturbed personalities, such as diagnosed narcissists, may achieve it; they just choose not to.[31] It would truly be ironic if scholars avoided developing a sense of empathy for everyday creators who are trying to have their voices heard and engage in civic dialogue. Paying inordinate attention to narcissists arguably fuels narcissism. Further, not all "boring" videos are created for the general public, even though the public has access to them. Vloggers' reactions to critiques about video quality give rise to the concept of viewership narcissism, which may be defined as viewers' toxically egotistical and unrealistic belief that a video should satisfy their unique preferences or it does not deserve attention. Yet videos may be banal to certain viewers because they were created for a specific group. Important aspects of content or subtle manipulations of form are lost on nontarget audiences.

Exhibiting empathy does not mean encouraging video makers to remain in stasis with regard to digital literacy skills. Nor does it require agreeing with or sanctioning inappropriate or harassing videos. However, even in such cases, it is certainly possible to use ethnography to "understand the lifeworlds of the 'repugnant other'" to analyze antagonistic interaction patterns.[32] As communication and digital technologies scholar Whitney Phillips argues, repugnant others, such as online trolls, are not as outré as is often assumed. In fact, they frequently engage with Western rhetorical practices that are fairly mainstream. Toxically aggressive messages appear, for instance, in nonanonymous, loud, and argumentative television journalism programs.[33] If it is possible to use ethnography even to understand works from "repugnant others," such as sexist, racist, and hater commentary, then surely it is possible to use empathy-driven ethnographic methods to understand why everyday creators feel that it is important to express the self through video.

Discourses of quality, in which video makers indicate a desire to improve and collaboratively share tips, routinely appear on the site.[34] YouTubers display awareness of the need for digital literacies and call on global audiences to develop them. In fact, YouTubers reflecting on their experience see increasingly professional work on YouTube and a much higher quality of videos—sometimes at the expense of sociality.[35]

Academics may hold heterogeneous online participants to standards that they would not demand of their own students. We expect students to improve over time; why not acknowledge that video makers and commenters with varying abilities may also do so? Consider a classroom in which the effectiveness of the traditional seminar discussion format is assessed—as in many digital research studies—at a single point in time, say the students' first papers. Deciding that the seminar format was useless because of a bad set of first papers would be absurd. Reasons for problematic papers may be numerous, including students' initial ability when they came into a class as well as a particular professor's facility with leading seminars. Students are mentored at least over a term with the conviction that they all may improve. Applying this pedagogical analogy, it is unduly pessimistic to judge video makers' abilities—as well as the usability of an entire site—only at a single point in time. It is perhaps unrealistic to pronounce definitive failure in participants' current and future ability by analyzing a few videos or comments.

YouTubers display overt awareness of their videos' aesthetic faults and are sometimes the first to call them out. They may *rhetoricize their visual literacies*, which means accounting for or apologizing for aspects of their video that they feel could be improved but that are not evident in the technical execution of a video.[36] For example, in one meet-up video the creator warns viewers that she might have used too many edits. Such warnings rhetoricize digital literacies by simultaneously displaying a sensitivity to the viewer as well as acknowledging that editing skills are important for making legible and interesting videos. Even though she garnered a small audience, she still felt the need to publicly express her technical knowledge about making videos. Public rhetoricizations of digital literacies were also observed among the youth whom I interviewed in *Kids on YouTube* (2014). Both young people and adults tend to perform their affiliations to ideas they assume to be important among video makers.

Many scholars and critics see online video making as frivolous, when in fact video-making skills are becoming increasingly important in core facets of life. Some people's life success now depends upon demonstrating an ability to manipulate media in networked environments. For example, one video blogger who had applied for a media job was told she needed to create a video about herself and post it online *as part of her job application*. I watched the video and admired her poise and confidence as she expressed herself quite well in front of a camera—skills that are not achieved overnight. Knowing how to create such a video or how to present the self when it counts takes time. Video bloggers and others who have long been aware of these trends have been developing skills by practicing in public and gauging different types of audience reaction to their work. Imagine a world in which video statements became as necessary for certain occupations as résumés. In such cases, more empathy and understanding might be extended to those who have spent considerable time developing mediated self-presentation skills.

Having empathy—at least initially—enables scholars to ask important questions that are crucial for the ethnographic enterprise, such as what message or purpose does a particular medium have? Why are certain objects or people chosen for emphasis? What kinds of participatory predicaments do people encounter when trying to learn in public? We may achieve more understanding by approaching everyday media making with sincere inquiry and empathy rather than hostility, elitist dismissal, and unrealistic temporal evaluations of media targeted for specific audiences.

Recognize Nuance

Despite the fact that many types of video are used in different ways across communities and contexts, scholars sometimes ignore vital nuances and backstories that shape creation, reception, and public sharing of videos. Misconceptions may be illustrated by sharing an observational vignette. At a scholarly conference on do-it-yourself digital media, a leading video blogger and public media figure named Ryanne Hodson presented her work to a largely academic audience. Hodson was a professional media maker who had previously worked as a television producer. She and other first-generation video bloggers had learned to use compression techniques to post videos to their own video blogs around the same time that YouTube launched in 2005 and in some cases even before then. To retain control over their work, they espoused the idea of having an independent video blog that was not part of a monetized platform such as YouTube. Hodson and other vloggers posted their videos to video blogging sites, staunchly avoiding YouTube. During Hodson's presentation, an audience member persistently referred to her videos as "YouTube videos," even though Hodson had not yet posted on the site. She was trying to achieve levels of quality, audience participation, and connection that she did not perceive to be likely on YouTube.

Metonymic substitutions such as these in which any online video is classified as a YouTube video is perhaps a testament to the site's successful branding and widespread uptake, but they are misleading categorizations in certain contexts. Not all public videos are YouTube videos, as there are many other sites and situations in which video is posted online. In fact, not even all YouTube videos are "YouTube videos" in the popular sense of exhibiting wacky virality and assumed rabid desires to commercialize and achieve stardom. YouTube's huge and ever-changing catalogue includes many types of videos, including professional, pre-professional, advanced amateur, everyday, and educational videos that garner millions of views. Many contexts exist to post online video, and they may have technical platforms, audiences, and intentions that differ quite distinctly from those that are stereotypically associated with YouTube.

From a knowledge acquisition perspective, it is important to recognize that nuances exist in terms of how a video is embedded within a site and how audiences interact with it in ways that arguably create new artifacts as the video lives on. A video that has no commentary may be received differently than a video with many enthusiastic comments and views. Or commentary may be blocked or ignored. Whether such differences actually influence viewers is an empirical question, but it is important to recognize how a video's situatedness may impact audiences. Admittedly, it is not always possible to have access to all nuances, but it is important to be attuned to their possible existence and effects.

Anthropology is distinguished by its comparative approach. Whether in traditional environments or new digital configurations, comparing and contrasting social arrangements yields analytical insights. Categories may come to light in ways that may be elided when one focuses on one group or website as a "field site." For example, in conducting research on video practices, I have elsewhere described comparisons between YouTubers who embraced the site and first-generation video bloggers such as Ryanne Hodson who vlogged before YouTube and who initially eschewed that site as a viable platform for distributing their work.[37] The comparison highlights salient analytical categories and practices, such as behind-the-scenes technical manipulations and self-idealizations. Analyses of video-sharing practices should consider the nuances of specific sites, including their cultural, social, technical, and commercial features, when understanding how videos are created for particular milieus. Whether different platforms actually produce alternative kinds of video experiences is a question best approached through systematic research. It is also possible that groups who avoid sites because of certain presumed features or philosophies may actually share more than they realize with the characteristics of the creators and sites they eschew. Many of the vloggers whom I encountered shared YouTubers' vision of democratic and social video sharing.

Anthropologists study artifacts, but nuanced media environments require theoretical reconsideration of what constitutes an "artifact." Is it a video alone, or the video plus accompanying text description and comments? Not all video-related information may be salient to every research project. Yet key descriptive commentary posted to a video is not always considered in scholarly analyses when it might be logical to do so. For example, one fellow scholar discussed an interview from one of my research videos as if the video had been created and posted by the YouTube interviewee. I explained in the text posted to my video that the comments were part of an ethnographic interview. Yet it was analyzed as if it were found footage created by the interviewee. A video created by a YouTuber versus one created within the context of an ethnographic interview are different genres of "data." How and when should scholars take into account the material surrounding and contextualizing the videos? What constitutes boundaries of so-called artifacts deserves theoretical consideration. Attending to nuances when analyzing new media environments not only invites sharper analyses of particular research questions but also prompts interdisciplinary teams to collectively question what is meant by the very foundational terms that undergird particular intellectual terrains.

Confront Diversionary Discourses

A discourse that ostensibly expresses concerns about media usage becomes diversionary when it fails to recognize more troubling underlying problems. In other words, diversionary discourses blame the wrong things for societal ills. Diversionary discourses tend to draw on stereotypical arguments in ways that intentionally or inadvertently divert attention from societal issues that are very difficult to identify and address. At root, not all discourses that become diversionary lack merit. For example, I agree that those who use media to fuel egotistical excess need to be helped. At the same time, labeling all genres of media that invite self-participation as "narcissistic" is to misunderstand how media are often used in social ways. Focusing only on obnoxious videos presents a skewed picture of how media are used in ordinary daily life. The YouTube case provided numerous examples of how videos were used to urge people to join a community. In this vein, Miller's team eloquently argues that "generalisations about new visual forms such as the selfie are often inaccurate. There are many varieties of the selfie which are often used to express group sentiment rather than individual narcissism."[38]

Diversionary discourses tend to cyclically reappear. For example, discourses about narcissism surfaced when the medium of video arrived, reemerged when video blogging entered the scene, and raised similar alarms when selfies appeared. Narcissism discourses arguably undergird a single concern, à la Sontag but perhaps as far back as Plato, which is general unease at expressing the self through media at all. Such discourses raise doubt about who has the right to use media. In examining the scholarly record, we find that diversionary discourses that criticize mediated interaction reflect underlying societal prejudices—such as those based on sex, gender, or technical ability. In one example, narcissism claims may be used in sexist ways to foreclose female expression. Exhibiting a circular quality, the argument is that women take selfies because they are said to be vain and narcissistic; thus selfies exude narcissism because women take them.[39]

Ability is a characteristic used to bolster diversionary narcissism discourses. Nonprofessionals are assumed to be terrible video makers. Vlogs are made by nonprofessionals, and therefore nonprofessionals are narcissists who draw inordinate attention to their undeserving vlogs. Amateur videos challenge professional media making and thus become targets of narcissistic discourses. Everyday videos threaten viewership of professional media because viewers are actually far more tolerant of the vernacular than is typically acknowledged. It is important to distinguish between true narcissism problems and the deployment of a diversionary discourse that demands unpacking the underlying societal prejudice that fuels it.

In addition to narcissism accusations, another diversionary discourse is the idea that mediated interaction is generally a degraded form of human connection. Yet this discourse may divert attention away from more pressing societal inequities about access. For example, Miller and his colleagues argue that "denigration of social media as inauthentic may in part be the practice of elites. Such groups, secure in their power to construct themselves offline, may seek to dismiss the attempts by less powerful populations to assert the authenticity of their self-crafting online."[40] Their conclusions in this context are in part based on the experiences of low-paid migrant workers in China who connect with other people and craft a digital identity portrayal that feels far closer to their beliefs and desires than what they can accomplish amid the socially limited and grim conditions in which they live. Despite decades of scholarship to the contrary, this folk myth about online inauthenticity persists but for different reasons across contexts. Miller's team, whose project was global in scope, keenly observed, "Whatever misgivings we may feel as academics about this dualistic terminology, it remains a primary mode by which people around the world understand and experience digital media."[41]

Another diversionary discourse revolves around blaming networked discourse problems on anonymity. This discourse often completely disregards the fact that many anonymous postings are often helpful and interesting. We would not want to prevent anonymous postings that are meaningful and that build a case for civic engagement among unknown members of coalitions. The real problem is not anonymity—or rather pseudonymity, as networked participants often exhibit recognizable behavior patterns[42]—but rather the fact that people hold and express underlying biased attitudes. As communication and digital technologies scholar Whitney Phillips argued in her book on subcultural trolling, the problem is not anonymity but the fact that people still hold racist, sexist, homophobic, weightist, ageist, and other biases that appear in digital environments.[43]

Anxiety over *accountability* for unacceptable behavior is understandable, but people who are anonymous to each other (or rather pseudonymous) may not be so to site administrators. At best, such discourses about the negative side of anonymity are well meaning because they attempt to identify interactional problems; at worst, these discourses become diversionary by actively discouraging vernacular voices in finding a public audience and for ignoring the fact that people need help with developing participatory literacies. They divert attention away from tackling more urgent but deeply entrenched infrastructural issues, such as societal prejudices and the reasons they are expressed at all.

Overgeneralizations about the ills of mediated behavior will quite likely persist. To some extent they may decrease as new generations experience media in more inter-threaded, less dualistic ways. Yet even when problems expressed in diversionary discourses are "resolved," new diversionary discourses will no doubt emerge. Researchers must work to unpack them and explain how they divert attention away from more fundamental issues that should be tackled if we are to create more equitable mediated environments.

Analyze Emplacement

Emplacement here refers to how interactions become tangibly or conceptually associated with a physical space. Meet-up experiences show how interactions continually weave back and forth through offline and digital milieus, as they have for decades. For these video makers, their interpretation of "YouTube" became dynamically emplaced in specific locations. The experiences were recorded and shared on YouTube, where place helped create shared histories that further cemented a social concept of YouTube. YouTube interaction was not emplaced or "fixed" in a few locations but rather dynamically emplaced as interaction fluidly moved across different media and in person. In these meet-up videos, places became "stars" in their own right. It is important to study how emplacements influence the creation and maintenance of social groups. Do they exhibit chronotopic orientations, as revealed in this case study? Or do they use other time-space metaphors to galvanize sociality? If they use different tactics, what are they and what are their consequences? Media scholarship should focus more intently on the role of place in digital interaction and the way it shapes and changes what is fundamentally meant by "the internet."

It is time to cease using binaries and focus more specifically on *degrees* and *types* of mediation that occur in particular encounters rather than refer only to the online and offline. To understand nuances of mediated participation, the book introduced the notion of different participatory levels of fungibility across different modalities, which weave across various forms of media. For example, in some cases YouTubers felt emotional fungibility between different degrees and types of mediated experiences. They felt strong emotional connections to people, whether they were discussing something through videos or at a meet-up. Yet at other times they did not encounter equivalences between experiences. It was difficult and expensive, for instance, to physically meet up, compared with conversing with someone via their computer. Attending gatherings required sacrifices of time and money. Combining notions of multiple modalities with participatory fungibility helps scholars to acknowledge and recognize salient differences without resorting to crude binary formulations.

Across media modalities, trade-offs are often deployed to accomplish social goals.[44] "The internet" is not a singular, monolithic entity; it is experienced quite differently all over the world and across different social groups.[45] Similarly, YouTube is not a singular entity; it is experienced in diverse ways. A productive next step is to understand how networked groups become dynamically emplaced and how place influences what constitutes individuals' perceptions of a digital milieu over time.

Respect Temporal Trajectories

In his work on rhythm analysis, Lefebvre argued that "the media day never ends, it has neither a beginning or end."[46] This study suggests that, on the contrary, particular media exhibit temporal trajectories that should be recognized and analyzed in order to understand interactive mediation. YouTubers know that videos have rhythms of viewership and commentary. After a certain window (usually a few days) interactivity dramatically dwindles—although engagement may asymptotically never completely disappear. On the other hand, bolstering Lefebvre's argument is the fact that months or even years later views and comments may surface. Dissipation of viewership does not always index a video's importance for an individual video maker or for friends in a video-sharing culture.

YouTubers attended to temporalities, thus exhibiting sensitivity to viewers. For example, one socially motivated YouTuber told me that he avoided posting too much within a short period of time so that his viewers' in-boxes were not flooded with his videos. Media are situated within an interactive chain in which expectations about their appearance and use are rooted in temporal assumptions and norms. Conflict ensues when expectations are either violated or people simply have different ideas about what constitutes appropriate media temporality.

Polyrhythmias or multiple temporalities could function in productive or pathological ways. Arrhythmias in media interaction occurred when people exhibited asymmetrically discomforting temporal expectations, thus producing social tension. For example, video makers sometimes deleted a video that bored them or exhibited unfortunate technical flaws that became more apparent as the vlogger became more experienced. When a video was deleted, so too were all the comments that were posted to it. Members of a vlogging community who had taken the time to watch the video and comment, perhaps providing emotional or technical support and advice, now saw all of their comments—which constituted time and effort—deleted as well. Creators and viewers might have different temporal expectations about how long media should remain on the site, thus creating participatory arrhythmias. Activities such as posting comments have been characterized as interactive "labor" in sites of creative production.[47] Interactive labor might be perceived as disrespected because of the (often legitimate) reasons that prompted a video maker to delete a video.

The point here is not to adjudicate who is right and who is wrong about ownership and dispensation of a video's existence, although videos arguably morph into a different kind of collective artifact when others view and take the time to comment on them. Rather, the goal is to discuss the fact that tensions ensue when video temporicities, or temporal meanings and interpretations about time, conflict. People may become sensitive to the shared histories that certain videos demarcate within a social collective and feel distraught when these videos are terminated through removals. Conversely, new generations of YouTubers may be unaware of these histories of features and choices and may establish new temporal engagements and expectations with collective media.

Ideally, both temporalities and temporicities should be analyzed in terms of how they influence co-creation of mediated social spaces. Temporalities refer to different cultural ways of experiencing time. Temporicities, following similar underlying principles for what scholars call historicities, refer to how different temporally driven participatory organizations become visible or are commercially or politically elided in particular interactive contexts.[48] Studying temporicities reveals how canonical forms of mediated, temporally based interaction receive widespread acceptance. Much about how YouTube "works" is hidden from ordinary use. For instance, YouTube reportedly did not always disclose changes to the site in timely ways. Temporicities, or interpretive, historicized, and evaluative aspects of temporal experience, provide important clues to video-sharing cultures. Temporicities should be studied, particularly when tacit temporal, participatory drivers and their effects are ignored or omitted in public and corporate discourses. What does it mean, for instance, when a high threshold of viewer "watch time" becomes a metric for monetization? What are the effects of this requirement on creators and viewers, both in terms of physical impact as well as creativity?

Of particular importance also is studying arrhythmias between humans, media, and posthuman collective forces. Tensions emerge when media trajectories and the life trajectories of those who made the media are no longer in sync. When people pass away, they often have strong feelings about the dispensation of their mediated legacy, and these media dispositions may conflict with those of loved ones. Ideological conflicts may result from tensions about how long media should remain and how they should be curated. Should all videos, including "frivolous" videos, remain or only the ones that portray video makers according to their preferred legacy? These temporal anxieties are likely to multiply exponentially as the rate of video production increases.

Studying temporalities exhibits challenges. As videos multiply and sites change, it will become increasingly difficult, if not impossible, to understand the specific technical and commercial contexts that video makers were operating within when they created and posted a video. When such changes occur, a platform conceptually becomes a different "site," with different features, options, and constraints at various points in time. As a thought experiment, imagine trying to understand the temporal contextualizations of YouTube partnerships. Consider a video that rants about YouTube's partnership program at the beginning of the program's launch in 2007 versus one in 2012, when the program was opened up and an entirely different model of monetization was in operation, including an ability to monetize single videos. In contrast, imagine a rant on monetization posted in 2017 or 2018 when YouTube further restricted the program to high performers.[49] These rants are temporally contextualized at points in which partnership had particular parameters, such as whether creators needed to obtain specific levels of overall viewership to apply.

Temporally contextualizing videos becomes complicated over time as they travel across platforms and are acontextually viewed. Consider the case in which a scholar encounters a rant about "partnership" years after it was posted. Imagine further that it was originally created in 2007 but reposted in 2012. Reposting videos due to glitches or the need to refresh one's channel are common facets of YouTube life. In some cases YouTubers are aware of the importance of these temporicities and carefully mark reposted videos with an original upload time stamp—say, in the text description to a video. Other YouTubers are less attentive to such temporicities and do not provide clues about their original temporal context of posting. In the example above, how will a scholar determine which parameters of "partnership" the video maker is complaining about if this information is not clarified in the video? Such contextualizations may require historical investigation that may not be easily tracked by participants or researchers.

Understanding how features change over time and across media generations will be difficult, given the pace of change and the fact that such alterations are not always made explicit to users. Newcomers will not necessarily perceive how new features provide different organizational frameworks for interaction. For example, in 2012 one pundit lamented YouTube's elimination of the temporal organization of video recommendations. In the past it was possible to see video categories, such as most viewed "today," "last week," "in the last year," and "all time."[50] Yet the pundit wondered if YouTube's elimination of temporal organization was an attempt to "erase history"—a fascinating observation of contested temporicities worth investigating.

New media generations on YouTube sometimes experience the site in profoundly different ways. Certain modifications will be visible and salient, while others will remain subtle or change too frequently to track. Viewers who used the temporal recommendation feature were part of a media generation that had conceptually oriented around time in order to view videos and share cultural experiences of temporally situated videos with other YouTubers. New media generations might not be aware that this type of organization is a possibility. The emergence and gestation for a particular media generation can be quite rapid. Indeed the word "generation" connotes human-life longevity, but media generations may involve very rapid cycles, lasting a few years, months, or even smaller increments of time, depending on the phenomena under study.

Rapid experiential temporicities have methodological implications. Anthropologists have traditionally based ethnographic research on the year-long cycle, in part because of a historical legacy of following communities across one full agricultural cycle of activity. Anthropologist Michael Scroggins references the term "ecological annum" to describe a temporicity that emerged from specific historical eras that privileged anthropological study of agriculturally framed or hunter-gatherer societies.[51] Scroggins advises researchers not to unreflectively rely on the "ecological annum" but rather to attend to the specific rhythms of an activity under study. Rather than conduct research privileging a historical temporal framework, he recommends "follow[ing] concrete action from start to finish and back." When studying laundry, he notes, one follows the process of how a shirt becomes "clean," which implies, of course, another cycle of how a shirt becomes "dirty."

Understanding temporalities has been central to this YouTube study, which demonstrated that media cycles may or may not map to traditional anthropological—or even human—rhythms. Indeed, media cycles may not be as predictable as is an "ecological annum" based on a local agricultural cycle. It is important to be attuned to multiple rhythms of phenomena and observe how new media "generations" respond to them.

At the same time, the long-term orientation of anthropologically motivated ethnography retains analytical force as a way of maintaining deep engagements that yield key insight into varied lifeways. It is instructive to watch action over the course of time, perhaps several years if possible, as insight is revealed when researchers track how interaction unfolds over time. A year of engagement may still provide a crucial long-range and temporally meaningful perspective that may not be visible through short-term visits to a site. The point is to attend to unexpected but salient temporalities. Whatever temporal cycles occur, scholars should analyze how media may operate according to multiple and unpredictable participatory rhythms. Researchers should study the moments when creators' and viewers' temporal expectations or mediated rhythms may dovetail or fall out of sync.

Reconsider the Ethnographer's Role

Renowned visual anthropologist Jay Ruby once asked whether researchers would be needed to document and tell the stories of future generations once it became commonplace to record one's own lifeways and messages.[52] He posited that visual production skills (and, I would add, digital literacies) would become more widespread among populations who would normally garner interest as subjects of research. In that event, people would have the tools to make their own media. Once people learned the appropriate technical, aesthetic, and rhetorical skills to mediate their message, he wondered, "Why would they need the outsider? Why wouldn't they want to make their own films?"[53] YouTube provides an open experiment that addresses Ruby's question. Are visual ethnographers needed now that video makers can make and circulate their own statements? Clearly, as "expert witnesses,"[54] YouTubers offer unique insights about the site and their participation. Indeed, YouTube contributes to anthropological analyses because it provides images in living color of certain public aspects of the intimate lives, interactions, and lifeways that researchers wish to understand. To suggest that scholars and media specialists are the only ones capable of recording and transmitting diverse cultural messages is arguably a form of elitism.

Nevertheless, visual ethnographers play a vital role in today's media-saturated world. Although video sites enable global distribution of people's own stories, individual videos are not guaranteed widespread viewership, nor will they necessarily receive in-depth consideration when they are viewed. Visual ethnographers must continue traditional activities, including creating, curating, contextualizing, and translating videos that deserve broader audiences because of the importance of their message and their illumination of diverse lifeways.

Curating videos with important messages functions as a form of civic engagement or what anthropologist Sarah Pink and others characterize as activism.[55] Calling attention to specific works and boosting their visibility may assist in transmitting messages, especially for those who are developing digital skills or hesitate to engage in self-promotion for fear of being labeled as narcissistic. Curation is a form of civic engagement because it involves selecting certain videos over others to receive attention and raise awareness about important issues and experiences. Despite the popular rhetoric about the assumed ability to craft one's best self online, people who post images or personal information do not always have complete "control" over their representation and reception. What people hope to show and what others interpret are not always aligned, as early bloggers learned when their character had been misconstrued. Young bloggers found that disclosing specific details leads to "frustration that audience members would essentialize their entire characters as being one way, simply because they chose to relay these aspects of themselves online."[56] Anthropologists and other media scholars can help contextualize and interpret the meaning and role of vernacular works in cultural contexts. Important everyday videos thus require *more* rather than less attention.

Anthropologists and ethnographers can provide commentary and other materials that translate ideas for the general public and provide contextualization about videos' merits. Translation has long been an important function of visual anthropologists. As anthropologists Howard Morphy and Marcus Banks have argued, even within the same cultural groups images may be interpreted in radically different ways.[57] Understanding which works have merit is a form of spectatorial literacy, and visual anthropologists can help educate publics about the importance of particular vernacular works, in part through ethnographically sensitive studies that contextualize videos within a group's lifeways.

Spectatorial literacies are often discussed in light of deciphering meaning, truth, and biases in visual and digital works. Yet fundamental elements of spectatorial literacies also include developing openness and tolerance to media when a message is worthy but production skills are not polished or professional. As digital divides are likely to persist, not only in terms of access to devices but to development of digital production skills, it will be advantageous to remain spectatorially open to different kinds of messages and ways of telling stories. People are increasingly shooting video on phones and handheld devices, and production quality may not resonate with all audiences, but it is important to understand and decipher when a message may be socially or politically significant.

Since Ruby asked about the necessity of visual documentarians in the early 1990s, countless films and videos have been made by professional anthropologists, ethnographers, and documentarians that reveal their continued importance in using visual means to understand lifeways. At the same time, everyday videography has risen dramatically, which presents challenges for older models of researcher-subject relations that assumed that the anthropologist always maintains control over mediating an interaction within a research context. The case of YouTube shows how the

FIGURE 8.1. A woman trains the camera on me at a meet-up in Toronto, August 8, 2008. Screenshot from a video recording by Patricia G. Lange.

proliferation of cameras in everyday life means that subjects will be both collaborating and at times competing for how an interaction will be publicly represented. As indicated in figure 8.1, as I was recording the action at a meet-up in Toronto, a woman saw me and trained her camera on me. Initially, we sat staring at each other for several humorously awkward moments. She eventually explained that her goal was to video record everyone she could find who was also recording the event. Clearly the visual anthropologist is not the sole mediator and interpreter of events.

Video-blogging norms included people operating their own cameras as they participated at meet-ups. It was common to see people video-record each other within the video-blogging idiom. Human-subject protocols often have language about how recordings will be controlled and protected by researchers. But how does one guarantee control within video-blogging milieus? In one instance, a man whom I interviewed during a meet-up trained his camera on me. I could have requested that he stop recording, but that would have been odd and socially out of step in a video-blogging milieu in which it was accepted for everyone to record their own social encounters. It would also have been physically impossible to enforce. Even if I made that request and interviewees respected it, I could not control the cameras of *all* the passersby who recorded my interactions. Indeed, a few meet-up videos on YouTube showed me interacting with and interviewing YouTube participants. In camera-heavy environments the researcher easily becomes a mediated subject.

Of course, one could conduct interviews solely in quiet, empty rooms. This would offer certain control in terms of access to responses. But such activity would count as formal interviews rather than qualify as participant-observation. Within the core idiom of video blogging, conversations occurred and were mutually recorded more informally during public socialization. Additionally, interviewing people at gatherings facilitates dialogue and comments about meet-up events in progress. I conducted research in public at video-themed events amid many camera-wielding video makers with their own ethics and agendas, each of which may or may not dovetail with my views on what is appropriate to record and distribute. For instance, at one meet-up I respected a lurker's request not to be recorded; YouTubers did not. The question becomes, how well do ethical recording principles generalize beyond controlled and overtly collaborative ethnographic projects?

Newer models of ethnographic interviewing forgo traditional sedentary approaches in ways that resemble interactive, mobile, and public characteristics of the video-blogging idiom. Of particular interest is the idea of the "walking interview" in which ethnographers studying place and other concepts may move around and walk with research participants during a recorded interview.[58] Active engagements may insightfully reveal interviewees' interpretations of place, rendering the traditional sedentary interview less useful in contemporary ethnographic contexts. Walking interviews of this type invite mobile—and often very public—recordings.

Much discussion has occurred about the ethics of using visual materials in digital anthropology. After one of his videos went viral and was reposted on over 1,000 blogs and websites, anthropologist Michael Wesch noted, "It is not hard to imagine the kinds of comments and graphics that might be added to ethnographic film that could not only degrade the quality of the work, but also violate the dignity of those portrayed in the video."[59] In my case I did not need to imagine it. Wesch's fears were realized in my study when a parody video appeared in which an interviewee's voice in one of my videos was altered to bark like a dog. Whole volumes have been rightly devoted to ethics in image making. For example, writing from an interdisciplinary perspective that draws on communication scholarship, film studies, and anthropology, Larry Gross, John Stuart Katz, and Jay Ruby discuss a range of concerns with respect to the rights of subjects, including how they are represented and whether informed consent is realistically achieved, especially amid video-surveilled societies.[60] Recent discussions about visual ethics continue at the American Anthropological Association meetings in which visual anthropologists explore the rights of subjects and the impact of images. Of particular concern is how forms of representation "are often used and understood in unanticipated ways outside and sometimes within their original anthropological frameworks of creation."[61]

Emphasis in these discussions has rightly focused on the subjects of research, and those dilemmas continue. However, we are now living in an era in which cameras are prevalent and we are all being recorded by parties with varying agendas. Some people believe that living among such widespread surveillance may be advantageous because recordings may be used to protect people from crimes (such as in banks) and expose potential abuses of those in power (such as police brutality). Augmented reality researcher Steve Mann has coined the term "sousveillance" to describe how people who are not in power turn the camera on those who do have control to monitor their behavior.[62] Turning the camera back on powerful people is not *sur*veillance, as in viewing something from above, but rather monitoring someone from "below," as the French word *sous* denotes. In an era in which cameras are prevalent in everyday life, anthropologists may find themselves under "sousveillance" when they study other people.

Sousveillance is said to counterbalance the power one individual may have over another, such as the power that a visual ethnographer may have in recording and shaping the story of other people. Writing from the perspective of video ethnography, Wesley Shrum and his colleagues define the "videoactive context" as the field in which social situations are influenced by the presence of a camera. They argue that it is important for the filmmaker to allow themselves to be recorded in order to conduct mutually respectful, collaborative research projects, especially those in which subjects have a stake in coproducing the research. In this context Shrum and his colleagues argue that "you must be willing to turn the camera on yourself—to let them film you, to signal your role as participant as well as observer. Finally, though it occurs less frequently, you must be willing to let the subjects fix the camera on you, allowing the subjects to play the role of filmmaker."[63]

Video bloggers and the ethical and methodological issues they raise are harbingers for visual ethnographers more generally; people increasingly consider it a normal part of life to record their encounters. Discussions need to consider the ethics of recording a *researcher* as well as interviewees. These discussions invite a host of important and complex questions about what it means to conduct visual projects in heavily mediated environments. What happens, for example, if casual footage taken from someone observing an ethnographic encounter is released into the wild? In these instances a visual ethnographer would normally omit sensitive or inappropriate footage in public videos. But if someone else takes the footage, a researcher would not be able to protect people in her study from those representations. However, a researcher cannot avoid all public research. As mentioned above, active, walking forms of visual ethnography may necessitate public interviewing to achieve insight—especially in place-based research contexts. What ramifications might this have for interviewees and the researcher? Who will protect the visual ethnographer from the release of footage that would, historically, never have seen the light of day?

In their original volume *Image Ethics* (1988), Gross, Katz, and Ruby concluded that the preponderance of images will complicate individual rights. Their subsequent volume, *Image Ethics in the Digital Age* (2003), is similarly pessimistic about subjects' image rights. However, the authors leave the matter open, stating that "it remains to be seen whether living in the digital age has improved our odds."[64] On the one hand, more individuals may see violative alters of their personae distributed beyond their control and may experience the kind of image-driven, posthuman tremendum discussed in chapter 6. On the other hand, as I have argued elsewhere, we may see a vast proliferation of images such that, aside from the deeply problematic or criminal, many people will have "awkward" images of themselves being circulated, which means that any individual image will lose rhetorical force.[65] If everyone has uncomplimentary images of themselves somewhere online, it will be hard for single individuals to use another person's image to damage that person's reputation (without risking retaliation). Conversely, a new type of digital divide has appeared based on whether people have an ability to erase problematic visual histories.

A key question is, to what extent does proliferation of mutual filming impact the filmmaker, the research subject, and other people in a visual field given today's ease of distribution? In this context I am reminded of an image in anthropologist Lucien Taylor's classic piece on "Iconophobia," which details scholarly anxieties about the status and truth value of imagery in visual anthropology.[66] Taylor discusses how certain film critics and scholars have debated the veracity and ability of images to speak for themselves in terms of representing reality. The article includes several images from visual anthropologists, including a photograph of a woman pointing a camera back at the viewer. The image is labeled "Filming the filmmakers: Longole, from *A Wife among Wives* (1982), pictured shooting David and Judith MacDougall." This image is included in the article without further description or contextualization, which raises a number of questions. For example, what is this image's main message? Is it meant to be an eerie preternatural prediction of the way that cameras have now become prevalent in everyday video contexts? Is it meant to suggest that filmmakers even in past eras had less control than one imagined? Or is it meant to quaintly and playfully depict an indigenous person experimenting with media in a way that ultimately ratifies the control that the professional ethnographic filmmakers David and Judith MacDougall likely had? What was the dispensation of Longole's raw footage in terms of its ultimate destination beyond its use in visual anthropology studies?

Writing from the perspective of information science, Helen Nissenbaum proposed the concept of "contextual integrity," which deals with expectations about what is meant to be shared and what is assumed to be private in interactive situations.[67] For instance, friends who share confidential information are assumed to keep such information private (although, of course people may breach that trust and gossip). Amid this framework the context of a YouTube gathering certainly does not invite expectations for privacy given that cameras are everywhere. Nevertheless, it may not be appropriate to circulate everything one sees and records. Communication and digital media scholar Graham Meikle calls for an "ethics of visibility" in which people should more carefully consider "who and what is valid for exposure," even when behavior occurs in public.[68]

Anthropologists become members of a community for a time. In mediated communities they may feel a responsibility to share and exchange footage for certain projects. Sharing footage is one way in which reciprocity can occur. Reciprocity is often seen as promoting more warm, mutual feelings of community. But what happens when community members request footage that an anthropologist may be reluctant to share for a variety of reasons, including protecting subjects, guarding against misinterpretation of video data, and degrading personal opportunities for professionalization of the footage? Relationships may sometimes be best preserved by not exchanging footage. Alternatively, sharing and discussing certain images may show the researcher's willingness to help people develop digital literacies and skills that facilitate transmission of people's own messages and stories.

As Ruby pointed out years ago, true *collaboration* (versus simply participating in and thus *cooperating* with a researcher in a media project) requires having access to and *control* of the technical and communicative aspects of the project. In truly collaborative efforts, each party "mutually determine[s] the content and shape" of media.[69] Additional challenges regarding collaboration include not only making media and assessing who has access to footage, but determining distribution and presentation of ethnographic material. Increasingly, people are sharing their stories on social media sites. Researchers must decide if such sites represent the appropriate venue for sharing anthropological knowledge.

A significant challenge involves expectations about social media sharing. On social media sites users are encouraged to share information about themselves. Wrestling with disclosing personal aspects of making media has been a part of anthropology since at least the discipline's reflexive movement. Yet how much should scholars share of themselves to resonate with people who are learning about anthropological concepts through media? Participation in digital environments is becoming increasingly important for young people to share information and circulate civic messages.[70]

To answer Ruby's question, visual anthropologists productively discover important patterns of mediation and provide perspective not apparent in videos alone.

Researchers make important contributions through anthropological analysis, creation of visual and textual ethnographies, and ethnographic contextualization of important vernacular works. Visual ethnography brings together both researchers' and video makers' voices to identify important general patterns about networked interaction. In addition, visual ethnographers create texts and visual works that communicate these analyses to diverse audiences. The role of the visual ethnographer continues amid—and in response to—the proliferation of everyday media. Visual ethnographers may also increase the visibility of videos that are not given sufficient attention in popular and scholarly discourses but that illustrate important cultural insights. The YouTube case demonstrates that the role of the visual ethnographer retains fundamental analytical vitality amid the explosion in vernacular video.

GOING FORTH IN STYLE

Drawing on research in linguistic anthropology, future studies might apply the concept of "style" to the study of new media sites. Insights about the human condition often come from linguistics and linguistic anthropology, fields that have widely influenced studies in cultural anthropology. In linguistics style is defined as "a social semiosis of distinctiveness." Style is a symbolic system that is recognizably different from other ways of engaging in activities, including things such as speaking, using text, or sharing videos.[71] The idea of speaking style appears as recognizably distinctive only when compared with other possible ways of speaking and their related social meanings. All styles are ideologically motivated in that they identify acceptable behaviors in particular social groups or institutions.[72] Styles are connected to particular aesthetics, which are organized around notions of relevant forms of value. Style may operate within a particular culture or internationally and cross-culturally, as members of a playful "YouTubia" envisioned.

Political scientist and historian Benedict Anderson once wrote, "Communities are to be distinguished, not by their falsity/genuineness, but by the style in which they are imagined."[73] His claim is interesting because it applies not only to the social arrangements that materialize from mediated interaction but also to technical platforms from which such communities emerge. Examining features and parameters of interaction across various sites in terms of style will quite likely shed analytical light on how websites and new media platforms facilitate or complicate imagined communities.

Focusing on style not only illuminates mediation's role in interaction; it also addresses critiques of the imagined community concept. For example, critics argue that the imagined community rubric suggests complete homogeneity and principally relies on mental ideations of collectivity generated through media. Yet these factors do not account for intensive loyalties that imagined communities suppos-edly yield. Studying the style in which communities are imagined provides oppor-tunities to address tensions as imagined communities are formed and contested. Exploring the concept of style may show how different groups bond across multiple modalities and even cultures, as the YouTube experience suggests.

As we move forward, key questions include, what are the distinctive properties that sites exhibit to facilitate interaction? What are the ideological motivations behind particular forms of distinctiveness and aesthetics? By thinking about style, one is forced to comparatively consider how different sites or the same site exhibits change in interaction over time. For example, Anderson's concept has been criti-cized for its emphasis on ideation, whereas "shared happenings" are seen as crucial for community formation. Are physical meet-ups important "shared happenings" for all mediated groups who seek community? What other methods might they use? When people gather in person, what mediated modalities do they prefer? Is wielding the camera important at all times? What about the style of a site's features and functionality? Do commercial features such as "subscription" models impair or facilitate sociality? Do creators engage in workarounds to achieve their ends, or do technical and commercial features produce competitive tensions? It is important to analyze how features are proposed and how they are adapted to serve particular agendas. Also of interest is how or whether video makers engage in or resist particu-lar styles of mediation within and across sites.

Style is a system of distinction. Moving forward, we should consider how style influences video creation and how videos are shared, received, and interpreted. *Thanks for Watching* represents an alternative narrative of how one socially oriented group used YouTube to interact in ways that respected and encouraged the vernacu-lar. Meaningful socialization and commercialization are not necessarily incompat-ible in creative social groups, but forethought is required to create user-friendly platforms. Like the fish who must "forget" the sea to adapt to land, media evolu-tion requires us to suspend our acceptance of YouTube's profitable march toward monetization if we wish to propose user-friendly platforms that support video sociality. No doubt future groups will emerge that accomplish their goals accord-ing to their own styles. Systematically studying new media generations and their choices will reveal innovative ways of using video for self-expression and collective interaction—at least for a time.

NOTES

CHAPTER 1: INTRODUCTION

1. Kirkpatrick 2007.

2. Kirkpatrick 2007.

3. O'Neill 2012.

4. YouTube changed its policy such that a channel would need 10,000 overall lifetime views in order to add advertisements and share in a video's advertising revenue. The move reportedly aimed to restrict channels that pirated material in an attempt to monetize. See Spangler 2017.

5. Under the rules established in early 2018, creators needed 4,000 hours of viewing within the past year as well as a minimum of 1,000 subscribers to their channel to qualify for partnership. See Levin 2018.

6. Appadurai [1990] 2006, 584–603.

7. Lange 2008a.

8. For more details see Lange 2015b.

9. YouTube's openness in accommodating vernacular and professional works encouraged diverse forms of participation. See Burgess and Green 2009.

10. Lipton 2014.

11. Warman 2012.

12. Warman 2013.

13. Nicas 2017.

14. Nicas 2017.

15. Warman 2013

16. Anderson 2015.

17. Jenkins 2009b, 187–212.

18. Burgess and Green 2009.

19. Clifford 1986, 1–26.

20. Driscoll and Paloque-Berges 2017.

21. The term was reportedly coined by the Portuguese writer Lucio Alberto Pinheiro dos Santos and adapted by Henri Lefebvre. See Lefebvre 2004, xiii and 9.

22. See Horton 2005, 157–159.

23. See Lee 2017.

24. Lefebvre 2004, 15.

25. Lefebvre 2004, 15.

26. Gingrich, Ochs, and Swedlund 2002, S3.

27. For example, MySpace was launched in 2003 but was superseded in popularity in 2010 by Facebook. See Gehl 2012.

28. Lefebvre 2004.

29. Burgess and Green 2009.

30. Kavoori 2011. Kavoori notes that close readings and proposed taxonomies of selected videos represent one particular "cut" or what Clifford would call a "partial view" of YouTube.

31. Strangelove 2010.

32. Strangelove 2010, 47.

33. For example, earlier digital ethnographers used participatory approaches to study MUDs, or multi-user domains, which were text-based games that technologists and others played online. Examples include Turkle 1984; Cherny 1999; Baym 2000; Kendall 2002; and Lange 2003.

34. Pink 2011.

35. Ruby and Chalfen 1974.

36. Morphy and Banks 1997.

37. Ruby 1991.

38. Lutkehaus and Cool 1999, 118.

39. Principal recording for the film occurred between 2007 and 2009. The film was screened in 2014 in Paris at Ethnografilm, a film festival that showcases the work of ethnographers and anthropologists that visually depict social worlds.

40. For ethnography on social media use outside of the United States, see the research project led by Daniel Miller at University College London called *Why We Post*. The research offers comparative insights through several publications about social media such as Facebook and Twitter in countries such as China, Brazil, Turkey, Chile, India, England, Italy, and Trinidad. See https://www.ucl.ac.uk/why-we-post.

41. Gielen 2015.

42. According to Wesch, 34.5 percent of total uploads came from the United States in 2008, followed by the UK at 6.9 percent and the Philippines at 3.9 percent. See Wesch 2008. Pundits similarly observed that from 2005 to 2010, the single country with the most uploads and viewers was the United States. See Geraldes 2010.

43. Basu 2010.

44. Statista Research Department 2016.

45. Blake 2015.

46. Robertson 2014; Blake 2015.

47. Kottak 2009, 4.

48. Appadurai 1996, 12.

49. Appadurai 1996, 13.

50. Katzmaier 2017.

51. For a more detailed explanation of this perspective, see Wellner 2016.

52. Wellner 2016, 16.

53. Wellner 2016.

54. Lange 2017. For an early influential work that discussed the problematics of mixing commerce, sociality, and education, see Seiter 2005.

55. Gillespie 2010, 347.

56. Mannheim and Tedlock 1995.

57. Mannheim and Tedlock 1995.

58. See Rheingold [1993] 2000; Herring 1996; Markham 1998; Cherny 1999; Baym 2000; Miller and Slater 2000; Kendall 2002; Wakeford 2003; Ito, Matsuda, and Okabe 2005; Boellstorff 2008; and Burrell 2012.

59. Warman 2014.

60. Markham 2003.

61. Scribner 2013.

62. Wilson and Peterson argue that scholars should attend to "deconstructing dichotomies of offline and online, real and virtual, and individual and collective." See Wilson and Peterson 2002, 456.

63. Geraci notes that even though everyday usage of the word "virtual" implies a kind of absence, "virtual worlds are most assuredly, real worlds" even if they are not "physical." Nardi seeks to "rehabilitate the term virtual, recognizing it not as indexing the exotic, dystopian, inauthentic, or unmoored . . . , or as one term in a false dichotomy, but as a genuine site of human activity supported by crafted objects that open possibilities for social and cultural development." See Nardi 2015, 19. See also Manning 2009; Geraci 2014. For a discussion about how prior terminology has complicated understanding of interaction, see Lange 2008c.

64. For example, Boellstorff argues that the virtual should not be seen as opposed to the "real" but to the "actual." See Boellstorff 2008, 21. Similarly, Zhao says that "virtual" experience is "real" but not "actual." See Zhao 2014.

65. Cool 2012.

66. Castronova 2005.

67. Drawing from computer interface research, Coleman uses the term "x-reality" to describe "an interlacing of virtual and real experiences." For Coleman, "x" represents a variable that stands in for people's different forms of reality that include networked mediation. See Coleman 2011, 19–20.

68. Nardi 2015, 20.

69. Coleman 2011, 19–20.

70. Coleman argues that defining true access only in terms of those who are "fully technologically engaged in media networks" reifies a neocolonialist view. In this view, voices do not count if they are only partially technically connected or not at all. See Coleman 2011, 37–38.

71. Coleman 2011, 20.

72. Miller et al. 2016, 7.

73. See "WhatsApp" n.d.

74. For a discussion on the problems of anonymity and discourse on YouTube, see Hess 2009.

75. See Hunter et al. 2012.

76. Kendall 2002.

77. Phillips 2015.

78. Coleman 2014.

79. Wellman and Gulia 1999, 177.

80. Security experts note that even when individuals use private mode when accessing online services, this act "does nothing to conceal your I.P. [Internet Protocol] address, a unique number that identifies your entry or access point to the Internet. So Web sites may not know your browsing history, but they will probably know who you are and where you are as well as when and how long you viewed their pages." See Murphy 2012.

81. Sharfstein 2015.

82. Goffman 1963.

83. Goffman 1959.

84. Warner 2002.

85. Krauss 1976.

86. Griffith and Papacharissi 2010.

87. Senft and Baym 2015.

88. Burgess and Green 2009.

89. Senft's Google searches for the term "voyeur" revealed usages that were far broader than originally conceived by psychologists. This contrasts to media makers who invite others to view them in public forums. See Senft 2008, 45.

90. See Lasch 1979; Twenge and Campbell 2009; and Twenge 2013.

91. See University of North Florida 2014.

92. Grijalva et al. 2015.

93. Bakhtin [1975] 1981.

94. Weiner 1992.

95. Turner 2002.

96. The video was featured on the welcome page for several days in early October 2007. It was also featured on YouTube's welcome page in Italy, where it had garnered over 550,000 views as of October 16, 2007.

97. Hayles 1999.

98. Lévi-Strauss used the term "to think with" when speaking about animal behavior. See Lévi-Strauss 1963, 89. Turkle invoked it to analyze metaphors of computer usage. See Turkle 1984.

99. Whitehead and Wesch 2012a, 1–10.

100. Bloustein 2003.

101. For example, a "view count" reportedly changes across sites. One YouTuber noted that Facebook's service counts a "view" after someone has watched a video for about three seconds, even if the sound is off. In contrast, the same video maker observed that YouTube's service counts a "view" after thirty seconds of viewership. Neither of them represents watching an entire video. It is also claimed that after thirty seconds only about 20 percent of viewers are actually still watching. See Green 2015.

102. Wellner 2016, 145.

CHAPTER 2: YOUTUBE INITIATION

1. Lange 2014.

2. Shrum et al. 2005.

3. Hampe 1997.

4. Shrum et al. 2005.

5. Shrum et al. 2005.

6. Grimshaw and Ravetz 2009, 119.

7. Grimshaw and Ravetz 2009, 119.

8. Shrum et al. 2005.

9. Evans and Jones 2011.

10. Jenkins et al. 2006.

11. Jenkins 1992.

12. Jenkins et al. 2006, 3.

13. Radway 1984.

14. Jenkins, Ford, and Green 2013.

15. Purcell 2013.

16. Researchers recognize the importance of commentary. Jones and Schieffelin argue that YouTube provides "an inherently dialogic forum in which young people and texting aficionados can display, develop, and co-construct the meaning of preferential stylistic and communicative practices." See Jones and Schieffelin 2009, 1075.

17. Lorraine subsequently deleted her account; current statistics on view counts and subscribers are unavailable.

18. Ito et al. 2010, 31.

19. Gauntlett 2011, 85.

20. See Müller 2009.

21. Gauntlett 2011, 87.

22. Stokel-Walker 2017.

23. Newlands 2015.

24. Gauntlett 2011.

25. Gauntlett 2011, 85.

26. "Peter Oakley—Obituary" 2014.

27. Sørenssen 2009.

28. Sørenssen 2009, 147. See also Harley and Fitzpatrick 2009.

29. Lange 2009.

30. Twenge and Campbell 2009, 121.

31. Damon and Louis 2011. Damon and Louis argue that people who are more narcissistic tend to post more online on YouTube, blogs, and social media. Narcissists tend to find content generation more gratifying. See also Panek, Nardis, and Konrath 2013.

32. Freud 1914.

33. Maddox 2017.

34. Twenge and Campbell 2009, 120–122.

35. Strangelove 2010.

36. Stetka 2016.

37. See Sheehy 2017.

38. Although aspects of Facebook, such as posting photos, positively correlated with narcissism, it was also found that "social media is primarily a tool for staying connected" rather than "for self promotion." See Alloway et al. 2014, 150. A counter discourse suggests that since personality is shaped before becoming a teenager, narcissism is fueled by patterns in homes and schools that promote an overinflated and precious sense of children's abilities. See Firestone 2012.

39. Lange 2009.

40. Lasch 1979, 32.

41. Senft and Baym 2015.

42. Lucy R. Lippard as quoted in Sims 1984, 47.

43. Griffith and Papacharissi 2010.

44. Griffith and Papacharissi 2010.
45. Stetka 2016.
46. Verdi and Hodson 2006.
47. Lange 2007c.
48. Lange 2009.
49. Wahlberg 2009.
50. Wahlberg 2009.
51. Lenhart et al. 2013.
52. Purcell 2013.
53. Purcell 2013.
54. Purcell 2013.
55. Lastufka and Dean 2009, 133.
56. Twenge and Campbell 2009, 120–122.
57. I proposed this term to describe the strong preferences people hold when making media or engaging in particular media activities. See Lange 2014, 35.
58. Lange 2014, 20.
59. Twenge and Campbell 2009, 108.
60. Lave and Wenger 1991; Wenger 1998.
61. Strangelove 2010, 126.
62. One month after the gathering, YouTubers reported that the Midwest Lurker still had no account.
63. Sontag 1977.
64. Sontag 1977, 24.
65. Williams 2014.
66. Amid the estimated 2.5 million annual US weddings, a majority of couples reportedly demand "the creation of a visual ideal for their wedding day." See Benzer 1996, 19. Most couples hire wedding photographers and cull photos from guests. See Douglas 2016.
67. Alexander 2013.
68. Gershon 2010.
69. See Mitchell 1986, 8.
70. Gonchar 2013.
71. Paumgarten 2014. Video bloggers' dreams of relatively inexpensive, body-mounted cameras have materialized in the GoPro camera.
72. Dedman and Paul 2006. The book provides technical vlogging tips as well as connecting to vlogging social groups.
73. Lange 2014, 169–184.
74. Bondanella 2002, 68.
75. The paparazzi industry is reportedly "booming," with celebrity photographs increasing. See McNamara 2011.

76. McNamara 2011.
77. Weisman 2012.
78. Mendelson 2007.
79. For example, McNamara argues that Paris Hilton's embodiment of a particular female identity resonated and attracted media attention. See McNamara 2016, 26.
80. McNamara 2016, 28.
81. Hallin 1992.
82. Goldhaber 1997.
83. Sontag 1977, 8.
84. Williams 2014.
85. Hiniker, Shoenebeck, and Kientz 2016.
86. DeWalt and DeWalt 2011, 28–29.
87. Paul 1953.
88. Behar 1996, 5.
89. Tedlock 1991.
90. Descartes [1637] 1998.
91. Hull 1998, 21–22.
92. Hull 1998, 39.
93. Lefebvre 2004, 16.
94. Hull 1998, 21.
95. See Wellner 2016.
96. Hull 1998, 22.
97. Hull 1998, 21.
98. Müller 2009, 126–139.
99. Lange 2014.

CHAPTER 3: GROWING CLOSER

1. Pink 2015, 28.
2. Markham 1998, 125.
3. Bakhtin [1975] 1981.
4. For information about purposeful sampling, see Coyne 1997.
5. Gupta and Ferguson 1997.
6. Pink 2015.
7. Pink 2015, 46.
8. Pink 2015, 80.
9. A more precise term might be "*en*placement." According to the dictionary, the *en-* prefix suggests "making" something, which emphasizes changing states and acts of co-creation. Examples appear in words such as enable, enact, and envision. The concept

of "*en*placement" might help to disassociate from "emplacement's" connotations of spatial fixity.

10. See Turkle 1984; Markham 1998; Cherny 1999; Baym 2000; Rheingold [1993] 2000; and Kendall 2002.

11. Graham 2012.

12. See Wakeford 2003. See also Burrell 2012.

13. Ingold 2008.

14. Miller and Slater 2000, 1.

15. Christensen 2003.

16. An excellent example is found in Lieberman 2003.

17. Miller et al. 2016, 12.

18. Appadurai [1990] 2006.

19. Appadurai [1990] 2006, 591.

20. Marcus 1995.

21. According to "Stickam" n.d., the site was a live video-sharing chat service that ran from 2005 to 2013. It enabled people to see and communicate with several other people in video feeds simultaneously. Interviewees said they often preferred Stickam because it felt more "live" and present than the asynchronous videos that characterized YouTube's functionality at the time.

22. Pink draws on Ingold's ideas of "meshwork" in this sense. See Pink 2015, 37. See also Ingold 2008.

23. Hamedy 2015.

24. See "The Mary Tyler Moore Show Opening Sequence" n.d.

25. "Minneapolis Gets Mary Tyler Moore Statue" 2002; Rodell 2013.

26. Turner 2002.

27. YouTube's beta phase lasted from May to December 15, 2005. See Dickey 2013.

28. Meltzer and Phillips 2009.

29. Stelter 2008.

30. Boots 2016.

31. Ikeda 1998, 162.

32. See "Christmas Truce" n.d.

33. Sobchack 1999.

34. Sokolowski 2000.

35. Bakhtin [1975] 1981, 198.

36. Perrino 2015.

37. Bakhtin [1975] 1981, 243.

38. Dyck 2002.

39. Bakhtin [1975] 1981, 84.

40. Lefebvre 2004, 18.

41. Lange 2011.

42. Dyck 2002.

43. Lange 2015a.

44. See Gal 2002. For a discussion of how the public and private relationship fractalizes in social media and video, see Lange 2007b.

45. Chalfen 1987.

46. Zimmerman 1995.

47. Pini 2009.

48. Pini 2009, 85.

49. Weston 1992.

50. Weston 1992; Moran 2002.

51. Pini 2009.

52. See Dicks et al. 2011.

53. Postill and Pink 2012.

54. Early research assessing functionality of modalities focused on factors such as synchronous or asynchronous interaction, characteristics that may have limited value for evaluating fungibility of interactions, which were largely inter-threaded between so-called online and offline experiences for YouTubers. More recent research further suggests that in-person discussions preceded by mediated conversation (whether synchronous or asynchronous) are reportedly more productive than those conducted only in person. See Dietz-Uhler and Bishop-Clark 2001.

55. Edwards 2010, 84.

CHAPTER 4: SYNCING UP THROUGH RECIPROCITY

1. Dodaro 2011.

2. Offer 1997, 452.

3. Douglas 1990, vii–xviii; see also Sahlins 1972.

4. See Sahlins 1972 and Weiner 1992 for analyses of reciprocity's complications.

5. For information about first-generation vloggers who began posting videos to their own video blogs outside of YouTube prior to 2005, see Lange 2014. See also Berry 2018.

6. See, for instance, Mark Day's video *Greetings from VidCon*, posted on July 10, 2010.

7. Scott 2011.

8. Blip.tv removed low-earning videos after Maker Studios acquired it in 2013. Blip.tv shut down in August 2015. See "Blip (website)" n.d.

9. Kollock 1999.

10. Kollock 1999.

11. Barak and Gluck-Ofri 2007.

12. Lange 2007c.

13. boyd 2010.

14. "The Anatomy of a Forgotten Social Network" 2014.

15. "The Anatomy of a Forgotten Social Network" 2014. See also Chang et al. 2014.

16. Pelaprat and Brown 2012.

17. Pelaprat and Brown 2012.

18. Pelaprat and Brown 2012.

19. Goldhaber 1997.

20. Gouldner 1960.

21. Blau [1964] 1986, 88–114.

22. Offer 1997.

23. Gouldner 1960.

24. Gouldner 1960.

25. Commenters sometimes compete to be the first to post, often with the declaration "First!"

26. Dreier 2012.

27. Narotzky 2007.

28. Twenge and Campbell 2009, 240.

29. Twenge and Campbell 2009, 240.

30. See Yarow and Angelova 2010.

31. Sahlins 1972, 194–195.

32. Pelaprat and Brown 2012.

33. Sahlins 1972, 194.

34. Sahlins 1972, 194.

35. Lovink 2011, 54.

36. Unlike social media connections, which are publicly visible, YouTube allows viewers to keep their subscription preferences private. A video maker can see only the subscribers who have agreed to be identified. When I click on my list of subscribers, YouTube's interface returns the message, "Only subscribers who share their subscriptions publicly are shown. Subscribers who have their subscriptions set to private don't show here, even if the account is subscribed to your channel."

37. Marwick and boyd 2010, 116.

38. Yan 1996, 210–238.

39. YouTube operates in a market economy in which videos may be commercialized through advertising. Sub-for-sub arrangements that seek monetization through mutual exchange render videos as commodities that may monetarily benefit platform operators and creators.

40. Yan 1996, 218.

41. Mauss 1990.

42. Marwick and boyd 2010, 114.

43. Wesch 2009, 23.

44. Pelaprat and Brown 2012.

45. Pelaprat and Brown 2012.

46. See Lastufka and Dean 2009, 133.

47. Nalty 2010, 195.

48. Twenge and Campbell 2009.

49. Joseph Walther long ago observed the impact of time on the timbre of interactions. "One-shot" studies attributing negative interactions to the effects of a medium did not consider the influence of anticipation of *ongoing* interaction on behavior. He stated: "[Computer-mediated communication] appears to be more interpersonally positive when used by members who at least think that their association will have some longevity." See Walther 1994, 495.

50. Sahlins 1972, 195.

51. See Carter et al. 2014. Carter et al. characterize the "like for like" hashtag as "overtly narcissistic." See also Andren 2016.

52. boyd 2010.

53. Park, Li, and Kim 2016.

54. Veszelszki 2016.

55. Andren 2016.

56. Lefebvre 2004, 78.

57. Lefebvre 2004, 78.

58. Lefebvre 2004, 99–100.

59. Lange 2010.

60. See Weiner 1992; Godelier 2002.

61. Godelier 2002.

62. Weiner 1992, 6.

63. Pelaprat and Brown 2012.

64. On social media sites, "follow blasts" occur when participants follow many accounts to entice people into following back. Follow blasts ostensibly work because they parlay a user's impulse to follow people in return when they discover a new follower. However, follow blasts exhibit risks. They are easily detected and may result in an account being banned or having privileges removed for sending spam. For a pundit's description of the Law of Reciprocity on Twitter as well as on follow blasts and their risks, see Dogan 2010.

65. Twenge and Campbell 2009, 112.

66. Marwick and boyd 2010.

67. Sahlins 1972, 193–194.

68. Sahlins 1972, 194.

69. Lange 2003, 2014.

70. See, for instance, the video *Zen Archer*, posted on February 15, 2015, on YouTube by ogier1.

71. MacCormack 1976.

72. Kolm 2006.

73. Simmel 1950, 389.

74. Appadurai [1990] 2006.

75. Sahlins 1972, 193–194.

CHAPTER 5: WHAT DEFINES A COMMUNITY?

1. See Curtis [1992] 1997; Cherny 1999; and Rheingold [1993] 2000.

2. Althusser 1971.

3. Juhasz 2009.

4. Boellstorff et al. 2012, 126–128. See also Fetterman 1987.

5. de Seta 2018a.

6. Lovink 2011, 52.

7. Lovink 2011, 57.

8. The removal may have resulted from comments that were excessively flagged by viewers as inappropriate, were spam, or had been posted by commenters with now-deleted accounts. Hater comments containing insults and profanity still remained as of July 2018 as part of the 552 comments.

9. Moreau and Alderman 2011.

10. According to one manual for dealing with graffiti, "Removing graffiti as soon as it appears is the key to its elimination—and recurrence." See Weaver 1995. Repainting graffiti to leave a clean surface tends to attract additional graffiti. See Eck and Martinelli 1998.

11. See de Seta 2018b.

12. Cohen 1985, 11.

13. Hillery 1955.

14. Redfield 1955, 113.

15. Gupta and Ferguson 1997.

16. Cohen 1985, 12.

17. Wellman and Gulia 1999, 187.

18. Wellman and Gulia 1999, 187.

19. Amit 2002c, 16.

20. Silverstone 1999, 104.

21. Amit 2002c, 3.

22. Lange 2008b; Gruzd, Wellman, and Takhteyev 2011.

23. Anderson 1983, 6.

24. Anderson 1983.

25. Silverstein 2000, 124.

26. Amit 2002b.

27. Amit 2002a; Silverstein 2000.

28. Mitchell et al. 2016.

29. Burgess and Green 2009, 90.

30. Eldon 2011.

31. Rotman and Preece 2010, 330.

32. Rotman and Preece 2010, 322.

33. Cunningham and Craig 2016, 5413.

34. Cohen 1985, 98.

35. Rheingold [1993] 2000, xxxi.

36. Lange 2008a; Burgess and Green 2009; and Rotman and Preece 2010.

37. Strangelove 2010, 105.

38. Bauman 1996, 15.

39. Strangelove 2010, 105; Douglas 1992, 133.

40. Strangelove 2010, 120–121.

41. Subscribers received alerts when a video maker posted a new video. From its inception until the present writing in 2018, subscribing to a YouTube channel was free of charge and merely involved clicking a yellow Subscribe button on a YouTuber's page.

42. Dyck 2002.

43. Lange 2007a.

44. Nip 2004.

45. Pink et al. 2017, 176.

46. According to Althusser's concept of interpellation, a person being hailed acknowledges the hail, thus identifying themselves as the subject of the hail. A classic example occurs when a police officer calls "Hey you!" down a busy street. Those who turn to answer interpellate themselves as subjects of the hail. Similarly, those who commented on community interpellated themselves as stakeholders in the discussion about prospects for digital community. See Althusser 1971.

47. Holmes and Marcus 2008, 595.

48. Holmes and Marcus 2008, 597.

49. Reagle 2015, 181.

50. Anderson 1983.

51. Silverstein 2000.

52. Amit and Rapport 2002.

53. Uldam and Askanius 2013.

54. Martínez 1995, 208.

55. Pink 2011, 229.

56. YouTube introduced video annotations in 2008. The site reportedly eliminated them in 2017, in favor of a feature called End Screen and Cards, a mobile and desktop tool that apparently enables similar functionalities, such as linking to other videos and polling viewers.

Some 60 percent of YouTube's watch time is reportedly from mobile devices. Annotation use, which was available only as a desktop feature, fell by 70 percent over the years. See Statt 2017.

57. Wogan 2006.

58. Wogan 2006, 29.

59. Hunter et al. 2012.

60. Herring 1996.

61. Papacharissi 2004.

62. Hutchens et al. 2015, 1210.

63. This post was not coded as a hater comment. Should it have been?

64. O'Sullivan and Flanagin 2003.

65. Kendall 2002, 112–113.

66. See Hill 2012.

67. In one example, a man threatened a congressman. The perpetrator was not anonymous because he put his face on camera. Officers eventually found him by examining identity indexes such as IP addresses. See Anderson 2010.

68. Reagle 2015, 175–176. See also Amadeo 2015.

69. Names that people provide consistently on social media do not always map to legal names. See Lil Miss Hot Mess 2015.

70. Reagle 2015, 175.

71. Kelly 2013.

72. Hern 2013.

73. Lovink 2011, 46.

74. Lovink 2011, 47.

75. Miller et al. 2016, 36. Miller et al. noted that concerns about social media and privacy are "parochial," meaning that they differ according to place. While people in some countries express concern about privacy, people in India and China may use social media to construct private social spaces.

76. The case of Kathryn Knott demonstrates how some people feel comfortable posting racist messages online under their official names. See Murray 2014.

77. Merlan 2015.

78. Reagle 2015, 181.

79. Kendall 2002, 112–113.

80. Coleman 2014.

81. As of July 2018, the accounts of teddieppl77 and microwavefishsticks could not be located on YouTube.

82. A similar point is made in Natanson 1986.

83. Mosendz 2015.

84. Garfinkel 1967, 116–185.

85. Kennedy 2006.

86. Warner 2002.

87. Granovetter 1973.

88. Pink et al. 2017.

89. Reagle 2015, 119.

90. See Juhasz 2008; Hess 2009; and Buckingham, Willett, and Pini 2011.

91. Hess 2009.

92. PR Newswire 2015.

93. Uldam and Askanius 2013.

94. Uldam and Askanius 2013.

95. Altucher 2013.

96. Radsch 2016.

97. Radsch 2016, 38.

98. YouTube has been referred to as the internet's comment "cesspool." See Slutsky 2014.

99. Perez 2016.

100. Perez 2016.

101. Reagle 2015, 174.

102. Reagle 2015, 183, 185.

103. Ash's Twitter account calls her "pronoun indifferent." Her partner refers to Ash in videos as "she."

104. Mediakix 2018.

105. Rouch 1975.

106. Pink 2011, 231.

107. Pink 2011.

108. Geertz [1972] 2005.

109. Miller et al. 2016.

110. Juhasz 2008, 133.

111. Juhasz 2009.

112. Juhasz 2008, 135.

113. Wali 2010, 147.

114. Wesch 2007.

115. Wesch 2011, 23.

116. Palmer 2007.

117. Wesch 2011, 26.

118. Nahon and Hemsley 2013.

119. Nahon and Hemsley 2013, 16.

120. Jenkins, Ford, and Green 2013, 16–23. For a summary, see Jenkins 2009a.

121. Nahon and Hemsley 2013.

122. Nahon and Hemsley 2013, 11.

123. For information about promoting interest-driven learning, see the work of Mizuko Ito and others in the Connected Learning initiative: https://clalliance.org/about-connected -learning/.

124. Newman 2008.

125. Vernallis 2013, 149–150.

126. Rotman and Preece 2010.

127. Postill 2011.

128. Postill and Pink 2012, 131–132. See also Amit and Rapport 2002.

129. Amit 2002a.

130. Amit 2002a, 14.

131. Appadurai 1996; Ito et al. 2010.

132. Appadurai 1996, 8.

133. Amit 2002d, 161–166.

134. Rapport 2002, 169.

135. Lovink 2011, 58.

CHAPTER 6: PORTALS TO THE POSTHUMAN

1. Hayles 1999.

2. Bollmer 2013.

3. Plato [370 BCE] 1973.

4. Poletti and Rak 2014.

5. Hayles 1999, 2–3.

6. Wesch 2012.

7. Beth Coleman proposes the term "avatar" in a similar context. In computer science an avatar is a visual representation of the self in a virtual environment. The term also connotes behaviorally representative forms such as text messaging and uses of social media. See Coleman 2011, 12.

8. Gingrich, Ochs, and Swedlund 2002.

9. Miller et al. 2016, x.

10. Whitehead and Wesch 2012b.

11. For information on actor-network theory, see Latour 2005.

12. Hayles 1999, 286.

13. Hayles 1999, 291.

14. Kennedy 2006, 874.

15. Whitehead and Wesch 2012a.

16. Hayles 1999, 291.

17. McNeill 2012.

18. Hayles 1999, 3.

19. Kincaid 2010.

20. Knight 2012.

21. In 2006, prior to the partnership program, YouTube introduced an account category called YouTube Director, which enabled users who had been vetted to be given director status for free. Directors could upload videos that were longer than ten minutes. See YouTube Team 2006.

22. Before 2010, all videos for standard accounts were reportedly limited to ten minutes. Due to technological improvements, as of July 29, 2010, standard accounts could post videos up to fifteen minutes long. See Eash n.d.

23. McNeill 2012.

24. Hayles 1999.

25. Hayles 1999, 255.

26. Coleman 2011, 41.

27. Coleman 2011, 137.

28. See Rheingold [1993] 2000, 139.

29. See Boellstorff 2008.

30. Phillips 2015.

31. Phillips 2015, 24.

32. Phillips 2015, 25.

33. For instance, Amazon.com's algorithms incorrectly pulled tens of thousands of gay-friendly fiction books from its sales lists. Such decisions have emotional, political, and financial impact on authors. See Gillespie 2014. For details on the misclassification of gay-themed books, see Flood 2009.

34. In examining "video assemblages" or groups of creators, videos, processes, and platforms on YouTube and other sites such as Facebook, Hondros observed that participants exhibited similar frustrations about automated processes, such as how posts were filtered and how automated bots served take-down notices. Video creators were often "left with assemblages that were inadequate with regard to their objectives as video producers." See Hondros 2016, 222.

35. Strangelove 2010, 68. See also Wright 2008.

36. Strangelove 2010; Wright 2008.

37. For community guidelines, see https://www.youtube.com/yt/about/policies/#community-guidelines. For information on hate speech, see https://support.google.com/youtube/answer/2801939.

38. For information about harassment and cyberbullying, see https://support.google.com/youtube/answer/2802268.

39. Coleman 2011, 41.

40. Other observed ratings were 2 stars (Nothing special), 3 stars (Worth watching), and 4 stars (Pretty cool).

41. Lohensohn 2010.

42. Lange 2014.

43. Gayle 2012.

44. Latour 2005, 75.

45. Hayles 1999, 256.

46. Cole Perriman is an amalgam of the authors' names: Wim Coleman and Pat Perrin. See Coleman and Perrin 1994.

47. Brubaker and Cooper argue that scholarship should move beyond the idea of "identity" and focus on processes of identification. See Brubaker and Cooper 2000.

48. Couser 2004.

49. Henwood et al. 2001.

50. Couser 2004.

51. Lange 2014.

52. See http://cc.au.dk/en/research/research-programmes/cultural-transformations /cultures-and-practices-of-death-and-dying/dorn/.

53. Leaver and Highfield 2018, 30–31.

54. Goffman 1959.

55. Lever and Highfield 2018, 32.

56. McNamara 2016, 1–8.

57. Even diaries intended for private consumption may circulate beyond an assumed audience. See Kitzmann 2004. For a discussion of misinterpreted Web pages, see Stern 2008.

58. McNeill 2012, 76.

59. See Christensen and Gotved 2015.

60. Christensen and Gotved 2015.

61. See Leaver 2013.

62. Ryan 2012.

63. Lopes 2015.

64. Fowler 2013.

65. See Myers 2011, 35; Carroll and Romano 2011, 146–147.

66. Bollmer 2013.

67. Leaver 2013.

68. Leaver 2013, 2.

69. Lefebvre 2004, 99–100.

70. Gershon 2010.

71. Bollmer 2013.

72. See Christensen and Gotved 2015, 5. For more information on the concept of the deathstyle, see Davies 2005; Davies and Rumble 2012.

73. Ryan 2012.

74. Bollmer 2013, 150.

75. Christensen and Gotved 2015.

76. Fowler 2013.

77. Margaret Gibson as quoted in Gotved 2014, 117. See Gibson 2007.

78. Hanks 2012.

79. Leaver 2013.

80. Stine Gotved observed that the "continuing bonds" theme was common in research studies. See Gotved 2014.

81. See Wahlberg 2009; Ryan 2012; and Bollmer 2013. See also the collection of papers for the panel "Coping with Death and Grief through Technology" presented at Internet Research 14.0, the fourteenth international conference of the Association of Internet Researchers, October 23–26, 2013, Denver, Colorado.

82. Lefebvre 2004, 46.

83. Gielen 2015; AdOps 2018.

84. TubeMogul 2013.

85. Discussions of migration in gaming communities noted that participants sometimes reached a moment in which loyalty to other players superseded the need to play a particular game. See Pearce 2009.

86. Another conceptualization is the idea of "digital diaspora," in which groups migrate to different sites. For anthropologists, diaspora are groups who mourn the violent or sudden loss of a homeland and long to return. The term digital diaspora may encompass a range of emotions from intensive feelings of loss to more casual responses to changes in media use. See Boellstorff 2008.

87. See "TheWineKone" n.d.

88. Stickam operated from February 2005 until January 2013. It offered live streaming video enabling several participants to connect simultaneously in a video chat room. See Constine 2013. See also "Stickam" n.d.

89. Burgess and Green 2009, 65. Burgess and Green observed that many YouTubers maintained their YouTube account names on Stickam.

90. Siegel 2011.

91. Constine 2013.

92. Blip.tv (2005–2015) was a media platform that offered web hosting. See "Blip (website)" n.d.

93. Jackson 2014.

94. Jackson 2014.

95. See Holpuch 2012.

96. This term is adapted from Arjun Appadurai and is discussed in more detail in chapter 3. See Appadurai [1990] 2006.

97. Lange 2008c.

98. Driscoll and Paloque-Berges 2017.

99. Driscoll and Paloque-Berges 2017, 49.

100. Guo and Lee 2013.

101. Raun 2016.

102. Naslund et al. 2014.

103. Cunningham and Craig 2016.

104. Niemeyer and Gerber 2015.

CHAPTER 7: LIVING WITH ARRHYTHMIA

1. Lefebvre 2004.

2. Neff and Stark 2002.

3. An announcement about eliminating friending appeared by YT Kendall on December 6, 2011, on the YouTube Help Forum site, with an update on December 12, 2011; see Kendall 2011.

4. Faeth 2012.

5. A rubric addressing these dynamics is "mediatization," which includes "institutional practices that reflexively link processes of communication to processes of commoditization." See Agha 2011.

6. Mitroff and Martin 2017.

7. Calabro 2017.

8. YouTube's beta phase lasted from May to December 15, 2005. See Dickey 2013.

9. Palladino 2017.

10. Hudson 2015.

11. Pathak 2018.

12. YouTube 2018a.

13. See YouTube 2018b.

14. Rosenblatt 2018.

15. See "Patreon" n.d.

16. See "#79 John Green." 2014; Leather 2018.

17. Hudson 2015.

18. Kirkpatrick 2007.

19. O'Neill 2012.

20. Pew Research Staff 2012.

21. Kaufman 2014.

22. Popper 2017.

23. Musil 2018.

24. Ram 2018.

25. Zaher 2018.

26. Zaher 2018.

27. Thompson 2016.

28. della Cava 2013

29. Kaufman 2014.

30. Kozlowski 2013.

31. Crushell 2018. See also Cunningham, Craig, and Silver 2016.

32. See Associated Press 2014.

33. Pacheco 2014.

34. Shields 2014.

35. Shields 2014.

36. Gutelle 2014. Zappin filed suit in 2013, alleging he had been forced out of Maker Studios, and again in 2014 to block the Disney acquisition of Maker Studios. Both cases were dismissed, and Zappin reportedly earned $25 million from the sale. See Reim 2016.

37. D'Anastasio 2017.

38. For a discussion of the benefits of networks, see Mueller 2013.

39. D'Anastasio 2017.

40. Becker 1982.

41. Prangley 2015.

42. Li 2015.

43. Metzger 2017.

44. Cannon 2017.

45. Dryden 2016.

46. Weiss 2017a.

47. Villarreal and Pierson 2016.

48. VidCon Europe launched in 2017 and took place in Amsterdam in 2018. See Crushell 2018. VidCon Australia was held September 2017 and August–September in 2018 in Melbourne. See Weiss 2017b; "VidCon" n.d.

49. Walsh 2016.

50. See Bilton 2015.

51. Spangler 2018.

52. Latinx (pronounced La-teen-ex) is a non-gender-specific term that collectively refers to Latinos and Latinas. See Logue 2015.

53. Her words echo the sentiments of those expressed by Mr. Safety (also known by his YouTube channel name of SMPFilms), who made similar remarks at a meet-up in Hollywood.

54. See Jarvis 2016.

55. BET Staff 2018. For an analysis of the "Chocolate Rain" phenomenon, see Burgess 2008.

56. One pundit observed that VidCon moved away from its initial roots of being a "classic YouTube gathering," which originally served creators by emphasizing "networking, learning, and seeing familiar faces." He lamented that VidCon became more expensive and less

accessible and that it compromised networking by concentrating on teen fan events. See Smith 2014.

57. As of 2018, YouTube provided a time stamp for posted comments at several increments. For instance, a time stamp might note that a comment was posted "38 minutes ago." As time passes, the time stamp converts to approximate hours, days, weeks, months, and years. After one year, the time stamp provides no additional specificity beyond the number of years since its posting.

58. Popken 2018.

59. Popken 2018.

60. Dave 2018.

61. Popken 2018.

62. Companies that track YouTube viewing metrics apparently corroborate this perception. Videos that are ten minutes or longer generally gain more views than those that are five minutes or less. See Gielen and Rosen 2016.

63. MacInnes 2018.

64. Rockrapid 2018.

65. Alexander 2018b.

66. Alexander 2018b.

67. Kaufman 2014.

68. Stokel-Walker 2017.

69. Alexander 2018a.

70. Cunningham, Craig, and Silver 2016.

71. Portelli 1991, 51.

72. Cunningham, Craig, and Silver 2016, 377.

73. Cunningham and Craig characterize the new YouTube ecology as "relatively frictionless" in comparison with "national broadcasting and systems of film and DVD licensing by territory." See Cunningham and Craig 2016, 5411. However, participatory complications and frictions routinely occur on YouTube. For instance, a YouTuber might upload copyrighted content under "fair use" to exhibit for review or critique, but such content may be flagged and removed. For a discussion about participatory challenges on YouTube, see Lange 2017.

CHAPTER 8: CONCLUSION

1. Paul 2016.

2. Meissner 2015.

3. Wellner 2016, 16.

4. Goodson 2012.

5. Panzarino 2013.

6. Vossen n.d.

7. See Kavoori 2011, who provides one "cut" of YouTube. Michael Strangelove notes that *"Watching YouTube* cannot capture all of the 'Tube' but it does provide an overview of YouTube's social features." See Strangelove 2010.

8. Miller et al. 2016.

9. Miller et al. 2016, 9.

10. boyd and Ellison 2007.

11. Miller et al. 2016, 15.

12. LaFrance and Meyer 2014.

13. See "Twitter" n.d.

14. Dean 2010, 98. See also Cheng and Evans 2009.

15. Burgess 2015.

16. Ginsburg 2012.

17. The adjective "cultural" is increasingly used rather than the noun "culture," which connotes homogeneity. See Appadurai 1996.

18. Kottak 2009, 500.

19. Driscoll and Paloque-Berges 2017, 48.

20. Driscoll and Paloque-Berges 2017, 50.

21. Post-phenomenology attempts to take a middle path between studying subjective experiences and analyzing technologized objects. See Rao et al. 2015, 454.

22. Wellner 2016.

23. Wellner 2016, 145.

24. Wellner 2016, 145.

25. Lang 2015.

26. Niemeyer and Gerber 2015.

27. See Naslund et al. 2014; Raun 2016.

28. Fish 1980, 14–17.

29. Moran 2002.

30. For details about my experiences, see Lange 2015b.

31. Cameron, Inzlicht, and Cunningham 2015.

32. Boellstorff 2008, 193. See also Harding 1991.

33. Phillips 2015.

34. Müller 2009.

35. See Stokel-Walker 2017.

36. Lange 2012.

37. Lange 2014. See also Berry 2018.

38. Miller et al. 2016, xvi.

39. Senft and Baym 2015.

40. Miller et al. 2016, 112.

41. Miller et al. 2016, 100.

42. People interacting online tend to exhibit consistent behavior under persistent pseudonyms. See Kendall 2002.

43. Phillips 2015.

44. Mirca Madianou and Daniel Miller use the term "polymedia" to refer to how people choose from a range of media according to how each one fulfills social and emotional needs. See Madianou and Miller 2012.

45. See Miller and Slater 2000; Postill 2011; Burrell 2012; and Miller et al. 2016.

46. Lefebvre 2004, 36.

47. Terranova 2000.

48. Inoue 2004.

49. See Musil 2018. Part of the stricter guidelines emerged as a result of the uploading of inappropriate, non-ad-friendly content such as graphic videos, hate speech, extremist videos about al-Qaeda, and videos depicting child endangerment or sexual abuse. See Dave 2018.

50. Scott 2012.

51. Scroggins 2012.

52. Ruby 1991.

53. Ruby 1995, 81.

54. Ruby 1991.

55. Pink 2011.

56. See Stern 2008, 111.

57. Morphy and Banks 1997.

58. Evans and Jones 2011.

59. Michael Wesch, as quoted in Pink 2011, 211.

60. Gross, Katz, and Ruby 1988, 2003.

61. See Perry and Marion 2010, 97.

62. Mann, Nolan, and Wellman 2003.

63. Shrum et al. 2005.

64. Gross, Katz, and Ruby 2003, xxii.

65. Lange 2014.

66. See Taylor 1996.

67. Nissenbaum 2004.

68. Meikle 2016, 92.

69. Ruby 1991, 56.

70. In a Pew survey of US teens between the ages of twelve and seventeen, Lenhart et al. found that 62 percent of online teens receive information about politics and civic events online. See Lenhart et al. 2010.

71. Irvine 2001.

72. Irvine 2001, 22.

73. Anderson 1983, 6.

REFERENCES

"#79 John Green." 2014. *Forbes*. June 13. https://www.forbes.com/profile/john-green-3
/#78a64ff117f5.

AdOps. 2018. "Is There a Mobile Video Primetime in the United States?" *AdOpsBuzz.com*.
September 8. http://www.adopsbuzz.com/is-there-a-mobile-video-primetime-in-the
-united-states/.

Agha, Asif. 2011. "Meet Mediatization." *Language & Communication* 31: 163–170.

Alexander, Julie. 2018a. "YouTube's Lesser-Known Creators Worry for the Future after
Major Monetization Changes (Update)." *Polygon*. January 17. https://www.polygon
.com/2018/1/17/16900474/youtube-monetization-small-creators-adsense.

Alexander, Julie. 2018b. "YouTube's Top Creators Are Burning Out and Breaking Down En
Masse." *Polygon*. June 1. https://www.polygon.com/2018/6/1/17413542/burnout-mental
-health-awareness-youtube-elle-mills-el-rubius-bobby-burns-pewdiepie.

Alexander, Valerie. 2013. "Stop Capturing the Moment and Just Enjoy It." *Huffington Post*.
October 3. http://www.huffingtonpost.com/valerie-alexander/stop-capturing-the
-moment_b_3992335.html.

Alloway, Tracy, Rachel Runac, Mueez Qureshi, and George Kemp. 2014. "Is Facebook
Linked to Selfishness? Investigating the Relationships among Social Media Use,
Empathy, and Narcissism." *Social Networking* 3: 150–158.

Althusser, Louis. 1971. *Lenin and Philosophy and Other Essays*. New York: Monthly Review
Press.

DOI: 10.5876/9781607329558.c009

Altucher, James. 2013. *Choose Yourself!* Austin, TX: Lioncrest Publishing.

Amadeo, Ron. 2015. "Google Officially Ends Forced Google+ Integration—First Up: YouTube." *Ars Technica.* July 27. https://arstechnica.com/gadgets/2015/07/google -officially-ends-forced-google-integration-first-up-youtube/.

Amit, Vered. 2002a. "Anthropology and Community: Some Opening Notes." In *The Trouble with Community: Anthropological Reflections on Movement, Identity and Collectivity,* Vered Amit and Nigel Rapport, 13–25. London: Pluto Press.

Amit, Vered, ed. 2002b. *Realizing Community: Concepts, Social Relationships and Sentiments.* London: Routledge.

Amit, Vered. 2002c. "Reconceptualizing Community." In *Realizing Community: Concepts, Social Relationships and Sentiments,* ed. Vered Amit, 1–20. London: Routledge.

Amit, Vered. 2002d. "Vered Amit Responds to Nigel Rapport." In *The Trouble with Community: Anthropological Reflections on Movement, Identity and Collectivity,* Vered Amit and Nigel Rapport, 161–166. London: Pluto Press.

Amit, Vered, and Nigel Rapport. 2002. *The Trouble with Community: Anthropological Reflections on Movement, Identity and Collectivity.* London: Pluto Press.

"The Anatomy of a Forgotten Social Network." 2014. *MIT Technology Review.* March 31. https://www.technologyreview.com/s/525966/the-anatomy-of-a-forgotten-social -network/.

Anderson, Benedict. 1983. *Imagined Communities.* London: Verso.

Anderson, Chris. 2006. *The Long Tail.* New York: Hyperion.

Anderson, Monica. 2015. "5 Facts about Online Video, for YouTube's 10th Birthday." *Pew Research Center.* February 12. http://www.pewresearch.org/fact-tank/2015/02/12/5 -facts-about-online-video-for-youtubes-10th-birthday/.

Anderson, Nate. 2010. "How the FBI Busted One YouTube Nutjob in under a Day." *Ars Technica.* March 30. http://arstechnica.com/tech-policy/2010/03/how-the-fbi-busts -youtube-terrorists-in-under-a-day/.

Andren, Eric. 2016. "I Can So I Will, Now We Must: A Creative Response to Selfie Culture." M.F.A. thesis, Iowa State University.

Appadurai, Arjun. 1996. *Modernity at Large: Cultural Dimensions of Globalization.* Minneapolis: University of Minnesota Press.

Appadurai, Arjun. (1990) 2006. "Disjuncture and Difference in the Global Cultural Economy." In *Media and Cultural Studies: Key Works,* ed. Douglas M. Kellner and Meenakshi Gigi Durham, 584–603. Malden, MA: Blackwell Publishing.

Associated Press. 2014. "Disney Buys Channel Operator Maker Studios for $500M." *CBC.* March 25. http://www.cbc.ca/news/business/disney-buys-youtube-channel-operator -maker-studios-for-500m-1.2585241.

Bakhtin, M. M. (1975) 1981. *The Dialogic Imagination*. Austin: University of Texas Press.

Barak, Azy, and Orit Gluck-Ofri. 2007. "Degree of Reciprocity of Self-Disclosure in Online Forums." *CyberPsychology & Behavior* 10 (3): 407–417.

Basu, Saikat. 2010. "5 Most Subscribed Channels on YouTube." *MakeUseOf.* November 22. https://www.makeuseof.com/tag/5-subscribed-channels-youtube/.

Bauman, Gerd. 1996. *Contesting Culture: Discourses of Identity in Multi-Ethnic London.* Cambridge: Cambridge University Press.

Baym, Nancy. 2000. *Tune In, Log On: Soaps, Fandom, and Online Community.* Thousand Oaks, CA.: Sage.

Bear, Greg. 1985. *Blood Music*. London: Orion.

Becker, Howard S. 1982. *Art Worlds*. Berkeley: University of California Press.

Behar, Ruth. 1996. *The Vulnerable Observer*. Boston: Beacon Press.

Benzer, Lili Corbus. 1996. "'Devine Detritus': An Analysis of American Wedding Photography." *Studies in Popular Culture* 18 (2): 19–33.

Berry, Trine Bjørkmann. 2018. *Video Blogging before YouTube*. Amsterdam: Institute of Network Cultures.

BET Staff. 2018. "I Went Viral: Tay Zonday." *BET.com*. April 13. https://www.bet.com /celebrities/exclusives/tay-zonday-i-went-viral.html.

Bilton, Nick. 2015. "At VidCon, Small-Screen Stars and Big-Time Fame." *New York Times*. July 22. http://www.nytimes.com/2015/07/23/style/at-vidcon-small-screen-stars-and -big-time-fame.html?_r=0.

Blake, Roberto. 2015. "What Makes a YouTube Channel Successful?" *Medium.com*. January 31. https://medium.com/@robertoblake/what-makes-a-youtube-channel -successful-3477e3dfad66.

Blau, Peter M. (1964) 1986. *Exchange and Power in Social Life*. New York: John Wiley and Sons.

"Blip (website)." n.d. *Wikipedia*. https://en.wikipedia.org/wiki/Blip_(website).

Bloustein, Gerry. 2003. *Girl Making: A Cross-Cultural Ethnography on the Processes of Growing Up Female*. New York: Berghahn Books.

Boellstorff, Tom. 2008. *Coming of Age in Second Life: An Anthropologist Explores the Virtually Human*. Princeton, NJ: Princeton University Press.

Boellstorff, Tom, Bonnie Nardi, Celia Pearce, and T. L. Taylor. 2012. *Ethnography and Virtual Worlds: A Handbook of Method*. Princeton, NJ: Princeton University Press.

Bollmer, Grant David. 2013. "Millions Now Living Will Never Die: Cultural Anxieties about the Afterlife of Information." *The Information Society: An International Journal* 29 (3): 142–151.

Bondanella, Peter. 2002. *The Films of Federico Fellini*. Cambridge, UK: Cambridge University Press.

Boots, Michelle Theriault. 2016. "A YouTube Star Takes on Alaska." *Anchorage Daily News.*
May 31. https://www.adn.com/anchorage/article/youtube-star-takes-alaska/2014/10/26/.

boyd, danah. 2010. "Friendship." In *Hanging Out, Messing Around, and Geeking Out: Kids
Living and Learning with New Media*, ed. Mizuko Ito, Sonja Baumer, Matteo Bittani,
danah boyd, Rachel Cody, Becky Herr-Stephenson, Heather A. Horst, et al., 79–115.
Cambridge, MA: MIT Press.

boyd, danah, and Nicole Ellison. 2007. "Social Network Sites: Definition, History, and
Scholarship." *Journal of Computer-Mediated Communication* 13 (1). https://doi.org/10
.1111/j.1083–6101.2007.00393.x.

Brubaker, Rogers, and Frederick Cooper. 2000. "Beyond Identity." *Theory and Society* 29:
1–47.

Buckingham, David, Rebekah Willett, and Maria Pini. 2011. *Home Truths? Video
Production and Domestic Life*. Ann Arbor: University of Michigan Press.

Burgess, Jean. 2008. "'All Your Chocolate Rain Are Belong to Us?' Viral Video, YouTube
and the Dynamics of Participatory Culture." In *Video Vortex Reader: Responses to
YouTube*, ed. Geert Lovink and Sabine Niederer, 101–109. Amsterdam: Institute of
Network Cultures.

Burgess, Jean. 2015. "Twitter (Probably) Isn't Dying, but Is It Becoming Less Sociable?"
Medium.com. November 5. https://medium.com/dmrc-at-large/twitter-probably-isn-t
-dying-but-is-it-becoming-less-sociable-d768a99968982#.eeobyk72h.

Burgess, Jean, and Joshua Green. 2009. *YouTube: Online Video and Participatory Culture.*
Cambridge, UK: Polity Press.

Burrell, Jenna. 2012. *Invisible Users: Youth in the Internet Cafés of Urban Ghana.*
Cambridge, MA: MIT Press.

Calabro, Eileen Bien. 2017. "YouTube Red vs. YouTube TV: What's the Difference?" *PC
Magazine*. September 11. https://www.pcmag.com/article/355611/youtube-red-vs
-youtube-tv-whats-the-difference.

Cameron, Darryl, Michael Inzlicht, and William A. Cunningham. 2015. "Empathy Is
Actually a Choice." *NewYorkTimes.com*. July 10. http://www.nytimes.com/2015/07/12
/opinion/sunday /empathy-is-actually-a-choice.html.

Cannon, Bradley. 2017. "Here's What Happened at the First #YouTubeBlack FanFest." *Blavity.*
October 19. https://blavity.com/heres-what-happened-at-the-first-youtubeblack-fanfest.

Carroll, Evan, and John Romano. 2011. *Your Digital Afterlife*. Berkeley, CA: New Riders.

Carter, Marcus, Martin Gibbs, Bjorn Nansen, and Michael Arnold. 2014. "#FUNERAL."
Paper presented at the Association of Internet Researchers Conference, October 22–24,
Daegu, Korea.

Castronova, Edward. 2005. *Synthetic Worlds: The Business and Culture of Online Games.*
Chicago: University of Chicago Press.

Chalfen, Richard. 1987. *Snapshot Versions of Life*. Bowling Green, OH: Bowling Green State University Press.

Chang, Yi, Lei Tang, Yoshiyuki Inagaki, and Yan Liu. 2014. "What Is Tumblr? A Statistical Overview and Comparison." *arXiv.org*. July 30, 2014. http://arxiv.org/abs/1403.5206.

Cheng, Alex, and Mark Evans. 2009. "Inside Twitter." *Sysomos Inc*. June 2009. https://sysomos.com/inside-twitter.

Cherny, Lynn. 1999. *Conversation and Community: Chat in a Virtual World*. Stanford, CA: CSLI Publications.

Christensen, Dorthe Refslund, and Stine Gotved. 2015. "Online Memorial Culture: An Introduction." *New Review of Hypermedia and Multimedia* 21 (1–2): 1–9.

Christensen, Neil Blair. 2003. *Inuit in Cyberspace: Embedding Offline Identities Online*. Copenhagen: Museum Tusculanum Press.

"Christmas Truce." n.d. *Wikipedia*. https://en.wikipedia.org/wiki/Christmas_truce.

Clifford, James. 1986. "Introduction: Partial Truths." In *Writing Culture: The Poetics and Politics of Ethnography*, ed. James Clifford and George E. Marcus, 1–26. Berkeley: University of California Press.

Cohen, Anthony. 1985. *The Symbolic Construction of Community*. London: Routledge.

Coleman, Beth. 2011. *Hello Avatar: Rise of the Networked Generation*. Cambridge, MA: MIT Press.

Coleman, Gabriella. 2014. *Hacker, Hoaxer, Whistleblower, Spy: The Many Faces of Anonymous*. London: Verso.

Coleman, Wim, and Pat Perrin. 1994. *Terminal Games*. New York: Bantam.

Constine, Josh. 2013. "Scene Kids Cry as Streaming Site Stickam Shuts Down." *TechCrunch*. January 31. http://techcrunch.com/2013/01/31/scene-kids-cry-as-streaming-site-stickam-shuts-down/.

Cool, Jennifer. 2012. "The Mutual Co-Construction of Online and Onground in Cyberorganic." In *Human No More: Digital Subjectivities, Unhuman Subjects, and the End of Anthropology*, ed. Neil L. Whitehead and Michael Wesch, 11–32. Boulder: University Press of Colorado.

Couser, G. Thomas. 2004. *Vulnerable Subjects: Ethics and Life Writing*. Ithaca, NY: Cornell University Press.

Coyne, Imelda T. 1997. "Sampling in Qualitative Research. Purposeful and Theoretical Sampling; Merging or Clear Boundaries?" *Journal of Advanced Nursing* 26: 623–630.

Crushell, Denis. 2018. "5 Takeaways from VidCon Europe 2018." *Tubular Insights*. April 5. http://tubularinsights.com/vidcon-europe-2018/.

Cunningham, Stuart, and David Craig. 2016. "Online Entertainment: A New Wave of Media Globalization?" *International Journal of Communication* 10: 5409–5425.

Cunningham, Stuart, David Craig, and Jon Silver. 2016. "YouTube, Multichannel Networks and the Accelerated Evolution of the New Screen Ecology." *Convergence* 22 (4): 376–391.

Curtis, Pavel. (1992) 1997. "Mudding: Social Phenomena in Text-Based Virtual Realities." In *Culture of the Internet*, ed. Sara Kiesler, 121–142. Mahwah, NJ: Lawrence Erlbaum Associates.

Damon, Chi-Him Poona, and Wing-Chi Leung Louis. 2011. "Effects of Narcissism, Leisure Boredom, and Gratifications Sought on User-Generated Content among Net-Generation Users." Paper presented at the Eighth International Telecommunications Society (ITS) Asia-Pacific Regional Conference, June 26–28, Taipei, Taiwan.

D'Anastasio, Cecilia. 2017. "Some YouTubers Are Overjoyed That Maker Studios Is Firing Them." *Kotaku*. March 1. https://kotaku.com/some-youtubers-are-overjoyed-that-maker-studios-is-firi-1792854530.

Dave, Paresh. 2018. "YouTube Deletes 5 Million Videos for Content Violation." *Reuters*. April 24. https://www.reuters.com/article/us-alphabet-youtube/youtube-deletes-5-million-videos-for-content-violation-idUSKBN1HV29H.

Davies, Douglas. 2005. *A Brief History of Death*. Oxford: Blackwell.

Davies, Douglas, and Hannah Rumble. 2012. *Natural Burial: Traditional-Secular Spiritualities and Funeral Innovation*. London: Continuum.

Day, Mark. 2010. *Greetings from VidCon*. https://www.youtube.com/watch?v=tnQSjCnSimo.

Dean, Jodi. 2010. *Blog Theory*. Cambridge, UK: Polity Press.

Dedman, Jay, and Joshua Paul. 2006. *Videoblogging*. Indianapolis, IN: Wiley Publishing.

della Cava, Marco R. 2013. "YouTube Gives Creators Space to Grow." *USA Today*. January 1. https://www.usatoday.com/story/life/tv/2013/01/01/you-tube-los-angeles-space/1792517/.

Descartes, René. (1637) 1998. *Discourse on Method*. Indianapolis, IN: Hackett Publishing.

de Seta, Gabriele. 2018a. "Three Lies of Digital Ethnography." anthro{dendum} (blog). February 7. https://anthrodendum.org/2018/02/07/three-lies-of-digital-ethnography/.

de Seta, Gabriele. 2018b. "Trolling, and Other Problematic Social Media Practices." In *The Sage Handbook of Social Media*, ed. Jean Burgess, Alice Marwick, and Thomas Poell, 390–411. London: Sage.

DeWalt, Kathleen M., and Billie R. DeWalt. 2011. *Participant Observation: A Guide for Fieldworkers*. Lanham, MD: AltaMira Press.

Dickey, Megan Rose. 2013. "The 22 Key Turning Points in the History of YouTube." *Business Insider*. February 15. https://www.businessinsider.com/key-turning-points-history-of-youtube-2013-2.

Dicks, Bella, Rosie Flewitt, Lesley Lancaster, and Kate Pahl. 2011. "Multimodality and Ethnography: Working at the Intersection." *Qualitative Research* 11 (3): 227–237.

Dietz-Uhler, Beth, and Cathy Bishop-Clark. 2001. "The Use of Computer-Mediated Communication to Enhance Subsequent Face-to-Face Discussions." *Computers in Human Behavior* 17: 269–283.

Dodaro, Melonie. 2011. "The Power of the Law of Reciprocity in Social Media." *Top Dog Social Media*. December 6. https://topdogsocialmedia.com/law-of-reciprocity-and -social-media/.

Dogan, Dino. 2010. "Top 5 Most Indispensable Twitter Tools for Marketers." *socialmedia- examiner.com*. August 23. http://www.socialmediaexaminer.com/indispensable-twitter -tools/.

Douglas, Mary. 1990. "Foreword: No Free Gifts." In *The Gift*, ed. Marcel Mauss, vii–xviii. New York: W. W. Norton.

Douglas, Mary. 1992. *Risk and Blame: Essays in Cultural Theory*. London: Routledge.

Douglas, Matt. 2016. "Part 1: The Past, Present and Future of the Wedding Industry." *Huffington Post Business*. February 24. http://www.huffingtonpost.com/matt-douglas /part-1-the-past-present-f_b_9294420.html.

Dreier, Troy. 2012. "Nalts Offers Video Newbies Tips on Earning a Living on YouTube." *OnlineVideo.net*. August 21. http://www.onlinevideo.net/2012/08/nalts-offers-video -newbies-tips-on-earning-a-living-on-youtube/.

Driscoll, Kevin, and Camille Paloque-Berges. 2017. "Searching for Missing 'Net Histories.'" *Internet Histories* 1 (1–2): 47–59.

Dryden, Liam. 2016. "The Complete Guide to EVERY Major YouTube Event Happening in 2016." *WeTheUnicorns.com*. January 19. https://www.wetheunicorns.com/features /every-youtube-event-in-2016/.

Dyck, Noel. 2002. "'Have You Been to Hayward Field?' Children's Sport and the Construction of Community in Suburban Canada." In *Realizing Community*, ed. Vered Amit, 105–123. London: Routledge.

Eash, Dan. n.d. "Is There a Size Limit for YouTube?" *Small Business Chron.com*. http:// smallbusiness.chron.com/there-size-limit-youtube-26654.html.

Eck, Ronald W., and David R. Martinelli. 1998. "Assessment and Mitigation Measures for Graffiti on Highway Structures." *Transportation Research Record: Journal of the Transportation Research Board* 1642: 35–42.

Edgar, Don, Leon Earle, and Rodney Fopp. 1993. *Introduction to Australian Society*. Sydney: Prentice-Hall of Australia.

Edwards, Paul N. 2010. *A Vast Machine: Computer Models, Climate Data, and the Politics of Global Warming*. Cambridge, MA: MIT Press.

Eldon, Eric. 2011. "YouTube's New Homepage Goes Social with Algorithmic Feed, Emphasis on Google+ and Facebook." *TechCrunch*. December 1. https://techcrunch .com/2011/12/01/newyoutube/.

Evans, James, and Phil Jones. 2011. "The Walking Interview: Methodology, Mobility and Place." *Applied Geography* 31: 849–858.

Faeth, Bill. 2012. "Gary Vaynerchuk: If Content Is King, Then Context Is God." *Inbound Marketing Blog*. September 1. http://www.inboundmarketingagents.com/inbound -marketing-agents-blog/bid/214177/Gary-Vaynerchuk-If-Content-is-King-then-Context -is-God.

Fetterman, David M. 1987. "Ethnographic Educational Evaluation." In *Interpretive Ethnography of Education at Home and Abroad*, ed. George Spindler and Louise Spindler, 81–108. New York: Psychology Press.

Firestone, Lisa. 2012. "Is Social Media to Blame for the Rise in Narcissism?" *Psychology Today*. November 29. https://www.psychologytoday.com/blog/compassion-matters/ 201211/is-social-media-blame-the-rise-in-narcissism.

Fish, Stanley. 1980. *Is There a Text in This Class? The Authority of Interpretive Communities*. Cambridge, MA: Harvard University Press.

Flood, Alison. 2009. "Amazon Apologises for 'Ham-Fisted' Error That Made Gay Books 'Disappear.'" *The Guardian*. April 14. https://www.theguardian.com/books/2009/apr /14/amazon-gay-sex-rankings-apology.

Fowler, Geoffrey A. 2013. "Google Lets Users Plan 'Digital Afterlife' by Naming Heirs." *Wall Street Journal*. April 11. http://blogs.wsj.com/digits/2013/04/11/google-lets-users -plan-digital-afterlife-by-naming-heirs/.

Freud, Sigmund. 1914. "On Narcissism: An Introduction." In *The Standard Edition of the Complete Psychological Works of Sigmund Freud*. Vol. 14. Translated by James Strachey, 67–104. London: Hogarth Press.

Gal, Susan. 2002. "A Semiotics of the Public/Private Distinction." *Differences: A Journal of Feminist Cultural Studies* 13 (1): 77–95.

Garfinkel, Harold. 1967. *Studies in Ethnomethodology*. Englewood Cliffs, NJ: Prentice-Hall.

Gauntlett, David. 2011. *Making Is Connecting*. Cambridge, UK: Polity Press.

Gayle, Damien. 2012. "YouTube Cancels Billions of Music Industry Video Views after Finding They Were Fake or 'Dead.'" *Daily Mail*. December 28. http://www.dailymail .co.uk/sciencetech/article-2254181/YouTube-wipes-billions-video-views-finding-faked -music-industry.html.

Geertz, Clifford. (1972) 2005. "Deep Play: Notes on the Balinese Cockfight." *Daedalus* 134 (4): 56–86.

Gehl, Robert W. 2012. "Real (Software) Abstractions on the Rise of Facebook and the Fall of MySpace." *Social Text* 30 (2): 99–119.

Geraci, Robert M. 2014. *Virtually Sacred Myth and Meaning in World of Warcraft and Second Life*. Oxford, UK: Oxford University Press.

Geraldes, Joao. 2010. "2005–2010 YouTube Facts & Figures (History & Statistics)." *Social Media & Marketing Strategy*. September 9. https://joaogeraldes.wordpress.com/2010 /09/09/2005-2010-youtube-facts-figures-history-statistics/.

Gershon, Ilana. 2010. *The Breakup 2.0: Disconnecting over New Media*. Ithaca, NY: Cornell University Press.

Gibson, Margaret. 2007. "Death and Mourning in Technologically Mediated Culture." *Health Sociology Review* 16 (5): 415–424.

Gielen, Matt. 2015. "Want to Know the Best Days and Times to Post YouTube Videos? Here's a Yearly Calendar." *Tubefilter.com*. January 12. http://www.tubefilter.com/2015/01 /12/best-days-times-to-post-youtube-videos-yearly-calendar/.

Gielen, Matt, and Jeremy Rosen. 2016. "Reverse Engineering the YouTube Algorithm: Part I." *Tubefilter*. June 23. https://www.tubefilter.com/2016/06/23/reverse-engineering -youtube-algorithm/.

Gillespie, Tarleton. 2010. "The Politics of 'Platforms.'" *New Media & Society* 12 (3): 347–364.

Gillespie, Tarleton. 2014. "The Relevance of Algorithms." In *Media Technologies: Essays on Communication, Materiality, and Society*, ed. Tarleton Gillespie, Pablo Boczkowski, and Kirsten Foot, 167–194. Cambridge, MA: MIT Press.

Gingrich, Andre, Elinor Ochs, and Alan Swedlund. 2002. "Repertoires of Timekeeping in Anthropology." *Current Anthropology* 43 (S4): S3–S4.

Ginsburg, Faye. 2012. "Disability in the Digital Age." In *Digital Anthropology*, ed. Heather Horst and Daniel Miller, 101–126. London: Berg.

Godelier, Maurice. 2002. "Some Things You Give, Some Things You Sell, but Some Things You Must Keep for Yourselves: What Mauss Did Not Say about Sacred Objects." In *The Enigma of Gift and Sacrifice*, ed. Edith Wyschogrod, Jean-Joseph Goux, and Eric Boynton, 19–37. New York: Fordham University Press.

Goffman, Erving. 1959. *The Presentation of Self in Everyday Life*. Garden City, NY: Doubleday.

Goffman, Erving. 1963. *Stigma: Notes on the Management of a Spoiled Identity*. New York: Simon & Schuster.

Goldhaber, Michael H. 1997. "The Attention Economy and the Net." *First Monday* 2 (4–7). https://firstmonday.org/article/view/519/440.

Gonchar, Michael. 2013. "Does Technology Make Us More Alone?" *New York Times*. September 4. http://learning.blogs.nytimes.com/2013/09/04/does-technology -somehow-make-us-more-alone/?_php=true&_type=blogs&_r=0.

Goodson, Scott. 2012. "If You're Not Paying for It, You Become the Product." *Forbes.com*. March 5. https://www.forbes.com/sites/marketshare/2012/03/05/if-youre-not-paying -for-it-you-become-the-product/#711a443a5d6e.

Gotved, Stine. 2014. "Research Review: Death Online—Alive and Kicking!" *Thanatos* 3 (1): 112–126.

Gouldner, Alvin W. 1960. "The Norm of Reciprocity: A Preliminary Statement." *American Sociological Review* 25 (2): 161–178.

Graham, Mark. 2012. "Geography/Internet: Ethereal Alternate Dimensions of Cyberspace or Grounded Augmented Realities?" *Geographical Journal* 179 (2): 177–182.

Granovetter, Mark S. 1973. "The Strength of Weak Ties." *American Journal of Sociology* 78 (6): 1360–1380.

Green, Hank. 2015. "Theft, Lies, and Facebook Video." *Medium.com*. August 2. https:// medium.com/@hankgreen/theft-lies-and-facebook-video-656boffed369.

Griffith, Maggie, and Zizi Papacharissi. 2010. "Looking for You: An Analysis of Video Blogs." *First Monday* 15 (1). http://firstmonday.org/ojs/index.php/fm/article/view/2769/2430.

Grijalva, Emily, Daniel A. Newman, Louis Tay, M. Brent Donnellan, P. D. Harms, Richard W. Robins, and Taiyi Yan. 2015. "Gender Differences in Narcissism: A Meta-Analytic Review." *Psychological Bulletin* 141 (2): 261–310.

Grimshaw, Anna, and Amanda Ravetz. 2009. *Observational Cinema: Anthropology, Film, and the Exploration of Social Life*. Bloomington: Indiana University Press.

Gross, Larry, John Stuart Katz, and Jay Ruby, eds. 1988. *Image Ethics: The Moral Rights of Subjects in Photographs, Films, and Television*. New York: Oxford University Press.

Gross, Larry, John Stuart Katz, and Jay Ruby, eds. 2003. *Image Ethics in the Digital Age*. Minneapolis: University of Minnesota Press.

Gruzd, Anatoliy, Barry Wellman, and Yuri Takhteyev. 2011. "Imagining Twitter as an Imagined Community." *American Behavioral Scientist* 55 (10): 1294–1318.

Guo, Lei, and Lorin Lee. 2013. "The Critique of YouTube-Based Vernacular Discourse: A Case Study of YouTube's Asian Community." *Critical Studies in Media Communication* 30 (5): 391–406.

Gupta, Akhil, and James Ferguson. 1997. *Anthropological Locations: Boundaries and Grounds of a Field Science*. Berkeley: University of California Press.

Gutelle, Sam. 2014. "Maker Studios Co-Founders Lisa and Ben Donovan Leave the Company." *Tubefilter*. August 8. https://www.tubefilter.com/2014/08/08/lisa-nova-ben -donovan-leave-maker-studios/.

Hallin, Daniel C. 1992. "Sound Bite News: Television Coverage of Elections, 1968–1988." *Journal of Communication* 42 (2): 5–24.

Hamedy, Saba. 2015. "Fans Are Amped after VidCon Announces 2016 Conference Dates." *Mashable.com*. November 4. http://mashable.com/2015/11/04/vidcon-sets-2016-dates /#QcLbfQ2dOuqN.

Hampe, Barry. 1997. *Making Documentary Films and Reality Videos: A Practical Guide to Planning, Filming, and Editing Documentaries of Real Events*. New York: Henry Holt and Company.

Hanks, Henry. 2012. "A Death in the iReport Family." *CNN iReport*. July 3. http://ireport .cnn.com/blogs/ireport-blog/2012/07/03/a-death-in-the-ireport-family.

Harding, Susan. 1991. "Representing Fundamentalism: The Problem of the Repugnant Other." *Social Research* 58 (2): 373–393.

Harley, Dave, and Geraldine Fitzpatrick. 2009. "YouTube and Intergenerational Communication: The Case of Geriatric 1927." Special Issue. *Universal Access in the Information Society* 8 (1): 5–20.

Hayles, N. Katherine. 1999. *How We Became Posthuman*. Chicago: University of Chicago Press.

Henwood, Flis, Gwyneth Hughes, Helen Kennedy, Nod Miller, and Sally Wyatt. 2001. "Cyborg Lives in Context: Writing Women's Technobiographies." In *Cyborg Lives? Women's Technobiographies*, ed. Flis Henwood, Helen Kennedy, and Nod Miller, 11–34. York, UK: Raw Nerve Press.

Hern, Alex. 2013. "YouTube Co-Founder Hurls Abuse at Google over New YouTube Comments." *The Guardian*. November 8. https://www.theguardian.com/technology /2013/nov/08/youtube-cofounder-why-the-fuck-do-i-need-a-google-account-to -comment.

Herring, Susan. 1996. "Bringing Familiar Baggage to the New Frontier: Gender Differences in Computer-Mediated Communication." In *CyberReader*, ed. Victor Vitanza, 144–154. Boston: Allyn & Bacon.

Hess, Aaron. 2009. "Resistance Up in Smoke: Analyzing the Limitations of Deliberation on YouTube." *Critical Studies in Media Communication* 26 (5):411–434.

Hill, Kashmir. 2012. "The Dogged Digital Detective Work That Busted an Online Harasser." *Forbes*. July 18. http://www.forbes.com/sites/kashmirhill/2012/07/18/the -dogged-digital-detective-work-that-busted-an-online-harasser.

Hillery, George A. 1955. "Definitions of Community: Areas of Agreement." *Rural Sociology* 20: 86–118.

Hiniker, Alexis, Sarita Y. Shoenebeck, and Julie A. Kientz. 2016. "Not at the Dinner Table: Parents' and Children's Perspectives on Family Technology Rules." *CSCW 2016*, February 27–March 2, 2016, San Francisco, CA.

Holmes, Douglas R., and George E. Marcus. 2008. "Para-Ethnography." In *The SAGE Encyclopedia of Qualitative Research Methods*, ed. Lisa M. Given, 595–597. Thousand Oaks, CA: Sage.

Holpuch, Amanda. 2012. "MySpace Re-Enters the Social Media Ring with Yet Another Rebrand." *The Guardian*. September 25. https://www.theguardian.com/technology/us -news-blog/2012/sep/25/myspace-social-media-rebrand.

Hondros, John J. 2016. "Problematizing the Internet as a Video Distribution Technology: An Assemblage Theory Analysis." *Information, Communication & Society* 19 (2): 221–233.

Horton, David. 2005. "Review of Rhythmanalysis: Space, Time and Everyday Life." *Time & Society* 14 (1): 157–159.

Hudson, Skye. 2015. "4 Reasons YouTube Red Is Bad for the YouTube Community." *Makeuseof.com*. October 26. https://www.makeuseof.com/tag/4-reasons-youtube-red -bad-youtube-community/.

Hull, Arthur. 1998. *Drum Circle Spirit: Facilitating Human Potential through Rhythm.* Gilsum, NH: White Cliffs Media.

Hunter, Dan, Ramon Lobato, Megan Richardson, and Julian Thomas, eds. 2012. *Amateur Media: Social, Cultural and Legal Perspectives.* London: Routledge.

Hutchens, Myiah J., Vincent J. Cicchirillo, and Jay D. Hmielowski. 2015. "How Could You Think That?!?!: Understanding Intentions to Engage in Political Flaming." *New Media & Society* 17 (8): 1201–1219.

Ikeda, Keiko. 1998. *A Room Full of Mirrors: High School Reunions in Middle America.* Stanford, CA: Stanford University Press.

Ingold, Tim. 2008. "Entanglements of Life in an Open World." *Environment & Planning* 40 (8): 1796–1810.

Inoue, Miyako. 2004. "Introduction: Temporality and Historicity in and through Linguistic Ideology." *Journal of Linguistic Anthropology* 14 (1): 1–5.

Irvine, Judith. 2001. "Style as Distinctiveness." In *Style and Sociolinguistic Variation*, ed. Penelope Eckert and John R. Rickford, 21–43. Cambridge, UK: Cambridge University Press.

Ito, Mizuko, Misa Matsuda, and Daisuke Okabe. 2005. *Personal, Portable, Pedestrian: Mobile Phones in Japanese Life.* Cambridge, MA: MIT Press.

Ito, Mizuko, Sonja Baumer, Matteo Bittani, danah boyd, Rachel Cody, Becky Herr-Stephenson, Heather A. Horst, et al. 2010. *Hanging Out, Messing Around and Geeking Out: Kids Living and Learning with New Media.* Cambridge, MA: MIT Press.

Jackson, Erick. 2014. "Facebook Is Dead, Long Live Facebook." *Forbes*. February 20. http://www.forbes.com/sites/ericjackson/2014/02/20/facebook-is-dead-long-live -facebook/.

Jarvis, Jeff. 2016. "What I Learned at VidCon." *Medium.com*. July 29. https://medium .com/whither-news/what-i-learned-at-vidcon-168e26f34970#.60wwg53xv.

Jenkins, Henry. 1992. *Textual Poachers*. New York: Routledge.

Jenkins, Henry. 2009a. "If It Doesn't Spread, It's Dead (Part One): Media Viruses and Memes." *Confessions of an Aca-Fan*. February 11. http://henryjenkins.org/2009/02/if_it _doesnt_spread_its_dead_p.html.

Jenkins, Henry. 2009b. "Why Mitt Romney Won't Debate a Snowman." In *Satire TV: Politics and Comedy in the Post-Network Era*, ed. Jonathan Gray, Jeffrey P. Jones, and Ethan Thompson, 187–212. New York: New York University Press.

Jenkins, Henry, with Katie Clinton, Ravi Purushotma, Alice J. Robison, and Margaret Weigel. 2006. *Confronting the Challenges of Participatory Culture: Media Education for the 21st Century*. Chicago, IL: MacArthur Foundation. http://digitallearning.macfound .org/atf/cf/%7B7E45C7E0-A3E0–4B89-AC9C-E807E1B0AE4E%7D/JENKINS_ WHITE_PAPER.PDF.

Jenkins, Henry, Sam Ford, and Joshua Green. 2013. *Spreadable Media: Creating Value and Meaning in a Networked Culture*. New York: New York University Press.

Jones, Graham M., and Bambi B. Schieffelin. 2009. "Talking Text and Talking Back: 'My BFF Jill' from Boob Tube to YouTube." *Journal of Computer Mediated Communication* 14: 1050–1079.

Juhasz, Alexandra. 2008. "Why Not (To) Teach on YouTube." In *The Video Vortex Reader*, ed. Geert Lovink and Sabine Niederer, 133–140. Amsterdam: Institute of Network Cultures.

Juhasz, Alexandra. 2009. "Learning the Five Lessons of YouTube: After Trying to Teach There, I Don't Believe the Hype." *Cinema Journal* 48 (2): 145–150.

Katzmaier, David. 2017. "YouTube TV Adds AMC, BBC America and More, as Promised." *CNET*. May 16. https://www.cnet.com/news/youtube-tv-adds-amc-bbc-america-and -more-as-promised/.

Kaufman, Leslie. 2014. "Chasing Their Star, on YouTube." *New York Times*. February 1. http://www.nytimes.com/2014/02/02/business/chasing-their-star-on-youtube.html.

Kavoori, Anandam. 2011. *Reading YouTube: The Critical Viewers Guide*. New York: Peter Lang.

Kelly, Heather. 2013. "YouTube Faces Backlash for Google+ Integration." *CCN.com*. November 8. https://www.cnn.com/2013/11/08/tech/social-media/youtube-comment -backlash/index.html.

Kendall, Lori. 2002. *Hanging Out in the Virtual Pub: Masculinities and Relationships Online*. Berkeley: University of California Press.

Kendall, Y.T. 2011. "[Update] Friends and Subscriptions Merge—Addressing Feedback." YouTube Help Forum. December 12. https://productforums.google.com/forum/?hl=en #!category-topic/youtube/sharing-and-connecting-on-youtube/qHCnTh2t8dE.

Kennedy, Helen. 2006. "Beyond Anonymity, or Future Directions for Internet Identity Research." *New Media & Society* 8 (6): 859–876.

Kincaid, Jason. 2010. "YouTube Begins to Remove Its Video Time Limits." *TechCrunch*. December 9. https://techcrunch.com/2010/12/09/youtube-time-limit-2/.

Kirkpatrick, Marshall. 2007. "YouTube Partner Program Opens to All; Chocolate Rain Guy Gets Ad Deal." *ReadWrite.com*. December 10. http://readwrite.com/2007/12/10/youtube_partner_program_opens.

Kitzmann, Andreas. 2004. *Saved from Oblivion: Documenting the Daily from Diaries to Web Cams*. New York: Peter Lang.

Knight, Shawn. 2012. "YouTube Now Letting Anyone Monetize their Videos through AdSense." *Techspot.com*. April 13. http://www.techspot.com/news/48182-youtube-now-letting-anyone-monetize-their-videos-through-adsense.html.

Kollock, Peter. 1999. "The Economies of Online Cooperation: Gifts and Public Goods in Cyberspace." In *Communities in Cyberspace*, ed. Marc A. Smith and Peter Kollock, 220–239. London: Routledge.

Kolm, Serge-Christophe. 2006. "Reciprocity, Its Scope, Rationales, and Consequences." In *Handbook on the Economics of Giving, Reciprocity, and Altruism*, ed. Serge-Christophe Kolm and Jean Marcier Ythier, 375–408. Oxford, UK: Elsevier.

Kottak, Conrad Phillip. 2009. *Anthropology: The Exploration of Human Diversity*. 13th ed. Boston: McGraw-Hill.

Kozlowski, Lori. 2013. "Multi-Channel Networks 101." *Forbes*. August 30. https://www.forbes.com/sites/lorikozlowski/2013/08/30/multi-channel-networks-101/.

Krauss, Rosalind. 1976. "Video: The Aesthetics of Narcissism." *October* 1: 50–64.

LaFrance, Adrienne, and Robinson Meyer. 2014. "A Eulogy for Twitter." *The Atlantic*. April 30.

Lang, Derrik J. 2015. "YouTube: 'Minecraft' Videos Are Most Popular in History of Site." *San Jose Mercury News*. May 13. http://www.mercurynews.com/business/ci_28106744/youtube-minecraft-videos-are-most-popular-history-site.

Lange, Patricia G. 2003. "Virtual Trouble: Negotiating Access in Online Communities." PhD diss., Ann Arbor: University of Michigan.

Lange, Patricia G. 2007a. "Commenting on Comments: Investigating Responses to Antagonism on YouTube." Paper presented at the annual conference of the Society for Applied Anthropology, March 27–31, Tampa, Florida. http://sfaapodcasts.files.wordpress.com/2007/04/update-apr-17-lange-sfaa-paper-2007.pdf.

Lange, Patricia G. 2007b. "Publicly Private and Privately Public." *Journal of Computer-Mediated Communication* 13 (1). https://onlinelibrary.wiley.com/doi/epdf/10.1111/j.1083-6101.2007.00400.x.

Lange, Patricia G. 2007c. "The Vulnerable Video Blogger: Promoting Social Change through Intimacy." *Scholar and Feminist Online* 5 (2). http://sfonline.barnard.edu/blogs/lange_01.htm.

Lange, Patricia G. 2008a. "Living in YouTubia: Bordering on Civility." Paper presented at the Southwestern Anthropology Association Conference, April 11, 2008, Fullerton, California.

Lange, Patricia G. 2008b. "(Mis)Conceptions about YouTube." In *Video Vortex Reader: Responses to YouTube*, ed. Geert Lovink and Sabine Niederer, 87–100. Amsterdam: Institute of Network Cultures. http://networkcultures.org/wpmu/portal/files/2008/10/vv_reader_small.pdf.

Lange, Patricia G. 2008c. "Terminological Obfuscation in Online Research." In *Handbook of Research on Computer Mediated Communication*, ed. Sigrid Kelsey and Kirk St. Amant, 436–450. Hershey, PA: IGI Global.

Lange, Patricia G. 2009. "Videos of Affinity." In *The YouTube Reader*, ed. Pelle Snickars and Patrick Vonderau, 228–247. Stockholm: National Library of Sweden.

Lange, Patricia G. 2010. "Achieving Creative Integrity on YouTube: Reciprocities and Tensions." *Enculturation* 8 (2010). http://enculturation.net/achieving-creative-integrity.

Lange, Patricia G. 2011. "Imaging and Imagining YouTube: Chronotopes of Meeting Up." Paper Presented at the annual meeting of the American Anthropological Association, November 16, Montreal, Canada.

Lange, Patricia G. 2012. "Rhetoricizing Visual Literacies." Paper presented at the annual conference of the International Communication Association, May 25, Phoenix, Arizona. http://www.patriciaglange.org/page4/assets/Lange%20ICA%202012%20Final%20Paper.pdf.

Lange, Patricia G. 2013. *Hey Watch This! Sharing the Self through Media*. 58 minutes.

Lange, Patricia G. 2014. *Kids on YouTube: Technical Identities and Digital Literacies*. Walnut Creek, CA: Routledge.

Lange, Patricia G. 2015a. "Typing Your Way to Technical Identity: Interpreting Participatory Ideologies Online." *Pragmatics* 25 (4): 553–572.

Lange, Patricia G. 2015b. "Vlogging toward Digital Literacy." *Biography* 38 (2): 297–302.

Lange, Patricia G. 2017. "Participatory Complications in Interactive, Video-Sharing Environments." In *The Routledge Companion to Digital Ethnography*, ed. Larissa Hjorth, Heather Horst, Anne Galloway, and Genevieve Bell, 147–157. New York: Routledge.

Lasch, Christopher. 1979. *The Culture of Narcissism*. New York: W. W. Norton.

Lastufka, Alan, and Michael Dean. 2009. *YouTube: An Insider's Guide to Climbing the Charts*. Sebastopol, CA: O'Reilly Media.

Latour, Bruno. 2005. *Reassembling the Social*. Oxford, UK: Oxford University Press.

Lave, Jean, and Etienne Wenger. 1991. *Situated Learning: Legitimate Peripheral Participation*. Cambridge, UK: Cambridge University Press.

Leather, Ariel. 2018. "The Highest Paid YouTubers—2018 List." *Gazette Review*. January 3. https://gazettereview.com/2016/05/the-highest-paid-youtubers/.

Leaver, Tama. 2013. "A Death on Facebook? Social Media and Posthumous Profiles." Paper presented at Internet Research 14.0, the fourteenth international conference of the Association of Internet Researchers, October 23–26, Denver, Colorado.

Leaver, Tama, and Tim Highfield. 2018. "Visualising the Ends of Identity: Pre-Birth and Post-Death on Instagram." *Information, Communication & Society* 21 (1): 30–45.

Lee, Siew-Peng. 2017. "Ethnography *In Absentia*: Applying Lefebvre's Rhythmanalysis in Impossible-to-Research Spaces." *Ethnography* 18 (2): 257–276.

Lefebvre, Henri. 2004. *Rhythmanalysis*. London: Continuum.

Lenhart, Amanda, Kristen Purcell, Aaron Smith, and Kathryn Zickuhr. 2010. *Social Media and Mobile Internet Use among Teens and Young Adults*. Washington, DC: Pew Research Center. http://files.eric.ed.gov/fulltext/ED525056.pdf.

Lenhart, Amanda, Sandra Cortesi, Urs Gasser, Maeve Duggan, Aaron Smith, and Meredith Beaton. 2013. *Teens, Social Media, and Privacy*. Washington DC: Pew Research Center. http://www.pewinternet.org/2013/05/21/teens-social-media-and-privacy/.

Levin, Sam. 2018. "YouTube's Small Creators Pay Price of Policy Changes after Logan Paul Scandal." *The Guardian*. January 18. https://www.theguardian.com/technology/2018/jan/18/youtube-creators-vloggers-ads-logan-paul.

Lévi-Strauss, Claude. 1963. *Totemism*, translated by Rodney Needham. Boston: Beacon Press.

Li, Anita. 2015. "YouTube's First North American FanFest Attracts Thousands, but Wants to Stay 'Grassroots.'" *Mashable*. May 2. https://mashable.com/2015/05/02/youtube-fanfest-north-america-toronto/#OcrMrnVWhaqi.

Lieberman, Kim-An. 2003. "Virtually Vietnamese: Nationalism on the Internet." In *AsianAmerica.Net: Ethnicity, Nationalism, and Cyberspace*, ed. Rachel C. Lee and Sau-ling Cynthia Wong, 71–97. New York: Routledge.

Lil Miss Hot Mess. 2015. "Facebook's 'Real Name' Policy Hurts Real People and Creates a New Digital Divide." *The Guardian*. June 3. https://www.theguardian.com/commentisfree/2015/jun/03/facebook-real-name-policy-hurts-people-creates-new-digital-divide.

Lipton, Josh. 2014. "Google's Best and Worst Acquisitions." *CNBC*. August 19. http://www.cnbc.com/2014/08/19/googles-best-and-worst-acquisitions.html.

Logue, Josh. 2015. "Latina/o/x." *Inside Higher Ed*. December 8. https://www.insidehighered.com/news/2015/12/08/students-adopt-gender-nonspecific-term-latinx-be-more-inclusive.

Lohensohn, Josh. 2010. "YouTube's Big Redesign Goes Live to Everyone." *CNET*. March 31. http://www.cnet.com/news/youtubes-big-redesign-goes-live-to-everyone/.

Lopes, Marina. 2015. "Facebook Users Finally Have Say over Their Account after Death." *PBS News Hour*. February 12. http://www.pbs.org/newshour/rundown/facebook-users -finally-say-account-death/.

Lovink, Geert. 2011. *Networks without a Cause: A Critique of Social Media*. Cambridge, UK: Polity Press.

Lutkehaus, Nancy, and Jennifer Cool. 1999. "Paradigms Lost and Found: The 'Crisis of Representation' and Visual Anthropology." In *Collecting Visible Evidence*, ed. Jane M. Gaines and Michael Renov, 116–138. Minneapolis: University of Minnesota Press.

MacCormack, Geoffrey. 1976. "Reciprocity." *Man* 11 (1): 89–103.

MacInnes, Paul. 2018. "What's Up Pewdiepie? The Troubling Content of YouTube's Biggest Star." *The Guardian*. April 5. https://www.theguardian.com/tv-and-radio/2018/apr/05/ whats-up-pewdiepie-the-troubling-content-of-youtubes-biggest-star.

Maddox, Jessica. 2017. "'Guns Don't Kill People . . . Selfies Do': Rethinking Narcissism as Exhibitionism in Selfie-Related Deaths." *Critical Studies in Media Communication* 34 (3): 193–205.

Madianou, Mirca, and Daniel Miller. 2012. *Migration and New Media: Transnational Families and Polymedia*. Abingdon, UK: Routledge.

Mann, Steve, Jason Nolan, and Barry Wellman. 2003. "Sousveillance: Inventing and Using Wearable Computing Devices for Data Collection in Surveillance Environments." *Surveillance & Society* 1 (3): 331–355.

Mannheim, Bruce, and Dennis Tedlock. 1995. "Introduction." In *The Dialogic Emergence of Culture*, ed. Dennis Tedlock and Bruce Mannheim, 1–32. Urbana: University of Illinois Press.

Manning, Paul. 2009. "Can the Avatar Speak?" *Journal of Linguistic Anthropology* 19 (2): 310–325.

Marcus, George E. 1995. "Ethnography in/of the World System: The Emergence of Multi-Sited Ethnography." *Annual Review of Anthropology* 24: 95–117.

Markham, Annette N. 1998. *Life Online: Researching Real Experience in Virtual Space*. Walnut Creek, CA: AltaMira Press.

Markham, Annette N. 2003. "Metaphors Reflecting and Shaping the Reality of the Internet: Tool, Place, Way of Being." Paper presented at the Association of Internet Researchers Conference, October 16–19, Toronto, Canada. http://annettemarkham .com/writing/MarkhamTPW.pdf.

Martínez, Wilton. 1995. "The Challenges of a Pioneer: Tim Asch, Otherness, and Film Reception." *Visual Anthropology Review* 11 (1): 53–82.

Marwick, Alice, and danah boyd. 2010. "I Tweet Honestly, I Tweet Passionately: Twitter Users, Context Collapse, and the Imagined Audience" *New Media & Society* 13 (1): 114–133.

"The Mary Tyler Moore Show Opening Sequence." n.d. *Wikipedia*. http://en.wikipedia
.org/wiki/The_Mary_Tyler_Moore_Show_opening_sequence.

Mauss, Marcel. 1990. *The Gift*. New York: W. W. Norton.

McNamara, Kim. 2011. "The Paparazzi Industry and New Media: The Evolving Production
and Consumption of Celebrity News and Gossip Websites." *International Journal of
Cultural Studies* 14 (5): 515–530.

McNamara, Kim. 2016. *Paparazzi: Media Practices and Celebrity Culture*. Cambridge, UK:
Polity Press.

McNeill, Laurie. 2012. "There Is No 'I' in Network: Social Networking Sites and
Posthuman Auto/Biography." *Biography* 35 (1): 65–82.

Mediakix. 2018. "The 13 Most Popular Types of YouTube Videos." *Mediakix.com*. April 16.
http://mediakix.com/2016/02/most-popular-youtube-videos/.

Meikle, Graham. 2016. *Social Media: Communication, Sharing and Visibility*. New York:
Routledge.

Meissner, Jenna. 2015. "I Liked His Instagram Photo from 90 Weeks Ago . . . Now What?"
The Odyssey Online. July 21. https://www.theodysseyonline.com/liked-instagram-photo
-from-90-weeks-agonow-what.

Meltzer, Tom, and Sarah Phillips. 2009. "From the First Email to the First YouTube Video:
A Definitive Internet History." *The Guardian*. October 23. https://www.theguardian
.com/technology/2009/oct/23/internet-history.

Mendelson, Andrew L. 2007. "On the Function of the United States Paparazzi: Mosquito
Swarm or Watchdogs of Celebrity Image Control and Power." *Visual Studies* 22 (2):
169–183.

Merlan, Anna. 2015. "The Cops Don't Care about Violent Online Threats. What Do We
Do Now?" *Jezebel*. January 29. http://jezebel.com/the-cops-dont-care-about-violent
-online-threats-what-d-1682577343.

Metzger, Clarice. 2017. "#YouTube FanFest Finally Lands in the U.S." *The Hilltop*.
October 16. http://thehilltoponline.com/2017/10/16/youtube-fanfest-finally-lands-in
-the-u-s/.

Miller, Daniel, and Don Slater. 2000. *The Internet: An Ethnographic Approach*. Oxford,
UK: Berg.

Miller, Daniel, Elisabetta Costa, Nell Haynes, Tom McDonald, Razvan Nicolescu, Jolynna
Sinanan, Juliano Spyer, Shriram Venkatraman, and Xinyuan Wang. 2016. *How the World
Changed Social Media*. London: University College London Press.

"Minneapolis Gets Mary Tyler Moore Statue." 2002. *Cbcnews*. March 20. http://www.cbc
.ca/news/world/minneapolis-gets-mary-tyler-moore-statue-1.346053.

Mitchell, Amy, Jeffrey Gottfried, Michael Barthel, and Elisa Shearer. 2016. *The Modern
News Consumer*. July 7. Washington, DC: Pew Research Center. http://assets

.pewresearch.org/wp-content/uploads/sites/13/2016/07/08140120/PJ_2016.07.07 _Modern-News-Consumer_FINAL.pdf.

Mitchell, W.J.T. 1986. *Iconology: Image, Text, Ideology*. Chicago: University of Chicago Press.

Mitroff, Sarah, and Taylor Martin. 2017. "Everything You Need to Know about YouTube Red." *CNET*. October 27. https://www.cnet.com/how-to/youtube-red-details/.

Moran, James. M. 2002. *There's No Place Like Home Video*. Minneapolis: University of Minnesota Press.

Moreau, Terri, and Derek H. Alderman. 2011. "Graffiti Hurts and the Eradication of Alternative Landscape Expression." *Geographical Review* 301 (1): 106–124.

Morphy, Howard, and Marcus Banks. 1997. "Introduction: Rethinking Visual Anthropology." In *Rethinking Visual Anthropology*, ed. Marcus Banks and Howard Morphy, 1–35. New Haven, CT: Yale University Press.

Mosendz, Polly. 2015. "'I Am a Woman,' Bruce Jenner Says in Diane Sawyer Interview." *Newsweek.com*. April 24. http://www.newsweek.com/i-am-woman-bruce-jenner-says -diane-sawyer-interview-325283.

Mueller, Bryan. 2013. *Participatory Culture on YouTube: A Case Study of the Multichannel Network Machinima*. M.Sc. thesis, London School of Economics and Political Science.

Müller, Eggo. 2009. "Where Quality Matters: Discourses on the Art of Making a YouTube Video." In *The YouTube Reader*, ed. Pelle Snickars and Patrick Vonderau, 126–139. Stockholm: National Library of Sweden.

Murphy, Kate. 2012. "How to Muddy Your Tracks on the Internet." *New York Times*. May 2. https://www.nytimes.com/2012/05/03/technology/personaltech/how-to-muddy-your -tracks-on-the-internet.html.

Murray, Rheana. 2014. "Police Chief's Daughter Fired from Hospital after Tweets Go Viral." *ABC News*. September 25. http://abcnews.go.com/US/police-chiefs-daughter -fired-hospital-tweets-viral/story?id=25758122.

Musil, Steven. 2018. "YouTube Tightens Rules for Tapping into Ad Money." *CNET*. January 16. https://www.cnet.com/news/youtube-adds-stricter-rules-for-creator-ad -monetization/.

Myers, Patricia. 2011. *Embracing the Teardrops*. Bloomington, IN: Xlibris Corporation.

Nahon, Karine, and Jeff Hemsley. 2013. *Going Viral*. Cambridge, UK: Policy Press.

Nalty, Kevin. 2010. *Beyond Viral: How to Attract Customers, Promote Your Brand, and Make Money with Online Video*. Hoboken, NJ: John Wiley & Sons.

Nardi, Bonnie. 2010. *My Life as a Night Elf Priest: An Anthropological Account of World of Warcraft*. Ann Arbor: University of Michigan Press.

Nardi, Bonnie. 2015. "Virtuality." *Annual Review of Anthropology* 44: 15–31.

Narotzky, Susana. 2007. "The Project in the Model: Reciprocity, Social Capital and the Politics of Ethnographic Realism." *Current Anthropology* 48 (3): 403–424.

Naslund, John A., Stuart W. Grande, Kelly A. Aschbrenner, and Glyn Elwyn. 2014. "Naturally Occurring Peer Support through Social Media: The Experiences of Individuals with Severe Mental Illness Using YouTube." *PLOS ONE* 9 (10): 1–9. http://journals.plos.org/plosone/article?id=10.1371/journal.pone.0110171.

Natanson, Maurice. 1986. *Anonymity: A Study in the Philosophy of Alfred Schutz.* Bloomington: Indiana University Press.

Neff, Gina, and David Stark. 2002. "Permanently Beta: Responsive Organization in the Internet Era." Working Paper, Institute for Social and Economic Research and Policy, Columbia University.

Newlands, Murray. 2015. "YouTube Star Olga Kay Can Juggle What It Takes to Be an Entrepreneur." *Forbes.* November 1. https://www.forbes.com/sites/mnewlands/2015/11/01/youtube-star-olga-kay-can-juggle-what-it-takes-to-be-an-entrepreneur/#4918eb9b3f4f.

Newman, Michael Z. 2008. "Ze Frank and the Poetics of Web Video." *First Monday* 13 (5). http://firstmonday.org/article/view/2102/1962.

Nicas, Jack. 2017. "YouTube Tops 1 Billion Hours of Video a Day, on Pace to Eclipse TV." *Wall Street Journal.* February 27. https://www.wsj.com/articles/youtube-tops-1-billion-hours-of-video-a-day-on-pace-to-eclipse-tv-1488220851.

Niemeyer, Dodie J., and Hannah R. Gerber. 2015. "Maker Culture and Minecraft: Implications for the Future of Learning." *Educational Media International* 52 (3): 216–226.

Nip, Joyce Y. M. 2004. "The Queer Sisters and Its Electronic Bulletin Board: A Study of the Internet for Social Movement Mobilization." In *Cyberprotest: New Media, Citizens and Social Movements,* ed. Wim van de Donk, Brian D. Loader, Paul G. Nixon, and Dieter Rucht, 233–258. London: Routledge.

Nissenbaum, Helen. 2004. "Privacy as Contextual Integrity." *Washington Law Review* 79 (1): 101–158.

Offer, Avner. 1997. "Between the Gift and the Market: The Economy of Regard." *Economic History Review* 3: 450–476.

Ogier1, 2015. Zen Archer. https://www.youtube.com/watch?v=z-qx1sm_Rfs&t=80s.

O'Neill, Megan. 2012. "YouTube Opens Partner Program to Everyone, Drama Ensues." *AdWeek.* April 16. https://www.adweek.com/digital/youtube-opens-partner-program-to-everyone/.

O'Sullivan, Patrick B., and Andrew J. Flanagin. 2003. "Reconceptualizing 'Flaming' and Other Problematic Messages." *New Media & Society* 5 (1): 69–94.

Pacheco, Carlos. 2014. "MCN 101: Everything You've Always Wanted to Know about Multi-Channel Networks." *CMF Trends*. July 10. https://trends.cmf-fmc.ca/blog/mcn _101_everything_youve_always_wanted_to_know_about_multi-channel_networks.

Palladino, Valentina. 2017. "I Used YouTube Red for Months—Here's Why I Cancelled My Subscription." *Ars Technica*. March 16. https://arstechnica.com/staff/2017/03/i-used -youtube-red-for-months-heres-why-i-cancelled-my-subscription/.

Palmer, Parker J. 2007. *The Courage to Teach. Exploring the Inner Landscape of a Teacher's Life*. San Francisco: Jossey-Bass.

Panek, Elliot T., Yioryos Nardis, and Sara Konrath. 2013. "Mirror or Megaphone? How Relationships between Narcissism and Social Networking Site Use Differ on Facebook and Twitter." *Computers in Human Behavior* 29: 2004–2012.

Panzarino, Matthew. 2013. "Google Dumps Video Responses from YouTube Due to Dismal .0004% Click Through Rate." *TechCrunch*. August 27. https://techcrunch.com /2013/08/27/google-dumps-video-responses-from-youtube-due-to-dismal-0004-click -through-rate/.

Papacharissi, Zizi. 2004. "Democracy Online: Civility, Politeness, and the Democratic Potential of Online Political Discussion Groups." *New Media & Society* 6 (2): 259–283.

Park, Minseok, Hanxiang Li, and Junmo Kim. 2016. "HARRISON: A Benchmark on HAshtag Recommendation for Real-World Images in SOcial Networks." School of Electrical Engineering, South Korea. https://pdfs.semanticscholar.org/5009/93a8852 f766d4bac7b5039b9072b587e4d09.pdf.

Pathak, Priya. 2018. "YouTube Red vs. YouTube Music Premium vs. YouTube Premium: All the Differences." *India Today*. May 21. https://www.indiatoday.in/technology/features /story/youtube-red-vs-youtube-music-premium-vs-youtube-premium-all-the-differences -1237952-2018-05-21.

"Patreon." n.d. *Wikipedia*. https://en.wikipedia.org/wiki/Patreon.

Paul, Benjamin D. 1953. "Interview Techniques and Field Relationships." In *Anthropology Today: An Encyclopaedic Inventory*, ed. A. L. Kroeber, 430–451. Chicago: University of Chicago Press.

Paul, Kari. 2016. "Does the 'Like' Mean Anything Anymore?" *NYMag.com*. May 5. http:// nymag.com/selectall/2016/05/does-the-like-mean-anything-anymore.html.

Paumgarten, Nick. 2014. "We Are a Camera: Experience and Memory in the Age of GoPro." *New Yorker*. September 22. http://www.newyorker.com/magazine/2014/09/22 /camera.

Pearce, Celia. 2009. *Communities of Play: Emergent Cultures in Online Games and Virtual Worlds*. Cambridge, MA: MIT Press.

Pelaprat, Etienne, and Barry Brown. 2012. "Reciprocity: Understanding Online Social Relations." *First Monday* 17 (10). http://www.firstmonday.dk/ojs/index.php/fm/article /view/3324/3330.

Perez, Sarah. 2016. "YouTube Upgrades Its Comments System to Give Creators More Control." *TechCrunch*. November 3. https://techcrunch.com/2016/11/03/youtube -upgrades-its-comments-system-to-give-creators-more-control/.

Perrino, Sabina. 2015. "Chronotopes: Time and Space in Oral Narrative." In *The Handbook of Narrative Analysis*, ed. Anna De Fina and Alexandra Georgakopoulou, 140–159. Malden, MA: John Wiley & Sons.

Perry, Sara, and Jonathan S. Marion. 2010. "State of the Ethics in Visual Anthropology." *Visual Anthropology Review* 28 (2): 96–104.

"Peter Oakley—Obituary." 2014. *The Telegraph*. March 25. https://www.telegraph.co.uk /news/obituaries/10722373/Peter-Oakley-obituary.html.

Pew Research Staff. 2012. *YouTube & News*. July 16. Washington, DC: Pew Research Center. https://www.journalism.org/2012/07/16/youtube-news/.

Phillips, Whitney. 2015. *This Is Why We Can't Have Nice Things*. Cambridge, MA: MIT Press.

Pini, Maria. 2009. "Inside the Home Mode." In *Video Cultures: Media Technology and Everyday Creativity*, ed. David Buckingham and Rebekah Willett, 71–92. London: Palgrave Macmillan.

Pink, Sarah. 2011. "Digital Visual Anthropology: Potentials and Challenges." In *Made to Be Seen: Perspectives on the History of Visual Anthropology*, ed. Marcus Banks and Jay Ruby, 209–233. Chicago: University of Chicago Press.

Pink, Sarah. 2015. *Doing Sensory Ethnography*. 2nd ed. Los Angeles: Sage.

Pink, Sarah, John Postill, Kerstin Leder Mackley, and Nadia Astari. 2017. "Digital Visual Stakeholder Ethnography." *Sociological Research Online* 22 (4): 174–192.

Plato. (370 BCE) 1973. *Phaedrus and Letters VII and VIII*. London: Penguin Books.

Poletti, Anna, and Julie Rak. 2014. "Introduction." In *Identity Technologies: Constructing the Self Online*, ed. Anna Poletti and Julie Rak, 3–22. Madison: University of Wisconsin Press.

Popken, Ben. 2018. "As Algorithms Take Over, YouTube's Recommendations Highlight a Human Problem." *NBC News Digital*. April 19. https://www.nbcnews.com/tech/social -media/algorithms-take-over-youtube-s-recommendations-highlight-human-problem -n867596.

Popper, Ben. 2017. "YouTube Will No Longer Allow Creators to Make Money until They Reach 10,000 Views." *The Verge*. April 6. https://www.theverge.com/2017/4/6 /15209220/youtube-partner-program-rule-change-monetize-ads-10000-views.

Portelli, Alessandro. 1991. *The Death of Luigi Trastulli and Other Stories: Form and Meaning in Oral History*. Albany: State University of New York Press.

Postill, John. 2011. *Localizing the Internet: An Anthropological Account*. New York: Berghahn Books.

Postill, John, and Sarah Pink. 2012. "Social Media Ethnography: The Digital Researcher in a Messy Web." *Media International Australia* 145 (1): 123–134.

Prangley, Smay. 2015. "My Thoughts on YouTube Conventions." *Smay Jay*. August 18. https://smayjay.wordpress.com/2015/08/18/my-thoughts-on-youtube-conventions/.

PR Newswire. 2015. "Increasing Percentages of Americans Are Ready for Legal Marijuana." *PRNewswire.com*. May 7. http://www.prnewswire.com/news-releases/increasing -percentages-of-americans-are-ready-for-legal-marijuana-300079417.html.

Purcell, Kristin. 2013. *Online Video 2013*. Washington DC: Pew Research Center. http:// www.pewinternet.org/files/old-media//Files/Reports/2013/PIP_Online%20Video %202013.pdf.

Radsch, Courtney C. 2016. "Laws, Norms and Block Bots: A Multifaceted Approach to Combatting Online Abuse." In *OSCE New Challenges to Freedom of Expression: Countering Online Abuse against Female Journalists*, Vienna, Austria, Office of the Representative on Freedom of the Media, Organization for Security and Co-operation in Europe. https://papers.ssrn.com/sol3/papers.cfm?abstract_id=2745717.

Radway, Janice A. 1984. *Reading the Romance: Women, Patriarchy, and Popular Literature*. Chapel Hill: University of North Carolina Press.

Ram, Aliya. 2018. "YouTube Announces It Has Removed 8.3m Videos from Website." *Financial Times*. April 23. https://www.ft.com/content/b08fb628-470f-11e8-8ae9 -4b5ddcca99b3.

Rao, Mithun Bantwal, Joost Jongerden, Pieter Lemmens, and Guido Ruivenkamp. 2015. "Technological Mediation and Power: Postphenomenology, Critical Theory, and Autonomist Marxism." *Philosophy & Technology* 28 (3): 449–474.

Rapport, Nigel. 2002. "Nigel Rapport Responds to Vered Amit." In *The Trouble with Community: Anthropological Reflections on Movement, Identity and Collectivity*, Vered Amit and Nigel Rapport, 167–175. London: Pluto Press.

Raun, Tobias. 2016. *Out Online: Trans Self-Representation and Community Building on YouTube*. Oxford, UK: Routledge.

Reagle, Joseph M., Jr. 2015. *Reading the Comments: Likers, Haters, and Manipulators at the Bottom of the Web*. Cambridge, MA: MIT Press.

Redfield, Robert. 1955. *The Little Community and Peasant Society and Culture*. Chicago: University of Chicago Press.

Reim, Garrett. 2016. "Content Firm Draws Suitors." *Los Angeles Business Journal*. November 14. http://labusinessjournal.com/news/2016/nov/14/content-firm-draws -suitors/?page=2.

Rheingold, Howard. (1993) 2000. *The Virtual Community: Homesteading on the Electronic Frontier*. Cambridge, MA: MIT Press.

Robertson, Mark R. 2014. "3 Metric Ratios to Measure Your YouTube Channel Success." *Tubular Insights*. September 18. http://tubularinsights.com/3-metrics-youtube-success/.

Rockrapid. 2018. "Everything You Need to Know about YouTube's Controversial 10 Minute Trick." *Rockrapid.com*. June 17. http://rockrapid.com/everything-you-need-to -know-about-youtubes-controversial-10-minute-trick/.

Rodell, Chris. 2013. "Look Out, RoboCop! Statues from Yoda to Rocky Lure Tourists to Cities." *Nbcnews.com*. http://www.nbcnews.com/id/41769254/ns/travel-destination _travel/t/look-out-robocop-statues-yoda-rocky-lure-tourists-cities/#.VBCHtEh2k_U.

Rosenblatt, Bill. 2018. "Google Tries, Tries Again with New YouTube Music Service." *Forbes*. May 27. https://www.forbes.com/sites/billrosenblatt/2018/05/27/google-tries -tries-again-with-new-youtube-music-service/#2b323355ce2c.

Rotman, Dana, and Jennifer Preece. 2010. "The 'WeTube' in YouTube—Creating an Online Community through Video Sharing." *International Journal of Web Based Communities* 6 (3): 317–333.

Rouch, Jean. 1975. "The Camera and the Man." In *Principles of Visual Anthropology*, ed. Paul Hockings, 79–98. New York: Mouton.

Ruby, Jay. 1991. "Speaking For, Speaking About, Speaking With, or Speaking Alongside—An Anthropological and Documentary Dilemma." *Visual Anthropology Review* 7 (2): 50–67.

Ruby, Jay. 1995. "The Moral Burden of Authorship in Ethnographic Film." *Visual Anthropology Review* 11 (2): 77–82.

Ruby, Jay, and Richard Chalfen. 1974. "The Teaching of Visual Anthropology at Temple." *Society for the Anthropology of Visual Communication Newsletter* 5 (3): 5–7.

Ryan, Jenny. 2012. "The Digital Graveyard: Online Social Networking Sites as Vehicles of Remembrance." In *Human No More: Digital Subjectivities, Unhuman Subjects, and the End of Anthropology*, ed. Neil L. Whitehead and Michael Wesch, 71–87. Boulder: University Press of Colorado.

Sahlins, Marshall. 1972. *Stone Age Economics*. New York: Aldine de Gruyter.

Scott, Jeremy. 2011. "YouTube Friends and Subscriptions Are Merging, Kind Of." *Tubular Insights*. December 2011. http://tubularinsights.com/youtube-friends-and -subscriptions/.

Scott, Jeremy. 2012. "Is YouTube Trying to Erase the Past? Browse Page Eliminates Date Filter." *ReelSEO.com*. February 13. http://www.reelseo.com/youtube-erase-browse-page -eliminates-date-filter/.

Scribner, Herb. 2013. "Blurred Lines: How People's Lives Have Become an Online and Offline Experience." *Deseret National News*. December 19. https://www.deseretnews .com/article/865592731/Blurred-lines-How-peoples-lives-have-become-an-online-and -offline-experience.html.

Scroggins, Michael. 2012. "The Ecological Annum." *Ethnography.com*. August 3. http:// www.ethnography.com/2012/08/the-ecological-annum/.

Seiter, Ellen. 2005. *The Internet Playground*. New York: Peter Lang.

Senft, Theresa M. 2008. *Camgirls: Celebrity and Community in the Age of Social Networks*. New York: Peter Lang.

Senft, Theresa M., and Nancy K. Baym. 2015. "What Does the Selfie Say? Investigating a Global Phenomenon." *International Journal of Communication* 9: 1588–1606.

Sharfstein, Daniel J. 2015. "Rachel Dolezal's 'Passing' Isn't So Unusual." *New York Times Magazine*. June 15. http://www.nytimes.com/2015/06/25/magazine/rachel-dolezals -passing-isnt-so-unusual.html?_r=0.

Sheehy, Gail. 2017. "At Yale, Psychiatrists Cite Their 'Duty to Warn' about an Unfit President." *New York Magazine*. April 23. http://nymag.com/daily/intelligencer/2017 /04/yale-psychiatrists-cite-duty-to-warn-about-unfit-president.html.

Shields, Mike. 2014. "Meet Maker Studios' Top Five YouTube Channels." *Wall Street Journal*. April 1. https://blogs.wsj.com/cmo/2014/04/01/meet-maker-studios-top-five -youtube-channels/.

Shrum, Wesley, Ricardo Duque, and Timothy Brown. 2005. "Digital Video as Research Practice: Methodology for the Millennium." *Journal of Research Practice* 1 (1). http://jrp .icaap.org/index.php/jrp/article/ view/6/12.

Siegel, Joshua. 2011. "YouTube Is Going LIVE." *YouTube Official Blog*. April 8. https:// youtube.googleblog.com/2011/04/youtube-is-going-live.html.

Silverstein, Michael. 2000. "Whorfianism and the Linguistic Imagination." In *Regimes of Language: Ideologies, Polities, and Identities*, ed. Paul V. Kroskrity, 85–138. Santa Fe, NM: School of American Research Press.

Silverstone, Roger. 1999. *Why Study the Media?* London: Sage.

Simmel, Georg. 1950. "Faithfulness and Gratitude: Negativity of Collective Behavior; the Stranger; Metropolis." In *The Sociology of Georg Simmel*, ed. Kurt H. Wolff, 377–395. New York: Free Press.

Sims, Lowery. 1984. "Body Politics: Hannah Wilke and Kaylynn Sullivan." In *Art & Ideology*, ed. New Museum of Contemporary Art, 45–56. New York: New Museum of Contemporary Art.

Slutsky, Mark. 2014. "Sad YouTube: The Lost Treasures of the Internet's Greatest Cesspool." *Buzzfeed News*. January 20. https://www.buzzfeednews.com/article/markslutsky/how -the-youtube-comments-section-became-our-cultures-secret.

Smith, Andy. 2014. "Is VidCon Pushing Away Creators in Favor of the Teen Fans?" *ReelSEO.com*. July 2. http://www.reelseo.com/vidcon-pushing-away-creators/#ixzz4 DBl11zs6.

Sobchack, Vivian. 1999. "Toward a Phenomenology of Nonfictional Film Experience." In *Collecting Visible Evidence*, ed. Jane M. Gaines and Michael Renov, 241–254. Minneapolis: University of Minnesota Press.

Sokolowski, Robert. 2000. *Introduction to Phenomenology*. New York: Cambridge University Press.

Sontag, Susan. 1977. *On Photography*. New York: Anchor Books.

Sørenssen, Bjørn. 2009. "Breaking the Age Barrier in the Internet Age: The Story of Geriatric1927." In *The YouTube Reader*, ed. Pelle Snickars and Patrick Vonderau, 140–151. Stockholm: National Library of Sweden.

Spangler, Todd. 2017. "YouTube Cracks Down on Fake Channels by Setting 10,000-View Minimum before Serving Ads." *Variety*. April 6. https://variety.com/2017/digital/news /youtube-fake-channels-10000-view-limit-ads-1202025260/.

Spangler, Todd. 2018. "Viacom Announces Acquisition of VidCon Internet-Video Conference." *Variety*. February 7. https://variety.com/2018/digital/news/viacom -acquires-vidcon-conference-official-1202690303/.

Statista Research Department. 2016. "Leading Countries Based on Number of Monthly Active YouTube Users as of 1st Quarter 2016 (in millions)." *Statista*. May. https://www .statista.com/statistics/280685/number-of-monthly-unique-youtube-users/.

Statt, Nick. 2017. "YouTube to Discontinue Video Annotations Because They Never Worked on Mobile." *The Verge*. March 16. https://www.theverge.com/2017/3/16/1495 3756/youtube-annotations-feature-discontinue-cards-end-screens.

Stelter, Brian. 2008. "YouTube Videos Pull In Real Money." *New York Times*. December 10. https://www.nytimes.com/2008/12/11/business/media/11youtube.html.

Stern, Susannah. 2008. "Producing Sites, Exploring Identities: Youth Online Authorship." In *Youth, Identity, and Digital Media*, ed. David Buckingham, 95–118. Cambridge, MA: MIT Press.

Stetka, Bret. 2016. "Psychiatrists Reminded to Refrain from Armchair Analysis of Public Figures." NPR.org. August 13. http://www.npr.org/sections/health-shots/2016/08/13 /489807468/psychiatrists-reminded-to-refrain-from-armchair-analysis-of-public-figures.

"Stickam." n.d. *Wikipedia*. https://en.wikipedia.org/wiki/Stickam.

Stokel-Walker, Chris. 2017. "More than a Decade Later, How Do Original YouTube Stars Feel about the Site?" *Ars Technica*. June 11. https://arstechnica.com/features/2017/06 /youtube-changed-my-life-a-pair-of-original-videostars-ponder-a-life-lived-online/.

Strangelove, Michael. 2010. *Watching YouTube: Extraordinary Videos by Ordinary People*. Toronto: University of Toronto Press.

Taylor, Lucien. 1996. "Iconophobia." *Transition* 69: 64–88.

Tedlock, Barbara. 1991. "From Participant Observation to the Observation of Participation: The Emergence of Narrative Ethnography." *Journal of Anthropological Research* 47 (1): 69–94.

Terranova, Tiziana. 2000. "Free Labor: Producing Culture for the Digital Economy." *Social Text* 63 (18): 33–58.

"TheWineKone." n.d. *Wikipedia*. https://en.wikipedia.org/wiki/TheWineKone.

Thompson, Laura. 2016. "YouTube Space for Video Creators Expands to Canada." *CBC*. April 26. http://www.cbc.ca/news/entertainment/youtube-space-for-video-creators -launches-first-canadian-studio-1.3553839.

TubeMogul. 2013. "Is There a Mobile Video Primetime in the United States?" *TubeMogul. com*. http://www.tubemogul.com/marketing/research/TubeMogul_MobilePrimetime _US_ Q2_2013.pdf.

Turkle, Sherry. 1984. *The Second Self: Computers and the Human Spirit*. New York: Simon & Schuster.

Turner, Victor. 2002. "Liminality and Communitas." In *A Reader in the Anthropology of Religion*, ed. Michael Lambek, 326–339. Malden, MA: Blackwell Publishing.

Twenge, Jean. 2013. "Social Media Is a Narcissism Enabler." *New York Times*. September 24. http://www.nytimes.com/roomfordebate/2013/09/23/facebook-and-narcissism/social -media-is-a-narcissism-enabler.

Twenge, Jean M., and W. Keith Campbell. 2009. *The Narcissism Epidemic: Living in the Age of Entitlement*. New York: Atria.

"Twitter." n.d. *Wikipedia*. https://en.wikipedia.org/wiki/Twitter.

Uldam, Julie, and Tina Askanius. 2013. "Online Civic Cultures: Debating Climate Change Activism on YouTube." *International Journal of Communication* 7: 1185–1204.

University of North Florida. 2014. "New Social Media Study Investigates Relationships among Facebook Use, Narcissism and Empathy." *Science Daily*. July 3. www.sciencedaily .com/releases/2014/07/140703102510.htm.

Verdi, Michael, and Ryanne Hodson. 2006. *Secrets of Videoblogging: Videoblogging for the Masses*. Berkeley, CA: Peachpit Press.

Vernallis, Carol. 2013. *Unruly Media: YouTube, Music Video, and the New Digital Cinema*. Oxford, UK: Oxford University Press.

Veszelszki, Ágnes. 2016. "#time, #truth, #tradition. An Image-Text Relationship on Instagram: Photo and Hashtag." In *In the Beginning Was the Image: The Omnipresence of Pictures: Time, Truth, Tradition*, ed. András Benedek and Ágnes Veszelszki, 139–150. Frankfurt am Main: Peter Lang.

"VidCon." n.d. *Wikipedia*. https://en.wikipedia.org/wiki/VidCon.

Villarreal, Yvonne, and David Pierson. 2016. "VidCon, the Annual Video Star Convention, Has Gotten So Big It's Expanding Globally." *LA Times*. June 22. http://www.latimes .com/entertainment/envelope/cotown/la-et-ct-vidcon-expansion-20160613-snap-story .html.

Vossen, Chad. n.d. "Discontinued: YouTube Ends Video Response Option and Why You Should Care." *522productions.com*. http://www.522productions.com/discontinued -youtube-ends-video-response-option-and-why-you-should-care.

Wakeford, Nina. 2003. "The Embedding of Local Culture in Global Communication: Independent Internet Cafés in London." *New Media & Society* 5 (3): 379–399.

Wahlberg, Malin. 2009. "YouTube Commemoration: Private Grief and Communal Consolation." In *The YouTube Reader*, ed. Pelle Snickars and Patrick Vonderau, 218–235. Stockholm: National Library of Sweden.

Wali, Alaka. 2010. "Ethnography for the Digital Age: http://www.YouTube/Digital Ethnography (Michael Wesch)." *American Anthropologist* 112 (1): 147–148.

Walsh, Julie. 2016. "VidCon Announces International Expansion for 2017." *StreamingMedia.com*. June 23. http://www.streamingmedia.com/PressRelease/VidCon-Announces-International-Expansion-for-2017_41874.aspx.

Walther, Joseph B. 1994. "Anticipated Ongoing Interaction versus Channel Effects on Relational Communication in Computer-Mediated Interaction." *Human Communication Research* 20 (4): 473–501.

Warman, Matt. 2012. "YouTube Uploads Hit 60 Hours per Minute." *The Telegraph*. January 24. http://www.telegraph.co.uk/technology/news/9033765/YouTube-uploads-hit-60-hours-per-minute.html.

Warman, Matt. 2013. "YouTube at 8: 100 Hours Uploaded Every Minute." *The Telegraph*. May 13. http://www.telegraph.co.uk/technology/news/10068258/ YouTube-at-8-100-hours-uploaded-every-minute.html.

Warman, Matt. 2014. "Real World v. Online World: Teens Do Not Distinguish." *The Telegraph*. April 27. http://www.telegraph.co.uk/technology/news/10791922/Real-world-v-online-world-teens-do-not-distinguish.html.

Warner, Michael. 2002. "Publics and Counterpublics." *Public Culture* 14 (1): 49–90.

Waters, Malcolm, and Rodney Crook. 1993. *Sociology One*. 3rd ed. Melbourne: Longman Cheshire.

Weaver, Martin E.1995. "Removing Graffiti from Historic Masonry." Washington, DC: National Park Service. http://www.nps.gov/tps/how-to-preserve/preservedocs/preservation-briefs/38Preserve-Brief-Graffiti.pdf.

Weiner, Annette B. 1992. *Inalienable Possessions: The Paradox of Keeping While Giving*. Berkeley: University of California Press.

Weisman, Aly. 2012. "These 10 Celebs Give Paparazzi the Biggest Paydays." *Business Insider*. April 18. https://www.businessinsider.com/celebs-who-make-paparazzi-the-most-money-2012-4.

Weiss, Geoff. 2017a. "Playlist Live Orlando Sells Out, Will Welcome 13,000 Guests and 500 Creators." *Tubefilter*. April 28. https://www.tubefilter.com/2017/04/28/playlist-live-orlando-sells-out-13000-attendees/.

Weiss, Geoff. 2017b. "VidCon Australia Confirms Return to Melbourne Next Year." *Tubefilter*. September 20. https://www.tubefilter.com/2017/09/20/vidcon-australia-returns-next-year/.

Wellman, Barry, and Milena Gulia. 1999. "Virtual Communities as Communities: Net Surfers Don't Ride Alone." In *Communities in Cyberspace*, ed. Marc A. Smith and Peter Kollock, 167–194. London: Routledge.

Wellner, Galit P. 2016. *A Postphenomenological Inquiry of Cell Phones: Genealogies, Meanings, and Becoming.* Lanham, MD: Lexington Books.

Wenger, Etienne. 1998. *Communities of Practice: Learning, Meaning, and Identity.* Cambridge, UK: Cambridge University Press.

Wesch, Michael. 2007. "What Is Web 2.0? What Does It Mean for Anthropology? Lessons from an Accidental Viral Video." *Anthropology News* 48 (5): 30–31.

Wesch, Michael. 2008. "YouTube Statistics." *Digital Ethnography.* March 18. http:// mediatedcultures.net/thoughts/youtube-statistics/.

Wesch, Michael. 2009. "YouTube and You: Experiences of Self-Awareness in the Context Collapse of the Recording Webcam." *Explorations in Media Ecology* 8 (2): 19–34.

Wesch, Michael. 2011. "The Art of Loving and Learning: Erich Fromm and the Learning (of) Transformation." In *Inspiring Academics: Learning with the World's Great University Teachers*, ed. Iain Hay, 23–28. Berkshire, UK: Open University Press.

Wesch, Michael. 2012. "Anonymous, Anonymity, and the End(s) of Identity and Groups Online." In *Human No More: Digital Subjectivities, Unhuman Subjects, and the End of Anthropology*, ed. Neil L. Whitehead and Michael Wesch, 89–104. Boulder: University Press of Colorado.

Weston, Kath. 1992. "The Politics of Gay Families." In *Rethinking the Family: Some Feminist Questions*, ed. Barrie Thorne and Marilyn Yalom, 119–139. Boston: Northeastern University Press.

"WhatsApp." n.d. *Wikipedia.* https://en.wikipedia.org/wiki/WhatsApp.

Whitehead, Neil L., and Michael Wesch. 2012a. "Introduction." In *Human No More: Digital Subjectivities, Unhuman Subjects, and the End of Anthropology*, ed. Neil L. Whitehead and Michael Wesch, 1–10. Boulder: University Press of Colorado.

Whitehead, Neil L., and Michael Wesch, eds. 2012b. *Human No More: Digital Subjectivities, Unhuman Subjects, and the End of Anthropology.* Boulder: University Press of Colorado.

Williams, Alex. 2014. "A Defining Question in an iPhone Age: Live for the Moment or Record It?" *New York Times.* September 26. http://www.nytimes.com/2014/09/28 /fashion/a-defining-question-in-an-iphone-age-live-for-the-moment-or-record-it.html? _r=0.

Wilson, Samuel M., and Leighton C. Peterson. 2002. "The Anthropology of Online Communities." *Annual Review of Anthropology* 31: 449–67.

Wogan, Peter. 2006. "Audience Reception and Ethnographic Film: Laughing at First Contact." *Visual Anthropology Review* 22 (1): 14–33.

Wright, Karen. 2008. "Dare to be Yourself." *Psychology Today*. May 1. https://www
.psychologytoday.com/articles/200805/dare-be-yourself.

Yan, Yunxiang. 1996. *The Flow of Gifts: Reciprocity and Social Networks in a Chinese Village*.
Stanford, CA: Stanford University Press.

Yarow, Jay, and Kamelia Angelova. 2010. "Chart of the Day: The Half-Life of a YouTube
Video Is 6 Days." *Business Insider*. May 27. http://www.businessinsider.com/chart-of-the
-day-the-lifecycle-of-a-youtube-video-2010-5.

YouTube. 2018a. "Introducing YouTube Premium." *YouTube Official Blog*. May 16. https://
youtube.googleblog.com/2018/05/introducing-youtube-premium.html.

YouTube. 2018b. "YouTube Music, a New Music Streaming Service, Is Coming Soon."
YouTube Blog. May 16. https://youtube.googleblog.com/2018/05/youtube-music-new
-music-streaming.html.

YouTube Team. 2006. "Introducing YouTube Director." *YouTube Blog*. April 10. https://
youtube.googleblog.com/2006/04/introducing-youtube-director.html.

Zaher, Amany. 2018. "MENA's First YouTube Space Launched in Dubai." *Forbes Middle
East*. March 18. https://www.forbesmiddleeast.com/en/menas-first-youtube-space
-launched-in-dubai/.

Zhao, Yupei. 2014. "Virtual Experience Is Real but Not Actual." *Journal of Political Science
and Public Affairs* 2 (2): 117–119.

Zimmerman, Patricia. 1995. *Reel Families: A Social History of Amateur Film*. Bloomington:
Indiana University Press.

INDEX

accountability, 170, 171; anonymity and, 22; anxiety over, 269

activities, 73; cultural, 64; mediated, 259; profit-making, 249, 250; social, 5, 97

actor-network theory, 191, 299n11

advertisements, 115, 229–30, 231, 243, 247, 250; lifetime views and, 283n4; overlay, 227; placing, 232; revenue sharing with, 234; video, 85

aesthetics, 97, 148, 183, 197, 198, 225, 237, 247, 264, 274, 281, 282; creative, 212; participatory, 65; vernacular, 263

Affleck, Ben, 58

Affleck, Violet, 58

AKT Enterprises, 238

algorithms, 187, 189, 190, 192, 194, 197, 199, 202, 234, 247, 249, 250, 251, 259; automated, 183; demands of, 228; viewing, 28–29

alters: connections through, 28; digital, 208; posthuman, 29, 212; violative, 194–97; YOUTUBE, 222, 223, 224

Althusser, Louis, 296n46

Amazon.com, 300n33

American Anthropological Association, 277

Amit, Vered, 153, 184

Anaheim Convention Center, 81, 238

anakin1814, 39–40, 42, 78, 96; media of, 221; posting by, 77

analysis, 3, 7, 10, 12, 65, 70, 149, 150, 154, 167; anthropological, 274, 281; discourse-based, 159; rhythm, 8, 9, 108, 270; temporal, 135

Anderson, Benedict, 164, 282; analysis of, 154, 167; on communities, 153, 281; community and, 152

Anderson, Chris, 41

Andren, Eric, 127

Angelcheeks (video), 136, 137

Angelcheeks Foundation, 136

annotations, 168, 296–97n56

anonymity, 28, 145, 147, 255, 269, 286n74; accountability and, 22; discourse and, 169–74; importance of, 21–23; obsession with, 174; partial, 174; relative, 23; unmasking, 169–74

anthropological concepts, 4, 7, 12, 29, 30, 150, 255, 280

anthropological record, 16, 117, 129, 140, 143, 144, 145, 147, 152, 183, 255

anthropological studies, 16, 116, 188

anthropology, 12, 28, 30, 33, 63, 74, 107, 108, 144, 145, 153, 165, 192; cultural, 281; cyborg, 7; digital, 11, 277; linguistic, 281; Malinowskian tradition of, 158; public, 147, 173; reconsiderations of, 152; shared, 179;

traditional, 273; visual, 11, 168, 179, 275, 276, 279, 280–81
Anthropology Video Blog, 12
AnthroVlog, 12, 13, 34, 35, 109–11, 130, 140, 144, 147, 198, 217; Bulletin, 110; comments on, 118
anti-memory, 31, 257–61
anti-Semitism, 28, 195, 196
anxiety, 23, 28, 117, 201, 207, 269, 279; algorithmic, 197–200; temporal, 272
Appadurai, Arjun, 77, 78, 302n96
arrhythmias, 9, 129, 146, 166–68, 206, 228, 230, 232, 235, 240, 250, 251, 252, 270, 271, 272; participatory, 248, 249; social, 246
As One, 84
Ask a Ninja DVD, 12
Askanius, Tina, 166
Association of Internet Researchers, 302n81
attention economy, 60, 113, 114
audiences, 176, 188, 228, 249; mass, 39, 115, 129
augmentation, 195; advantageous, 196; asymmetrical, 199–200

Bakhtin, Mikhail, 89–90, 92
Banks, Marcus, 11, 275
Basilio, Ryan, 246; death of, 210–12, 214, 245
Baym, Nancy, 44, 75
Bear, Greg, 194
Becker, Howard S., 238
Behar, Ruth, 63
behavior, 11, 75, 113, 125, 166, 172, 221, 239, 256, 268; acceptable, 281; antisocial, 10; interaction on, 294n49; monitoring, 269, 278; narcissistic, 24; online/offline, 20, 21, 99; problematic, 157, 169, 196; quid pro quo, 127; self-centered, 132; social, 99; video-blogging, 62
Bernard, Michael, 194, 195
Beverly Hills City Council, 245
Beyond Viral: How to Attract Customers, Promote Your Brand, and Make Money with Online Video (Nalty), 115, 248
Biella, Peter, 179
binaries, 20, 53, 97, 99, 269; Cartesian, 254; formulation of, 270; online-offline, 70, 77, 96, 102, 103
blaggabloogy, 165, 166
Blake, Roberto, 126, 127, 249–50, 251; subscriptions and, 132
blip.tv, 109, 111, 292n8, 302n92

blogging, 39, 72, 169, 173, 177, 233, 237, 288n31, 289n71
Blood Music (Bear), 194, 202
bnessel1973, 47, 79, 118, 119–20, 135, 136, 137; gratitude for, 142; video by, 121, 141
Boellstorff, Tom, 10, 150, 196
boh3m3, 94, 95
Bollmer, Grant David, 207
bonds, 85, 102, 183, 205, 223; communal, 108; continuing, 210, 215; interpersonal, 111
bots, 131, 200, 300n34
boyd, danah, 112, 122, 124, 127, 257
Brian, 118, 121, 142; reciprocity by, 119–20
Brittney, 178–79
BRITTNEYLEESAUNDERS, 178
BroJo Ghost, 53, 54, 55; photo of, 54
Brown, Barry, 113, 133; reciprocity and, 112, 121, 124, 130
Burgess, Jean, 10, 221, 258
burnout, 30, 227, 249–51, 252
Butler, Shay Carl, 236, 239

CafePress, 115
cameras, 36, 37, 56, 60, 91, 94, 112, 138, 235, 239, 278; being on, 49; body-mounted, 289n71; GoPro, 41, 189n71; high-end, 35; observing through, 57–58, 64; participation and, 61, 64–65; photo of, 276; privacy and, 280; proliferation of, 276; video, 51, 54, 204
cavwondagainsti69, 165, 166
celebrities, 23, 96, 289n75; interviews with, 176; orientation toward, 241; YouTube, 5–6, 7, 130, 156, 230, 239, 240, 241, 242, 243, 248, 257
Center for Disease Control, 136
Chagnon, Napoleon, 179
Chalfen, Richard, 11, 97
chat service, 19, 220, 291n21, 302n88
Cherny, Lynn, 75
Chocolate Rain (video), 242
"Chocolate Rain" song, 242, 304n55
Christensen, Dorthe Refslund, 204, 207, 208
"Christmas Truce," 88
chronotopes, 12, 26, 70, 71, 92–93, 94, 98, 105, 106, 253, 269; commemorative, 91; concept of, 89–90; literary conventions and, 90
civic issues, 12, 22, 162, 174
civic messages, 136, 212, 280
Clifford, James, 6, 284n30
CNN.com, 211

Cohen, Anthony, 152, 155

Coleman, Beth, 20, 195, 286n70, 299n7

Coleman, Wim, 301n46

collaboration, 91, 94, 185, 203, 276, 277, 278, 280; birthday, 136; ethnographic, 277; heartfelt, 134

collective, 184, 281, 282; needs of, 201–2; post-human, 215, 272

Coming of Age in Second Life (Boellstorff), 10

commenters, 48, 51, 110, 112, 117, 119, 141, 172–73, 180, 246; anonymous, 170; gratitude from, 142; identities of, 174; interactive, 159–60; postings by, 158–68; rating system of, 177

comments, 7, 35, 90, 97, 115, 134, 140, 142, 160–61, 166, 167, 185–86, 200, 261, 264, 266, 271; anonymous, 21; answering, 110; constructive, 169–70, 173; contributing, 38, 193; controversial, 151; corpus of, 173; cruel, 157; encouraging, 130, 152; expectations for, 174–77; gaming, 248; generic, 125; hater, 157, 177, 263; inappropriate, 175, 176–77; inclusion/exclusion of, 177; mean, 199, 295n8, 297n63; moderating, 151, 176; negative, 177; neutral, 160, 163; popularity of, 122; positive, 170, 175; problematic, 160, 177; public, 13; random sample of, 161, 161 (table); reciprocity and, 110, 117–22; removing, 177, 199; threatening, 169; video, 104–5, 113, 180, 184

commerce, 188, 206, 230–31, 285n54

commercial events, 239, 240, 243, 266, 282

commercialization, 3–4, 10, 16, 17, 85, 233, 238, 240, 246, 252; meaningful, 282; move toward, 256

communication, 10, 19, 97, 112, 166, 167, 199, 230, 251, 280; computer-mediated, 294n49; electronic, 162; mass, 183; political, 169; sociality and, 15; structuring, 61

communitainment, 154, 223–24

communitas, 27, 84–86, 106

community, 3, 7, 12, 14, 39, 42, 50, 77, 85, 86, 124, 129, 145–46, 173, 194, 218, 231, 233, 252, 254, 259, 262, 280; achieving, 150, 178, 185; Asian/Asian American, 223; building, 146, 148, 164, 166, 182, 183, 282; concept of, 27, 147, 164, 184, 186, 281; defining, 155, 161, 163–65; digital, 129, 160, 296n46; discussions of, 147, 155, 179, 185; ethos of, 154, 223; formation, 8, 146, 158, 159, 163, 244; imagined, 29, 152, 153, 164, 185, 282; media generations and, 147; mediations on, 177–79; models of, 162; notions of, 27–28, 255; online, 111–12; parameters of, 147; as processual,

182–86; prospects for, 28, 152, 155–58, 160–63, 179; rhetorical aspects of, 165; term, 184, 255; trans YouTube, 223; tropes of, 170

conceptualizations, 25, 105, 188, 189

conflicts, 238; ideological, 272; interpersonal, 197; participatory, 9; processual, 197

connections, 159, 182; internet and, 76; interpersonal, 25, 117; mutual, 108; visual, 36

content: action-worthy, 123; cultural, 146; democratized, 247 extreme forms of, 247; moderating, 234; temporal padding of, 248

contextualization, 229, 230, 275, 279–80, 281

conversations, 50, 175; mediated, 182, 292n54

corporate entities, 66, 164–65, 166, 228, 253, 254

Craig, David, 151, 154, 223, 251, 305n73

creativity, 27, 122, 129, 271, 277

Creator Academy, 235

Crisis Avoided—THANK YOU (video), 139

Crook, Rodney, 163

cultural contexts, 23, 71

cultural forms, 17–18, 26, 259, 266

cultural groups, 11, 76, 275

cultural patterns, 177, 261

cultural practices, 16, 259

culture, 10, 23, 45, 61, 71, 76, 78, 137, 191, 209, 232, 274; celebrity, 6; defining, 16; employee, 159; multiple, 282; participatory, 29, 33, 36–37, 50, 51, 53, 55, 65, 68, 196; pop, 83; processual view of, 184–85; public, 263; technical, 138; video, 32, 189; video-sharing, 25, 49, 55, 138, 142, 188, 261–81, 270, 271; visual, 56

Cunningham, Stuart, 151, 154, 223, 251, 305n73

curation, 210–12, 274, 275

Curtis, Sonny, 83

cyberbullying, 79, 199, 300n38

cyborg studies, 191

CyndieRae, 136

Cyworld, 257

DaleATL2, 100–101, 119, 134–36; diversity and, 156

danbergam, 162

data, 187, 195; collecting, 13, 15, 180, 182, 243; creating, 151; digital, 187; ethnographic, 183, 188, 227; friction, 102, 103–4; genres of, 267

Dave & Buster's, 69

Day, Mark, 109

de Seta, Gabriele, 150, 151, 182

Dean, Jodi, 258

death, 8, 28, 208; cultural rituals of, 207; digital, 204, 205, 206–7

Death Online Research Network, 203, 204

deathstyle, 207, 208, 222, 301n72

Dedman, Jay, 57

Definitive Way to Go Gluten Free (Rignola), 79

DeFranco, Philip, 236

Deleuze, Gilles, 261

demographics, 15, 70, 86, 222, 257, 258

desire, 9, 17, 22, 42, 52, 53, 55, 98, 103, 104, 113, 133, 165, 172, 188, 202, 207, 210, 251, 254, 264, 266, 268; chronotopic chain of, 96, 97, 105, 106; digital, 29; human, 212; posthuman, 209

dialogue, 12, 151, 166, 168, 263, 288n16

diaspora, 76, 152; digital, 302n86

Digital Ethnography, 14, 181

digital media, 9, 11, 14, 20, 51, 76, 101, 204, 265, 275; contexts of, 262; death and, 206–7; reciprocity in, 111–13, 130

Disappearing YouTubers (video), 219

discourse, 28, 31, 79, 255, 257, 259; anonymity and, 21, 169–74; diversionary, 267–69; engaged, 211; narcissistic, 268; networked, 268–69; online, 21, 23; popular, 6, 18; positive, 170; productive, 18; public, 17, 199

Discussion page, 13, 114, 115, 130

Disney, 236, 304n36

Disneyland, 238

disposition, 112, 177; media, 30, 169, 272; mediated, 51, 62

diversity, 60, 86, 87, 148, 156; lack of, 238; vernacular, 66

Donovan, Ben, 236, 237

Donovan, Lisa, 125, 236, 237

Douglas, Mary, 108, 155

Down with Robtran (video), 197

Driscoll, Kevin, 222–23, 224, 260

drum circles, 33–34; photo of, 66; video, 65–68

dynamics, 64, 240; community, 148, 185; cultural, 142; emotio-temporal, 119; emplacement, 70, 75–76, 78; force-based, 33; interactive, 16, 253; interpersonal, 4, 97, 109, 144; meet-up, 71–73; posthuman, 197; reciprocity, 140; vernacular, 26

Earle, Leon, 163

ecology, 273, 305n73; interaction, 21; media, 39, 44, 189, 220, 221; mediated, 216; screen, 251

Edgar, Don, 163

Edwards, Paul, 102

"888," 26, 91

elites, 24, 67, 94, 263, 268

Ellison, Nicole, 257

emotion, 48, 101, 201, 216; community and, 155; raw, 209, 210; sociality and, 27

empathy, 30, 36; emphasizing, 262–65

emplacement, 12, 30, 79–83, 84, 257, 290n9; analyzing, 269–70; chronotopic, 90, 92, 106; dynamics of, 70, 74–76, 78; sociality and, 75; video making and, 74

End Screen, 296n56

engagement, 166, 174–75, 225; active, 174, 277; analytical, 159; civic, 175, 268, 275; community, 256; levels of, 150; principal forms of, 159; public, 180; reciprocal, 109; temporal, 271; video, 24

environment: arrhythmic, 252; commercial, 228; digital, 10, 11, 27, 117, 269, 280; discursive, 155; financial, 229; hybrid, 252; media, 266, 267; mediated, 228, 258–59, 269; networked, 264; posthuman, 195; social-commercial, 144; video-sharing, 27; YouTube, 39–40, 234, 237

ethics, 203, 254, 277, 278

Ethnografilm, 284n39

ethnography, 11–14, 27, 36, 64, 68, 70, 73, 74, 76, 89, 109, 168, 216, 253, 262, 263; anthropological, 273–74; digital, 10, 147, 150, 158; forms of, 62; internet, 75; role of, 274–81; stakeholder, 158; textual, 281; video, 35, 278; visual, 26, 33, 35, 63, 224, 274, 278, 281

Ethnography and Virtual Worlds (Boellstorff), 150

eurhythmia, 65

exchange, 107; forms of, 129–31; immediate, 134; media, 17, 32, 66

exhibitionism, 43, 46, 48, 60, 62

experience, 3, 6, 27, 30, 73, 85, 95, 106, 153, 189; asymmetrical, 228; authentic, 61; chronotopic chains of, 253; collective, 201; communal, 154; cultural, 273; embodied, 55–56; enlivening, 101; fan, 243, 244; lived, 30, 35; mediated, 56, 60, 70, 270; online-offline, 18, 70; posthuman, 189, 194, 206–7; pure versus inauthentic, 56

Experience: As One Gathering (video), 93

expression, 20, 23, 114; cultural, 16, 17, 18; encouraging, 144; facial, 212; self, 193

Facebook, 5, 29, 99, 176, 204, 205, 211, 214, 216, 219, 221, 222, 234, 257

FanFest, 238
fans, 45, 243, 244
Fatpandas, 162, 163
feedback, 39, 50, 129, 180
Fellini, Federico, 58
fiction, 88, 153, 189, 191, 192, 199, 263; gay-friendly,
    300n33; posthuman, 222
film studies, 42, 277, 279
"Filming the filmmakers: Longole," 279
footage, 12, 26, 57, 93, 94, 101, 113, 116, 117, 119,
    150, 209, 213, 267, 278, 279; home mode, 97;
    inappropriate, 278; interview, 149; meet-up,
    4, 27, 82, 84, 98, 104; observational, 35; shar-
    ing, 134–38, 142, 280
Fopp, Rodney, 163
Ford, Sam, 182
*4 Reasons YOUTUBE RED IS GOING TO
    FAIL|Rant* (video), 230
frameworks, 26, 222, 273
Francis, Pope, 56
Frank, Ze, 109
fredrika27, 159
FreeWingz, 214, 215
Freud, Sigmund, 43, 46
frictions, participatory, 99–105
friendships, 15, 23, 41, 110, 152, 228–29, 237, 238,
    303n5; connotations of, 253; trajectory of, 103
fungibility: emotional, 71, 99–100, 106, 270;
    experiential, 101, 102; media, 99, 102; partici-
    patory, 99–105, 270; physical, 71, 102, 106

Gambito, Christine, 223
gaming, 20, 230, 248, 302n85
Garner, Jennifer, 58
Gates, Bill, 229
gatherings, 12, 18, 19, 37, 72, 75, 79, 90, 93, 96, 103,
    220, 242, 280; activities at, 73; As One, 84;
    attending, 104; chronotopes of, 92; classic,
    304n56; commercial, 81; early, 26; grassroots,
    81, 82, 239, 246; large-scale, 69, 73; observa-
    tions at, 87; private, 115–16; reunions and, 86;
    YouTube, 86, 91, 105, 106, 218. *See also* meet-ups
Gauntlett, David, 41
Geertz, Clifford, 179
GeneticBlend, 79, 80, 98, 135, 136
Geraci, Robert M., 285n63
Gershon, Ilana, 56, 206
Gharaibeh, Kassem, 236
ghostinvestigator, 167

Ginsburg, Faye, 258–59
globalization, 93, 121, 164
Godelier, Maurice, 129
Goffman, Erving, 22, 204
Going, Ben, 95
Google, 111, 171, 198, 236; advertisements and,
    232; algorithms of, 247; policy by, 205–6;
    purchase by, 5; YouTube and, 229
Gotved, Stine, 204, 207, 208, 210, 302n80
Gouldner, Alvin, 113
Graceffa, Joey, 230, 240
graffiti, 151, 295n10
Granovetter, Mark, 174
grassroots, 71, 235, 240, 241, 245, 246
gratitude, expressing, 138–41, 142
GreasyGuide.com, 176
Green, Hank, 81, 231, 238
Green, John, 81, 231, 238
Green, Joshua, 10, 182, 221
Griffith, Maggie, 45, 46
Gross, Larry, 277, 279
Guattari, Félix, 261
Gulia, Milena, 21, 152

Hampe, Barry, 35
Hanner, Jill, 76–77, 119
HappySlip, 223
harassment, 170, 172, 176, 196, 199
hate speech, 28, 176, 199, 234
haters, 8, 21, 28, 42, 156, 157, 159, 160, 170, 173, 177,
    195, 196, 198, 199, 201, 202, 211
Hayles, N. Katherine, 194, 202
healing, forms of, 45–48
Hecox, Ian Andrew, 230
Hemsley, Jeff, 181, 182
Herring, Susan, 169
heteromorphic reciprocity, 114, 130, 137, 140, 255
Hey Watch This! Sharing the Self through Media
    (video), 12, 51, 101, 206, 233
Higa, Ryan, 223
Highfield, Tim, 203, 204
Hilton, Paris, 157, 290n79
history, 90, 91, 199; alternative, 260; erasing, 273;
    media, 39; shared, 71, 94; visual, 279
Hodson, Ryanne, 46, 57, 265, 266
Holmes, Douglas, 158
homeomorphic reciprocity, 114, 130, 144, 255
homogeneity, 155, 164, 184, 281
homophobia, 21, 169, 177

Hondros, John J., 300n34
Hugs for Jacey Campaign, The (video), 200, 201
Hulu, 229
human spirit, 188–89, 234
humanity: death of, 190; future, 209; mediated, 207
Hutchens, Myiah, 169
Huynh, Tony, 219

I hate what youtube has become (video), 233
"Iconophobia" (Taylor), 279
identity, 7, 13, 21, 23, 28, 139, 169, 174, 195; change, 203; collective, 16, 129, 153; common, 163; construction of, 11, 192; digital, 268; ends of, 204; fluid, 191; gender, 199; individual, 188, 189; informational patterns and, 28; interpretations of, 204; Latinx, 241; participatory, 78, 193; performative, 191; perpetrator, 170; post-human, 192, 203; public, 197, 200; virtual, 22
ideology, 282; media, 56, 60, 61, 62, 64, 68
idioms, 108, 192; mediated, 7, 28, 83, 206; video-blogging, 51, 61, 276, 277
Illuminatta, 98
Image Ethics (Gross, Katz, and Ruby), 279
Image Ethics in the Digital Age (Gross, Katz, and Ruby), 279
images, 60, 191, 199, 277; alternative, 197; awkward, 279; digitized, 20; home mode, 97; maximizing, 35; posting, 275; public, 59; rights to, 279; uncomplimentary, 279; visual, 7
imagination, 5, 184, 251, 252; popular, 18, 117, 153, 185
information, 23, 153, 168, 175, 179, 195, 238; collecting, 181, 182; contact, 206; demographic, 15; discussing, 159; identity, 22, 28; imparting, 182; logistical, 95; personal, 275; quantitative, 150; sharing, 23, 257, 258, 262, 280; withholding, 170
infrastructure, 75, 153, 185, 269; commercialized, 182; communicative, 75; digital, 43; drum circle, 67; economic, 16; technical, 16, 180
Ingold, Tim, 291n22
Instagram, 29, 219, 236, 255
interaction, 50, 51, 62, 65, 78, 94, 96–97, 114, 125, 138, 142, 143, 187, 204, 244, 276; chronotopic, 89–92, 106, 254; collective, 282; digital, 18, 21, 22, 112, 269; emplacement and, 269; history of, 141; in-person, 19; inter-threaded, 72, 75, 76; mediated, 20, 23, 74, 75, 100, 228, 261;

modalities of, 18, 76, 111; networked, 20; online, 19, 20, 172; participatory, 36, 111; promoting, 134, 181; reciprocity and, 111, 121, 134, 140; rhythms of, 8; social, 16, 43, 92, 124, 156, 260; sociality and, 75; third-person, 144
interactivity, 35, 65, 66, 76, 92, 143, 159, 161, 179, 188; constructive, 165–66; cycle of, 134
internet, 56, 57, 62, 77, 103, 125, 212, 222, 223, 260; connections and, 76; studies, 75, 203; third wave of, 17; trajectories of, 223; usage, 5
internet cafés, research on, 75
Internet Protocol, 286n80
Internet Research4.0, 301n81
interpretation, 22, 37, 62, 152, 269, 271
interviewees, 4, 35, 38, 42, 74, 84, 104, 115, 123, 143; behavior and, 75; reciprocity and, 121–22; researchers and, 36; video sharing and, 23; YouTube experience and, 3
interviews, 13, 35, 49, 53–54, 67, 74; conducting, 277; ethnographic, 208, 243, 267; reciprocal, 50; remarks, 113, 142; semistructured, 14; video, 67; walking, 277
Introduction to Australian Society (Edgar, Earle, and Fopp), 163
"invisible wall" approach, 35, 36
iReporter, 211
ItalianStallionette, 88, 91, 92, 196
Ito, Mizuko, 299n123

Jacey, 200, 201
Jane, 48, 119; data friction and, 103–4; memorial by, 47
Jenkins, Henry, 6, 36, 50, 67, 182
JennaMarbles, 239, 240
Jenner, Bruce/Caitlyn, 174
Jones, Graham M., 288n16
Juhasz, Alexandra, 180, 182

K80Blog, 119, 217, 218
Karim, Jawed, 84, 171
Katz, John Stuart, 277, 279
Kavoori, Anandam, 10, 284n30
Kay, Olga, 40, 41, 49, 239
Kendall, Lori, 21, 75
Kendall, YT, 303n3
Kennedy, Jamie, 157
kenrg, 93, 94, 136
KevJumba, 223

Kids on YouTube (Lange), 11, 42, 51, 138, 200, 244, 264
Kjellberg, Felix, 248
Knott, Kathryn, 297n76
knowledge, 261; anthropological, 280; cultural, 85; exchange, 9, 169; generational, 212–13; technical, 264
Kollock, Peter, 111–12

La Dolce Vita (Fellini), 58
landscapes, 203; YouTube, 228–51
Lange, Patricia G., 92, 137, 208; photo of, 244
Lasch, Christopher, 44
Law of Reciprocity, 294n64
learning: collaborative, 223; by going viral, 179–82
Learning from YouTube (class), 180
Leaver, Tama, 203, 204, 205, 206, 211
Lefebvre, Henri, 9, 25, 91, 141, 143, 166–67, 177; analysis by, 8, 65, 167, 270; arrhythmias and, 129, 228; media and, 216; model of, 185; rhythmic patterns and, 8, 146, 270; rubric of, 8, 227; temporalities and, 142, 164, 256, 270
Lefebvrian cycle, 30, 32, 69, 130, 146, 185, 188, 256
legacy: digital, 29, 187, 188, 203–16, 223; historical, 273; media, 206; mediated, 272; social, 209; video, 207, 213
Lemelson, Robert, 179
lemonette, 157; attention for, 59, 60, 64; described, 57–58; photo of, 59
Lennyfoshenny, 163, 164
"Let's Play" videos, 223
Lévi-Strauss, Claude, 287n98
lifeways, 4, 63, 273, 274, 275
LindaSVorhies, 119–20
linguistics, 169, 281
LinkedIn, 5
LisaNova, 49, 125, 236
literacy: developing, 67; digital, 37, 40, 66, 151, 199, 263, 264, 280; participatory, 269; spectatorial, 275; visual, 264
Little YouTube #community (video), 178
Long Tail, The (Anderson), 41
Los Angeles County Planning Commission, 245
Los Angeles Space, 235
"Love Is All Around" (song), 83
Lovink, Geert, 122, 151, 171, 185–86
loyalties, 153, 155, 210, 237, 282
Lurker6-7-8, 53
lurkers, 25, 50, 51, 52, 53, 133, 277

MacArthur Foundation, 14
MacDougall, David, 279
MacDougall, Judith, 279
Machine Is Us/ing Us (video), 180–81
Machinima MCN, 236
Maddox, Jessica, 43, 46
Madianou, Mirca, 307n44
Maggothon, 161, 165
Maker Studios, 236, 237, 239, 292n8, 304n36
Mann, Steve, 277
Marcus, George, 78, 158
Markham, Annette, 75, 709
Martinez, Wilton, 168
Marwick, Alice, 122, 124
Mary Tyler Moore Show, The (television show), 69, 83
mash-ups, 195, 197; videos of, 28–29, 196
Mauss, Marcel, 124
McNamara, Kim, 290n79
McNeill, Laurie, 204
MCNs. *See* multi-channel networks
Mean Kitty Song, The (video), 84–85
media, 14, 16, 51, 56, 83, 86, 102, 189, 204, 212, 224, 252; collectivity and, 281; corporatized, 23; creating, 11, 50, 143, 253; democratized, 107–8; different forms of, 188; do-it-yourself, 24; everyday, 10; grassroots, 183; home mode, 97; inappropriate, 22; inter-threadedness of, 19; markers, 12; mass, 5, 6, 37, 39; messages, 37; migration to, 9; news, 83; posthuman, 254; professional, 6, 49, 118, 268; psychology of creators and, 46; rhythmic patterns of, 9; ritualized, 153; self and, 43–44; sensory, 99; sociality and, 6, 144, 152; socially motivated, 256; technologized, 192; temporal evaluations of, 265; types of, 100; vernacular, 263
media generations, 30, 179, 234, 255, 256, 282; community and, 147; determining, 262; features and, 272–73; monetization and, 232; support for, 235; vloggers and, 226
media making, 4, 12, 16, 39, 44, 50, 56, 57, 126, 259; democratized, 86; participation and, 8; reciprocity and, 144
media sharing, 4, 125, 227, 280; engaging in, 200; forms of, 256, 262; global public and, 263
mediascapes, 4, 89, 93, 96, 98, 222; communicative, 216; constructing, 76–79; interactive, 80, 99

mediation, 9, 10, 11, 21, 31, 33, 47, 51, 64, 74, 100, 102, 150, 155, 177–79, 184, 281; analysis of, 7; expecting, 62; experience and, 60; impact of, 58; interactive, 270; interpersonal, 61; lack of, 58; moment and, 60; observational, 35; online/offline, 269; participation and, 55–61; patterns of, 258; place and, 26; self-focused, 48; sociality and, 68; suspicion of, 56; technologized, 26; time/place and, 70; types of, 19, 99, 269, 282; video, 25, 28
meet-and-greet events, 238, 243
Me at the Zoo (video), 84
meet-ups, 12, 13, 14, 15, 25, 33, 38, 41, 69, 70, 77, 84, 85, 88, 91, 96, 99, 100, 101, 111, 114, 115, 118, 131, 133–34, 136, 137, 140, 156, 158, 212, 214, 217; attending, 49, 72–73, 98, 104, 127; character of, 76; chronotopic, 26, 90, 93; commercialized, 239; data friction at, 102–3; democratizing spirit of, 245; diversity at, 87; dynamics of, 71–73; future, 104–5; grassroots, 241, 242, 246; importance of, 26; inter-threaded aspect of, 93; monetization of, 30, 238–51; origins of, 71–73; social side of, 205; videos of, 72, 79, 94–95, 97, 98, 106, 209, 269, 270, 276
Meikle, Graham, 280
memorials, 47–48; digital, 209, 210; posthuman, 215–16
memories, 86, 136, 139; collective, 71; covering, 138
meshworks, 75, 291n22
metrics, 182, 232; monetization, 233, 247; viewing, 81, 123, 126, 131, 305n62; watch-time, 251
Meunier, Jean-Pierre, 88
microwavefishsticks, 172, 173, 297n81
Middleton, Kate, 58–59
Midwest Gathering, 72, 90, 91, 104–5; photo of, 54
Midwest Gathering Shindig (video), 55
Midwest Lurker, 51, 52, 53, 289n62
migration, 9, 30; conceptual, 189, 216, 217, 218; digital, 8, 12, 28, 189, 216–20; radical, 216–17
milieus, 36; community and, 183; digital, 19, 23, 32, 49, 53, 142, 143, 144, 169, 217, 255, 270; mediated, 17, 33, 75; social, 9, 33, 146, 253; video-blogging, 276; video-making, 31; video-sharing, 32, 256
Miller, Daniel, 76, 180, 257–58, 267, 268; on internet, 75; polymedia and, 307n44; social media and, 20, 171–72
Minecraft, 223, 262

Mitchell, W.J.T., 56
modalities, 28, 67, 99, 111, 142, 270; functionality of, 292n54; interactive, 18, 71; inter-threaded, 25; maximizing, 18–21; mediated, 70, 102; multiple, 270, 282; sensory, 100; sociality and, 70; types of, 105; video-blogging, 96
monetization, 4, 7, 8, 81, 124, 126–27, 130, 132, 178, 188, 224, 227, 228, 229, 252, 256, 257, 260, 261, 272; activating, 234; boosting opportunities for, 122; impact of, 233; MCNs and, 235–37; media generations and, 232; meet-ups and, 238–51; policies about, 5; reaction to, 29–30; single-video, 232; sociality and, 233, 250; socialization and, 231–35
Moore, Mary Tyler, 82–83
Moosh Walks, 40–41, 249
Moran, James M., 263
Morphy, Howard, 11, 275
Mourey, Jenna Nicole, 239
Müller, Eggo, 67
multi-channel networks (MCNs), 235–37
multi-user domains (MUDs), 284n33
music, 39, 40, 41, 55, 69, 77, 82, 83, 95, 183, 200, 213, 219, 229, 231, 242, 243; enjoying, 65; quality of, 67; video, 136
musoSF, 96, 119, 127, 128, 136; video making and, 41–42
My Life as a Night Elf Priest (Nardi), 10–11
My YouTube Story (video), 118–19, 141
MySpace, 39, 205, 218, 221, 222, 234, 284n27
MysteryGuitarMan, 239, 243, 244

Nahon, Karine, 181, 182
nalts, 115, 116, 136, 248
Nalty, Kevin, 115–16, 125, 248
narcissism, 23, 24, 29, 113, 125, 143, 199, 254, 263; claims of, 44–48; discourses of, 55, 68; diversionary, 268; fears about, 208; female sexuality and, 45; fueling, 34, 263; individual, 267; overstating, 33; rethinking, 43–55; self and, 44; selfies and, 45; sociality and, 33; term, 43, 44; unwarranted attention and, 47; video, 25, 52, 132; vloggers and, 45–46
Nardi, Bonnie, 10–11, 20, 285n63
narratives, 37, 88, 152, 156, 216, 220; alternative, 7, 257–61; departure, 189; diversity in, 148; fall from grace, 251; historical, 260; teleological, 260
nbwulf, 119, 212, 213, 218–19

Netflix, 252

networks, 17–18, 95, 147, 181, 223; business strategies of, 236; communication, 75; digital, 19, 205; internet, 75, 260; multichannel/multiplatform, 30; profit-oriented, 237; social, 121, 181, 258; technological, 207; video-based, 72

new media, 55, 148, 150–51, 178, 227, 255, 256, 267

Newman, Michael, 183

nickynik, 129

nigahiga, 223

Nissenbaum, Helen, 279–80

nitrofreakmanho, 167

NorCalCorsello, 93, 94, 121, 130

NutCheese, 16

NYC Gathering 777 (video), 79, 98

Oakley, Peter, 42

observation, 62, 95, 96, 129; participation and, 26, 63–64, 65, 254. *See also* participant-observation

obsessive-compulsive disorder (OCD), 24

Offer, Avner, 107

offline, 18; online and, 19, 20

OhCurt, 77, 78, 136, 137–38, 232, 233

OlgaKay, 40, 41, 49, 239, 249

On Photography (Sontag), 56

OneTakeAsh, 178

online, 8, 18, 229; accounts, 187; offline and, 19, 20

Ontario Science Centre, 65, 69, 72, 78, 85, 242, 244; meet-up at, 73; photo of, 66

Ontus, 123–24

otherness, stereotypes of, 168

Padilla, Daniel Anthony, 230

Palmer, Parker J., 181

Paloque-Berges, Camille, 223, 224, 260

Papacharissi, Zizi, 45, 46, 169

paparazzi, 57–58, 59–60, 61, 64, 204, 254, 289n75

para-ethnography, 158, 159, 160, 163, 173, 180, 183

parentrazzi, 62

participant-observation, 7, 12, 25–26, 68, 277; criticism of, 64, 254–55; interrogating, 62–65

participants, 3, 5, 22, 33, 42, 61, 65, 74, 98, 130, 137, 167, 176, 232, 254, 276; emplacement and, 79; modalities and, 99; online, 101–2, 264; role of, 36

participation, 4–5, 9, 11, 25, 33–37, 50, 60, 66, 68, 82, 87, 96, 152, 175, 177, 190, 193, 197, 209, 211, 216; agentive, 189; arrhythmic, 185; broadening, 44; cameras and, 61, 64–65; centrality of, 165; collective, 146; contexts of, 251–52; defining, 105; democratized, 242; digital, 7; discussing, 95; ethnographic, 150; framing, 106; influences on, 75; intensity of, 8, 44, 167, 216; interactive, 36, 116; invitations for, 133–34; meaningful, 254; media-making and, 9; modal, 144; motivations for, 39, 43; networked, 30; observation and, 26, 55–61, 63–64, 65, 254; online, 112; positive, 151; problems with, 176; rhythm analysis and, 9; social rules of, 116; sociality and, 34; socially driven, 138; subscriptions and, 131; trajectories of, 37–43, 49, 55, 67, 188, 260; video making and, 36–37, 50; WordPress, 110; YouTube, 9, 14, 32, 38, 39, 43, 51, 52, 55, 62, 66, 71, 105, 106, 110, 116, 213, 219, 249

partnership programs, 231, 232, 250–51, 272, 300n21

Patreon, 231

Paul, Benjamin, 63

PayPal, 5

pedagogy, 170, 179, 180–81, 264

Pelaprat, Etienne, 112, 113, 121, 124, 130, 133

Penna, Joe, 243; photo of, 244

performances, 138, 191, 238, 250

Perriman, Cole, 202, 301n46

Perrin, Pat, 301n46

personal stories, 40, 42, 143

personhood, 191, 195, 207, 212; agentive, 193; idealized, 202; partial dimensions of, 187

Pew Research Center, 5, 37, 49, 53, 307n70

PewDiePie, 248

Phillips, Whitney, 196, 263, 268

photography, 39, 56, 187, 238, 289n66, 289n75

Pillow Talk 1:888 Toronto Meet-up (video), 96

Pinheiro dos Santos, Lucio Alberto, 284n21

Pini, Maria, 97

Pink, Sarah, 99, 158, 168, 179, 184, 274, 291n22; emplaced ethnography and, 70; on place, 74

Pixelodeon, 12

place, 70; creating, 83; emplacement and, 74; mediation and, 26; physical, 77; representations of, 76

platforms, 66, 100, 139, 145, 184, 192, 193, 223, 249; alternative, 260; changes for, 228; interaction, 218, 257; networked, 18; neutral, 257; news, 258; participatory, 259; public, 103;

social media, 234, 258, 281; technical, 266;
user-friendly, 282; video-sharing, 71, 180
Plato, 188, 267
Playlist Live, 238, 239, 240
*Playlist Live 2013—@shanedawson Hello,
@Harto, @JoeyGraceffa* (video), 240
Playlist LIVE Highlights w/Pillow Fights
(video), 239
PlaystationVUE, 229
Poehler, Amy, 235
politics, 156, 157, 169, 307n70; cultural, 10
polyrhythmic, 9, 206, 270
populism, 107, 117
Portelli, Alessandro, 251
posthuman, 9, 29, 188, 190, 194, 197, 201–2, 203,
206, 207, 213, 215, 216, 220, 245, 249; analyzing,
193; clashes with, 224; concept of, 191; connective aspect of, 189; experiences of, 28; mediated
self and, 191–92; social media and, 192
posthumanism, 190–92, 207, 220, 254; absorbative, 202; contact/collision with, 192
Postill, John, 99, 184
posting, 5, 229, 249, 293n25
post-phenomenology, 17, 306n21
post-YouTube, thoughts on, 220–24
Preece, Jennifer, 154
prejudice, 21, 169, 172, 173, 268, 269
PresOfWeb, 164
PrincessDiana161, 205, 212
privacy, 172, 204; cameras and, 280; legal issues
and, 21; policies about, 5; social media and,
297n75
production, 40, 237; creative, 271; cultural, 263;
visual, 7, 274
professionalism, 6, 16, 17, 183, 224, 243, 264, 280
proudyke, 156, 157
pseudonyms, 13, 21, 103, 170–71, 193, 269
Psychology Today, 199
Public Broadcasting System (PBS), 46

rabidzebu32, 165
racism, 10, 21, 169, 177, 242
Radsch, Courtney, 176
Rant Response for Renetto, A (video), 232, 233
Rapport, Nigel, 184
ratings, 200–201, 300n40; commenter, 177;
participatory, 257
Reagle, Joseph, 160, 171, 177
reciprocity, 7, 12, 108, 166, 184, 231, 254, 280;

anthropological studies of, 27, 109, 116;
attentional, 131; comments and, 110, 117–22;
dialogue and, 121; digital media and, 111–13;
dimensions of, 26–27; engaging in, 26, 27, 110,
120; eschewing, 110, 125–29; expressing, 112–13,
140; forms of, 107–8, 122, 123, 142; generalized, 120, 134, 138; heteromorphic, 114, 137;
homeomorphic, 114, 130, 144, 255; idealization
of, 133; inclinations toward, 112; insider's view
of, 142–44; interactions and, 111, 121, 134, 140;
invoking, 124, 143; lessons about, 255; liking,
140; losing, 26, 121, 138; meaning of, 141; media
makers and, 144; mediated, 108; mutual, 231;
negative forms of, 108–9, 126, 143; as obligation, 27; as participatory law, 129; patterned,
131–34; positive forms of, 117, 143; reworkings
of, 255; roots of, 140–42; social media and, 109,
112; sociality and, 108, 122, 143; subscriptions
and, 126, 132; video, 26, 110, 113, 115, 116–40,
141, 261; video making and, 139; video sharing
and, 114–16, 117; visual, 122–25, 125–29
Red Top Mountain State Park, photo of, 81
relationships, 10, 97, 113, 141, 280; building, 92,
127; community, 153; ethics governing, 163;
future, 22; interpersonal, 24, 123; long-term,
124; maintaining, 86, 107; political, 124;
public/private, 292n44; social, 124
"Remembering Ryan Basilio," 214
renetto, 94, 95
Renetto + Boh3m3 = YouTube History 101 (video),
94
representations, 188, 203–4, 224, 252, 277;
controlling, 275; ethnographic, 74; false, 29;
posthumous, 210; visual, 190
reputation, 112, 177, 193, 279; manipulating,
200–201
research, 10–11, 225, 247; anthropological, 74,
75–76, 148, 158, 202–3; communication, 277;
comparative, 258; digital, 70; ethnographic,
75–76, 148, 174; media, 33, 262, 269; primary,
71; protocol, 13; sociological, 174; subjects of,
64, 278; systematic, 266; visual, 165
Response to Vlog Brothers Vidcon Is a Ripoff!
(video), 245
reunions, 86–89, 90, 106
Rheingold, Howard, 75, 155, 196
rhetoric, 51, 52, 162, 166, 263
rhythms, 4, 146, 203; analysis, 8, 9, 108, 270;
anthropological, 273; behavioral, 8; collective,

91; conflicting, 9, 167; cultural, 9; interactive, 14; mediated, 9, 274; multiple, 228; participatory, 7–9, 29, 274; polymorphic, 65; public, 91; social, 9; temporal, 128

Richards, Mary, 82–83

Rignola, Joe, 79

Robinett, Paul, 95

robtran, 131–32, 193–94; anxiety for, 198–99, 201; mediated self of, 202; ratings and, 200–201; on reciprocity, 132; representation of, 196, 197; videos by, 195–96

Rocky (film), 90–91

Rotman, Dana, 154

Rouch, Jean, 179

rubrics, 7, 8, 11, 19, 22, 28, 64, 74, 77, 105, 153, 189, 255; community, 281; conceptual, 32, 35, 147; Lefebvrian, 29, 188, 227; participant-observation, 62; posthuman, 169, 190, 196, 201–2, 204; theoretical, 152

Ruby, Jay, 11, 179, 275, 277, 279, 280–81

Ryan Edit, 46

SadieDammit, 200, 201

Safety, Mr., 304n53

Sahlins, Marshall, 120, 126

Sanders, Chris, 230–31

Sandler, Adam, 95

Schieffelin, Bambi B., 288n16

Scroggins, Michael, 273

Seaman, Gary, 179

Second Life, 10, 196

Secrets of Videoblogging (Verdi and Hodson), 46

self, 147, 203; agentive, 191; construction of, 202; expressing, 263; media and, 43–44; mediated, 191–92, 202; narcissism and, 44; sharing, 39, 108; self-aggrandizement, 51, 62; self-centeredness, 24, 25, 53, 108, 123, 132, 143

self-expression, 24, 131, 166, 170, 195, 203, 229, 282; forms of, 45–48

self-perception, 189, 194, 198

self-promotion, 45, 85, 88, 92, 125, 127, 158; aggressive, 49–50; community and, 165; de-emphasizing, 24; encouraging, 179; sociality and, 18, 23–25

selfies, 23, 44, 55, 267, 268; fan, 45, 244; narcissism and, 45; video, 254

Senft, Theresa, 24, 44, 286n89

sentiment, 28, 105, 197, 267; community of, 184; posthuman, 209

"777," 26, 91

sexism, 10, 21, 169, 177

sexual orientation, 156, 199

shared happenings, 90, 158, 282

Shay Carl, 236, 239

ShortbusMooner, 111, 145, 155, 156

ShrinerMcbitey, 162

Shrum, Wesley, 35, 36, 278

Silver, Jon, 251

Simmel, Georg, 141

SimplySadie, 200

skills, 67, 280; creational, 34; development of, 37, 265; digital, 274–75; editing, 40, 41; filmmaking, 131, 181, 194; musical, 40; participatory, 11, 40; production, 235, 274; rhetorical, 162, 263; self-presentation, 265; technical, 40, 55; video-making, 253

Skype, 42, 221

Slater, Don, 75

Smart Brown Voices (podcast), 176

Smosh, 230

SMPfilms, 84, 304n53

Snapchat, 219

Sobchack, Vivian, 88, 89

social arrangements, 74, 266, 281

social atmosphere, 116, 117, 233

social bonds, 84, 146, 185

social circles, 68, 146, 178

social collective, 147, 271

social connections, 23, 121, 129, 217, 262; establishing, 113; facilitating, 38; strengthening, 143

social encounters, 116, 123, 142, 276

social formations, 147, 185

social groups, 16, 24, 51, 149, 158, 167, 185, 188, 226, 257, 258, 270, 282

social intensity, 146, 223

social issues, 23, 24, 25, 50, 176, 267

social media, 4, 12, 13, 15, 20, 24, 76, 107, 113, 117, 124, 125, 127, 132, 171–72, 175, 176, 180, 189, 190, 204, 205, 208, 217; engines, 206; entertainment, 223; ephemeral, 187; migration and, 219; narcissism on, 43, 288n31; posthuman and, 192; privacy and, 297n75; production on, 9; publications about, 284n40; reciprocity and, 109, 112, 256; research on, 62; sensory deprivation and, 56; sharing, 280; shelf life of, 258; sites, 221; videos and, 238

social phenomena, growth phase of, 108

social support, 36, 42, 167

social uses, 257, 260
social ways, 178, 256
sociality, 4, 7, 9, 11, 17, 18, 20, 26, 32–33, 40, 48, 50, 78, 80, 123, 133, 134, 137–38, 165, 229, 237, 238, 243, 244, 246, 247, 251, 252, 253, 254, 260, 261, 262, 264; chronotopic chains of, 71, 92–94, 104, 240; collaborative, 105; collective, 156; communication and, 15; democratized, 106; development of, 146; emotion and, 27; emplacement and, 75; facilitating, 37, 85, 179, 234, 256, 258; frames of reference and, 71; grassroots, 245; human, 31, 90, 248; instrumentality and, 124; intensification of, 30, 70, 90, 111, 116, 179; interaction and, 75; internet, 167; interpersonal, 60; investment in, 144; maintaining, 113, 126, 129; meaningful, 108; media and, 61, 144, 152; mediated, 7, 68, 108; modalities and, 70; monetization and, 233, 250; narcissism and, 33; participation and, 34, 71; reciprocity and, 108, 122, 143; self-promotion and, 18, 23–25; subscriptions and, 130; technical competition and, 138; temporality and, 26, 94–98; VidCon and, 242
socialization, 7, 70, 157, 228, 240, 243, 276, 282; monetization and, 231–35
society, 156; fraction of, 164; in miniature, 87; small-scale, 7; sociology, 35, 150, 152, 163
Sociology One: Principles of Sociological Analysis for Australians (Waters and Crook), 163
Sontag, Susan, 55, 56, 62, 63
Sørenssen, Bjørn, 42
sousveillance, 278
South by Southwest, 218
SouthTube, 57, 59, 69, 80, 90, 114, 139, 148, 155; events at, 87; meet-up at, 38; photo of, 59, 80, 81, 149
spaces: creative, 228; creator, 235; digital, 33, 174; mediated, 259, 260; networked, 147; social, 67, 271; time and, 70; video-sharing, 33
spam, 28, 125, 159, 160, 294n64, 295n8
sponsorships, 115, 126, 250
spricket24, 123
stakeholders, 153, 158, 173, 180, 183; epistemological, 163; investment from, 185
stars. *See* celebrities
STEELPOT1, 164
stereotypes, 96, 156, 168
Stickam, 78, 100, 220, 221, 291n21, 302n89

Strangelove, Michael, 10, 52, 155, 199, 305n7
streaming service, 229–31, 234
Street, Mike, 176–77
sub for sub, 122–23, 126, 127, 132, 261, 293n39
sub4sub (video), 123
subscribers, 44, 126, 126–27, 130, 134, 157, 221, 230, 239, 248, 250
subscriptions, 114, 122, 127, 215, 259, 260, 282; comparative, 126; original videos and, 131; participation and, 131; reciprocity and, 126, 132; sociality and, 130; value of, 130, 131
Summer in the City, 238
support: community, 214–16; emotional, 47, 271; expressing gratitude for, 138–40; technical, 271
Susan, 214, 215; media making by, 44, 45
SuziNess1968, 120
symbolism, 251, 252, 281

Tajen: Interactive (documentary), 179
Talkin' about OhCurt (video), 77
Taylor, Lucien, 279
TayZonday, 242
technology, 12, 112, 181, 188, 190, 191, 193, 199, 205, 257, 261; digital, 268, 280; emergence of, 23; humans and, 216; involvement with, 7; language and, 20; social media, 124
teddieppl77, 172, 173, 297n81
Tedlock, Barbara, 63, 64
television, 5, 17, 36, 113
tempi, 118, 250, 251
temporality, 26, 30, 33, 56, 115, 117, 143, 146, 215, 220, 228, 246, 272, 274; asymmetrical, 9; cultural dynamics and, 142; effect of, 44–48; experiential, 8; media, 270; multiple, 270; sociality and, 94–98; term, 8; understanding, 273; video, 271
temporicities, 271, 272, 273
ten-minute trick, 248
Terminal Games (Coleman and Perrin), 202
terms of service, 139, 158
thetalesend, 233, 234, 245, 246
thewinekone, 219–20
30 percent rule, 175
Thor, 208, 209, 210, 217, 236–37, 239
time stamps, described, 305n57
timur1lenk, 161
trajectories, 17, 103, 119, 146, 223, 235; media, 95, 272; participatory, 37–43, 49, 55, 67, 188, 260; temporal, 51, 95, 270–74

trebuchet1221, 154

tremendum, posthuman, 202–3, 224, 254, 279

tributes, 136, 139, 156, 157, 196

trolls, 157, 196, 198, 219, 263

truesign, 170

Tumblr, 112

Turkle, Sherry, 75

Turner, Victor, 27, 84, 85–86

Turner Based Gamer, The, 115

Twitter, 5, 12, 29, 112, 122, 132, 211, 216, 217, 219, 221, 234, 257; groups on, 153; launching, 258; Law of Reciprocity on, 294n64; migration to, 218; variations in, 258; YouTubers and, 222

2008 Philadelphia YouTube Gathering, The (video), 91

Uldam, Julie, 166

Usenet groups, 169

values, 92, 130, 131; cultural, 108, 177; production, 37, 40, 197

Vaynerchuk, Gary, 229

vernacular, 17, 24, 26, 29, 31, 37, 224, 268, 275, 281

Vernallis, Carol, 183

Veronica, 38, 47, 209, 210

Viacom, 238

VidCon, 12, 71, 82, 232, 304n48, 304n56; budget of, 245; celebrities at, 242, 243; early, 246; growth of, 240–41; photo of, 82; sociality and, 242; ticket prices for, 81; Viacom and, 238; videos of, 239

Vidcon What a Rip Off (video), 245

video bloggers, 57, 62, 216, 218; issues of, 264–65, 278; photo of, 61

video blogging, 23, 25, 34, 35, 36, 46, 53, 54–57, 61, 96, 109–10, 131, 151, 199, 208, 210, 238, 265, 267; characteristics of, 276, 277; maintaining, 12

video games, 38, 55, 262

video makers, 15, 27, 32, 34, 35, 51, 52, 59, 95, 97, 98, 113, 116–17, 122, 123, 128, 133–34, 143, 159, 193, 227, 232, 235; accounts of, 225–26; celebrity and, 96; commercial sponsors and, 81; commitment of, 201; cultural forms and, 17–18; emotional fungibility and, 106; emplacement and, 79; engagement by, 67, 118; ethic/agendas of, 277; individual, 270; legacy of, 188; media and, 9; meet-ups and, 73; monetization and, 29–30; narcissism and, 25; portrayal of, 272; promotions by, 66–67; reciprocity and,

114, 133; resources for, 260; rhythms of, 230; variety of, 16; viewers and, 228

video making, 3, 8, 11, 12, 35, 37–38, 39, 41–42, 51, 55, 65, 67, 72, 84, 101, 109, 149, 188, 193, 199, 203, 233, 250, 251; approach to, 32–33; cycles of, 249; emplacement and, 74; experience of, 83; increased, 40, 217; online, 264; participation and, 36–37; process of, 10; reciprocity and, 139; skills for, 40; techniques for, 197; trajectory of, 235

Video Reciprocity (video), 110

video sharing, 8, 17, 23, 28, 31, 49, 71, 72, 73, 134, 148, 199, 228, 234, 245, 256, 260; cultural practices of, 259, 261–62; dynamics of, 109; migration from, 30; parameters of, 227; practices of, 7, 261; reception of, 265; reciprocity and, 114–16, 117; researching, 261–81; social, 228, 266; temporalities of, 141

video streaming, 30, 227, 229–30, 233

Videoblogging (Dedman and Paul), 57

videochick770, 73, 78

videos: authentic, 28–29; birthday, 39, 47, 96, 134–35, 140; blimp, 44; causal, 49; celebrity-driven, 23; collaborative (collabs), 16, 26, 134, 136, 137, 138, 178, 261; comedic, 3, 38–39, 42, 115, 128, 134, 187–88, 224; commercial, 261; content of, 131; cool, 55, 85; deleting, 199, 206, 212, 271; educational, 179, 180, 266; feature-length, 11; half-life of, 225; hater, 195, 199; meet-up, 72, 79, 94–95, 97, 98, 106, 209, 269, 270, 276; offensive, 189, 198–99; parodic, 193; political, 156; popular, 5, 10, 206, 233; posting, 14, 37, 49, 73, 226, 272; promoting, 200, 259; promotional, 72, 73; public, 266, 278; quality, 41, 129, 264; reflection, 96; religious, 44; return, 225, 226, 249, 250; sharing, 4–5, 11, 49, 281; special-effects, 215; tagging, 205; thank you, 134, 135; trial, 84; tribute, 156, 157, 196; uploading, 32, 256; vernacular, 10, 44, 154, 183, 281; viral, 39, 181, 232, 242, 257; visibility of, 10; watching, 5, 6, 9, 11, 15, 242; YouTube, 15, 37, 94, 113, 265–66. *See also* mash-ups

view counts, 15, 104, 111, 124, 156, 197, 198, 200, 232, 287n101, 288n17

viewership, 178, 216, 234, 247, 274; commitment to, 122; creators and, 271; dissipation of, 270; sociality and, 250

viewing practices, 5–6, 10, 128, 247, 305n62

viral, 7, 10, 181, 182

virtual, 20, 153, 285n63

visibility, 67, 85, 232; ethics of, 280; mutual, 34, 66

Visiting Maker Studios Los Angeles California (video), 237

VLog to GOD—PART ONE—(The Voices of Creation) (video), 215

VLog to GOD—PART TWO—(Walking with Satan) (video), 215

vlogbrothers, 81, 231, 238

vloggers, 13, 47, 68, 109, 112, 144, 154, 157, 263, 266, 271; early, 262; interviews by, 56–57; media generations and, 226; narcissism and, 45–46; popular, 139; support from, 48; vernacular, 249; WordPress and, 111

vlogs, 11, 14, 15, 24, 26, 34, 38, 46, 47, 53, 58, 61, 77, 79, 81, 95, 96, 109, 116, 126, 129–30, 131, 156, 176, 187–88, 203, 211, 213, 215, 217, 219, 221, 225, 230, 233, 236, 237, 239, 240, 246; camera-address, 112; comedic, 100, 115, 134, 157; creating, 250, 253; lack of, 244; picture, 47; religious, 44

Wahlberg, Malin, 48

Walther, Joseph, 294n49

War on Robtran (video), 197

War on Capitalism (video), 175

Washington Square Park, 79, 91

Waters, Malcolm, 163

websites, 13, 220, 224, 253; demise of, 222; existential cycles of, 221; user-friendly, 234; video-sharing, 3

Weiner, Annette, 27, 129

Wellman, Barry, 21, 152

Wellner, Galit P., 261

Wesch, Michael, 14, 124, 181–82, 277, 285n42; communities of truth and, 183; sociality/communication and, 15; video by, 180–81

What Defines a Community? (video), 21, 27, 35, 147, 148, 150, 152, 168, 182

What I Have Done So Far to Block Vidcon 2010 (video), 245

WhatsApp, 20

WHY I TOOK A BREAK FROM YOUTUBE (video), 249

Why We Post (Miller et al.), 76, 180, 284n40

Why YouTube Sub4Sub Is Bad (video), 126

Wife among Wives, A (film), 279

Wikipedia, 13, 220

Williams, Cory, 84, 85

Wilson, Rainn, 235, 285n62

Wired Magazine, 41

Wogan, Peter, 168

WordPress, 12, 34, 109, 111

World of Warcraft, 11

WpgPeanut, 119, 120, 128, 129, 136

Wright, Karen, 199

Wu, Kevin, 223

Yahoo IM, 221

Yan, Yunxiang, 124

Yanomamö Interactive CD-ROM, 179

Yo'Tube, 90–91

You People Are CRAZY (and GREAT)!!! Thank You So Much! (video), 134

YouTube Black FanFest, 238

YouTube Community: Season 2 (video), 40, 221

YouTube Directors, 300n21

YouTube Etiquette (video), 115, 116

YouTube Music, 231

YouTube Music Key, 229

YouTube Music Premium, 231

YouTube Premium, 231

YouTube Red, 229, 230, 231

YouTube Space, 235

YouTube TV, 229

YouTube welcome page, 27, 173

You Tube Your Way (vlog), 176

YouTubers, 4, 8, 9, 13, 14, 18, 19, 21, 23, 26, 36, 52, 68, 77, 85, 87, 89, 92, 99, 100, 104; celebrities and, 242; chronotopic chains and, 93; community and, 152, 216; creative spaces and, 228; cultural expressions and, 16; data friction and, 102–3; events and, 97–98; experiences of, 70, 292n54; gatherings of, 81, 82; inspiration for, 34, 45; media generations and, 226; narratives and, 152; observation by, 62–63; orienting concepts of, 106; photo of, 61, 80, 81, 86, 89, 101, 133, 149, 241; posthuman identities of, 203; reciprocity and, 143; relationships among, 86; self-reflection by, 6; sociality and, 7, 48, 50, 237, 240, 245; starting over by, 35; stories of, 5, 31; support for, 250; video sharing and, 17; work of, 21, 95

YouTubia, 4, 14–17, 18, 261, 281

Zappin, Danny, 236, 237, 304n36

ZenArcher, 130, 139, 157, 162

Zhao, Yupei, 285n64

ingramcontent.com/pod-product-compliance
ning Source LLC
>ersburg PA
'031217050326
?CB00009B/1367